Whose Woods These Are

A History of the Bread Loaf Writers' Conference
1926 – 1992

Editors

David Haward Bain and Mary Smyth Duffy

Text by

David Haward Bain

With a Preface by

Marvin Bell

THE ECCO PRESS

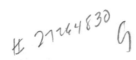

27264830 G

All rights reserved
THE ECCO PRESS
100 West Broad Street
Hopewell, NJ 08525
Published simultaneously in Canada by
Penguin Books Canada Ltd., Ontario
Printed in the United States of America

Designed by Richard Oriolo

First Edition

Library of Congress Cataloging-in-Publication Data

Whose woods these are : a history of the Bread Loaf Writers'
Conference, 1926–1992 / edited by David Haward Bain and Mary Smyth
Duffy ; text by David Haward Bain ; with a preface by Marvin Bell.
p.   cm.
Includes bibliographical references (p.   ) and index.
ISBN 0-88001-323-0 (cloth)
1. Bread Loaf Writers' Conference of Middlebury College.
I. Bain, David Haward.   II. Duffy, Mary S.
PN133.U5W46   1993
808'.02'07152—dc20   92-43688
CIP

CONTENTS

INTRODUCTION TO BREAD LOAF

by Marvin Bell

This is the Writers' Conference, blankingly overhead
as those who will attend anticipate the sky.
What will be the first word on the empty page,
the final word that may occur before the poem ends?
We are the vessels into which the old wine is poured.
We are the forms of silence between the lines,
the crunching of type as it descends the page
to coalesce in a dome enclosing a small fire.
You, writer, seeking the one metaphor, in the field
beyond the stone wall, listening for the resonance
where you linger in slat-back chairs on the lawn,
attendant to the long arc of ideas that preceded you
to this edge of your seat—you, writer, who are you?

First, you will want us to say who we are, will you?
I am the ghost of Robert Frost. He, also, is Frost.
That one is Walt Whitman, and that one Dr. Williams,
who read here, as you might, in the Inn, as you might,
to a small audience. I am Williams and Whitman too,
the solitary Dickinson, Neruda, Marianne Moore
in a big hat, Stevens in the snow, Jiménez in prison,
Vallejo dying in Paris, we are each of them and others.
We agree with all of them, we contradict everyone.
We will be at our worst and our best for you.
Are you ready? Do you prefer the one or the other?
Sorry, the good stuff and the bad stuff
are all part of the stuff: good, bad and in between!

You will have heard the one about the student who fled
into the forest, not to reappear until the dreaded
conferencing was past, and the one about the conferee
who walked across the rafters in the barn. I myself
observed a poet trying to kill a tree with his bare hands,
and heard firsthand the jewel thief with the telltale heart.
I witnessed the last days of writers, fantastic lust,
the overheard, overstated, written-down and written-up.
You who arrive under these open skies, you too may receive
such imprints of eye, ear, nose, tongue and touch:
moments that may lie in the recesses of your unconscious
until the day they rocket upwards into place,
breaking the surface of the formerly unconsidered.

Once, there may have been a writer who considered
fresh bread, beyond the loaf, long after the baker
had gone to sleep. Turning a slice in his hand,
he felt the time it took to rise, the mystery
of air that it could so infiltrate a solid,
and the magical properties of water that can melt
a mouthful in the lightest tide of saliva. And,
if time, space and water were new in the hand,
there was also a hint of the oven, in the smell
still encased in the remnants of fire which earlier
had transformed the designs of gas and liquid
into the architecture of bread, ready if touched
to quiver everywhere, like a spider's web, like a poem.

To a writer, one slice of bread is plenty,
nearly too much, where from a fragment of crust
all things may be deduced, and even from the spat-out
last bite of the burned base-edge of a loaf cooked
too long, from the putty of refusal, laden with spit,
a narrative of composition grows to maturity.

From the crumbs, one may sense the sparrow.
From the lingering taste of a sandwich, the writer
may end his or her days still digesting the past.
What are poems made from? Bits of string
and thread, and some dust from under the bed.
And even these may seem extravagant should one
be forced to look hard at the night, or the sun.

How did we begin? We began by trying to make
a thing that had eyes to see the other side of
the universe, a thing with a nose for those odors
locked into inert materials, a thing that hears the past
as it comes into being in the still undulating
frequencies of outer space, a thing of exquisite taste
for metals, liquids and gases, a thing that could touch
the feelings of another without leaving a mark.
You should have seen us experimenting at night,
mixing delirium, fatigue and spiritual hungers
into a love potion too strong to be taken straight.
You can't imagine the syllables we distributed
just to get "I love you" into a form that could hold it.

How long did it take? Each poem, finished or abandoned,
took exactly how long we had been alive, without
regard to the birth of those particular words, though
it's always hard to say when a fire begins or ends.
I tell of that Yellowstone Ranger during a blaze
whose home the flames encircled every day,
and who went out each night to fight the fire
yet could not find it. Like a fire, when the poem
is underway, you cannot get near it. Thus, this talk
is of the history of a kind of being, and you must

trust me when I tell you that when we were the fire
we wrote like the fire, and when we were the chasm
we wrote like the chasm, and it was all in the timing.

Since assignments are expected, I recommend you try
to understand what it means to be the capital letter A
with its dunce cap and its role as constant beginner,
and next you live a year at the bottom of a well
on bread and water, and after that you write by using
the buttons on your coat sleeve, not forgetting
to take from the diner the napkin on which you composed
that dreaded tidal flood of truth and fancy
that will come and go for the rest of your life.
Try to think of silence as an interval, consider a pulse
a variation on a tone, and work to understand
that figures of speech are innumerable, but the poem
is the true metaphor, and the true image must be abstract.

But writing, itself, is sexual. Like an ocean of roses,
like a coverlet quilted with stars, like a forest of tresses—
you cannot keep the sentiment or the thinking
out of your system. They will rise up, they will burrow in.
The spasms of phrasing, the syllables combining
and then dividing, a new metabolism that starts up
accidentally, improvising the future as it evolves—
do you want to know so much, that you will put an ear
to a lover's breast to record the anticipation,
or say the thousand things aloud that mean only,
words will not do? Poems are last words of the living,
words that *must* do, passed mouth to mouth
as we go, by writers like you, just like you, just like you.

GROUP PORTRAIT–
CREATIVE WRITERS AND COMMUNITY:
The Bread Loaf Writers' Conference, 1926–1992

a narrative by

David Haward Bain

The most important spot

in an artist's geography

is not necessarily the

place where he pays

his taxes.

—*Vermont: A Guide to the Green Mountain State,*
U.S. Works Progress Administration, 1937

PRELUDE

H e would have stepped out onto the front veranda from the dining room of the Inn in an excess of self-confidence. Afloat in the witty conversation of the friends and admirers surrounding him, John Chipman Farrar would have found himself a throne from which he could preside over his entourage and the spectacular sunset just beginning above the western foothills. Not yet in his eminence as an editor and publisher, but clearly on the mark, Farrar would have extracted from his suit jacket a long, pencil-thin Corona Corona as chairs scraped across the painted pine floorboards of the Bread Loaf Inn to flank the founding director, and the fast, brilliant talk would have resumed.

It was August 1926. If there was anticipation in the air it would not have been for the launching of a grand literary establishment nor for the decades to come, but merely for two weeks of country air and sunlight, a croquet game or two, and easy lectern talk about the literary world of 1926 and how, perhaps, to enter it. The world seemed new, everyone was rich, and the weight of years and of tradition was not yet impelling them on. They were experimenting. It had never been done before.

Behind and above those writers and editors circled on the veranda, the windows of the old Victorian Inn would begin to radiate a warm yellow kerosene glow. The first day of the first Bread Loaf Writers' Conference would gracefully move toward its close.

The Bread Loaf Inn, c. 1875 (University of Vermont)

The Annex building, late 1870s (University of Vermont)

The Bread Loaf Inn in one of its many revisions, 1870s (University of Vermont)

A Mountain, An Inn

A bove all there is the mountain. Situated along the main range of Vermont's Green Mountains and rising some 3,835 feet, bearing a striking resemblance to the staple baked for generations in rural stone hearths, Bread Loaf Mountain is part of the ancient margin of what plate tectonic geologists have termed "Proto–North America"—the edge of the continental shelf existing from the Eocambrian to Early Ordovician Ages, more than 500 million years ago. Across this margin of billion-year-old basement rock—gneiss and quartzite—the warm tides of the Proto–Atlantic Ocean coursed on their way shoreward to the Adirondacks. The closing of this ocean, culminating during the Devonian Age in the collision of the North American and African continents about 360 million years ago, thrust and folded Bread Loaf and its companions to their present prominence.

Bread Loaf Mountain presides over an upland valley that is about six square miles in area and roughly diamond-shaped, hemmed by a hilly spur of the Green Mountains, and beyond which is the floor of the Champlain Valley, just to the west. The surface of this thousand-foot-high plateau, as well as its attending mountains, has been repeatedly and strongly affected by glaciation. The last of the Pleistocene ice sheets retreated from Vermont about 13,000 years ago, reshaping the mountain passes and streambeds and leaving behind a scoured fabric of thin, bouldery soil below Bread Loaf Mountain.

By the late eighteenth century the valley was densely carpeted with towering spruce, yellow and cherry birch, hemlock, balsam, beech, maple, white and black ash, and basswood; tamaracks inhabited the marshy places; it was untouched and virtually unvisited. Still, from East Middlebury, a hamlet situated in the Champlain Valley against the foothills, one could gain access to that isolated upland plateau by following the narrow little Middlebury River upstream through a winding, precipitous, six-mile-long gorge, ascending six hundred feet to the lower edge of the plateau.

There was little reason to make the difficult climb even in 1781, when a group of speculators obtained a charter and called the parcel "Riptown." For twenty years they could entice no one to settle there. Finally, in desperation, the proprietors let slip a rumor in the taverns and stores of Middlebury, twelve miles away and the seat of Addison County, that they would grant title for a homestead to the first child born in the township. Immediately in that November of 1801 the impoverished Mr. and Mrs. Ebeneezer Collar, she nine months pregnant, fought their way up the frosty, boulder-choked gorge and through the dense, already wintery forest and constructed the roughest of shelters. Mrs. Collar bore a baby girl, but they never got any land, for of course the proprietors repudiated their own rumor. By the next summer, though, others had followed the miserable Collars' lead to what would soon be called "Ripton." In 1803, laborers began to scrape a road grade up the gorge from East Middlebury, across the plateau and under the shadow of Bread Loaf, and finally up along the South Branch of the Middlebury River to a gap elevated at 2,144 feet, from which it descended along the eastern slope of the Green Mountains alongside the Hancock Brook toward the White River. Completed in 1808, the road became known as the Center Turnpike—it ran from the courthouse in Middlebury to the same in Woodstock, with a branch to Royalton.

The town of Ripton was organized in 1828. It was never anything but sparsely populated. Struggling with a short growing season and eternally cursing the glacially deposited boulders, farmers coaxed oats, wheat, and potatoes from the rough ground. Dirt tracks branched off the turnpike, mostly following streams until they dead-ended at mill-sites. During the 1830s a dozen sawmills operated, replaced in time by four more efficient circular sawmills. By the time of the Civil War, the rich forestland of the Bread Loaf plateau and surrounding mountains, rapidly diminishing, seemed poised for complete devastation. It was then that a young man rode up the gorge, intending to stay only a short while. It would stretch into a lifetime, and the stamp of Joseph Battell would be left upon Vermont, the Green Mountains, Bread Loaf, and—finally—upon the Writers' Conference.

H e grew up in an atmosphere of gloom and redemptive Puritanical toil, with no mother and only his older sister for a friend. Born in Middlebury on July 15, 1839, Joseph Battell was the son of Philip and Emma Hart Seymour Battell. Both parents were of wealthy backgrounds; Philip, an attorney, came from a prominent family in Norfolk, Connecticut, while Emma was raised in Middlebury, the daughter of Horatio Seymour, an attorney and two-term United States senator, associate of Webster and Clay. She died of tuberculosis while Joseph was still an infant.

The children were brought up by their father in the stately Seymour mansion on Main Street in Middlebury, just across the street from the Congregational church, of which they were members. Joseph recalled his father as "a Puritan by faith and a strict disciplinarian." Partly because of Philip's strictness and partly because of his natural disposition, Joseph had few associations outside of the household. "My sister was my only acquaintance," he recalled, "my only confessor. . . . Thanks to her company I was contented and happy. I cared for no other, sought for no other." A daguerreotype taken when he was ten shows a strikingly somber boy—he was formally dressed and stiffly seated as was the necessity; still, Joseph's face looks three times its age, his eyes even older. One finds it difficult to imagine the boy doing anything impulsive or mischievous; instead of scampering through the echoing rooms of that imposing brick house with its four high chimneys, he would have walked; instead of climbing trees, he would have sat primly on a horsehair sofa, the windows shutting

Joseph Battell, Paris, 1865. (Sheldon Museum)

out street noise and dust, the curtains drawn against the light, reading something his father had decided was morally uplifting.

Apparently, as an adolescent a little of his reticence wore off—writings refer to fishing excursions in the mountains, skating parties, "sleigh rides with the girls, and buffalo robes." But he remained painfully shy, emotionally impulsive only when it seemed utterly safe. At fifteen he fell in love for the first time, but it was with an older girl who was a friend of his sister's, and she was soon to be leaving town. Sophy Chloe Allen was also of a prominent Middlebury family, and for a time she responded to his emotional onslaught. "We would sit whilst her little hand laid in mine and her head rested upon my shoulders," he recalled, "and she would lay plans for the future." She quickly outgrew him when she went away to school. For two years he pined away but was too shy to actively pursue her, both then and upon her return to Middlebury. She soon married another.

"Unfortunately," he would write only a few years later, "someone else married my wife." It was a theme he would sound a number of times in his life, and not just about Sophy Allen, and it betrays Battell's unconscious fear of intimacy and all that it represented. He seems to have passively, chastely, rapturously waited out his late teens and twenties for one young woman or another. Only when it was too late would he announce his deepest feelings in the densest Victorian prose, these sentiments often seasoned with scripture and vague references to "Principle." More than once he fell for someone on the brink of engagement. In the most notable case, he wrote his florid epistles to an about-to-be-married "Dear Cornelia," waited in vain for an encouraging word, and meanwhile let slip "the only woman I ever saw that I knew I should like for my wife, who is lost to me now." Her name was Ellen. We shall hear her name again.

It seems that Battell may have studied for a time at the West Brattleboro Academy before enrolling at Middlebury College, just up the hill from his father's house, in 1856. He did not graduate; the young man suffered from the then-common complaint of "weak lungs" and dropped out after completing his junior year. It being suggested that travel was not only a form of education but a way in which to regain one's health, Battell embarked upon a two-year walking tour of Europe.

His travel diary, published as *The Yankee Boy from Home* soon after his return in 1863, traced his route: Paris, Tours, Geneva, Pau, Switzerland, the south of France, the Rhine, the Pyrenees, back to Paris followed by Rotterdam, thence to Scotland, Ireland, and England. Having sailed from New York three weeks before the election of Abraham Lincoln and six months before the firing on Fort Sumter, Battell peppered his diary with naive speculations about the conflict at home. But more often, as he recorded observations of the European countryside—a succession of cathedrals and picturesque country lanes—he presented the reader with what Theodore Morrison has termed "staggeringly juvenile and virginal responses to female attractiveness at a safe distance." It seems he possessed a spyglass—and rather than employ it as would any self-respecting twentieth-century Peeping Tom, Battell delighted in staring for vast stretches of time at distant milkmaids or serving girls as they went about their work in broad daylight. Any Freudian would delight in the following passage, recorded at the head of the Glen of Glencoe:

Inverness is eighty miles to the north of me. Since I wrote last our travelling party has resumed the road: my sack, umbrella, myself, and spyglass. The sack does all it promised to. The umbrella has had active service daily, and even the spyglass, which has been sulky since leaving its Helen at the—Inn, near Inverness, saw yesterday another lass, going alone through a large field toward an especially pleasant-looking farmhouse. . . . When it found she was pretty, it grew better natured; I

hope it will soon get over its pique about leaving the other. . .

Elsewhere in the Isles:

I had arranged my spyglass to see the old castle [ruin], and distinguished a single female in a black riding-habit and a pretty plumed hat. . . . She stood in the perspective, and, so far as I was concerned, completely covered the castle. She didn't seem to care for the castle or for its environs—neither did I; but she walked about the lawn, and finally seated herself on the decline of the grass. I myself was lying on a bank of heather, some thirty feet above the road, my glass resting upon its summit. . . . Perhaps fifteen minutes passed, when the damsel rose, gathered quickly her long robe, and commenced a rapid run down the green. My glass moved with its object, and soon caught the form of two bright little girls coming to meet her.

And so on. But castles and cathedrals and girls observed at a safe distance ultimately paled. "This is the great fault I find with this Highland scenery," he wrote, "and why it can never equal kindred landscapes in America. There's a magnificence in our original forests that nothing I have seen in Europe can supply. The snow or greatness of the Alps won't do it, nor the beauty of the Pyrenees, nor now again the heather-covered and fern-waving hills of Scotland. Would that the day might never come when our mountains shall lose their greenness, or America her woods and forests!"

Not all of us are able to act upon such sentiments, though try we might. Joseph Battell did, though via a circuitous route. He returned to Middlebury in January 1863—the month of Lincoln's Emancipation Proclamation, and some months before Chancellorsville and Gettysburg. It is likely that Philip Battell paid Joseph's conscription exemption bounty of $300 when it came due that spring. At any rate, though he had learned a smattering of French during his tour, Joseph's health was not improved and he did not resume college studies; instead he looked after some of his father's commercial interests in town and did a bit of traveling as he tried to set himself into the Ayshire cattle business. A New York publisher issued *The Yankee Boy from Home* in 1864. His older sister, Emma, found all of Joseph's references to girls and spyglasses so distasteful that she had nearly the entire press run bought up and destroyed—by then she had married the eminent John W. Stewart of Middlebury, later a Vermont governor and United States senator. Joseph persevered by issuing a slightly abridged second printing.

In the summer of 1865, Ezra Brainerd, a school friend who later served a long and distinguished term as president of Middlebury College, suggested that Battell's weak lungs might be improved by some light exercise, some hunting and fishing, in the mountain air around the hamlet of Ripton. Thus Joseph Battell drove up the narrow, fern-fringed and tree-overhung old stagecoach road through the gorge, passing through Ripton where very likely the sounds of many sawmills reached his ears. Some few miles farther, the young man reached a humble, isolated farmhouse where he boarded with the family of one Joseph Parker. Sure enough, his health improved. Liking the area, he bought it.

Records show that the three-hundred-acre parcel changed hands on April 4, 1866, and Battell must have been very busy that spring, supervising additions and hiring help—he had decided to open his house to the public. It would be called the Bread Loaf Inn. His eminent father and even wealthier uncle and namesake, whose resources must have been tapped for this venture, were appalled to hear that Joseph wanted to engage in such an ungentlemanly calling. "Perhaps we are going to be disappointed in the result," the elder Joseph Battell wrote, "and find that one of the Battells, of the Dedham branch . . . is capable of keeping a hotel." There isn't a generous tone in this correspondence; it was as if they expected failure out of anything the young man tried. He was determined, though, to succeed.

He opened his doors on June 25, 1866. Soon he erected ("by the aid of half a dozen men and a bottle of California wine," it was reported) an oval, gilded sign depicting the massif that rose behind the Bread Loaf Inn. Seldom did he lack for company. During a two-week period that July he registered forty-three guests; one week in mid-August saw thirty-six—and they came up to Bread Loaf not just from Middlebury, but from as far away as Boston, New York City, Philadelphia, Chicago, and St. Louis. Battell was forced to discontinue a weekly stage from Middlebury in favor of daily service.

Reports of Joseph Battell's success appeared regularly in the weekly *Middlebury Register,* both in the editorial columns and in small advertisements. Trout dinners pulled out of the nearby streams were the Inn's mainstay at seventy-five cents, raised to a dollar after a month. Moreover, Battell had furnished his inn with a piano "with several volumes of carefully chosen songs," with a library and all the periodicals, with a "very choice" collection of photographic slides, with chess sets, cards, croquet equipment, footballs, quoits, fishing tackle, and even—please note—a "superior spy-glass." He attached a livery service from which guests could rent a horse and carriage for five dollars per day or a saddle horse for three dollars. He marked walking trails into the surrounding forests and

mountains, from which one could view not only adjoining peaks but also Lake Champlain and the Adirondacks. "The situation of the Bread Loaf Inn is peculiarly adapted to enjoyment," he boasted in one lengthy advertisement. "One finds oneself removed here to a higher atmosphere of entirely different life from that which he has been accustomed to. The novelty charms, the freshness fascinates, the decided character pleases, the walks delight, the mountains impress, and their air cool, clear, bracing, invigorates." Not only that: "In its culinary department," he maintained, the Inn would "henceforth rank with Hyde's Hotel as one of the best in the country."

After the early mountain frost closed him for the season, Battell counted himself a success even if he showed no profit. All during that winter and for several winters thereafter he labored in his surrounding forest with his grounds manager, John Houston (who was to work for him for at least forty-five years), cutting firewood to sell in Middlebury and Brandon to erase his debts in time for the following summer.

Debts notwithstanding, Battell continued. The Inn grew like a living organism; in the inimitable New England style, the original one-and-a-half-story farmhouse sprouted connected wings and outbuildings, several of which would be jacked up and moved around like dominoes as he added improvements. By his third season he announced he could accommodate fifty permanent boarders and the same number in transient guests, such to be charged fifty dollars per month, fifteen per week, or $2.50 per day; his celebrated trout dinners remained a dollar. Truly, and within a short number of years, Battell's modest enterprise grew beyond the limitations of the farm. His formerly doubting, ever wealthy uncle rewarded his diligence by buying him a huge wooded tract, including the western slope of Bread Loaf Mountain—starting Joseph Battell on a spree and giving him a cause that was to last his lifetime. In Vermont, one could not fail to see that the Green Mountain slopes were quickly being stripped of their primeval forests. Battell surely had read the extraordinarily popular book *Man and Nature,* published in 1864 and written by his fellow Vermonter George Perkins Marsh.

Marsh was a true Renaissance man—a scholar, attorney, and foreign diplomat—whose book has come to be known as (in Lewis Mumford's words) "the fountainhead of the conservation movement." It turned current notions—that the earth existed for humankind's pleasure and industry—on their heads. For Marsh, his native Vermont was a perfect example of how unbridled logging and unplanned farming, how ignoring the environment and not understanding how plants and animals and soil and water interacted, could swiftly devastate the landscape. "Every middle-aged man who revisits his birthplace after a few years of absence," Marsh wrote, "looks upon another landscape than that which formed the theatre of his youthful toils and pleasures." Such transformation had to be heeded at humanity's peril, he said. Extinction was the sure result if practices were not changed. "Even now we are breaking up the floor and wainscoting and doors and window frames of our dwelling, for fuel to warm our bodies and seethe our pottage."

Sensitive restoration and maintenance of the earth was of paramount importance, said Marsh. On his upland plateau, Joseph Battell heeded him. Over the years he increased his land holdings a hundredfold from the original 300-acre parcel, making sure that the vista viewed from his Inn would never be altered—and that a sizable portion of his beloved Green Mountain forests would be spared the axe. John Houston, manager of the Bread Loaf grounds, carried blank deeds in his pocket, and when he met anyone willing to sell his woodland they would settle the matter at once. When confronted by two men claiming to own the same land, Houston would sidestep court battles by buying both claims. "'Some folks go to Europe," Battell would often say, "and pay $10,000 for a painting and hang it up in their home where none but their friends can see it. I buy a mountain for that money and it is hung up by nature where everybody can see it. And it is infinitely more handsome than any picture ever painted."

Such ambitions were certainly made possible by family largesse, particularly that of his uncle Joseph Battell, who left him a bequest amounting to some $19,000 per year—a fortune in that solid, pretax era. His centerpiece, the Bread Loaf Inn, dramatically changed in 1882 when Battell hired the local architect Clinton Smith, who transformed the rambling structure into a marvelous Victorian wonder—two clapboard stories topped with the latest wood-shingled, cornice-bracketed mansard roof in the Second Empire style, which in turn was crowned by a belvedere. Defying the mountain winds, a flagpole topped this confection, from which flapped the largest American flag in the state of Vermont. In the rear an ell housed a Music Hall, a men's smoking lounge, and a bowling alley. A series of cottages was erected along the road for his friends, joined by two three-story structures for suites with private fireplaces and baths. Their ornate, stacked porches made them look like nothing else than a pair of Mississippi River steamboats. In 1884 Battell removed his barn from across the road—where it blocked a view of sunsets over the western foothills—to a spot a hundred yards behind the Inn, where the barn grew twice its size and acquired a stately, bracketed Mansard roof, rather fancy digs for the Bread Loaf herds of Jersey cows and Morgan horses.

The latter became another of Battell's powerful fixations: the study and propagation of Justin Morgan's breed. In the 1870s he bought a farm down in Weybridge, in the Champlain Valley, and over the years lavished a fortune on its equine inhabitants; later he gave it to the United States government for research into the breed suitable for cavalry as well as for pack transport; today the Morgan Horse Farm continues under the direction of the University of Vermont. As publisher of *The Morgan Horse Register,* published in several volumes, Battell traveled around the United States to research Morgan lines. He fiercely defended his findings. In one famous case, one Wallace, the publisher of a monthly horse magazine, accused Battell of giving a false Morgan pedigree to the noted trotter Seeley's American Star. Battell sued Wallace for $50,000 in libel damages. When Wallace visited the Seeley stable and satisfied himself that the horse was indeed a Morgan through his dam, he sent a letter of retraction to Battell— but it was refused until Wallace agreed to make his apology in his own magazine. Sure enough, the retraction appeared in *Wallace's Monthly Magazine.* However, Wallace closed his statement by saying, "They lie so like hell in Vermont that one cannot tell when to believe them and when not to believe them."

Battell had other causes. With the earliest intrusion of the horseless carriage onto Vermont roads, he mounted a fierce campaign to ban the noisy and dangerous contraptions: If owners of the "death wagons," as he called them, wanted to ride, let them construct their own highways and byways. He himself had witnessed an accident on the narrow, winding road up the Ripton Gorge in which an automobile spooked a team of horses drawing a carriage, which overturned and pitched a young woman and her two children down the steep embankment. They survived, luckily, but to Battell the incident was a bugle summoning him to war. By then he owned the weekly *Middlebury Register,* a journal doing a creditable job in covering national as well as local news. From then on it was a rare edition that did not feature gruesome accounts of automobile accidents around the nation. More than once he was observed standing on the veranda of the Addison House in Middlebury cursing every passing motorist. He even briefly closed the road that ran past the Bread Loaf Inn to automobiles, though he was overruled by the authorities. So Battell had to be content to forbid any guest to arrive by car, leaving them to park down at Ripton Hollow and wait for someone at the Inn to fetch them by carriage. A longtime guest recalled that Battell "could often be seen in front of the Inn warning off a luckless intruder" who had pulled his runabout into the driveway "and telling him

The Bread Loaf Inn with 3-storey east wing, 1890s.

there was no admittance at Bread Loaf for such as he. 'What do you suppose they think of us?' asked one of the assembled guests watching the show from the veranda. 'They probably think this is a lunatic asylum and suppose we are the patients.'"

No longer young, Battell's idiosyncrasies had become more refined with time and purified by wealth and the power that it brought him. Up at Bread Loaf he was formidable indeed. "He was above average height, massively built, big-boned," recalled one longtime guest. "His head was set solidly on his strong neck, in keeping with the firm jaw, large mouth, and the keen blue eyes now flashing wrath, now kindly humor. One of his broad shoulders sagged perceptibly, owing to a siege of lung trouble in his college days. When he trod the veranda, one shoulder up, the boards trembled. So did any guest guilty of a possible infringement of the host's orders." Joseph Battell would forbid dogs or cats at the Inn so that he might enjoy watching chipmunks race across the veranda on a summer's day, refused to allow anyone but waitresses to set up the dinner tables or remove sweetpea blossoms from the flower garden, strictly forbid any sociabilities between his male guests and his female employees on pain of expulsion from the Mountain, and carried guests' reservations and his scattered invitations around in his increasingly absentminded head, to the chagrin of those employees who would have to find them rooms.

The Bread Loaf Inn attracted a solid upper-middle-class clientele with an accent on education and the arts—eminent scholars and writers were frequent guests, and ministers always received a discount. Battell counted many of the repeaters as close friends. But his essential loneliness never left him. Several acquaintances recall him "sitting for hours alone, his eyes fixed on the green hills." One guest said that "he lived much within himself. . . . [H]e never joined the guests in their gatherings in the music hall," though he often went there alone to sit at the piano and sing to himself old favorites such as "Old Black Joe," "Home Sweet Home," or "Mary of Argyle." Paradoxically, he had assured himself of an occupation that would keep him surrounded by people. They were, however imperceptibly, kept at an emotional distance—especially women, whom the lifelong bachelor always idealized beyond reach. One story offers a tantalizing note: For years the Music Hall behind the Inn was used as a general sleeping room for unmarried men, sometimes numbering thirty or forty. Folding cots would be unpacked at the close of each evening's music and theatricals. Battell used to sleep there, too. One night his old friend Ezra Brainerd awoke at 2:00 A.M. and spied Battell sitting before a table and writing. "What are you doing, Joe? Come to bed." Battell replied, "Sh-h, I'm writing to the prettiest girl in the world." No clue to her identity has survived, and it is likely that Battell did not even tell his friend Brainerd. But there is ample record of Battell's idealization, at least, of many women. He had, by then, traded in the spyglass of his youth for an unwieldy camera and tripod. Obsessively—and very properly, with chaperones nearby—he posed young girls in their frilly Victorian finery before every vista his extensive lands held. "His camera was his constant friend and companion," remembered one guest.

> He loved to turn it on a typical Vermont farm, on a distant mountaintop, or a choice bit of green woodland, and to achieve perfection the human element must be present. Was there anything lovelier in human nature than a fresh young girl poised on the threshold of life? So, at least, argued Mr. Battell. Standing in the sun while he studied the chosen spot from every possible angle to secure a viewpoint and its setting perfectly suited for the picture was often tiresome, and posing for Mr. Battell was no unmixed blessing. On the other hand, long drives over the country with a congenial chaperone and a fine dinner at some village Inn were by no means despised, but cordially welcomed by any young girl whom his eye had selected as a favorable subject for a picture.

What this old friend of Battell's seems to have missed is that this pastime (all in the name of art!) allowed Battell many hours' opportunity to stare and scrutinize young womanhood as he squinted through his lens or straightened up from behind his tripod to request a change in her demure pose. Always, always there was the capturing but distancing lens.

Many of these photographs he published, usually in venues in which the connection between photographic subject and editorial matter was unclear, such as in his *Middlebury Register* and its occasional supplements, in his *The Morgan Horse Register,* and in a mammoth tome he considered his greatest achievement. It was an eight-hundred-page pseudo-novel, *Ellen, Or, Whisperings of an Old Pine* (1901), a Socratic dialogue between Ellen, a sprightly young Vermont girl, and the Old Pine. Together this pair no doubt represented Battell himself, but we also know

that the name "Ellen" had repeatedly surfaced in his writings since his twenties when an unknown Ellen chose another man over Battell—if she ever knew of his attachment; late in life Battell was also to purchase a mountain in the adjacent township of Lincoln called Potato Hill and rechristen it Mount Ellen. To prepare for the book's nearly unreadable ruminations on science and philosophy, Battell hired a former Middlebury professor, Thomas E. Boyce (who was to serve as Battell's general manager and factotum), as a tutor. They spent several winters huddled over tables at the Library of Congress in Washington, D.C., reading transactions of the philosophical societies of London, Edinburgh, and other cities, from which Battell developed his unique views on the corpuscular theory of sound (it was a real substance, he thought, not merely a transmitted vibration) and on geometry (which he disbelieved). It is remarkable to note that in his book on his youthful European wanderings, published thirty-five years before *Ellen,* Battell had interrupted his travel narrative to include a precursive chapter about the Old Pine and his pupil. Perhaps these imagined conversations first appeared in a Middlebury College assignment. But whatever their origin, in their most mature incarnation, published in no fewer than two editions and at Battell's own expense, they are an "incredible hodge-podge," as the Works Progress Administration's guide to Vermont says in its edition of 1937. "The book did not, of course, sell," we are told in that federal guide, "and copies of it can still be found scattered about Bread Loaf Inn, where they serve as casters and doorstops."

Battell was always a generous philanthropist to individuals and institutions, to Middlebury both town and college; though he sometimes bruised sensibilities he left his stamp everywhere. After downtown Middlebury was devastated by fire in 1891, he constructed a grand fireproof business block that bore his name and that was crowned with a corner tower overlooking Main Street and Merchants' Row. It set a standard for architecture that other rebuilding businesses emulated. Then, nearby, the old wooden bridge over the cascading Otter Creek had also been destroyed by the 1891 fire, and town officials wanted to replace it cheaply. Battell held up town politics for a year arguing for a stone bridge that would suit the proper image. He finally contributed more than half of its cost and selected its graceful arching design—based on the Ponte Sant'Angelo in Rome, which had been constructed around A.D. 130 across the Tiber River to the tomb of Emperor Hadrian. Battell also donated farmland, located up the hill from the center of town, to Middlebury College, creating a large part of the institution's north campus, and gave generously to scholarship and building funds.

Politically, Battell counted himself a progressive Republican, becoming an ardent follower of Theodore Roosevelt. He served eight terms in the Vermont legislature, but when he stood for governor he was resoundingly defeated, nowhere as strongly as in his own Addison County—his fellow citizens seemed to like him where he was, where any statehouse eccentricities were over-shadowed by his advocacies, especially for the Vermont landscape. Now the largest private landowner in the state, owning most of Bread Loaf Mountain and also peaks like Camel's Hump, Lincoln, Grant, Roosevelt, Boyce, Worth, and Monastery, Battell delivered an impassioned plea in Montpelier in 1891. Vermont would be doomed, he orated, if citizens could not protect their forests from "timber butchers, lumber merchants and firebugs."

In those later years, he kept an apartment suite downtown in the Battell Block for those nights when he did not feel like riding back up to Bread Loaf. And oftentimes he spent the dead of winter in Washington, D.C., and Florida, because cold weather worsened his lung troubles. It was after forty-nine years of operating the Bread Loaf Inn, in the bitter winter of 1915 when the thermometer readings in Middlebury plummeted to forty-two degrees below zero, that Battell took his last train south. He did so suddenly and unexpectedly, without informing anyone but the boy he took to manage his trunks. His worried factotum, Thomas Boyce, knew Battell was ill and traced him as far as Washington, but the old man slipped away and went to Florida, where he remained alone for a few weeks. He grew restless, though, and bought a train ticket for Middlebury.

On Saturday, February 6, Battell stopped off in Washington where he visited a friend, Senator Frank Lester Greene of Vermont, and cashed a check for one hundred dollars. Back at Union Station, he forgot that his ticket home was in his pocket and stood in line to buy another ticket for Middlebury. By now he was noticeably dazed and confused and talking strangely. A detective saw Battell and arrested him. The old man, still a physically formidable figure, was unused to such treatment and became violent. Not only did he suffer the ignominy of being arrested and restrained and having his valuables taken away from him, but police took him away from Union Station in a motorcar.

An item in the newspaper reported that Battell had been arrested and conveyed to the locked, barred ward of the city charity hospital. This news alerted his friends. Police had been too stupid to look at his checkbook and papers to notify anyone. Senator Greene retrieved the old man and placed him at Georgetown Hospital. By then he was weak, demented, paranoid, and seriously ill with a kidney ailment. Boyce and several friends rushed to his side only to find him steadily declining. An operation was performed

on February 19—but he never recovered. Battell died on Tuesday, February 23, 1915, aged seventy-five. "So passed," a friend would write, "a great and lonely man."

The line between Joseph Battell and the Writers' Conference is short and straight. A few weeks after a properly large and dignified funeral (marred only by the fact that his coffin was borne to the cemetery in a motor-driven hearse), Battell's will was opened. He gave a number of bequests to individuals and institutions alike—including $1,000 per year for the education of Addison County girls, $1,500 for celebrating the annual Forefather's Day, $1,000 to the Middlebury Congregational Church, $5,000 to Middlebury College (which was also made residuary legatee). Then there was his real estate. Mount Ellen went to the federal government. A handsome hill outside Middlebury and a fund to maintain it as a park was donated to the town. And 30,000 acres of Green Mountain forests went to Middlebury College with strict instructions as to their care. Battell's Bread Loaf Inn, to be kept open with his cronies welcome as guests as long as they lived, passed into college hands, too. Thomas Boyce managed the Inn and farm for a couple more years, scaling back and selling off some of the farm animals and managing the forests. He planted forty-five thousand white pine, ninety thousand Norway spruce, and three hundred or four hundred white ash. But by 1919 the college had just about decided to get out of the innkeeping business because Bread Loaf had been a financial and managerial drain. The board of trustees instructed its agents to put the Bread Loaf Inn and its attending buildings up for sale or rent.

Thankfully, the order was rescinded. Instead, at the behest of some of its faculty and with the support of its president, the college decided to use the Bread Loaf Inn for a new summer graduate school of English language and literature that would follow models already in place for the summer study of foreign languages on the Middlebury campus. Investing it with this academic purpose justified its upkeep to the college trustees and thus saved it from the melancholy fate of so many nineteenth-century summer hotels. In 1920 the Bread Loaf School of English began the first of many successful seasons, offering master's level study in English and American literature, teaching methods, public speaking and debate, theory and practice in modern drama, and composition.

It is the instruction in "composition" that draws a line straight to the Writers' Conference. What happened next was a convergence of diverse elements: first, an administrative need; second, an educational vacuum; third, the vaguely expressed sentiments of several illustrious outsiders; and fourth, the active efforts of a number of people within and without the college. The administrative need, that of adding more revenue to the Inn's balance sheets, could be solved by extending or supplementing the six-week school session to keep the Inn nearer to capacity until shortly before Labor Day. Within the school curriculum, creative writing seemed best for this elaboration.

Certainly in the 1920s most of the teaching of creative writing was done by academics, not professional writers. As a course offering or a major field of study, creative writing would not come to its present national popularity until after the Second World War, and it wasn't until the 1960s that many professional writers began to find retreats, even sinecures, inside the academic groves. Back in the twenties, as educators began to perceive a need, Middlebury officials entertained outside advice.

Directly after the first session of the School of English in 1920, Professor Wilfred Davison received a letter from a poet recently settled in South Shaftsbury, Vermont. Robert Frost had published three well-received volumes of verse and had recently resigned from Amherst College. As early as 1915 he had dreamed of owning a farm at which he could write in the winters and in the warm months entertain writers "in a sort of summer literary camp." His lifelong discomfort with the rigors of academe notwithstanding, Frost took an interest in the new summer school. He suggested to Davison that it might be at Bread Loaf, rather than in formal colleges, that more literature might be born. He offered himself as an instructor in the "Responsibilities of Teachers of Composition." The nebulous

position went unfilled, though Frost was to make brief reading appearances there in 1921 and 1923. Frost would stay for a few days at the Writers' Conferences of 1926 (reportedly), 1927, and 1929, and his name would be mentioned early in the latter year as a possible director. But it seems that his seminal influence in the creation of the conference was later exaggerated—which is not to neglect his thirty-year role as "spiritual godfather" of the matured conference, beginning in 1933. As a literary celebrity interested in the study of creative writing in a bucolic setting, Frost may have had as much influence upon the college as four writers who participated in the 1922 School of English session: Willa Cather, Katherine Lee Bates, Edwin Markham, and Louis Untermeyer. Cather, particularly, told students she dreamed of returning to Bread Loaf and occupying a little studio of her own, such as the humble, rustic "Tea Cabin" behind the clay tennis courts, to which she retreated to write while at Bread Loaf.

So it was probably in the summer of 1925, when College President Paul Dwight Moody turned to a young editor up from New York to lecture at the School of English and asked what *he* thought should be done with Bread Loaf's two vacant summer weeks, that the enterprising John Farrar replied with a suggestion that not only made eminent sense but had literally been in the air. With the encouragement of English Dean Wilfred Davison, Farrar organized a teaching staff and program for the 1926 Bread Loaf School of English "Conferences on Creative Writing."

The first faculty of the Bread Loaf Writers' Conference, 1926: (l-r, rear) John Farrar, Robert M. Gay, Edward Davison, Grant Overton; (front) {?}, Doris Halman, Harriet Monroe, {?}, {?}. (Courtesy Poetry Society of America)

Stephen Vincent Benét and Joseph Auslander, 1928

THE HAPHAZARD EXPERIMENT

Not for nothing was he known as publishing's fair-haired boy, even this early in his career. John Farrar, Yale '18, had started at the *New York World* as a reporter and feature writer. After only two years, the thin-faced, pale young man with red hair, owlish spectacles, and flashing gregariousness had become so visible that he was offered the editorship of *The Bookman,* the New York literary monthly published by the George H. Doran Company.

First published (beginning in 1895) by Dodd, Mead and Company and edited by the brilliant Harry Thurston Peck, the magazine took its name from the oft-repeated saying of James Russell Lowell—"I am a Bookman," displayed as the epigraph of each issue—and soon became a beloved institution for its incisive literary criticism and witty essays. Then Doran bought it, establishing Robert Cortes Holliday as its editor, who, along with the World War, drained the *The Bookman* of its vitality; it fell to young John Farrar to restore authority to the monthly, which he did almost instantly. "He has taken what was once a desuete and uninteresting house organ and made it a lively and interesting magazine," Farrar's greatest champion—himself—would write, "playing up to no clique or cult, fair, intelligent, well informed, steering a clear course between the radicals on the one side and the mossbacks on the other."

Born on February 25, 1896, in Burlington, Vermont, John Chipman Farrar was the son of an advertising man and a librarian, and he began publishing his own work early, with—at age fourteen, no less—the first of three plays he would issue in his home town before he was out of high school. At Yale he became a close friend of classmate Stephen Vincent Benét and his older brother, William Rose Benét, who was in New York then working as a publisher's reader. Their association would be a long and profitable one. He worked with Benét on the *Yale Literary Magazine,* Farrar serving as chairman, and together with John Andress and Pierson Underwood they edited *The Yale Book of Student Verse, 1910–1919.* Yale University Press published Farrar's first book of verse, *Portraits,* when he was only a sophomore, and his next collection, *Forgotten Shrines,* was issued in the Yale Series of Younger Poets in 1919. In the spring of that same year Yale produced a one-act play by Farrar entitled *Nerves.* It was based on his wartime experiences, for Farrar had interrupted college to serve in the Army Air Service as a first lieutenant from July 1917 to February 1919—his Yale degree was issued that spring, "as of" 1918.

Down in New York City, Farrar was already a habitué of its cafes and theatres by the time he emerged from Yale, his backslapping bonhomie and sharp intelligence easing him through his apprenticeship at the *World* toward the even more visible post editing *The Bookman.* There, he developed a large and loyal group of writers who appreciated his "grand-auntly" concern for their personal lives as well as their words. Farrar was always, as he boasted, "arranging love matches, furthering courtships, trying to straighten out marital difficulties, reconciling estranged couples, making young poets sign the pledge, trying to distract the sentimental attentions of ingenuous novelists

Margaret Farrar, John Farrar, Alexander Laing, 1927

ingly dubbed himself "the most socially amenable of party-hounds." Charlie Chaplin was there, as was Mary Astor. Young Village poet Charles Norman was suitably impressed, and not just by the celebrities. Farrar, he thought, "had the old-fashioned notion that new writers could be, or should be, helped on the road to fame by older and more established ones." Old-fashioned or not, in time the notion would become the chief raison d'être of the Bread Loaf Writers' Conference. In 1925, as Farrar ended his companionable evening with Charles Norman by instructing him to take his poems to two older, established poet friends, the forces were working toward the conference's formation; Farrar's brief lecture appearance at the 1925 session of the Bread Loaf School of English brought him full circle to that experimental gathering in the third week of August 1926—with one brief delay, in May 1926.

W̲e went there on our honeymoon. Luckily I had no great desire to see Niagara Falls," recalled Margaret Petherbridge Farrar many years later, "because this trip to Bread Loaf had been planned in advance, and our wedding day was chosen to coincide with the long Memorial Day weekend. So we were married on Friday, May 28th, and took the day train up to Middlebury on Saturday." Even around Memorial Day, Bread Loaf nights can get rather cold; the newlyweds' suite in Maple Cottage had a fireplace, which they put to good use during their ten-day sojourn. "We ate all our meals at the inn, in the kitchen," Margaret Farrar remembered, "and some mornings it was so cold that our hostess invited me to sit by one of the big stoves and put my feet in the oven in order to get them warmed up." They walked around the Bread Loaf campus and drove around the countryside with English School Dean Wilfred Davison, all the while planning curriculum and strategy for the coming Writers' Conference.

Farrar's announcement in the Bread Loaf bulletin in 1926 set forth the intention under which all future Writers' Conferences would be presented:

> The program will consist of background lectures on the writing of short stories, novels, articles, and poems, with practical suggestions on developing a prose style and the preparation and placement of manuscripts. Informal discussions on both the artistic and practical problems of creative writing, and group and individual conferences on manuscripts brought by the students, will furnish opportunity for professional criticism that should result in marketable writing.

Farrar emphasized the practical and professional in his idea of the Writers' Conference. Some inhabitants of the ivory

and playwrights away from dangerous women, advising fresh air, wholesome amusements, and hard work against the claims of temptresses, the flesh and the devil." One hopes he showed similar advocacy for women writers beset by confidence men, lounge lizards, and predatory critics and editors!

"Farrar was the most generous of editors," recalled Charles Norman, poet and biographer. "You could bring a poem to him, and he would read it, then call up the treasurer to make up a check; you waited, almost overcome by joy and pride, all the while regaled by his talk of the literary world, the problems of running a magazine, his own desire to continue writing poetry. He was also a generous friend." In his *Poets and People* (1972), Norman recalled how he shared a typical Farrar afternoon in his office at Doran, which moved to drinks and dinner at the Yale Club. Later there was a play by a new British playwright named Noel Coward, who also starred in it. And during intermission Farrar worked the lobby, Norman in tow, demonstrating, no doubt, why the editor had laugh-

tower would call it crass. But, as Wallace Stegner pointed out in his magisterial biography of Bernard DeVoto, *The Uneasy Chair* (1974), that practicality was balanced by the other side of the equation: The conference was held under the auspices of an academic institution, and some of the staff came from academe. Thus, at Bread Loaf, at least some of the academic community's standard of impartiality of education in promoting excellence in writing was grafted onto the goal of demonstrating how to earn a living from it. Not only was a sort of balance achieved, said Stegner, but the combination proved better than either of its components.

It was a solid, prosperous faculty, somewhat removed from the cutting edge of literature in the twenties but close enough to know what was what, that took up residence in the Bread Loaf Inn for the 1926 session—well respected in those days if somewhat forgotten now, perhaps heavier on the editorial side than in subsequent years—but by all reports the thirty-five literary yearners who paid their hundred dollars' tuition were satisfied. Farrar's greatest draw was Harriet Monroe, editor of *Poetry: A Magazine of Verse.* Fourteen years before, Monroe had been a published poet of limited talent whose career was in eclipse. After returning to her native Chicago from a trip around the world, she hit upon the idea of launching a magazine solely devoted to poetry. Too often, she felt, poets were made to feel like poor relations, hats in hand, at publishing's back doorstep—grateful when their work was squeezed as unpaid filler into the empty spaces between prose pieces. *Poetry* would embrace new names and new ideas, it would pay for published work, and it would give generous annual prizes. She found one hundred patrons to subsidize *Poetry*; its first issue appeared in October 1912. Over the next fourteen years it became a major force in American literature, aiding the careers of Carl Sandburg, Amy Lowell, T.S. Eliot, Ezra Pound, and Robert Frost. Harriet Monroe's stirring book *Poets and Their Art* had been issued the previous May, and it is likely that the frail but spirited editor drew upon it as she addressed the Bread Loaf assembly. "The people of America should learn," she had written, "that their poets cannot do their work alone. An artist must feel his neighbors behind him, pushing, urging, arousing him, if he is to achieve his utmost."

John Farrar would have applauded that sentiment, as would the rest of his faculty. There was Grant Overton, his associate at *The Bookman* and literary editor of *Collier's*; Arthur McKeogh of *McClure's*; Doris Halman, reader for the American Play Company of New York; Edward Davison, editor of *Cambridge Review*; and Robert M. Gay of Simmons College and the Bread Loaf School of English, the one teaching professional. In addition, visiting lecturers were to appear and disappear after a few days: Honorée

Willsie Morrow, who was former editor of the popular women's magazine *The Delineator,* wife of the publisher William Morrow, and author of a number of earnest, well-researched, but now thoroughly dated historical novels; Owen Davis, wide-ranging playwright of not only serious Broadway dramas such as *Icebound* but also of melodramas popular in the summer-stock circuit, like *Nellie: The Beautiful Cloak Model;* Isabel Paterson, a book columnist for the *New York Herald Tribune*; and finally William McFee, prolific writer of seafaring tales in the mold of Jack London, based on his own years on a United Fruit Company tramp steamer. In addition, Lawrance Thompson, biographer of Robert Frost, asserts that Frost delivered a reading at Bread Loaf in 1926; however, documentation of this is sketchy, so the poet of South Shaftsbury will be saved for later. It is Margaret Farrar's recollection that everyone on the faculty, including Farrar, worked without pay, getting only room and board and the beauties of Bread Loaf, perhaps receiving traveling ex-

Robert Malcolm Gay, 1930s (Simmons College)

penses—"because," she wrote, "everybody was rich and things were booming in those years . . . and we thought it would last forever."

The first conference was judged a success on all fronts, as can be seen in correspondence between Middlebury College President Paul Moody and Farrar and in a November 1926 column in *The Bookman,* in which the editor expanded on the developing Bread Loaf credo. "I am thoroughly convinced," Farrar said, "that it is only by direct contact with editors, publishers, critics, and writers that those who are trying to write will be able to diagnose their own cases and know whether or not they have any chance in their field." It would be among the last columns of *The Bookman* that Farrar would write, for Doran sold the magazine in April 1927 to Sewell Collins and Burton Rascoe, who took over the editorial helm. Farrar continued as a book editor at Doran, but of course in that spring he would also have been planning for the 1927 conference at Bread Loaf. It was comforting to know that the old mountain inn would finally be electrified, with the hazards of kerosene to vanish forever from the place.

Farrar's main choice for the full-term faculty was his friend Hervey Allen. Tall (six four), blond, florid, and possessing a bad limp earned during frontline infantry service in France, Allen had published six volumes of poetry (including one in the Yale Series); a war memoir, *Towards the Flame* (1926); and what was then considered the authoritative biography of Edgar Allan Poe, *Israfel* (1927). Much, though, was still ahead of him—he had begun work on a long adventure novel set in the Napoleonic era entitled *Anthony Adverse,* with the accompanying celebrity and wealth still five financially difficult years away. There would be quite a contrast between the end of his career in the 1940s, when Allen's lifetime sales would exceed three million, and the struggling but well-regarded poet of 1927. He was then teaching American literature at Vassar after a similar lecturing post at Columbia. Just weeks before Bread Loaf, the thirty-seven-year-old Allen had married one of his students; the conference continued their honeymoon, to the giggling delight of several romantic-minded participants. For a number of years to come, Hervey and Ann Allen would be a frequent presence at Bread Loaf whether or not the writer served on the faculty—such were his ties to many Bread Loafers.

One close and longtime friend of Allen's was Robert Frost, at fifty-three well into his eminence, readying *West-Running Brook* for publication, with the first of three Pulitzers already in hand, but many years short of the grandfatherly presence by which he is remembered. Still enjoying a cordial relationship with John Farrar (their famous feud would boil up soon enough), Frost was vividly portrayed in one of Farrar's columns in *The Bookman*—he

with his "eyes . . . bright blue, steady, gentle yet canny, two vivid lights in a face that is otherwise gray." The poet whose interest in the idea of Bread Loaf had predated it by six years, and whose future participation would number in the decades, was scheduled only to deliver an evening talk. Kid-glove treatment was already de rigueur—customers were explicitly warned not to impose themselves or their manuscripts upon him. And one assumes the sensitive Frost did not see an amusingly donnish note in the previous day's Bread Loaf newsletter, *The Crumb*: "This evening at eight Dean Davison will read from the poems of Mr. Frost, if there are any who care to hear them. . . . The Dean hopes that no one will come out of a sense of duty or courtesy merely."

If the rest of the full-term 1927 faculty did not have such a future ahead as Allen and Frost, still, for the time they were a solid lot. There was a Stanford writing professor, the birdlike Edith Mirrielees, who had already spent a quarter-century on that campus and would continue until well into the Second World War; her most dedicated Stanford student would be John Steinbeck. Mirrielees would anchor the teaching of fiction at Bread Loaf for twelve subsequent sessions. There was also Herbert Gorman, novelist and biographer of his friend James Joyce, and whose other friendships spread across quite a length of Anglo-American literature—Edwin Arlington Robinson, Vachel Lindsay, Elinor Wylie, Ford Madox Ford, and Padraic Colum. The perennially stagestruck Farrar invited the noted playwright Susan Glaspell, widow of George Cram Cook and one of the founders of the Provincetown Playhouse. Indicative of the more variegated politics of intellectual life in those days was one visiting lecturer, the radical journalist Floyd Dell, an editor at *The Masses* and author of several novels about disaffected youth in the jazz age. It was Dell, together with his colleague at *The Masses* Max Eastman, who helped inspire Frost's disdainful poem "Young, Sure and Twenty" after Frost was dragged down to the *Masses* office in New York to have his nose rubbed in radicalism by wealthy Marxist Louis Untermeyer, who never tired of puckishly provoking his conservative democratic friend. At Bread Loaf in that summer of 1927, there was little beyond literature that Floyd Dell could address without mentioning the two surpassing controversies of the moment—the presence of the U.S. Marines in Nicaragua, and the execution of Nicola Sacco and Bartolomeo Vanzetti, carried out at Charlestown State Prison, Massachusetts, on August 23, a day on which Edith Mirrielees lectured on "Analyzing a Situation" and Burges Johnson on "Conservation of Profanity."

Another unconventional presence during that session was the stocky, balding, and monocled adventurer Achmed Abdullah, who arrived at Bread Loaf with his agent, Jean

Wick. They occupied adjoining rooms. "There was a good deal of gossip around campus about their relationship," recalled Margaret Farrar, "which added further zest to the proceedings!" The couple, however, were soon to be married. Eton educated, of highborn White Russian– Afghani parentage, Abdullah dazzled all who encountered him. He walked the veranda like a polo player, was full of stories of his British cavalry days in India, China, and Tibet, and was ready at the drop of a glove with the sort of romantic adventure yarns that provided him with a good income from the slick magazines. *Steel and Jade* was the sort of title he went for in his novels, or *The Blue-Eyed Manchu.* Or *The Trail of the Beast.* Later Abdullah would find Hollywood— or vice versa—and his screenplays would help define the thirties era of adventure epics, including *The Lives of a Bengal Lancer* and *The Thief of Bagdad.* His picaresque and somewhat apocryphal autobiography was a few years down the line, but a passage from *The Cat Had Nine Lives* (1933) gives one an idea of Abdullah's monologues in the Bread Loaf dining room. His life was full of

> events, some polite and some less polite, in London's Mayfair, Oxford, New York, Hollywood, Outer Mongolia, Central America; on the Roof of the World, in Tibet, during Sir Francis Younghusband's expedition, where the temperature dropped to seventy below and a gale blowing, and on the West African coast where it was one hundred and twenty in the shade—and no shade to speak of—and where recruiting was carried on with the help of a rope and a rhinoceros-hide whip. Seeing one of my best friends killed in a duel over a worthless cocotte. Matching skill at poker with the King of Montenegro and damned near losing my shirt and a decade later, regaining my shirt, with interest, during a stud session at the Spokane Club. Meeting a baker's dozen of other kings and finding most of them frightfully middle-class—with the exception of King Ferdinand of Bulgaria who, with his jewels and perfumes, reminded me of a typical South American gigolo.

Vermont did not often see such colorful sights as the monocled Achmed Abdullah.

Both Robert Frost and Hervey Allen proved to be especially popular at Bread Loaf, but both would be absent from the conference in 1928—Frost was traveling in Europe, and Allen could not afford to leave his typewriter in Bermuda (or to pay for passage) and his manuscript of *Anthony Adverse.* However, two visiting lecturers created a stir among faculty and customers alike—in very different ways.

The first was Farrar's classmate from Yale, the thirty-year-old Stephen Vincent Benét, poised that month on the brink of unaccustomed fame and wealth and having at least

Achmed Abdullah, 1927

some mixed feelings about it. He had published five books of poetry (the first at age seventeen) but derived his meager living from a number of novels and stories in the popular magazines. In his second novel, *Young People's Pride,* there was a character named Johnny Chipman who was modeled on his longtime friend Farrar. Having grown up on a succession of army posts, Benét was always interested in American military history. For several years he had been obsessed with the idea of writing a book-length narrative poem about the Civil War, but he was unable to afford to do so until 1926, when he was awarded a Guggenheim Fellowship. He decided to stretch his dollars by relocating himself and his wife (Rosemary Carr Benét, also a writer) and family to Paris. There they lived in attenuated Left Bank–garret circumstances while he focused all of his time on the poem *John Brown's Body.* The ballad-form narrative begins back in the time of the slave ships, sweeps forward impressionistically through Brown's raid on Harper's Ferry, his execution, and the Civil War (in which the stories of fictional protagonists are interwoven with scenes in which figure Abraham Lincoln, Jefferson Davis, Ulysses S. Grant, and Robert E. Lee, among others), and ends with a meditation on the war's aftermath and the beginning of a new era for the rejoined nation. The editor instantly recognized the potential of the finished manuscript. By midsummer 1928, Farrar was full of good news—the Book-of-the-Month Club had gotten behind the book and the Garden City presses were rolling again—and of schemes for publicizing the "overnight success." (He would naturally nominate it for a Pulitzer Prize, which the book would win the following year.) Benét was leery, though, of any obvious commercialization; he resisted Farrar's idea to set the publication date to coincide with his appearance at Bread Loaf (with the press invited, of course, which would have been good not only for the young poet but for Farrar and Bread Loaf). "It seems," Benét argued, "too pat."

Nevertheless, by the time the still underfed-looking Benét arrived at the Inn, everyone on the Mountain had heard about the book's success. They were surprised to find the balding, bespectacled, moustachioed poet so youthful and unassuming, and so willing to read even the most amateurish manuscripts and offer serious commentary. When he delivered an evening reading from *John Brown's Body,* faculty member Robert Gay was struck by the chanting delivery and the surprising volume "from so meager a man." His sincerity, he decided, "after the attitudinizing and affectations of some poets we had heard, was very refreshing."

Quite a different effect was made by Sinclair Lewis, who came over from his nearby summer place, Twin Farms, in Barnard. The gaunt, bibulous novelist whose eyes burned dramatically from a face ravaged by scars and eruptions had already published most of the work for which he is remembered: *Main Street, Babbitt,* and *Arrowsmith.* The latter had been awarded a Pulitzer, which Lewis had scornfully declined in 1926, saying that the prize had been specifically set up to judge "Americanism," an inquiry that should have had no artistic bearing whatsoever. *Elmer Gantry* had been issued the previous year, and now Lewis was finishing up *Dodsworth.* Beyond that would be many more novels of decreasing quality and increasing sales. This was the first of a number of appearances at Bread Loaf, both at the School of English and the Writers' Conference, each of which would leave Bread Loafers buzzing for the rest of the sessions. Still, through whatever alcoholic fogs he navigated while on the Mountain, the serious teaching made an impression. Lewis would be speaking about both school

and conference in 1930 when, in Stockholm, he accepted the first Nobel Prize in Literature to be awarded to an American: "I know of only three educational institutions in America which teach literature as a living art—of these the Bread Loaf School of English is one."

When Lewis was in his drunken, manic mode, which usually came in between his novels—Carl Van Doren noted that when possessed by writing he showed "the industry of a bird building a nest"—the usual result was all-around embarrassment. He appeared at the 1928 Bread Loaf lectern "fantastically drunk," as his biographer Mark Schorer wrote, and there assured the literary hopefuls in his audience that they could never be taught creative writing and that if they were fortunate enough to become writers it would be downhill from then on—"writers are a bastard lot of human beings." One pronouncement after another left his audience nearly breathless. Later, while he withdrew to take one of his famous catnaps, the faculty whispered about how to get rid of him. But when Lewis appeared at his reception he was sober, deft, and witty, almost—but not quite—erasing his earlier impression as a man tragically out of control.

This was to be the last year that John Farrar would direct the conference, although his shadow would be on it for an additional five years or more. The reason for his resignation lay in the publishing events of the late 1920s. It was a dramatic time, a generational changing of the guard; young turks like Farrar and Marshall Best and (only slightly older) Alfred Knopf, Bennett Cerf, and Donald Klopfer were establishing their own names in the book trade. And it was a time of great literary excitement. Consider what had occurred in just a few years: *The New Yorker,* the Book-of-the-Month Club, and the Literary Guild had been founded; there was Ernest Hemingway's *The Sun Also Rises,* Willa Cather's *Death Comes for the Archbishop,* Thornton Wilder's *The Bridge of San Luis Rey,* and Eugene O'Neill's *Strange Interlude*; and Random House was readying William Faulkner's *The Sound and the Fury,* and Scribner's was about to publish Thomas Wolfe's *Look Homeward, Angel.* And magazines helped support the book business. "The 1920's were for all editors a time of very pleasant security," recalled *The Atlantic Monthly*'s Edward Weeks.

It was a time when fiction was ripe and plentiful. You never had to worry about the supply of good short stories or of good novels to serialize. It was a time brimming with poetry. Poems by Robert Frost, Edwin Arlington Robinson, Archibald MacLeish, Stephen Vincent Benét, Elinor Wylie, Carl Sandburg, Amy Lowell were coming to us at regular intervals. I remember how hard my chief, Mr. Sedgwick had to work to find anything to argue

Willa Cather at Bread Loaf, early 1920s

Farrar decided to throw in with his friends; they resigned en masse from the company. Their new business was to get under way that spring under the name of Farrar and Rinehart (announcing in its initial list the name of one Hervey Allen), with Stephen Vincent Benét as its principal reader. With such a new enterprise there could be no time for directing the Bread Loaf Writers' Conference.

Farrar's resignation from Bread Loaf unleashed an interesting succession of events, almost all behind the scenes at Bread Loaf and some of it betraying a struggle between academic and editorial approaches to the teaching of writing. Some academics complained to the college authorities about the direction Farrar's conference had been taking—too many editors and writers, to their minds, had been dispensing simply commercial advice, with not enough art (or, tellingly for the professors, criticism) on the discussion table. School of English Director Wilfred Davison, who held nominal responsibility, briefly entertained the idea of naming Robert Frost to succeed Farrar; Frost himself had privately grumbled about Farrar's style as he indicated his willingness to take over. Early bulletins even announced the poet as new director. One professor, Robert Gay, who had apparently wriggled uncomfortably next to Frost in the Bread Loaf Music Hall audience in 1928, wrote to congratulate him on January 16, 1929:

> The main thing seems to be to get rid of the commercial flavor of the Conference, and I do not think that will be hard. . . . The morning meetings of the Conference have as a rule been profitable, I am sure, but the afternoon "discussions" have not. The latter too often became merely one more lecture . . . and the subject "discussed" was trivial or commercial. . . . To sit there for hours, as we did, and discuss how to sell MSS, the "taboos" of editors, and so forth, seemed quite literally a desecration. . . . Your presence and influence alone will do much.

Apparently, though, President Paul D. Moody of Middlebury College stepped in to make a "safer," more conservative choice than Frost for director, someone with a reassuring doctorate and long pedagogical career who had taught at the School of English between 1925 and 1927 and at the Writers' Conference in 1926 and 1928: Robert Gay. Moody did have genuine faith in the idea of a more informal, less academic Bread Loaf, but for the moment there was Professor Gay.

This appointment ushered in a transitional period in the conference's history; from the beginning Gay's leadership was known to be temporary. Gay openly voiced his misgivings; the professor did not want tenure directing the

about. Prohibition was the one staple subject of controversy, divorce came next, and one or two of our economists were beginning to question the soundness of the credit structure and the pyramiding then rising to new heights in Wall Street. But no one worried about War, and no editor had ever heard of atomic energy.

Meanwhile, the hypnotic business boom with its illusion of endless growth—"Coolidge prosperity"—cycled upward toward the Crash. Many publishing businesses succumbed to the mania, being merged, bought out, and extracted of their vitality. Personnel wandered like gypsies. Over the winter of 1928–1929, the corporate changes stole into the household of John Farrar. George H. Doran Company had been merged with Doubleday in 1927. As two former Doran executives, the brothers Stanley and Frederick Rinehart, were being edged out of the company,

Writers' Conference. Born in Brooklyn, New York, and educated at the Polytechnic Institute, Columbia, and Dickinson, Gay was through and through a teacher, not a creative writer. He had taught at Goucher, Harvard, and Simmons, but he had no books of verse or prose of his own, nor had he expressed any interest in that area, nor had he any career ties to the editorial world. He did contribute regular book reviews to *The Atlantic Monthly* (conservative, judicious, and predictable reviews, though there were many of them). He was the author of a writing textbook and the editor of the popular *Riverside Book of Verse, 1250–1925,* and he was considered an expert on Emerson. He was an austere-looking man with a long nose and high forehead and was known for occasional flashes of humor. In his three years directing the Writers' Conference (he would also direct the School of English, between 1930 and 1936, following the unexpected death of Wilfred Davison), Gay did little to innovate it. Instead he offered a reassuring presence to his faculty and—more important, as the realities of the Great Depression sank in after Black Friday, October 1929—to the Middlebury trustees who were still carrying the money-losing conference.

Interestingly enough, both Frost and Farrar attended the 1929 conference as weekend lecturers, and it was at Bread Loaf that their formerly cordial relations came to an end—in public, in front of faculty and customers alike, in one of the new afternoon "roundtable" discussions in which there was to be general critical talk about published writers and writing. Frost's unsympathetic biographer Lawrance Thompson tells us that it was an "unpleasant verbal battle" and that Frost complained that Farrar ran Bread Loaf as a commercial literary agency, that he was "merely shopping for manuscripts." Frost was also resentful on a more paternal note; his high-strung daughter, Leslie, had gone to work for Farrar at Doubleday, Doran, and she had written home to complain of Farrar's "mistreatment" of her. One cannot imagine how their open quarreling was smoothed over by Robert Gay. Later, the poet was walking somewhere around Bread Loaf when he saw Farrar jump over a low hedge and stride purposefully toward him. Frost mistook his demeanor as aggressive and prepared himself for a fight. But when they were nose to nose, Farrar thrust a hand into a pocket, withdrew it with something, and said, "Have a cigar!"

Even such a peace offering as an expensive Corona Corona would not salve Frost's resentment—he did not heal easily. But at the 1929 conference the poet had a strong ally and loyal friend who must have made his Bread Loaf appearance more than merely tolerable: Louis Untermeyer. Forty-four, with a receding hairline and a magnificent beak of a nose, upon which rested a pince-nez, the wealthy Untermeyer had stepped down from an executive position in the successful jewelry manufacturing business founded by his father. He did so to follow his lifelong avocation, poetry. A high school dropout at fifteen, by 1929 Untermeyer had published six volumes of verse, a novel, and a number of parodies. His original work, however, made less of an impression upon the literary world than did his annual anthology, *Modern American Poetry,* which began appearing in 1919 and was widely recognized as a formidable arbiter of contemporary poetry and, of course, of the careers of those who wrote it. Being a centrist in the continuum of modern verse, he drew fire from both sides. Inevitably, as each new edition appeared to pay homage to the newest emerging poets, some names would have to be dropped. Who made it—and who didn't—spurred much comment in literary gatherings all over the country. As Robert Hillyer would write,

> Taste changes. Candid Louis Untermeyer
> Consigns his past editions to the fire;
> His new anthology, refined and thrifty,
> Builds up some poets and dismisses fifty.
> And every poet spared, as is but human,
> Remarks upon his critical acumen.

The friendship between Untermeyer and Frost was made up of equal parts of genuine affection, aesthetics, locker-room banter, male ego-posturing of the middle- and old-aged varieties, and self-promotion—and it was not even affected by Frost's constant anti-Semitic wisecracks, which Untermeyer absorbed (offering a few self-deprecating ones of his own) into the protective coloration necessary in the era. Untermeyer was to leave an indelible mark upon Bread Loaf, during this and nine later conferences, as teacher, tennis partner, inveterate punster, and amorist—his marital life, forever tangled, was uncomplicated compared to his extramarital life.

For the most part, between 1929 and 1931 Gay relied on a core of faculty and lecturers, influenced to a certain extent by Farrar, who came up for at least one weekend of each session. There were, however, fewer editors and more writers on his staff than had been on Farrar's. One editor who did come to those three sessions, and who remained a friend of the Writers' Conference for many years thereafter, was young Edward Weeks. Born the week that the U.S.S. *Maine* blew up in Havana Harbor in 1898, Weeks had graduated from Harvard and worked briefly as a salesman for Horace Liveright as that great publisher was beginning to go under. Then, at twenty-five, Weeks turned down an offer from Harold Ross and his about-to-be-launched magazine, *The New Yorker,* and instead joined *The Atlantic Monthly* as a first reader. Ambitiously, he waded through over-the-transom manuscripts and combed all the little magazines looking for new talent; one of his "discoveries" was a Yale graduate just a year younger than himself whose first novel had just appeared—Thornton Wilder. Weeks wrote to him and asked if he could serialize his next book. "In time he sent me the first half of his new manuscript entitled *The Bridge of San Luis Rey,*" Weeks remembered. "I was crazy about it, and was confident that it could be divided for effective use in *The Atlantic.* But to my bitter disappointment neither of my senior editors seemed to like *The Bridge.* They kept saying, 'No,' 'No,' and in the end the noes had it."

He was not always shot down. In 1927 Weeks received a short story from an expatriate midwesterner; he had, like Weeks, been an ambulance driver in France during the World War. His name was Ernest Hemingway. He had never been published in a national magazine. "Fifty Grand" had been turned down by *The Saturday Evening Post, Cosmopolitan, Collier's,* and *Scribner's,* but Weeks fought for it at *The Atlantic Monthly* and prevailed. Despite this and other successes, he nervously eyed his calendar; the policy at *The Atlantic Monthly* was that no first reader could hold the job for more than three years. However, instead of being fired when he reached that point in 1928, Weeks was promoted to editor-in-chief of Atlantic Monthly books, from which post he would publish James Hilton's *Goodbye, Mr. Chips,* Walter Edmond's *Drums Along the Mohawk,* and Charles Nordhoff and James Norman Hall's *Mutiny on the Bounty.* Ten years later he would become *The Atlantic Monthly*'s ninth editor.

Weeks, considered an expert on the currently burning subject of book censorship in New England, lectured on the essay and the magazine article at Bread Loaf in 1929, where he met Hervey Allen (still slogging away at *Anthony Adverse* though now able to leave his typewriter in Bermuda thanks to a $14,000 advance from John Farrar) and Robert Frost. "There was never any problem getting him started" to talk, Weeks recalled. "The problem was to get him to stop. He was a nighthawk who loved the stars, and he and Hervey would go on and on until two or three in the morning unless Mrs. Frost put her foot down." Weeks also witnessed another flare-up between Frost and Farrar. The editor delivered a rambling lecture in which he said that he liked to read poems aloud to his children and that his five-year-old daughter "responded much more eagerly to the music of Shelly than she did to Frost." He meant it as a joke, Weeks remembered, "but it was tactless and Robert was miffed—it took all of Bob Gay's diplomacy to bring about a temporary reconciliation."

Though his presence felt never very far away—so many of his friends would be present—Robert Frost would not make an appearance at the Writers' Conference for the next five years (he did deliver a talk at the 1930 dedication of the new library for the School of English). The separation

pained him greatly. Relations between him and the conference took on the aspect of a lovers' quarrel; the problem certainly went beyond his open disdain for John Farrar. At first, he knew he was not asked back because of his public intemperance. He could not mask his hurt and chagrin with sarcasm when he wrote Untermeyer to report that "I am left out of the Two Week Manuscript Sales Fair" and to urge that his friend be his "spy and agent provocateur." Later, when the angry episodes of 1929 were all but forgotten, there could still be no reconciliation between Frost and Bread Loaf because of that great stumbling block, pride. It would take someone of immense patience to patch the rift.

Others would still be there waiting for him when he returned. One of the writers sharing a cottage with Edward and Fritzie Weeks in 1929 and 1930 was Gorham Munson, literary journalist and critic. High-domed and sporting a fastidious little moustache and owlish glasses, Munson would be known in his later life chiefly as a lecturer at writers' conferences and as the main (some would say the last) proponent of Social Credit, but in 1928 Van Wyck Brooks had called him "the most important of younger American critics." (Brash young Edmund Wilson would satirize him unflatteringly as "Borem B. Bunsen" in a piece called "Gorgonzola: or the Future of Literary Criticism.") Some of his place was undoubtedly earned on the strength of a little review he founded in 1922 and coedited for two years—*Secession,* an exuberant journal of aestheticism and literary experimentalism that had published little-known poets such as Hart Crane, Marianne Moore, William Carlos Williams, E. E. Cummings, and Wallace Stevens. He had written critical praise of Frost and for a time he would be on the poet's short list of potential biographers. At Bread Loaf, Munson would be nearly a constant presence until 1939, becoming a sort of resident critic though spending perhaps too much conference time on his economic enthusiasms.

Gorham Munson had many connections in the publishing world and was always gracious about sharing them with others. One such instance, which took place in July 1929 at the Yaddo artists' colony, involved Munson and an emerging writer who was later to be seen up at Joseph Battell's old inn for many a year—Donald Davidson. The thirty-five-year-old Davidson, who was to be at the Writers' Conference in 1931, had heard about Munson from his friend Allen Tate, who had met him in New York in 1924. Tate's description of Munson helps to animate their conversation: He was "a much married young man. . . . He's a very nice fellow and excessively fantastic of visage: petite spiked mustaches and a huge tuft of hair on the back of his head; rather fat, mainly amidships. Like most uncompromising critics, he is very meek in conversation, but very precise in his statements—no fumbling; he knows his own mind."

Donald Davidson divided his time between teaching at Vanderbilt University and editing an influential weekly book page for the *Nashville Tennessean.* The page was also distributed to other southern newspapers, which helped to supplement his meager instructor's salary and gave him access to a multitude of free books. In such a position he occasionally talked about how he "settled wagers as to whether [the novelists] Du Bose Heyward and Julia Peterkin are white or colored," which says something unfortunate about the tenor of at least some literary discussions in Nashville in the twenties. Davidson had obtained his bachelor's and master's degrees from Vanderbilt and had published two volumes of verse. Louis Untermeyer remarked in his *Modern American Poetry* that Davidson's work had been "praised for its 'mysticism'" but that its "outstanding characteristic" was "its fiery localism."

It was that concern with southern localism that Davidson discussed with Munson. Davidson wanted to create a highly partisan symposia involving him and a number of his Vanderbilt friends—including John Crowe Ransom, Allen Tate, Cleanth Brooks, and Robert Penn Warren, all of them published by Davidson in the *Tennessean* columns and collectively known as the Fugitives after their little arts magazine, *The Fugitive,* published between 1922 and 1925. An anthology of poetry reprinted from *The Fugitive* was published in 1928. Davidson told Munson that his planned polemic would be titled *I'll Take My Stand* and that it would address "southern problems": self-determinative politics and preservation of southern traditions, religion, and art. Despite Munson's being an industrial sort of northerner, a Manhattanite from Amityville, New York, he was intrigued by Davidson's energy in outlining *I'll Take My Stand* and promised to buttonhole an editor at Doubleday, Doran, on its behalf.

By the time they encountered each other at Bread Loaf in August 1931, the collection had been out for a year and had created a vortex of controversy in literary gatherings north and south with its call for a return to traditions many critics felt had been overruled at Appomattox Court House. Still, adherents insisted that their political separatism would lead to a new aesthetic, and in such terms the matter would continue to be debated until the Second World War. Davidson referred to the collection and to his fellow Fugitives' other work in his lecture "Southern Poets and Current Issues," and it was perhaps at the faculty reception later that evening that Bread Loaf saw the genesis of the "Ten O'Clock Rule": It was forbidden that anyone could discuss the Civil War after ten at night, on pain of expulsion from the faculty club and payment of a fine, the

amount of which varied. It was a rule that Davidson would have to follow for many years to come. The Tennessean liked the New England surroundings and the company so much that he would buy a house within sight of the Inn and spend every summer from the Hoover to the Kennedy administrations teaching at the Bread Loaf School of English, frequently tarrying for the Writers' Conference and often sponsoring younger poets or budding critics at the institutions. So many of his Bread Loaf visitors and protégés would come up from Vanderbilt that Allen Tate would be moved to say in a 1940 School of English lecture "If anyone were to ask where the Nashville Fugitives came from, no one could answer, but if anyone were to ask whither have they flown, the answer would be 'to Bread Loaf.'" By no means would the Mountain become their northernmost outpost. But the remarkable fact was that regardless of how vigorously the Fugitives were opposed in that plethora of political self-expression in the literary community of that era—the social realists, the Marxists, the anticritics, the naturalists, the New Dealers—they were always treated with respect when they appeared.

There still would have been the odor of charred wood about the Inn in August 1931. Oddly enough, in the first sixty-two years that the Inn had operated, when it was lit by hundreds of kerosene lamps and when fireplaces were often used to take the chill off those late-season evenings, there had been no major fires. After the place was electrified, the fire came—and it began in the electrical plant behind the old Music Hall, on June 14, 1931. Word reached Middlebury College, twelve miles away, as President Paul Dwight Moody was delivering the baccalaureate address to seven hundred students and graduates. The assembly surged out of its chairs and ran pell-mell for automobiles, black academic robes flapping, with President Moody leading the vanguard. The rescue party raced up the perilous mountain road "in every form of conveyance from luxurious limousine to rattletrap automobiles and bicycles," reported the *Boston Herald,* with many students standing on running boards. When they reached Bread Loaf they saw that the annexes behind the Inn—the Music Hall, the "ell" dormitory and classrooms, the brand-new library, and the caretaker's cottage—were ablaze. Moody and a crowd of students ran into the Inn and began to carry out antiques; the Middlebury firetruck appeared, firemen found there was no water pressure, and they ran a mile-long hose to a stream; other towns' tank trucks responded and began to spray the mansard roof and facing clapboard walls of the main building to keep it from igniting. Meanwhile, the fire in the Music Hall was spreading toward the Inn along a covered and latticed walkway. The amateur firefighters tore it down with their bare hands. But if the wind had not propitiously shifted at that moment, it's likely that the main building would have gone up, too.

Viewing the smoking ruins, Moody vowed that the School of English would go on though it was to start in three weeks' time. Temporary quarters had to do for many of the school's functions, but by the time the Writers' Conference opened, the destroyed Music Hall had been replaced with a Little Theatre with a stage and a large brick fireplace, and other outbuildings, such as a sprawling dormitory and a caretaker's cottage, had been rebuilt. All were rendered handsomely enough in the popular colonial revival style, which somehow did not do violence to the charmingly old-fashioned Second Empire look of the rest of the grounds. Charred and blistered clapboards on the rear wall of the Inn testified to the narrowness of the old building's escape.

As little as Robert Gay altered or improved the Writers' Conference, his choices of Davidson for the English School and Edward Weeks and Gorham Munson for the Writers' Conference really took root. But in larger effect for the conference there would appear, in 1931, a young New Hampshireman with poetical leanings who had graduated magna cum laude from Harvard and worked for several years as manuscript reader and junior editor for *The Atlantic Monthly* and then for the Harvard graduates' magazine. Theodore Morrison's first book of poetry, a narrative entitled *The Serpent in the Clouds,* was published by Houghton Mifflin in 1931. He was then about to join the Harvard English Department, in which he would teach creative writing for forty-three years. Morrison would spend much of that time involved with Bread Loaf; when Robert Gay finally tendered his resignation as director after the 1931 conference, saying that he could not afford the time to teach at Simmons and run both Middlebury's Bread Loaf School of English and the Writers' Conference, he recommended that Ted Morrison be named—to incalculable effect, it turned out—to succeed him. "I had plenty of diffidence about accepting the job," Morrison recalled, but "like most of the world's families at any time, and especially in America in 1932, my wife and I needed any income we could scrabble together. Salaries at the bottom academic ranks did not stretch far. I agreed to try directing the Writers' Conference, and as it turned out, I kept on doing so for twenty-four years."

1935 staff and fellows: (rear) Gorham Munson, John Crowe Ransom, George Stevens, Ted Morrison, John Mason Brown; (center) William Harris, Victor Lowe, Victoria Lincoln Lowe, unknown, Avis DeVoto, Julia Peterkin, Catherine Brown, Bernard DeVoto, Raymond Everitt, Helen Everitt; (front) Mrs. Gorham Munson, Isabel Wilder, Shirley Barker, Gladys Hasty Carroll, Kay Morrison

(Above) Julia Peterkin, 1935; (above right) George Stevens, William Harris, Hervey Allen, 1935; (below right) John Farrar, 1934

THRIVING IN THE DEPRESSION

"I shall feel my clothes very much too big for me," Morrison wrote—in the self-effacing Cambridge manner he would affect all of his life—to Margaret Widdemer in March 1932, asking her to return to the Writers' Conference. "I think," he similarly wrote to John Farrar, "that there will be a good deal of vacant space in his boots when I step into them." Nonetheless, by dint of his energy and his fresh perspective on administration, teaching, and the inherent potential of Bread Loaf, Morrison easily grew into those clothes and those boots and soon needed a refitting.

To begin with, feeling that the conference could not simply wait up on the Bread Loaf plateau for someone to wander in nor depend on stay-overs from the English School, Morrison began to sculpt an image that was distinct from the school and decidedly public. He changed the format of conference literature, began to compare magazine advertising rates with circulation, schemed to get free editorial mention, and even wrote scores of publishers to ask that they mention Bread Loaf in their rejection slips (most wrote back that they would! life was simpler then and Bread Loaf had no competitors). It was important, too, that the conference be viewed as the independent and educational entity it was. Robert Gay had some advice: Morrison should state it in no uncertain terms that

> the conference is not a commercial venture, that it is conducted under the auspices of Middlebury College, and that it has always shown a deficit. You see, we do

not know how far the old impression persists that it was a little pet of John's, somehow connected with Doran or, later, with Doubleday, or now, with Farrar and Rinehart. That's an impression you must kill. I suggest, then, that you rather lay it on that the Conference is connected with no commercial interests, is entirely academic in its provenance, that the staff are mainly engaged in a labor of love.

And although the idea would take a few years to gain full acceptance by the college, Morrison began to explore ways to offer scholarship aid, either through outright grants or work arrangements. Hervey Allen and Robert Gay suggested that Morrison should even ask publishers to contribute tuition for their own promising writers. For the time being President Moody was willing to rescind the tuition of $125 in a few selected needy cases, requiring only that those students be responsible for their room and board at the Inn, about $60.

But the signal job Ted Morrison faced was putting together a faculty and securing visiting lecturers, which he was forced to do under the stringencies of the depression. His budget for this task was set at only $2,000, which meant he would be able to pay full-termers $200 for two weeks' work, plus free room and board, and evening lecturers $25. Morrison's salary was $350 for nearly an all-year job. "It is a source of embarrassment to me," wrote President Moody, "that nearly everyone who works at Bread Loaf has to do it partly as a charity." For his part, Morrison would ruefully admit many years later to not being up to coaxing (he would never demand) much more of a budget out of Middlebury College. Nevertheless, he began ambitiously. He wrote to Willa Cather (she would be in Europe, alas, as would Christopher Morley, another to decline). He wrote to Thornton Wilder and Julia Peterkin, both of whom would be busy. He tried to reach Pearl S. Buck. Hervey Allen was too close to finishing his novel to want to travel. Farrar, of course, would come up for a weekend, and Munson for the duration, and Ted Weeks, and there was Margaret Widdemer, an earnest poet and novelist who had once received a Pulitzer and who had been coming to Bread Loaf since 1928. Morrison walked down the hall at Harvard and secured his old teacher in freshman English, Robert Hillyer. A deeply conservative lyric poet of, in Morrison's recollection, "traditional forms, delicately turned stanzas, fastidious versification, and scrupulous rhyme schemes," with quite a number of books out, the stolid, personally troubled Hillyer was of a vanishing breed even in 1932. If his hearing had been more acute he might have heard the word "mossback" whispered behind his back by the youthful and experimental. He could be brought to boiling point by the mere mention of Eliot or Pound, and his later public diatribe against the modernists for corrupting poetry would embarrass his friends and sympathizers.

Representing quite a different breed was the forty-year-old Archibald MacLeish, brought up as a weekend lecturer. After Yale ('15) and Harvard ('19) he had successfully practiced law until he resigned to follow his Muse, which for the moment spoke to him as a modernist in the style of Pound and Eliot. Moving to Paris with wife and two children and intending to live not in the style of a Boston lawyer but as a penniless Left Bank poet, MacLeish had produced a number of volumes in the subjective postwar vein. Now back in the United States and earning a good salary from Henry Luce at *Fortune,* the poet had been increasingly turning toward politics and history. His seventh book, *Conquistador,* was just out; he had written the poetic narrative about the conquest of Mexico after having made a long solitary trip in the footsteps of Hernando Cortez. It would receive much attention and a Pulitzer. From his summer place in Farmington, Connecticut, the handsome and outgoing MacLeish would often appear on the Mountain in the 1930s, and Bread Loafers would continue to be as charmed by him as they were curious to see how he had developed since the last time they had seen him.

In August 1932, Bread Loafers were still discussing the kidnapping and murder of the Lindberghs' son and speculating about whether the recently nominated Roosevelt with his stirring talk of a "New Deal" would prevail over President Herbert Hoover in the elections. They, like the country, seemed ready for a change. Somewhat suspicious and not in the least afraid to show it was Ted Morrison's next-door neighbor in Cambridge and fellow low-echelon lecturer at Harvard, Bernard DeVoto, whose teaching at Bread Loaf—as well as his off-the-Mountain advocacy of it—was to leave an indelible stamp upon the conference.

The thirty-five-year-old DeVoto—looking somewhat like a goggle-eyed former boxer with a rearranged nose—was a dependable source of bootlegged Canadian whiskey, but that was the least of his attributes even at Bread Loaf. From Ogden, Utah, he had previously taught at Northwestern, where he married one of his students, Avis MacVicar. Until recently he had been editor of the *Harvard Graduates' Magazine.* He had published three unnoticed novels, a writing handbook, many slick short stories in *Redbook* and *The Saturday Evening Post,* and a multitude of biting, trenchant essays for H.L. Mencken's *American Mercury, The Saturday Review* (beginning in 1936, but for only sixteen months, he would become its editor), and *Harper's* (for which he would later contribute years' worth of monthly columns in "The Easy Chair"). He was always remembered as a strikingly good teacher of fiction writing, but DeVoto's own work in the genre was flat and formulaic. Considering himself primarily a novelist, he would struggle for years and never get it right, primarily because all of his characters spoke and acted like himself. Toward the end of his life he would confide in a friend that "he had solved his life when he gave up fiction writing." His true métier was nonfiction—hard-hitting essays and brilliant narrative histories, the latter still some years away from 1932. However, there was his forthcoming *Mark Twain's America,* set for fall publication. In it he would rescue one of our greatest writers from the clutches of intellectuals who had psychoanalyzed him into a Freudian corner; in it he would mercilessly pummel poor Van Wyck Brooks, previous "owner-biographer" of Twain, to the point that Brooks would attract any number of samaritans to aid him. *Mark Twain's America* was about to put DeVoto on the intellectual map even as it created for him a host of enemies.

If he was pugnacious DeVoto was also generous, though he was always a tough editor who believed religiously in the curative powers of revision ("Just run it through your typewriter again" was one of his stock phrases). "Bernard DeVoto was my valued friend," wrote the historian Catherine Drinker Bowen, often known as Kitty, many years after their first meeting at Bread Loaf in 1933. "I am among the host of writers who came to him for advice, for criticism, and for general renewal of spirit. In letters and by word of mouth DeVoto and I shouted at each other. But always, in the end, I sat still and listened to what he had to say. And after each encounter, I came away rejoicing in

Bernard DeVoto, Archibald MacLeish, Theodore Morrison, 1937

ist." He was sinewy and tall, somewhat peppery in editorial discussions, and he was a merciless opponent in the daily croquet matches held next to the Inn on the west lawn. Fisher and Eaton would also be steady presences at Bread Loaf, particularly in the early Morrison years.

It was with such people as these in 1932 that Morrison attempted to refine the experimental raw material of Bread Loaf, trying to find the ideal conjunction between the academic and publishing and writing spheres. He had already decided that two weeks of uninterrupted lectures was too much for anyone, henceforth dividing the conference into two sections, a week of lectures and discussions and a week of what were then called "manuscript clinics" and are now called by the less Aesculapian term "workshops"—theory neatly followed by practice in an organized, highly compressed atmosphere. "I don't think that we can conceal from ourselves that it is fundamentally a teaching business," he wrote to President Moody in October, knowing that Moody was planning to ask the advice of John Farrar, "and that its success has depended and will depend on teaching skillfully done, and if you like, skillfully concealed. I think that we have found the right *kind* of staff member in the man or woman who unites actual writing with experience as a teacher. I do not believe that a publisher could do what we do at the Conference. It is because the publishers cannot do it that we undertake the job." As Morrison saw it, the conference should not become "a shop for re-writing manuscripts," nor should it consider its success to depend on their sale. "I think that it has a real and abiding value as an unconventional little academy—a school whose pupils are professional writers and whose teachers are also writers with the added experience of the art of instruction." A few weeks later he put a fine point on it: "Now . . . the opposite magnetic poles symbolized by Robert Frost and John Farrar each exert an influence on it, and the conference is bound to be a more or less happy compromise between them. It cannot be wholly abandoned to one or the other."

He had innovations in mind back then. He proposed merging the conference and the English School into one summer-long program with the former taking precedence; he imagined having residencies for creative writers who might occasionally be persuaded to participate in the regular sessions; he conjured the idea of a little Bread Loaf quarterly to publish established and emergent writers alike. But there was another problem facing them all: the depression. Industry was down to half of its high volume of 1929. Unemployment would climb in 1932 to thirteen million. National wages were 60 percent less than in 1929; even the desperate Herbert Hoover had given himself and his cabinet a 20 percent pay cut. Similarly, in Vermont the Middlebury College staff was taking less and the Writers'

the existence of that vivid, generous, and diabolically intelligent presence."

Two other writers on Morrison's faculty in 1932 were Dorothy Canfield Fisher and Walter Prichard Eaton. Fisher, square-jawed, graying, and with deep-set blue eyes, was fifty-three and of Vermont pioneer stock; she had studied at the Sorbonne and Columbia and had spent much time abroad. Now she lived a quiet domestic life on a farm near Arlington, Vermont. Fisher had published nearly a book every year since 1907, novels and collections of short stories, and was an active champion of the Montessori method of teaching. At Bread Loaf she spoke about the taste of the American reading public; she was able to do so as an original editorial board member of the Book-of-the-Month Club, for which she read about 150 books a year. Walter Prichard Eaton was an all-around hand in nonfiction. In Theodore Morrison's recollection he was "a writer and lecturer of unusual versatility, a dramatic critic and skilled teacher of playwriting, a journalist, essayist, music critic, a gardener, a man whose love of unspoiled natural surroundings gave him the sympathies of a conservation-

Conference would have to follow. In August 1929 the customer enrollment had been a pleasing sixty-four, but since the 1929 Crash attendance had steadily declined—forty-six, thirty-six, and twenty-three between 1930 and 1932. Knowing that some sort of axe was going to fall, Morrison hastened to urge tolerance from President Moody. "The country is full of people who want to come to Bread Loaf," he wrote; "they can't afford to." At his suggestion the tuition was reduced from $125 to $100. But his staff budget was cut and the college suggested he drop most of his outside lecturers as an economy. This Morrison did not plan to do, anticipating that some staff members would surely decline payment.

Even so, national events in 1933 threatened to close down the conference. There were bank panics and "bank holidays" to keep them from closing, and tightened credit; there were Roosevelt's reassuring-in-retrospect fireside chats, emergency relief, and a new army of governmental agencies, but times were dire. Though the college received more inquiries about Bread Loaf than in any previous year, subsequent cancellations left only six firmly registered customers. President Moody wired Morrison, on vacation in Nova Scotia in July, to say that it seemed best to cancel the conference. Morrison quickly replied, fearing that even a one-year suspension would kill Bread Loaf. He persuaded Moody to wait until opening day—if they had fifteen registrations they should go ahead. On July 31, the enrollment had climbed only to nine; on August 4, fourteen; by opening day of August 16, twenty, and the conference went on.

Very often during that conference, dinnertime conversations focused on the bumpy time books were having—federal courts might have finally allowed *Ulysses* into the United States after years of an obscenity ban, but in Germany the troublesome Nazi party had taken to piling books in public places and setting them afire. It appeared to some, though, that there were two empty places at the faculty tables in the dining hall, at least figuratively. First, there was no Hervey Allen, and second, no Robert Frost, who had stayed away since 1929. The nation had been eminently ready for escape reading since the Crash, and when Allen's mammoth, picaresque *Anthony Adverse* finally appeared in 1933 the sales went through the ceiling—half a million in hardcover within two years alone, a tremendous record in those desperate years. With the exception of *Gone With the Wind,* Allen's book was the largest seller of the decade, and he would have to get used to a more generous life-style and the host of concerns, tax and otherwise, that success was to bring him. When he did return to Bread Loaf, in 1934, his friends were waiting for him on the veranda of the Inn, curious to see what changes wealth had made in him. Sure enough, a

Sinclair Lewis, 1930s

long black limousine purred up the hill and eased to a stop opposite them. The liveried chauffeur leaped out, opened the rear door with a flourish—to reveal only Ann Allen. Hervey was nowhere in sight. Then, the onlookers heard a "putt putt putt" down the road. A humble Ford flivver appeared, to their amazement driven by Hervey Allen.

In Frost's case, Ted Morrison had begun to make overtures in early 1933 by inviting him to deliver a reading at the conference. Apparently Frost was insulted by the depression pay of fifty dollars and made the college officials aware of his displeasure. Morrison was to apologize to the poet with a reasonable-sounding explanation—times *were* bad all around—but Bread Loaf was to remain Frostless while the conference director thought up another approach.

The twenty paying customers in 1933 did not lack for celebrities, however. There would be the genial Archibald MacLeish and the unpredictable Sinclair Lewis, whose novel *Ann Vickers* was to appear that year with its thinly disguised, unsympathetic portrait of his long-suffering wife, Dorothy Thompson, the career journalist whom Hitler had tossed out of Germany when she described him as "inconsequent and voluble, ill-poised, insecure." Bernard and Avis DeVoto had stopped by Twin Farms in Barnard on their way up to Bread Loaf from Massachusetts. DeVoto found Lewis drinking only beer and surmised that a return engagement would not be as scandalous as the visits in 1928 to the Writers' Conference and in 1929 to the English School. In the latter episode, Lewis had arrived before noon and delivered a decent talk to one of the classes. "After the evening meal," remembered a faculty member, Fred Lewis Pattee, "he went to his room in Maple Cottage and two strangers drove up and went in. . . . At 8 the audience room of the school was crowded. . . . No Lewis. Five minutes no Lewis, ten minutes, fifteen and the President son of Evangelist Moody went up. Lewis seeing him said, 'Here, Prexy, we've got the damnedest good gin. Have a drink.'" When he was finally conveyed to the lectern, it was to deliver, in one irate observer's words, "an inexcusably discourteous, shoddy performance by an inebriated celebrity."

DeVoto and Morrison hoped for a better showing in 1933; after all, Lewis was on the wagon. Put in charge of the last afternoon roundtable discussion, Lewis behaved himself but was unable to rouse the customers from a respectful torpor. By dinner the novelist had been fortified by a bottle of whiskey, and in a carrying voice, waving his silverware, his eyes seeming to burst from his reddened face, he launched into one of his famous poetic improvisations in a given poet's voice and meter. Ted Morrison recalled it as "an extraordinary tour de force, elaborated at surprising length, a kind of free-verse, Vachel Lindsay–like chant celebrating the hegira of Bernard DeVoto from Ogden, Utah, to the effete culture of the East. If DeVoto, listening close at hand, was in the least put out, he did not show it by a twitch." Lewis's address that evening was boozy, lackluster, and self-pitying. In two years his theme—"Random Thoughts on Literature as a Business"—would be set down in more cogent form for the *Yale Literary Magazine,* edited by young Brendan Gill. In it he advised young writers to have a trade, but not in advertising, teaching, or journalism, for the days of writers earning big money were over. At the Bread Loaf lectern, however, the audience was distracted from his words by his glassy eyes and slurred speech. Writing was a great art, Lewis assured them. But it was a lousy business. With all of his commercial success, as so many were going on relief, listeners were puzzled: What was Lewis talking about?

R ound about early August, returning Bread Loafers find themselves preoccupied (to the exclusion of much of their "real" lives) with anticipating their return to the Mountain. It was as much so in 1934, only the ninth annual gathering, as it is today. Bernard DeVoto, who would always write about the conference with jubilation only partially tempered by irony, confessed as much to his friend Kate Sterne. "When we can barricade ourselves away from the customers," he wrote,

we'll have a good time. At four P.M. on Thursday the entire gang will be in that pre-game jitters, deciding wholesale that it was a mistake to accept the appointment, quarreling with each other, and clamoring to poor Morrison for room transfers and transportation out, and drinking some luke-warm infusion of Hervey's made up of old tea, sweet vermouth, sugar syrup, Scotch, lemon peel, grenadine, cedar bark and table salt, and never wondering why they feel so bad. The bark of a Pontiac horn, a bellboy enters bearing ice, then silence and expectation for a space, and, the dust of Lincoln still on him, Benny is seen mixing martinis. At once she'll be driving six white horses and no one needs to tell me why I'm asked to Bread Loaf year after year.

Indeed, bearing certain arcane southern recipes for punch, Hervey Allen returned for a full-term engagement. He would get an opportunity to serve his concoctions in one of the cottages across the road from the Inn. Ted Morrison had decided that the conference needed a "tea room" for general socializing before and after meals and following the evening programs. The chosen cottage, named for the Treman family that had once occupied it in the Battell years, would not attract the numbers he'd hoped for in 1934 but would gain in popularity over the years. The next year the general social center was removed to the Fritz Cottage down the road, and Treman Cottage was restricted to faculty only, as a private lounge and retreat in which old friends could reacquaint and make new associations without feeling that they were performing onstage; it would free them, necessarily, for a few hours in each very public day from the incessant barrage of publishing questions and requests for favors that students naturally were eager to make—and did, during and between all public events. Allen was scheduled to conduct a roundtable discussion and to lecture on "The Rewards and Punishments of Writing." He was, in the words of fellow staff member Fanny Butcher of the *Chicago Daily Tribune,* "sort of pater squire of the mountain . . . always in the breach in the arguments about experimentation vs. classic methods, sitting hours on the side porch of his cottage trying to iron out the problems of the inexperienced, never losing his poise nor his patience." It would be noted in *The Crumb* that Farrar and Rinehart had been talking about *Anthony Adverse* and fourteen other national best-sellers published by the firm when it took out an advertisement in *Publishers Weekly*: "There are no bad seasons for good books."

Ted Morrison had worked overtime in the winter to publicize Hervey Allen's presence, hoping to swell the conference rolls, and he had announced with equal pride that he had finally secured Julia Peterkin to teach fiction writing after several years of encountering scheduling dif-

Hervey Allen, 1935

Sister Mary (1924), which received a Pulitzer Prize, meant "to present these people in a patient struggle with fate," Peterkin would explain, "and not in any race conflict." Her books, which fell into a category critics called "American Primitive," along with the works of DuBose Heyward, humanized the African-American in a southern liberal way without excoriating the southern system; they were banned anyway from many regional libraries. Other writers of the time were addressing American racism in other ways, such as Carl Van Vechten, who wrote of the Harlem Negro, and Langston Hughes and Richard Wright, who focused on the urban Negro proletariat. Julia Peterkin, though, "wrote what she knew" as she presided over the sprawling Lang Syne Plantation in South Carolina, which employed nearly five hundred African-Americans and raised not only cotton but asparagus, wheat, and oats. Donald Davidson had called *Black April* (1927) "perhaps the first genuine novel in English of the Negro as a human being." *Scarlet Sister Mary* not only made her a national reputation but, when dramatized, afforded Ethel Barrymore her first—and last—opportunity to play a role in blackface. At Bread Loaf, Peterkin's "progress down the white marble paths was that of a queen with her court," recalled Fanny Butcher, "or of a surgeon and his gallery."

There was something new in the air at the conference—in fact, one might have called it a celebration of the new. Among the other regulars was Archibald MacLeish, who in his usual boostering way was talking about his latest enthusiasm, a young unknown poet by the name of James Agee, for whose book (in the Yale Series) MacLeish had just written an introduction. Agee was not present, but other emerging writers were, and they were accorded a special status. Ted Morrison had beaten the bushes of Publishers' Row for seed money and nominations. He had also continued to urge the college's support. Finally, in early 1934, he was able to announce a new Bread Loaf fellowship program. It was to be competitive, drawn from nominations by publishers, agents, writers, and teachers; that year twenty-two obliging editors nominated some thirty-seven writers. (John Farrar kept out of it; "I think it would be a bad idea," he wrote to Morrison in February, "for us to recommend any one for the scholarships. Somehow we are identified closely enough.") Initially the program was to be administered by Morrison, DeVoto, and Weeks. DeVoto, too, became a sort of dean of fellows at the conference, watching out for them and introducing them around. The fellowship program was one that newspapers would continue to oblige the conference by publicizing for decades to come. First-timers would be given a sort of mountaintop coming-out party with established writers offering their advice and contacts.

One of the five fellows named that year was Catherine

ficulties. Tall and lithe, with striking long red hair, Julia Peterkin had broken into print (in H. L. Mencken's *Smart Set*) after Carl Sandburg discovered her; later there was the ambitious little southern magazine, Emily Clark's *Reviewer*. Peterkin devoted her professional career to writing about southern plantation blacks. Her mother had died when she was born, and Peterkin was raised by an African-American nanny who had acquainted her with folklore and with the Gullah dialect. Three books, particularly *Scarlet*

Drinker Bowen, a thirty-seven-year-old Pennsylvanian. She had published a novel and was shopping for a publisher for a volume of essays on music, *Friends and Fiddlers.* Bowen had registered as a student of the conference—her fellowship was awarded after she had showed herself and her work there and after she had made an enduring friend and patron in Bernard DeVoto, who would immediately find her a publisher in Little, Brown. She had begun to focus on the nonfiction genre for which she would later be known, biography. *Beloved Friend* was in preparation—the epistolary biography of Tchaikovsky and his patroness, Nadejda von Meck, would sell more than 150,000 copies after publication in 1937; after several other books, there would be her best-selling biography of Chief Justice Oliver Wendell Holmes, Jr., *Yankee From Olympus* (1944), and a biography of John Adams. Throughout there would be the advice and support of DeVoto—one of whose unceasing maxims in 1934 Bowen took courage from and never forgot: "[T]o be a writer you have to push out into the open and take knock after knock."

DeVoto befriended another Bread Loaf fellow in 1934, a lovely waif named Josephine Johnson who had been nominated by *The Atlantic Monthly* for her realistic novel of bleak life on a Missouri farm, *Now in November,* set for publication that September. DeVoto contributed a blurb for the book ("In the ten years of my existence before the public," he wrote John Farrar, "I have been able to report only two quotable blurbs—the one I did for Josephine Johnson because I thought her book altogether fine and beautiful.") As a latter-day Joseph Battell, it seems—in "a fury of admiration," in Wallace Stegner's words, but remaining at a focal-plane distance—DeVoto snapped a number of portraits of Johnson around the Bread Loaf campus. Later he campaigned to have his protégée named to the regular faculty. It was easy to justify—the novel won a Pulitzer in 1935. "She is a sensitive little thing," said Fanny Butcher, "destined, so everyone agreed, to be really great."

Success for another 1934 fellow came more quickly. *The Crumb* announced that California novelist Scott O'Dell had just sold motion picture rights to his first novel, *Woman of Spain.* After Stanford, the descendant of Sir Walter Scott had worked in Hollywood during the silent era as a cameraman, where he had filmed several of Gloria Swanson's movies as well as the original *Ben Hur* and *Son of the Sheik* with Rudolph Valentino (whose mobbed funeral in New York, it is interesting to note, had taken place during the first Bread Loaf conference in 1926). O'Dell showed a career-long interest in the downtrodden; he would write four other novels for adults before turning to a distinguished list of children's books, including *Island of the Blue Dolphins* (1960). He had driven to Vermont from California, and he took an active part in the evening entertainments; Fanny Butcher wrote that he was "the best looking and most engaging young gentleman on the range."

One somber note was felt only by a few people close to Julia Peterkin. She had commanded rapt attention from her audiences and attracted small groups of the devoted; she would sometimes "sprawl and drawl" on the lawn and smoke a cigarette. One day near to the end of the conference she received a telegram that a close friend and collaborator, Doris Ullman, had just died. She finished all of her teaching obligations that day. At dinner one observer found her "sweet and grave." She left soon after on a night train for New York.

In 1917, a young field artillery officer serving in France by the name of John Crowe Ransom was giving at least some of his thoughts to literature. He had trusted a sheaf of poems to his friend in New York, Christopher Morley, who placed a few in magazines but had difficulty finding a publisher for the book-length manuscript *Poems About God.* While it was being examined at Henry Holt and Company, Ransom decided that if his book was rejected he would withdraw it for revision after the war was over. But the outside reader to whom Holt sent the poems liked them and urged their publication. His name was Robert Frost, and upon his advice Holt published Ransom's first book in 1919. Frost and Ransom would not meet for many years—not until after Ransom had begun teaching at Vanderbilt, after he had met his student and later colleague Donald Davidson, and after they had published *The Fugitive* (in which Ransom had admired Frost's deft poetic use of irony). In the mid-thirties, Ransom invited Frost down to Nashville for a well-received, exhilarating reading. After the evening reception, which lasted until 3:00 A.M., Ransom drove his guest back to his hotel. "There before the front entrance—both still in tuxedos—and in the lobby," wrote Ransom's biographer, Thomas Daniel Young,

> the two poets talked until daylight. Milkmen were on the street, Ransom recalled many years afterwards, before they went inside, and "there we stood in our dress clothes, in the morning sun, still talking. People passing by must have thought it funny." Just before he was due at school for an eight o'clock class, Ransom rushed home to change clothes. His wife, whom he had dropped off on his way downtown, was awakened and heard him complain as he searched for appropriate clothing, "I must go to class, but Robert Frost can sleep."

Thus forged, their friendship would continue for many years despite their personal and poetic differences; Frost would be speaking about his friend Ransom and the New Criticism when he said in 1940 to young Bread Loaf English student Peter Stanlis that "We murder to dissect"—he wished Ransom would return to his own poetry. He would be instrumental in 1937 in getting the neglected Ransom from Vanderbilt to Kenyon College where he was to flourish anew as teacher, editor, and critic. And nowhere would their association be so regularly renewed as at Bread Loaf; this tradition began after the Nashville reading at Bread Loaf's 1935 Writers' Conference, where John Crowe Ransom served as a full-term faculty member and where Robert Frost made a brief appearance a few days after delivering the commencement speech at the English School. (Frost's biographer Lawrance Thompson has been rightly criticized for getting most of the facts right but frequently missing the man; in the case of Frost and Bread Loaf, he got many of his facts wrong, including when the poet was present at the conference.) Moreover, in the 1940s, when Ransom became a regular faculty member of the Bread Loaf School of English and Frost had become a nearby summer resident, their association on the Mountain would continue. Then, as well as in 1935, the two continued Frost's habit of walking and talking the night away. Presumably Ransom would have been present when Frost delivered an informal talk on the west lawn adjacent to the Inn. "Those who sat in the sun that morning listening to him talk of life and writing and many things," reported *The Crumb*, "realize how pleasantly profitable are some of the most casual conversations. Bread Loaf is like that." In the evening, Frost's friends hosted a reception for him in the Little Theatre. Having Ransom there, and other friendly presences such as Julia Peterkin and Bernard DeVoto, subtly began to rebuild the ruined bridges between the poet and the Writers' Conference, to each party's benefit.

Certainly by 1935 Ransom had ceased to publish his most significant verse—though he primly read some of his older poems in his soft Tennessee accent—but he had come into his own as a critic. He carried this on in the lecture hall, talking on the subjects of "The Character of Artists," "Relativity in Poetry," answering the question, "Do Poets Communicate?" (yes, he said, and no), and leading a classroom verse clinic in constructing six cantos about points of view at Bread Loaf:

So many stories vibrate in a face,
Flame out of eyes, or flash along the halls,
So much of living centered in one place
Might fire the roof or pulverize the walls.

He was assisted in poetry by Ted Morrison and on one day by Stephen Vincent Benét, who had arrived for a visit with John Farrar—making for the most interesting conjunction of a Nashville New Critic, a Harvard Yard narrative poet, and an Americanist balladeer, presided over by "that most amiable of party hounds." Bread Loaf was like that.

It was the tenth anniversary of the Writers' Conference, and there was much to celebrate—it had weathered first its very evanescent, experimental nature and next the depression's wolf at the door, and at that midpoint in the 1930s there at last began to appear the first gleam of hope that times would not always be bad.

It may have been this session that found DeVoto and Ted Morrison sitting in the rear of the Little Theatre as Edith Mirrielees lectured on the novel. "Just call in all your outfielders," DeVoto whispered admiringly, "and let Edith pitch." Mirrielees was hardly an innovative teacher but she showed great skill in handling the diverse Bread Loaf audience and its reams of manuscripts. "She was a maiden lady of impeccable taste and refinement," recalled Ted Morrison,

a gentlewoman if ever there was one. But with the gentleness went a quick wit and a tough intelligence and a stamina undaunted by the crudities of life or of less fastidious characters. She had in remarkable degree the capacity to prick bubbles of pretense or absurdity without leaving the victim scarred or humiliated. She was not curt with bores, though she had her own way of handling them. Once we had at the conference a man with such a singular gift for *non sequiturs* that it amounted to a special genius. He was always intervening during lectures with questions or remarks that threw the discussion so far off track as to have an effect that was paralyzing. I asked Edith how she dealt with his interruptions when she was on the stand. "I just enclose them quietly in parentheses," she said, "and go right on."

Another time, Mirrielees was sitting in the dining hall when a woman of considerable size and presence gushed at her, "Oh, Miss Mirrielees, I did so enjoy your lecture this morning. I simply hung on your word. I hope they supported you," Edith Mirrielees replied.

Four emerging writers were chosen for fellowships from a pool of forty-five candidates nominated by twenty-six publishers. The one we shall mention here was Howard Fast, the nineteen-year-old son of a factory worker, who had published his first novel at eighteen. *Two Valleys*, set during the American Revolution, set his pattern for powerful, realistic historical novels. *Citizen Tom Paine, April Morning*, and *Spartacus*, among many others, were still years away. So was his membership in the Communist party, his repudiation of it, the blacklist, and his prison term for defying the House Un-American Activities Committee. "I was a tough working class kid" in 1935, he recalled. "I'd

Outside the Little Theatre: Fletcher Pratt, Edith Mirrielees, Kay Morrison, Avis DeVoto, Lovell Thompson (BDV)

never been in that kind of environment before. One day I came out of my room and found John Mason Brown, the drama critic for *Theatre Arts* and *The New York Post*." Brown was a Harvard man and Fast was assuredly not—he had dropped out of high school, had been a hobo and a day laborer, and had furthered his education as a page at the New York Public Library. He was then, he recalled, somewhere to the left of Stalin. "Rather like college, isn't it," Brown had said to Fast. "Not like any school I've ever seen," the young man retorted. The sights alternately amazed and enthralled him: Julia Peterkin, "very lovely, gentle and kind"; Gorham Munson, chain-smoking from stub to stub; the young post-Prohibition sophisticates and the "forward" young women, "drowning themselves in gin—I'd never seen that before, I'd been in a couple of working-class saloons but never to a nightclub." He gladly gulped down the institutional Bread Loaf food, wondered how a great poet like Robert Frost could read "like his mouth was full of marbles," and spent a day walking in the woods with the New England novelist Gladys Hasty Carroll. "Some younger people made cracks about what we were doing," Fast recalled. "I wouldn't have known what to do." Carroll shared some of Fast's feelings of alienation. At the Treman faculty lounge she found Bernard DeVoto to be bumptious and profane, and she later wrote a schoolmarmish letter of

complaint to Middlebury President Moody. But, as Wallace Stegner has pointed out, it was DeVoto who returned to Bread Loaf in subsequent years, and Carroll who stayed in Maine.

In some ways the Bread Loaf of 1936 was a stand-pat sort of session: Why tamper with the known quality? Voters were feeling that way about Franklin Roosevelt, and Ted Morrison was of a similar mind about his faculty. Dean of fellows DeVoto was glad to get his literary ward, Josephine Johnson, back to Bread Loaf on the faculty; she hated, though, to talk before audiences, and her best memories were saved for moments away from the lectern, not only for time spent with associates but also for the astounding wildflowers all around the campus. Peterkin came up for her third and last session. Ransom and Davidson were not present but they sent up a young protégé, George Marion O'Donnell, to represent the Fugitives as a Bread Loaf fellow. Robert Hillyer also returned to lecture on the techniques of verse. His poured-on-thick poem, "A Letter to Robert Frost," was published that month by editor DeVoto in *The Saturday Review*. At Bread Loaf Hillyer showed another poem—more personal and polemic, taking aim at leftists and symbolists and linking the author's sentiments with his editor's. When DeVoto published it later in the year, it would prompt *The New Masses'*

Gladys Hasty Carroll, 1935

Granville Hicks to respond, also in rhymed couplets, with an acid attack on Hillyer, Frost, DeVoto, and "the Bread Loaf gang." (Hicks's response would never be fully published, although a truncated version found its way a year later into *The New Republic.*)

Robert Frost and John Farrar were the only nonfaculty speakers; due to a timely illness Farrar's appearance was rescheduled from the first weekend, when Frost would be present, to the second. Frost had not been eager to go at all. His latest collection, *A Further Range,* had appeared in the spring to great commercial success (the Book-of-the-Month Club took it, and it received a Pulitzer the next year) but to hostile critical notices, chiefly by liberal and left-wing critics riled by his moralistic light versifying against the New Deal, Marxism, and internationalists. Frost winced when friends at Bread Loaf lavished expressions of sympathy upon him—he distrusted their motives—and not even the presence of his friend Louis Untermeyer and the chance to do amiable battle on the

bumpy clay tennis courts could assuage him. As soon as he could he took his leave. Ted Morrison remembered standing with his wife, Kay, as they shudderingly watched Robert and Elinor Frost at the end of their stay "wobble down the road with Robert at the wheel of a car which he managed to drive by a series of spasms rather than any rapport with the engine." Frost erupted all over with shingles when he got back home.

Shingles plaguing a noted poet makes for a good story, as do occasions of cultural infighting in the editorial columns—but one cannot minimize how the political, the personal, and the creative had merged in the arts of that time, and one cannot neglect what happened off the Mountain before, during, and after the conference. It had become utterly impossible, anywhere, to ignore the menace of fascism. Sinclair Lewis's *It Can't Happen Here* appeared in 1936, as did Victor Wolfson's *Bitter Stream,* both predicting that the price of American apathy could end in dictatorship over its own shores. One could scrutinize the lower appeal of Governor Long or Father Coughlin—or, for a real nightmare, one could look toward Europe. In Spain, the rightist military rebellion against the popularly elected left-wing coalition Republican government had surged beyond control in July, with Hitler agreeing to aid General Franco's Nationalists. In the declining weeks of August, the daily Boston and New York newspapers dispensed at Bread Loaf began to report on the closed Spanish border, the progress of the fascists' march on Madrid, the massacres in Badajoz, and the divisive, ominous "nonintervention" policy of the European nations. By the time the Bread Loaf Inn hosted the next session in August 1937, three thousand Americans, a number of them writers, were fighting or reporting on the Spanish Civil War, and many others wrote about it at home. Two books, *Authors Take Sides* and *Writers Take Sides,* collections of hundreds of statements about Spain, were published in 1937 and 1938. And, in most geographical gazetteers of the mind, the names of Jarama, Guernica, and Brunete had found their indelible place.

The sight of someone goose-stepping and fascist-saluting across Bread Loaf's west lawn in August 1937 was taken in the whistling-past-the-graveyard spirit in which it was offered by one James T. Farrell, visiting lecturer. He was a hearty and outspoken antifascist who, like many intellectuals, was breaking ranks with leftists for their excessive doctrinairism. He had attended the crowded Second Congress of the League of American Writers in New York earlier in the summer, during which the recently returned Hemingway spoke of Spain and "the problems of a writer in wartime." Farrell saw intellectual lock-stepping there at Carnegie Hall and wrote about it for DeVoto's *Saturday Review.* But politics aside for the moment, Farrell had come a long literary way. He had lived on Guggenheim money for a year and he had just received a $25,000 Book-of-the-Month Prize for his trilogy *Studs Lonigan.* That was quite a distance from 1932, when his first novel, *Young Lonigan,* had been published by James Henle's Vanguard Press. The naturalistic, stream-of-consciousness portrait of the mind of a teenaged street kid contained so much sexually explicit material that Vanguard feared obscenity statutes; it issued the book in a plain dust jacket with only this statement: "This novel is issued in a special edition, the sale of which is limited to physicians, surgeons, psychologists, psychiatrists, sociologists, social workers, teachers, and other persons having a professional interest in the psychology of adolescence."

The novel and its two successors had found genesis in a creative writing course at the University of Chicago in 1929, where Farrell was a sometime student. "Although I read continuously and rather broadly," he later remembered, "after my sophomore year I could not maintain a steady interest in any of my courses except in composition, where I could write as much as I pleased. I would cut other classes, day after day, finally dropping out, heedless of the loss of credit and the waste of money I had spent for tuition." Most of what he wrote related, as he said,

to death, disintegration, human indignity, poverty, drunkenness, ignorance, human cruelty. They attempted to describe dusty and deserted streets, street corners, miserable homes, pool rooms, brothels, dance halls, taxi dances, bohemian sections, express offices, gasoline filling stations, scenes laid in slum districts. The characters were boys, boys' gangs, drunkards, Negroes, expressmen, homosexuals, immigrants and immigrant landlords, filling-station attendants, straw bosses, hitch hikers, bums, bewildered parents.

Exactly the locales and characters he would be known for later. One of these short stories, entitled "Studs," is the story of a wake told by one of the mourners who has come to view an Irish-Catholic friend with whom he had roamed Chicago's mean streets, now dead at the age of twenty-six. The composition was praised by Farrell's professors. After he left school he lived a shabby, lonely, and frustrating life, supporting his writing with miserable jobs, including one in an undertaking parlor, as the college short story grew into one novel and then two and three.

Short, rumpled, and poker-faced, Farrell spent much of his time at Bread Loaf with Bernard and Avis DeVoto, returning more than once to the martini pitcher at Treman. He never reached the heights set by Sinclair Lewis during his appearances but, in the words of Ted Morrison, "my recollection is that cups of black coffee and a supervised walk in the fresh air formed a part of Farrell's lecture preparation." The talk, a long one on realism in the modern American novel, was widely attended. But, Morrison wrote, "he read it in a drone with his nose never far above his manuscript."

Paul Green, up from Chapel Hill to teach Bread Loafers drama, did better in front of audiences. In his lecture on "The Movies and the Theatre," he contrasted his unhappy year in Hollywood writing for Will Rogers and George Arliss with his many good experiences writing and producing for the New York stage. There had been *Abraham's Bosom,* awarded a Pulitzer in 1928, and *The Field God* and *Roll, Sweet Chariot,* all set in North Carolina, the place where he felt most at home: "Back with my own folks, and I mean black and white," he had written,

I can't help feeling that they are experiencing life that no art can compass. . . . There among them I felt at home as I'll never feel at home elsewhere. The smell of their sweaty bodies, the gusto of their indecent jokes, the knowledge of their twisted philosophies, the sight of their feet entangled among the pea-vines and grass, their shouts, grunts and belly-achings, the sun blistering down upon them, and the rim of the sky enclosing them forever, all took me wholly, and I was one of them—neither black nor white but one of them, children of the moist earth underfoot.

The previous year Green (who early on had been acclaimed as the nation's best playwright after O'Neill) had teamed with Kurt Weill to write *Johnny Johnson* for the Group Theatre, and he had just opened an ambitious, experimental "symphonic drama" about the Lost Colony of Roanoke that would involve 150 actors and singers and run for decades on that North Carolina island. "If he sometimes had to be almost shovelled out of bed to meet an early lecture hour," Ted Morrison recalled, "on the tennis court he commanded a backhand that exploded like a high velocity shell."

Among the five fellows in 1937 was an odd little man given to shockingly loud shirts and ties, a former welterweight boxer by the name of Fletcher Pratt: "half genius," as his friend DeVoto would say, "and half rodent." The first to admit that he would "write anything for anybody, anytime," Pratt had published widely—journalism and other prose, notably science fiction in the pulp magazines. That year, and in eighteen subsequent sessions as "dean of nonfiction," Pratt was fond of listing how many celebrated authors had written for the cheap periodical press. A satirical couplet in *The Crumb* in 1937 purported to quote Pratt:

Don't try to drink success in highbrow gulps:
Remember, Arnold Bennett wrote for pulps.

Fletcher Pratt, Inga Pratt, Edith Mirrielees, late 1930s

Pratt often used a sporting maxim learned from his days dancing on canvas to justify his relentless marketing advice to the customers: "Never fight out of your weight." They were words that totally missed two other fellows who by chance roomed together, the poets Robert Francis and James Still. They found, however, much in common. Both had published their first books the previous year and, mirroring their poetic styles, both lived reflective, hermetic lives. Francis had built a two-room cabin, which he called "Fort Juniper," in the woods outside of Amherst; Still inhabited an old log cabin on Dead Mare Branch of Little Carr Creek in Kentucky. Francis had come up to Bread Loaf hoping to see Robert Frost (lecturing at the conference), who had befriended him a few years before. Frost would later call Francis "the best neglected poet." Their association, along with that of Frost and Charles H.

Foster and Peter Stanlis over the next few years, at least partially refutes the commonly held belief that Frost could not be generous even to younger poets who offered him no competition.

This is not to say that Robert Frost had no meanness in his soul. One cannot appreciate Frost the man without accommodating both the light and the dark sides of his personality. He could smolder in resentment for years, with it surfacing in biting offhand remarks or remaining hidden in references about people made in private correspondence to trusted friends like Untermeyer. Or it could flash out in abrupt storms of temper. Sometimes it was provoked, sometimes not. Only occasionally was it premeditated or purposeful. But nowhere did it so famously reach the heights as it did at Bread Loaf in August 1938.

FROST HEAVES

In March 1938, in Gainesville, Florida, the world caved in for Robert Frost when his wife of forty-two years, Elinor, died after a series of heart attacks. She had never been well, and in fact her marriage to the mercurial Frost, with its dirt-poor early years and her six childbirths, had done much to weaken her. He was almost paralyzed with grief and guilt. Hervey Allen and Louis Untermeyer were among the close friends who immediately went to comfort the poet, and sympathy letters poured in from others whom he treasured, such as Bernard DeVoto. "I expect," Frost responded to DeVoto, "to have to go depths below depths in thinking before I catch myself and can say what I want to be while I last. I shall be all right in public, but I can't tell yet how I am going to behave when I am alone."

Later, in July 1938, after he had closed up their house in Amherst and moved to the farmhouse in South Shaftsbury, Vermont, he received a note from the Morrisons inviting him to a kind of public refuge at Bread Loaf for the two weeks of the Writers' Conference. He had been scheduled, as for the previous sessions, as a weekend visitor and lecturer. But now he was invited to do as many or as few talks and readings as he liked. Accordingly, they agreed he would deliver an evening reading, three morning lectures, at least one manuscript clinic, and the conference's concluding remarks—the most involvement that Frost had ever had at the conference. But in the weeks before Bread Loaf, matters became more involved.

Still brooding and awash with guilt and loneliness, the poet presented a shaky front. Kathleen (Kay) Morrison had known him since her Bryn Mawr student days when her writing club had brought Frost to the campus for three days in 1920; that slight acquaintance, renewed periodically at Bread Loaf, had been solidified beginning in 1936 at Harvard when the Morrisons had hosted the receptions after his Norton lectures. Now, solicitously, Mrs. Morrison met him several times at a mutual friend's country place and they took long walks in which Frost poured out his doubts and troubles. Her father had recently died; many years later she would say that the comparatively aged Frost filled a certain empty place for her. But from that same late period, nearly ten years after Frost was dead, Kay Morrison wrote that she was astounded when one day the poet abruptly declaimed his love for her, voicing almost a demand that she leave her husband (and small children) and marry him. She refused him, Kay wrote, with all the grace she could muster. But the Writers' Conference loomed.

Putting up in one of the little cottages between the Inn and Treman, which he would share for a few days with the Untermeyers, Frost was constantly attended by friends who saw he was still teetering near nervous collapse. Before his evening reading, on August 18, he was in an ominous frame of mind. "I've had a queer feeling all day that this is the last time I'd speak here," he muttered to friends, "and I've been reminiscing like a drowning man, remembering things as fast as I could. It's a strange feeling."

The combined lecture and reading began with some impromptu, free verse poems. "They weren't really poems in any sense," recorded a witness, Frances Fox Sandmel, "just loosely woven, reflective speaking, simple, sincere, said with silver haired ease, and somehow pathos." He finished with a good number of more formal poems. It was, in the words of young Charles Foster, a poet serving as the first Elinor Frost Fellow, "the best lecture I have ever heard him give. His mind was seething and rolling with metaphors and humor and he was exhausted when he was finished."

Outside, to Ted Morrison, Frost confessed he'd felt strange all day. Sandmel was standing nearby when a breathless young southern woman got the poet to sign her book. "Now I feel that heaven has come right down on earth," she later told Sandmel. "He autographed my book. But he said, 'It's the last time.'"

He was unpredictable, especially to his friends, talking bitterly of his "badness" and abruptly stalking away, drinking hard liquor for the first time that any could remember. "Frost told me," wrote Charles Foster in his journal, "that he was a God-damned son-of-a-bitch, a selfish person who had dragged people rough-shod over life. People didn't understand [him] who wanted to make him good. His rebellion looked so good, he said, but he was always a person who had his way, a God-damned son of a bitch, Charlie, and don't let anyone tell you different." But he did muster the courtesy to attend some of his friends' lectures and readings and became the center of a little nightly vortex of involved conversation on the Treman porch. Avis DeVoto and—bravely, one supposes, under the circumstances—Kay Morrison conducted him on long walks in the surrounding forest; to Mrs. Morrison, he apparently kept up his appeals to leave his host, her husband. Her repeated answer, according to her book, *Robert Frost: A Pictorial Chronicle,* was "No"—the most she said that she would agree to beyond friendship was to type his backed-up correspondence at the close of the conference.

Meanwhile, despite these distractions, the conference was proving to be one of the most brilliant in its thirteen years. Frances Sandmel was moved to write to a friend that "Mr. Morrison, Mr. DeVoto, and Mr. Munson are all brilliant and trenchant thinkers, with a 'live and let very few others live' attitude, and a glorious intolerance for ineptitude and mediocrity. The atmosphere of the place was a strange mixture of incisive caustic canniness, and absolute acceptance of excellence where (if!) it can be found." DeVoto, in particular, was in outstanding form. On August 23, he who, as a younger man, had fled Utah in angry dismay delivered a thumping lecture on the errors of the Mormon Church, "The Angel and the Book." Ted Morrison remembered what happened:

I hear DeVoto bellowing out, "The fountains of the great deep shall be unloosed," the Biblical words immediately followed by a close flash of lightning and a crack of

thunder fit, in Lear's phrase, to "Strike flat the thick rotundity of the earth." I have seen speakers at Bread Loaf forced helplessly to give up by the noise of a cloudburst on the roof of the one-story lecture hall, even without the accompaniment of thunder and lightning. Not so DeVoto. He finished a coherent and impressive lecture despite darkness and celestial fireworks.

One of the junior faculty members exulting in DeVoto's performance was a twenty-nine-year-old alumnus of the University of Utah, Wallace Stegner. It had been after his postgraduate studies at Iowa, while he was an instructor at Utah, that he had seen an announcement of a novella contest conducted by Little, Brown; he wrote one, *Remembering Laughter,* entered, and won. DeVoto was one of the judges. Stegner wrote to thank him, "the kind of asking-for-advice letter that young writers are always writing older writers—and I got back a very decent and very intelligent response." The next year, in 1937, Stegner was teaching at the University of Wisconsin and met DeVoto at the annual convention of the Modern Language Association. And after the 1938 conference their association would solidify, for Wallace and Mary Stegner were on their way to Cambridge and Harvard—by way of their farm in Greensboro Bend, Vermont, which Stegner had bought from his royalty advance—and the DeVotos were in Cambridge. Stegner would, many years later, recall that time as exhilarating

because for the first time in my life I was moving among people who really rattled my brains. Benny was always happy to act as a guru. When I told him I had to write some stuff for money, because we were just too poor to make it otherwise, he took me over one afternoon and said, "My boy, here are my files." He showed me all the files of his *Collier's* stories, how you did it, and laid me out formulas. I could never write to a formula, but I thought that was decent of him.

Stegner would return to Bread Loaf during seven subsequent sessions either as a full-time instructor of fiction or as a visiting lecturer, and nowhere has Bread Loaf been written about as vividly or with as much comprehension as in *The Uneasy Chair,* his biography of Bernard DeVoto.

Stegner's comprehension of the storms of 1938, though, came later after comparing notes with others present—he was after all a junior faculty member, had not known Frost before, and was not sensitive to the nuances of words and deeds that others could interpret by second nature. This was especially so on Saturday, August 17, after *The Crumb* announced that the evening lecture would be given by Archibald MacLeish, Pulitzer Prize winner in poetry.

MacLeish had come up from his summer place in Farmington, Connecticut, arriving for lunch with no idea of the ambush that awaited him amidst the genteel Victorian surroundings. That evening after dinner, people filed into the Little Theatre to hear him read and talk—among them was Robert Frost, who sat in the rear. In his heart he still harbored nearly twenty-year-old resentments against MacLeish and his postwar expatriate friends and as much disliked his new ones, welfare-dispensing New Dealers whose chief in the White House would soon nominate MacLeish to be Librarian of Congress. He thought MacLeish's new verse was less poetry than poster—addressing *subjects,* something always guaranteed to raise Frost's hackles. "Of all the poets who had been on the mountain that summer," recalled Wallace Stegner, "he was the only one who could have been said to rival Frost, though neither he nor his most fanatical admirers would have made any such claim. But without intending to, he dimmed the local sun, and the dimming was less tolerable because MacLeish's politics, though definitely opposed to those who said Comrade, seemed to Frost mawkish with New Deal welfare sentiments."

As the speaker began to talk, Frost picked up some loose papers from an empty seat and rolled them into a tube, which he used, along with a raised eyebrow or an occasional nudge of the elbow, to punctuate some of MacLeish's pronouncements. "He seemed to listen," Stegner recalled, "with an impartial, if skeptical, judiciousness," but halfway through the ninety-minute-long program he began to get restless, shifting his weight around on his little wooden folding chair and muttering. The people around him found this funny and there were charitable smiles. Then Frost leaned over and in a stage whisper audible to the others in the back of the hall, he complained: "Archie's poems all have the same *tune.*" Soon the oblivious MacLeish announced he would read "You, Andrew Marvell." "It was a favorite," Stegner wrote. "Murmurs of approval, intent receptive faces. The poet began. Then an exclamation, a flurry in the rear of the hall. The reading paused, heads turned. Robert Frost, playing around like an idle, inattentive boy in a classroom, had somehow contrived to strike a match and set fire to his handful of papers and was busy beating them out and waving away the smoke."

Charles Foster later found Frost in the kitchen of Treman Cottage where he had filled a tumbler with whiskey. "Ted Morrison asked him to be good," wrote Foster, "and he said he'd be all right when he put what he had in his hand where it should go." In the living room, where a reception was under way, the tension was palpable and Foster saw that "Benny DeVoto was pacing around the room like a captain on the quarter-deck." Thinking that as

the host he should refocus the spotlight on his evening guest, Morrison insisted that MacLeish read a new poem composed for radio and based on events in Spain, "Air Raid." This was a blunder in such a small and crowded room only one pace away from an open bar. As MacLeish began to read to people sitting in chairs or on the floor, the ambient Treman hubbub began to rise—conducted most noticeably by Robert Frost, who began wisecracking in a friendly way but soon became openly hostile. MacLeish tried to ignore him as he doggedly worked his way toward the finish. The profoundly uncomfortable witnesses began counting the unread pages left in MacLeish's hands, having no idea what to do. Finally Bernard DeVoto did what they had no courage to do: "For God's sake, Robert," he pleaded, "let him read!"

The price of that rebuke would be their friendship, and though Frost would eventually storm out of the cottage at that and other perceived insults, one more episode just before the exit had a curiously friendly tone. After the room had returned to seeming normality, Foster had taken a seat next to Frost on a sofa. "After a time," Foster recorded, "Archie came over and sat on the arm of it. Frost had one arm around me, and, as more drinks were drunk, and discussion arose, Archie balanced himself with an arm around my shoulder. With Frost's arm around my back and Archie's around my neck and with both arguing and almost meeting before my nose, I felt—at least physically—in the center of American poetry." MacLeish was plainly in no mood for a literary and personal battle at Bread Loaf, and again and again he deferred to the older poet as they discussed the new literalness of modern poetry and Frost's part in it. "Archie then tried to make the conversation less personal," recalled the young man in the middle, "and Frost said, 'God-damn everything to hell so long as we're friends, Archie.' 'We are friends, Robert.'"

There was no peace to be had, however, for Frost did later storm out of the party. (He remained in a fury long enough that if MacLeish had blundered into sight he might not have survived to go to Washington, or, years later, to team up with Frost to spring Ezra Pound from Saint Elizabeths Hospital psychiatric ward.) Then Frost abruptly decided to hightail it out of there, demanding that his friend and fellow staff member, Hershell Brickell, drive him up to Concord Corners, three hours away in northern Vermont, where his daughter lived. Friends heard gossip that someone had seen Frost deliberately *eat* a cigarette. And they guiltily sighed with relief that he was off their hands. Not for long. The next day at Bread Loaf, Brickell received Frost's phone call and patiently went back up to fetch him.

The poet delivered the parting address of the conference after all, but the most pointed parting remark came from

Bernard DeVoto, who could not abide the reckless way in which Frost seemed bent on wrecking the Morrisons' marriage. Before they all returned to the Boston area, the poet was to move into the Morrisons' cottage where they would begin doing his unanswered correspondence. At Treman, as conference faculty members were saying good-bye, DeVoto and Frost shook hands. "You're a good poet, Robert," he was overheard saying. "But you're a bad man."

The marriage between Ted and Kay Morrison was not wrecked—it had begun in 1927 and would not end until Ted died in 1988, leaving Kay in a blissful Alzheimer's fog. Still, in 1938 it enlarged in private, unspecific ways to encompass the enormous, complex, and unruly personality of Robert Frost. Publicly, Kay became Frost's managing secretary, employing the firmness, the tenacity, and the protectiveness of a sheepdog in overseeing the personal and business details of his life until his death in 1963. For years after August 1938 her ward was buoyed and inspired by the love he felt for her; he dedicated in somewhat guarded language some of his published work to her and occasionally referred to the relationship in his most private correspondence. To Louis Untermeyer, on November 28, 1938, he wrote of their "unusual friendship," that he doubted if it had been dignified (as if to be in someone's "charge" was not), that she had "soothed my spirit like music," and that "I wish in some indirect way she could come to know how I feel toward her" (as if Untermeyer was supposed to play John Alden to Frost's Miles Standish, something he would certainly not do). This statement seemed to indicate something of the unrequited between them, but after all Frost was writing Untermeyer, the aging Lothario with whom Frost had felt cheerfully competitive for twenty-five years, on and off the tennis court. Was it merely empty, locker-room competitiveness with a wishful wink and a nebulous nod when he said he saw potential in the relationship "for me at my age in my position"? One might be led to think so; Frost was at bedrock a Puritan. He may have often talked to Untermeyer about his fantasy to run away with Kay to a South Sea island, as Untermeyer once confided to Stanley Burnshaw in 1953. Was that the fantasy of an unrequited lover?

The question is hard to put to rest. There has been much gossip over the decades about the relationship between Robert Frost and Kathleen Morrison but almost nothing in the historical record. Kay's memoir of Frost says that his attentions were turned away. Ted's book *Bread Loaf Writers' Conference: The First Thirty Years* (1976) skirts the issue entirely. Other writers with personal knowledge of the principals have chosen not to probe or pry. Then there was Lawrance Thompson, whose three-volume biography of

Robert Frost exhibits the sort of biographer's antipathy, the-glass-is-half-empty approach toward a subject that one can find in, for instance, Mark Schorer's book on Sinclair Lewis, or Joan Givner's on Katherine Anne Porter. Reportedly, while the final volume of Frost's biography *The Later Years, 1938–1963*, was still in preparation, Kay Morrison told a friend in the Ripton summer community that she planned to be out of the country when "that book" was published. She did not elaborate but her friend assumed she was referring to Thompson's revelations about Kay's relationship with Frost. But then Lawrance Thompson died. His book was finished by his research assistant, R. H. Winnick. And when Winnick completed the manuscript he took it up to the Morrisons and they made "substantial improvement," as he wrote in the acknowledgments. It has also been said by some who knew the principals that the Morrisons cut all unfavorable references to themselves, mostly about Kay's bossy protectiveness in Frost's late winter years—but they also excised anything about the ties between Frost and Mrs. Morrison beginning in 1938. With no known documents to follow, besides the impossible jumble of Thompson's papers and a few letters given by Kay to Dartmouth, it is hard to find a sure path through the underbrush. Following intuition—a dangerous guide—and listening to what survivors of that era believe for themselves, which may or may not be only gossip, it seems possible that for an undetermined but relatively short time, a sexual relationship existed between the two, and that they grew out of it.

Enough. It is between the three principals and they are all dead. The Morrisons—particularly Kay but also Ted, who remained a supportive friend throughout—brought order out of the chaos of Frost's life. In 1939 he would buy some Ripton land, the Homer Noble Farm, an easy walk away from the Bread Loaf Inn. Ted and Kay Morrison and their two children would spend their summers in the old farmhouse, paying a nominal rent. Frost lived in a tiny rustic cabin half a mile up a gentle slope, taking his meals with the Morrisons. And their unique friendship would cement Robert Frost to Bread Loaf for the last twenty-three summers of his life.

"Come to Bread Loaf," Frost would write Untermeyer in late November 1938, "and team up with me in poetry criticism. . . . We would make the poetry consultations and clinics a joint stunt to the nation. I got up this idea and Ted Morrison took to it like live bait. I needn't go into my mixture of motives except to say that they are all honorable by now. I am growing more and more honorable every time the moon comes safely through an eclipse." The rest of the team assembled by Morrison for

Robert Frost and John P. Marquand outside the Little Theatre, 1939

the 1939 session consisted of most of the then fairly permanent full-time staff, including DeVoto, Munson, Pratt, the novelist Eleanor Chilton (wife of Herbert Agar, transplanted Fugitive and frequent conference visitor), John Gassner of the Theatre Guild, Edith Mirrielees (whose textbook, *Story Writing,* with a preface by her former Stanford student John Steinbeck, would appear that year), and the publishing advisers Raymond Everitt (of Little, Brown) and Alan Collins (of the Curtis Brown literary agency). MacLeish would return, and Stegner and Walter Prichard Eaton, all as visiting lecturers—to be joined notably by John P. Marquand.

Marquand, the versatile author of *The Late George Apley,* a novel about a smug and snobbish Bostonian, had won a Pulitzer in 1937. His thirteenth novel, *Wickford Point,* to be published in 1939, had its roots in his boyhood summers at the Marquand summer place in Newburyport,

Massachusetts, where his great-aunt Margaret Fuller had once entertained her Transcendentalist friends. The book also lampooned the Harvard English Department to its great harrumphing chagrin; Ted Morrison's choice of Marquand for Bread Loaf, made before publication day in March, may have earned him some glares from his colleagues at Warren House. But to his credit he would have Marquand back for three successful sessions as a full-term faculty member in fiction.

Marquand had begun his writing career after a few years of newspaper work, first for the *Boston Transcript,* then for *New York Tribune Magazine,* and finally as an advertising copywriter for J. Walter Thompson. He spent a summer writing a novel "of the cloak and sword school" that later found a domicile in the *Ladies' Home Journal.* It was later explained to Marquand that the magazine bought his story because it had recently installed five-color printing presses, "and they wanted to do pictures of men with lace about their throats." Most of what he went on to produce would be in the slick pages of *The Saturday Evening Post*—the formulaic mystery stories of his Japanese detective, Mr. Moto, travel pieces, and the assortment of serialized novels about Bostonian society—but Marquand's stories were deceptively smooth, and as he got more serious they exhibited his knowledge of how ironically even genteel society worked. He was then beginning to conceive of his next novel, *H. M. Pulham, Esquire,* which mirrored a concurrent project, the twenty-fifth anniversary report of his Harvard class of 1915.

Marquand's experience at Bread Loaf fit in with his feelings of inadequacy as a writer; having written for the slicks for so many years, he had always chafed that academics stood as frowning gatekeepers to the temple of literary fame when they knew little about the actual writing process. After the critical and commercial success of *The Late George Apley,* this belief became especially true. His character Jim Calder in *Wickford Point*, modeled of course on Marquand himself, wrote "for the market," for real human beings, and was too often misunderstood and undervalued for it. Marquand would have liked what his fellow alumnus DeVoto—another unrequited suitor for Harvard's literary and social acceptance—wrote about literary standards. "There are two classes of writers who do not write for *The Saturday Evening Post*: those who have independent means or make satisfactory incomes from their other writing, and those who can't make the grade. Many of the former and practically all of the latter try to write for the *Post*." It is not recorded in *The Crumb* what Marquand read from at Bread Loaf in 1939, but often one draws from what one has just published—most naturally with a nod to the little bookstore waiting expectantly over at the Inn. From *Wickford Point,* Marquand might have read this speech of Jim Calder's:

It has never been my observation that education helps this [writing] talent. On the contrary, undue familiarity with other writers is too apt to sap the courage and to destroy essential self-belief. . . . Instead, a writer of fiction is usually the happier for his ignorance, and better for having played ducks and drakes with his cultural opportunities. All that he really requires is a dramatic sense and a peculiar eye for detail which he can distort convincingly. He must be an untrustworthy mendacious fellow who can tell a good falsehood and make it stick. It is safer for him to be a self-centered

egotist than to have a broad interest in life. He must take in more than he gives out. He must never be complacent, he must never be at peace; in other words, he is a difficult individual and the divorce rate among contemporary literati tells as much.

The slapping of other mavericks' knees in the audience might have been deafening.

It is no doubt appropriate so close on the heels of describing Robert Frost's uncontrolled "bad" behavior in 1938 to mention a friendship that began during the English School in 1939 and continued through both school and Writers' Conference for six years—that of Frost and young Peter Stanlis, a talented Middlebury sophomore who had been allowed to work on scholarship toward his master's degree as an undergraduate. From New Jersey, the precocious and well-read Stanlis had a camera for an eye and a phonograph for an ear. His dialogues with Frost took place often on the road between Frost's rented house in Ripton and the Bread Loaf campus as one walked the other home and then turned around to be conducted back. As transcribed by Stanlis, these dialogues show Frost's brilliant, opinionated, restless mind at work—he liked to think of himself, after all, as a sort of "Professor of Conversation," and when he had the right talking partner there was almost no evidence of the bad man. (Stanlis's notes, which appear in the *Robert Frost Centennial Essays,* do much to restore the generous parts of Frost's soul to the reputation left him by his unsympathetic biographer, Lawrance Thompson, who was already at work on his mammoth undertaking when he visited Bread Loaf in 1939 from Princeton.) It was the twenty-year-old Stanlis who utterly confounded Frost when he pointed out the poet's unintentional pun in his celebrated old poem, "Mending Wall":

Before I built a wall I'd ask to know
What I was walling in or walling out,
And to whom I was like to give offense.

As Stanlis was to record, the 1939 conference "ended on a very ominous note." The ink on the Munich agreement had been dry for eleven months, with the Sudetenland and Czechoslovakia under Nazi control; the Hitler-Stalin nonaggression pact was disclosed on August 24, a day of striking ordinariness at Bread Loaf but also a day when the fairyland isolation of the United States came to an end. Many conference-goers were still on their way home when the German armies crossed the border into Poland, precipitating the Second World War.

TRIPLETS, 1940

Emergent writers attending Bread Loaf on fellowships often do more than enhance the conference—they can make it transcendent, raising the temperature and the level of excitement in a way that is felt by all participants, from the most hard-bitten "pros" on the faculty all the way over to the most naive granny with a nine-hundred-page manuscript about her colonial forebears. To be sure, there have been quieter sessions, and those which included authors of first books who later disappeared into respectable academic careers, raised families, came up empty, or otherwise still await the nod of that fickle maître d', posterity. But the Bread Loaf session of 1940 was one in which the writers massing under the old maple trees could feel the vibrancy in the air. Among the six fellows that year were three first-timers who were clearly destined for great futures: Eudora Welty, Carson McCullers, and John Ciardi.

Welty was tall and blonde and thirty-one, with an easy smile and a dreamy, quickly averting gaze. Her first collection of short stories, *A Curtain of Green,* would not appear until the following year. She lived in the house in which she was born, in Jackson, Mississippi. She had always longed to be a writer. At age twelve she won the "Jackie Mackie Jingles Contest" held by the Mackie Pine Oil Specialty Company of Covington, Louisiana. Congratulating her with a check for twenty-five dollars, a pine oil executive wrote that he hoped Miss Welty "will improve in poetry to such an extent as to win fame." As a freshman at the University of Wisconsin, Welty took pains not to write about the only world she knew—Missis-

sippi—and strove for a worldliness that simply did not fit. Much later she wryly recalled the first line from one college story: "Monsieur Boule inserted a delicate dagger in Mademoiselle's left side and departed with a poised immediacy." As a graduate student at Columbia University, however, Welty went further afield, studying advertising. For a short while she even worked for an advertising agency—but she quit "because it was too much like sticking pins into people to make them buy things that they didn't need or really much want." Back home, she knocked about until she found a job in the Works Progress Administration as a publicity agent. For the next three years she roamed the state taking photographs and doing feature stories on the WPA, all the while writing short stories and collecting rejection slips. In 1935 she tried and failed to find a publisher for a book of Mississippi photographs, *Black Saturday*, but later sold a photograph to *Life.*

Welty's first story, "Death of a Traveling Salesman," was finally taken by a little magazine in Detroit, *Manuscript,* and published in June 1936. Then there were sales to *Prairie Schooner* and, notably, to *Southern Review,* where Robert Penn Warren, Albert Erskine, and Cleanth Brooks took a great interest in helping her career. Erskine's wife, Katherine Anne Porter, read the stories and invited Welty to visit her in Baton Rouge. It took the younger writer six months or a year to get up the nerve to make the visit—twice she turned back at Natchez—but by 1938 Welty had the four eminent literary figures trying to find her fellowships and a hardcover publisher; soon they were joined by Ford Madox Ford, who at Porter's behest had read some of Welty's stories. Still, the going was not easy. Houghton Mifflin turned her down for its literary fellowship program, which included publication, although later it inquired if she had a novel. Harcourt, too, rejected her short stories, wanting a novel. So would Putnam's and William Morrow: No one thought they could sell short stories between boards; they all wanted miniaturists to stop fooling around and leap to larger canvases. It was a constant temptation, and Porter warned Welty that it might lead her disastrously away from her central gifts.

A few days after Welty learned she would not be awarded a Guggenheim, things brightened. She received a letter from Theodore Morrison granting her a Bread Loaf fellowship on the strength of Porter's recommendation and her work. By the time she was taking the train up to Bread Loaf, Welty had begun talking to an editor at Doubleday, Doran, but she would not have the reassurance of a book contract until early in 1941.

The skinny, puckish, androgynous Carson McCullers was twenty-three. A native of Columbus, Georgia, as Carson Smith she had moved to New York in 1935 to study music at Juilliard but lost her tuition money on the subway. Instead, she enrolled for night classes at Columbia to study her other enthusiasm, writing, supporting herself with part-time jobs. Illness forced her to return to Columbus, but after recuperation she went back to New York where she eventually took a class from Whit Burnett at Columbia. Her teacher was also the editor of *Story* magazine, and he published her first story, "Wunderkind." Married in 1937 to Reeves McCullers, also an aspiring writer, hers was the stronger personality and her work won out. A partial manuscript and outline won her a Houghton Mifflin literary fellowship of $1,500 to complete it; apparently she had edged out Eudora Welty's *A Curtain of Green.* Her manuscript was completed and accepted in the spring of 1939. First entitled *The Mute,* and later renamed to the less documentary-sounding *The Heart Is a Lonely Hunter* and set for publication in 1940, the book was about a deaf mute who loses his only friend, another mute with whom he can communicate in sign language, and finds himself the sounding board for a young girl, an agitator on the skids, and an intellectual black physician. Reflecting the times, McCullers intended it as a parable of fascism.

McCullers wrote her second novel in only two months; her editor at Houghton Mifflin, Robert Linscott, set the gothic tale of a tortured homosexual army officer, *Reflections in a Golden Eye,* for publication the next year and sent off a warm fellowship recommendation to Ted Morrison. Two weeks before Bread Loaf, *The New Republic* reviewed her book. "Its interest lies in its angle of vision," wrote Richard Wright, "for its picture of loneliness is the most

desolate yet to emerge from the South, and McCullers is surely the first white Southerner to deal with Negroes easily and with justice. Indeed, McCullers' despair is more natural and authentic than Faulkner's, her characters are more lost than Anderson's, and her prose is more carefully neutral than Hemingway's." The reviewer, celebrated that year for his own *Native Son,* was soon to occupy what must have been the most electrifying brownstone in Brooklyn Heights, having as its tenants Carson McCullers, Christopher Isherwood, George Davis of *Harper's Bazaar,* Jane and Paul Bowles, Gypsy Rose Lee, and W.H. Auden.

McCullers was standing in a corridor off the lobby of the Bread Loaf Inn, examining notices on a bulletin board, when two large men brushed by her, one eyeing her thin frame, her drooping bangs, her starched white men's shirt. "Whose *enfant terrible?*" quipped the younger man to burly Richard Brown, a Middlebury English professor who for many years served as Ted Morrison's assistant director; the speaker was John Ciardi, at twenty-four as blunt and clever with language as he would ever be. Tall and physically at ease, his most prominent features were a magnificent Roman nose and a cruel, cynic's mouth. Hair usually dangled in his eyes. Ciardi was the child of Italian immigrant parents in Boston's North End; after her husband was killed in an automobile accident, his mother moved the family to Medford, where they lived near the bank of the Mystic River, and where Ciardi attended the public schools. Much of his youth he spent playing on the streets, becoming adept at fighting and getting into trouble and adopting a pugnaciousness and swagger he would find hard to shake. He just about flunked out of Bates College in Maine, where his roommate was Edmund S. Muskie, though one thoughtful professor told Ciardi he had received the highest grade of all who failed the course. Back at home, he attended Tufts College in Medford (working on summertime road gangs to make expenses), from which he graduated magna cum laude, missing Phi Beta Kappa by a few tenths of a point in 1938. His Tufts adviser, the wise and generous John Holmes, introduced him to Theodore Roethke, whom Ciardi later described as "the first living and breathing poet I'd ever met." Ciardi had seen Roethke's work in *The New Yorker* and in the green-ink-scrawled manuscript that Roethke had sent to his former colleague; Roethke would later trail Ciardi to Bread Loaf and stay in contact as long as both were alive. Ciardi "found the great satisfaction of writing poetry in his years at Tufts," recalled John Holmes. "He would bring not one, but five or six poems to the advanced writing class. We did not finish with his, but at the next class he was not interested in those. He had new ones, and better, he said. He began then to be a prolific, an eruptive writer, but one who grew fast, who advanced in skill with every new poem, ranging wider and further for new forms, new subjects, new metaphor, new vocabulary."

Ciardi next went to the University of Michigan for a master of arts degree, hoping that his poems would win some of the Hopwood Prize money. "He wrote that, being short of funds, he would send me a standard-form telegram if he won anything, 'May Easter bless you many years,' for fifteen cents," remembered Holmes. "But when the awards were made, a straight wire said, 'Ring out wild bells twelve hundred bucks.'"

Ciardi's first collection of poems, *Homeward to America* (1940), was drawn from material he wrote at Tufts and rewrote at Michigan. His work attracted the attention of Louis Untermeyer, who sponsored him to Bread Loaf. The two men enjoyed an easy, amusing, punning association in manuscript clinics and on the Treman porch, but the rake in Untermeyer focused a bit more attention on the charismatic McCullers, who obtained a generous blurb from him for *Reflections.*

The other associations there continue to startle. Katherine Anne Porter arrived to deliver a lecture, her piercing, luminous movie-star eyes no doubt registering with warm approval the presence of her protégée, Eudora Welty, for whom she would contribute an introduction to *A Curtain of Green.* Now separated from her husband and living near Yaddo, Porter's literary reputation—built largely on her first story collection of ten years before, *Flowering Judas,* had been enhanced the previous year by her superb *Pale Horse, Pale Rider,* consisting of three long stories. Porter's preparation for writing, she liked to tell people, consisted of long periods of brooding. She brooded excessively. Then she would usually rent a room somewhere where she was a stranger, stock it with oranges and coffee, and go to work—composing on a typewriter the way she had as a newspaper drama critic twenty years before—at rapid-fire pace. "The crystal clearness of her style, the perfect imagery," wrote the book columnist Robert Van Gelder in the *New York Times* in April 1940, "are achieved at white heat." She had written the three novelettes of *Pale Horse* in only three weeks. But it had become a saying in the publishing world that some of her other work would forever be "on its way": Her book about Cotton Mather had been in the works since the twenties. "Each season," wrote Van Gelder, "Harcourt, Brace hopefully announce the coming publication of her study of Cotton Mather. Each season publication is postponed." After an embarrassment of years, she would announce with asperity: "No more promises, no more announcements of publication." Another book, *Ship of Fools,* was by then likewise taking its time to be born. With its genesis in a voyage Porter took to Europe in 1931, the novel had been begun in the early forties and would not be published until 1962.

Following her Bread Loaf reading and talk on the techniques of fiction, Porter entertained questions from the audience, largely from Eudora Welty. It was, in the words of young Peter Stanlis, "a pleasant but searching dialogue," and "When the meeting broke up they converged, and as they drifted off with the rest of the staff to Treman Cottage they continued to talk. The visual image of these two ladies talking about fiction, while oblivious to everyone around them, is almost archetypal." Later, Wallace Stegner looked across the living room to see Porter enthroned in an armchair, holding forth in her soft Texas accent, with Welty sitting worshipfully at her feet. It is a marvelous image, often repeated.

Three nights later the featured visitor was fair-haired, hazel-eyed, introvertive Wystan Hugh Auden, still in the playful, flamboyant early stage of his long career; the Briton appeared younger than his thirty-three years and now, since war had broken out in Europe, was a permanent resident of the United States. Auden had driven an ambulance for the Loyalists in Spain, and he was still married to Thomas Mann's daughter Erika. At Bread Loaf, according to Richard Ellmann (who was working off his tuition in the dining room and on the grounds crew), Auden won over Robert Frost by confessing that he had been influenced by the older poet. But he did not rise much to the social occasion. "Auden was a very shy and self-conscious man," remembered Peter Stanlis, "most difficult to engage in conversation.

But when he stepped up to the podium to give his poetry reading he seemed to catch fire. He brought no book, but quoted his poems from memory in a rapid-fire, nonstop manner, which made it difficult for his audience to absorb what he said. Also, he distracted his listeners by his awkward way of standing at the podium. He lifted one leg almost halfway up the podium, and stood on the other leg and leaned heavily over the podium while he recited a poem. Between poems he would sometimes change legs. About halfway through Auden's performance a thunderstorm struck. The Bread Loaf Little Theatre has no partition between the roof and the hall, to absorb sound, and giant hailstones rained an incessant tattoo on the roof, so that no one could hear Auden beyond the first several rows of seats. After a while the podium was moved to the side of the hall, next to the fireplace, and chairs were swung around in a close semicircle. But it was still impossible to hear well, and as the storm continued Auden finally quit reciting his poems.

After the storm stopped, allowing the assembly to leave for the reception, Auden and McCullers appropriated Wallace Stegner's bottle of bourbon and retreated to a corner where they huddled and ignored everyone.

What no one could ignore, even at a session of such marked literary potential, was the war situation in Europe and the growing inevitability that Americans would sometime be swept into the conflict. Norway, the Low Countries, and France had all been overrun by Hitler's armies by early summer, and the Luftwaffe began pounding away at Britain on August 8; newspaper reports of the resulting devastation were passed from hand to hand at Bread Loaf, and on one evening wiry little Fletcher Pratt stood at the lectern in his recent authority as free-lance writer on the European war and as "military advisor to *Time, Fortune, The New York Post,* and the *St. Louis Post-Dispatch,*" among others, to fill the air with pipe smoke and answer questions about the European situation and America's national defense—Would Britain withstand an invasion? Could the Free French forces prevail against such odds? What might happen in Indochina, where Japanese aggression could not be ignored? Would the president's greatly expanded "two-ocean navy" be enough? Was not national service inevitable in the United States? (The answer to the last question would come a few weeks later with America's first peacetime program of compulsory military service.) Pratt cautioned his audience: "Political questions," he said, "will not be discussed," such as whether the nation would trade its sitting President Roosevelt for the Republican Wendell Willkie in the coming election. By the time of the November landslide, the lives of all those gathered writers at Bread Loaf would have begun to slide into the gravitational eddies of that expanding war.

THE WAR YEARS

When Fletcher Pratt next peered over the Bread Loaf lectern to talk of military matters, the question about war involvement had palpably shifted from "if" to "when"—the sweeping German victories, the Lend-Lease bill, the American declaration of an unlimited national emergency, the freezing of Axis assets in the United States, the embargoes on scrap iron and gasoline to Japan—all confirmed the direction. On the day in 1941 that Bread Loafers lined up to register for their rooms, August 18, President Roosevelt announced the new Selective Service Act with its expansion of the peacetime army and its lengthening of the required hitch in the service.

But the Bread Loaf schedule was as full as ever and even with war scratching insistently at the window the general mood could not and would not be dampened for the entire two weeks. Grinning, punning Untermeyer was there, in his most public personae ducking around his concern for the plight of European Jews, running poetry clinics, directing glee-clubbing harmonies, and hosting "Information Tease," the extemporaneous evening entertainment in parody of the popular radio quiz show. DeVoto came back after having skipped the 1940 session, still insisting that America should have joined its allies two years before when the Polish border had been trampled; besides cranking out his monthly essays for the "Easy Chair" column in *Harper's,* he was furiously finishing work on his historical tour de force *Year of Decision: 1846* and would draw from his research and manuscript for an evening lecture on Manifest Destiny.

Mutual friends noticed the cooler air between DeVoto and Frost—the differences opened in 1938 were widening with every contact between the two, on or off the Mountain, and DeVoto was seen to leave a group whenever Frost joined it. "Everyone was aware of their enmity and felt uncomfortable," recalled Peter Stanlis, who had stayed over from the English School to wait on tables. "DeVoto stayed at Treman cottage and spent all his spare time there, rather than around the campus and tennis courts, as in previous years," talking about war and history and writers' markets with Fletcher Pratt, who had decided to cultivate a wispy new beard. For his part, Frost was in good form, seemingly unperturbed by the crumbled friendship; perhaps it was then that he could tell John P. Marquand about a late-night encounter with a scruffy-looking intoxicated man near his apartment on Louisburg Square in Boston's Beacon Hill. The man accosted Frost for a handout, and when he was rebuffed he upbraided the poet: "Who do you think you are—the late George Apley?"

As before, Frost and Untermeyer conducted the poetry clinics. In one, a woman began to speak about Frost's poems with certitude as if they were wholly, exclusively autobiographical, but with his characteristic brusqueness in such circumstances he interrupted her discourse. "When I use the word *I* in a poem," he said impatiently, "surely you don't believe I mean *ME?*" Of course there was nothing more for her to say, but—typically—Untermeyer made a joke of it. He always had found it hard to speak without uttering a pun, something Frost often felt distracted not

Walter Prichard Eaton sits on the Inn veranda with his wife (r.) and an unknown conferee, 1940s.

Fletcher Pratt, Bernard DeVoto, William Hazlett Upson, 1940s

Fletcher Pratt at the lectern, late 1940s

reached into his pocket, pulled out a penny, tossed it nonchalantly on the tray, and said, "Have a tip." When the penny stopped spinning, and I saw the value of the coin, I responded: "Looie, what kind of an animal throws a cent?" Before Untermeyer could come back with a pun or a quip, and with the loud laughter of his young partner ringing deliciously in my ears, I slipped past him into the dining hall. Frost remarked on hearing this story that it was good enough to keep "Looie" subdued for a whole morning session.

Frost would remain studiously apart when William Carlos Williams paid a short visit to deliver a lecture on writing poetry in the American vernacular. Williams apologized to Ted Morrison, saying that he wanted to stay longer but had to return to his pediatric duties back in Rutherford, New Jersey. Williams's arrival created quite a stir of excitement—for more than three decades he had exerted influence with his stripped-down, sensory-laden poetry, and he was then at work on his magnum opus, *Paterson.* His lecture was well attended. Stanlis and Eaton were there despite being all but forbidden to go by Robert Frost, who did not want them to become "contaminated" by the wrong sort of poet. "Frost was politely unimpressed by Williams," wrote Peter Stanlis. Some of what the doctor said "was obvious," Frost contended, "and much of it was dubious." Eaton also witnessed Frost's scorn. "He would invite me up to his cabin for long and delightful talks, full of gossip, both witty and a little wicked," recalled Eaton, "in which he would 'tick off' the poets and the people he did not admire. He particularly did not like William Carlos William and warned me against associating with a man who wrote 'nothing but snippets of poems,' citing 'The Red Wheelbarrow' as a particularly odious example."

Nevertheless, Eaton and Williams did become friends for many years, though, as a poet, Eaton recalled, "I was not in any way to take his direction. . . . [U]ntil his death, he wrote to me and constantly encouraged the development of my confidence in my work. I shall always remember him as the warmest and most radiant of friends, and I learned a lot about compassion and generosity from him." This might have been a form of "contamination" to Frost, "but Bread Loaf did not contaminate me in any way. I had then, and still have, a great zest for human variety, and though Frost was mainly right in his judgments, I did not find it necessary to preclude from my life what might, and, in fact, did come to me from the best that was in all of the people I met."

Another person Eaton met while at Bread Loaf was the thirty-three-year-old Theodore Roethke, who also held a fellowship in poetry. His first book, *Open House,* which had

only him but the customers. Earlier in the year he had addressed the subject in a letter to Untermeyer in which he asked his friend to clown less and assume a "higher literary dignity." But entertainment was firmly ingrained in Untermeyer's character—especially at Bread Loaf. Charles Edward Eaton, who at the time was a young writing instructor at the University of Missouri and was attending the conference on a Robert Frost fellowship, recalled, "Bread Loaf would have been too staid for [Untermeyer] if he could not have kicked up his heels and gone off square dancing in the evening." Untermeyer's vitality "spilled over into countless amours and into 'having fun,'" wrote Eaton. "Though he was married at the time, I believe, to Esther Antin, he was courting rather heavily one of the Bread Loaf girls, and she later became his wife. He would corral me and my date, and the four of us would go off for a spirited evening." Frost did not approve, and his complaining about the man who was such a long and close friend surprised the young Eaton, who was his former student and protégé. The private irritability showed itself to Peter Stanlis, who saw that Frost could relish any time when, instead, the joke was on his jokester friend. "One day while waiting table," recalled Peter Stanlis,

I was asked to go upstairs with a dinner tray for a sick member of the conference. As I came back into the dining hall, Louis Untermeyer came past me through the door in company with a lovely writers' conferee. He

taken him ten painful years to complete, was published that year. Roethke had not been interested in writing poetry until he was a Harvard undergraduate—"I really wanted," he once confessed, "at fifteen and sixteen, to write a beautiful, a 'chiseled' prose as it was called in those days." Thinking about a career in advertising or the law, he showed his first three college attempts at verse to Robert Hillyer, who reportedly whirled about in his office chair and said, "Any editor who wouldn't buy these is a fool!" Thus encouraged, Roethke sold two of them to *The New Republic* and *Commonweal* and began his long trail. "I wasn't just a spoiled sad snob," he remembered thinking. "I could write and people I respected printed the stuff."

"He was a large man, both in height and bulk," recalled Eaton, "and moved around rather awkwardly, uneasily, I might say, in his big body, and conveyed both shyness and underlying strength, even aggressiveness, contemptuous as he was of the poets who did not believe in his fastidious use of form." He had toted a bulging briefcase up to Bread Loaf, and Eaton was surprised when Roethke showed him what was inside—his reviews and press clippings. "He would pull them out and read them to me for as long as he thought he could hold my attention," Eaton said, intrigued that all of the recognition the older man had already enjoyed, that early in his career, was not enough to suppress his underlying insecurity. Roethke was even leery of Frost, who equally respected and distrusted him. A few years later, talking at Bread Loaf with young Donald Hall, Frost would criticize Roethke "of all things," wrote Hall, "for being so competitive with other poets. Perhaps it was Roethke's *style* which bothered Frost; Roethke made his competitiveness obvious with a boyish enthusiasm." This was also true on the clay tennis courts at Bread Loaf; Roethke usually doubled as varsity tennis coach at any university he taught at—he moved like a dancing bear but with surprising quickness and agility, charging up and down the court and smashing to bits the pretensions of any opponent.

Roethke's poetry and his prowess diminished to some extent any flashes of his aggression—but this was not so for another fellowship holder, a Harvard student named Cedric Whitman. Seeing great promise in his work, his teacher Ted Morrison borrowed against the next year's fellowship account to get Whitman to Bread Loaf and saw to it that his student's small book of verse was published by the fledgling Bread Loaf Printers, a limited-edition enterprise that had been Morrison's dream for ten years. The book appeared during the conference to great celebration, and Whitman's talents were celebrated by many on the faculty, including Untermeyer and DeVoto. But Whitman could not handle the attention nor summon the gratitude that most would have felt at such a sponsored debut. Instead he got drunk, remained so, insulted everybody in sight, and left hurling rancor in his wake. "The best will in the world was expended on him," wrote Bernard DeVoto,

and, if he's got some stuff, he could have shortened his portage by several years. The sum may be trivial, he may have felt that Bread Loaf was absurd and that these people were making a pompous and absurd effort that should properly be classified with the uplift, or with whatever the literary young are despising this year. And he may have been right. But decent people were going out of their way to treat him as decently as they knew how, and it was up to him to be decent in return. He wasn't. Drunk or sober, he subjected them to an unjustified, and indecent affront. On my way out of Bread Loaf I heard him saying that he felt like a rat, and that was OK with me.

There was another untoward incident during that session—they always seem to occur in bunches, probably when the stars are out of alignment, which happens occasionally at Bread Loaf. It involved a seventeen-year-old office boy on vacation from his job at *The New Yorker*, the New Orleans–born Truman Capote. In Brendan Gill's marvelous memoir, *Here at the New Yorker*, he pictures Capote as "a tiny, round-faced, slender creature, as exotic as an osprey," who was given to eccentric dress. "I recall him sweeping through the corridors of the magazine in a black opera cape, his long golden hair falling to his shoulders: an apparition that put one in mind of Oscar Wilde in Nevada, in his velvets and lilies." In 1941, Capote's first novel, *Other Voices, Other Rooms*, a story of a homosexual young man's coming-of-age, was still years away from being written and seven years away from publication. Even then, though, with few professional attainments, Capote had a mastery of name-dropping, and he used his intern's connection with *The New Yorker* for all the mileage it would give him. It got him into the faculty lounge where, as Wallace Stegner has recalled, he could hold himself studiously aloof from Louis Untermeyer "after Untermeyer had lectured on contemporary poetry and called T. S. Eliot a writer of society verse." And later, during a crowded reading, the dramatic and precocious Capote could show the daylight between himself and Robert Frost by waiting until the eminence was a few minutes into his presentation and then starting up from his seat as if offended and noisily brushing past and over the knees of those row mates between him and the aisle. As much the master of the self-serving anecdote as any writer alive or dead, Capote would later rewrite the incident into a funnier story,

Fletcher Pratt and Theodore Morrison, late 1940s

with—of course—Frost as the offender who throws a book at Capote who has innocently bent over to scratch a mosquito bite and whom Frost thinks has fallen asleep. To Capote's credit, not as a reporter but as a seeker of higher truths, although that scene did not happen at Bread Loaf, it *could* have. Expunged, however, were the simple bad manners of a young poseur who had yet to show his later gifts.

But the incivilities were dwarfed, as usual, by the readings, the lectures, the square dances, the "Information Teases," the adrenalic associations, be they intellectual, platonic, or romantic, and the bright August sun and crisp mountain nights, just as the 1941 conference was to be dwarfed in the memories of participants only three months later by the Japanese sneak attack on Pearl Harbor. The world would truly be different for those Bread Loafers able to regroup for the next session, as well as, assuredly, for those who could not.

During the war sessions at Bread Loaf, 1942–1945, the conference was severely attenuated. Nonetheless, under Morrison's direction it carried on despite fewer customers, a reduced staff, almost no visiting lecturers, and few over-

night literary visitors from off the Mountain. Each annual May conference announcement would carry an ominous disclaimer: "Plans for the conference are subject to cancellation if war conditions prevent the use of Bread Loaf Inn," or, "Because of war conditions, the Administration reserves the right to make necessary changes without notice in program, staff, or other arrangements." That it carried on at all seems something of a marvel today. Morrison made up for the shrunken staff roster by enlisting local summering singers and musicians for evening classical recitals; additionally, the watercolorist Arthur K.D. Healy, in residence at Middlebury College, delivered talks and exhibited his work. If it was not literature, it nevertheless occupied minds prone to thinking about troubles off the Mountain. Then, between 1943 and 1945, the sessions of the English School and the Writers' Conference overlapped, with two directors, two faculties, two student bodies, and, inevitably, two shifts in the dining room.

Rationing sometimes had the effect of making a stay at the Inn seem like a camping trip. Food ration coupon books had to be turned in upon registration at the front desk and left there like passports until check-out time. "Any Conference member who has not turned in his ration book at the Inn desk should do so at once," warned *The Crumb* in 1944. "To fail to do so would involve the inn dietician in considerable difficulty." Shipments of meat and fish—when they could be obtained—were delayed, leaving the kitchen staff to concoct something out of vegetables. Somehow Fletcher Pratt would obtain a beefsteak—to be referred to, in code, as "Baby"—which would be broiled in secret for a few select members of the faculty. *The Crumb* conducted a poll in 1943: Would conference goers like to have butter at breakfast or at dinner? One choice was allowed, and breakfast won, 113–19. Fletcher Pratt, with his high connections in the Navy Department, stole the beloved chef of the Inn, Eddie Doucette, playing a hand in getting him shipped off to be a battleship admiral's chef in the Pacific. "It was," recalled Ted Morrison, "Fletcher's one disloyalty to the conference." Participants who had not taken the train to Middlebury, of course, were subject to gasoline rationing—and so, almost as soon as they arrived with luggage at the Inn, they were cautioned to apply for their return gasoline coupons from the local rationing board in Ripton. *The Crumb* noted that, beginning in 1942, the Inn had been limited to 50 percent of its 1941 consumption of tea and coffee, a true stringency. "It is still hoped," wrote the editor, "that inn guests and conference members will still prefer Bread Loaf to the Solomon Islands."

Indeed. The reference to strife in the South Pacific was probably an unnecessary reminder. Life on Bread Loaf Mountain often conveyed a sense of isolation, which had much to do with making the conference what it was, but there were the daily newspapers and, of course, car radios—around which small knots of listeners were wont to gather at the appointed hours. As the Bread Loaf Inn opened for the Writers' Conference on August 17, 1942, American B-17's were flattening the Rouen railroad yards; on April 19, over Dieppe the skies were raining Allied paratroopers; Corregidor had been surrendered for three months; the battles in the Coral Sea and at Midway were likewise over, but the marines were dug in for the long fight on Guadalcanal; meanwhile, in Africa, Rommel had been checked outside Alexandria. And at Bread Loaf, Fletcher Pratt rose to speak on "Books and the War." In August 1943, the African war was long over, the German summer offensive in Russia was being turned away, and Anglo-American troops were finishing the invasion of Sicily; the U.S. Navy was busy in the South Pacific, while the Aleutians had been emptied of Japanese. And Fletcher Pratt spoke on "What the War Has Done to Books," subtitled, "Forty Thousand Copies of Walden." By August 1944, islands in the Central and Southwest Pacific had been invaded and occupied by American forces, the naval and air battles of the Philippine

Sea had resulted in the resignation of Premier Tojo, Europe had been softened and Berlin bombed, the Normandy invasion had given way to the battle of France, and Fletcher Pratt spoke on "Is It Still Our War?" Yes. And when the Writers' Conference opened on August 13, 1945, Hitler and Mussolini had gone to their rewards, Germany was occupied, and irradiated survivors in Hiroshima and Nagasaki were picking through their ruins; Fletcher Pratt's customary lecture, scheduled far ahead, as it happened, on V-J Day, was instead given by Colonel Joseph I. Greene, editor of the *Infantry Journal*. Deliriously, the topic, "Writing in the Armed Forces," seemed finally somehow redundant.

Frost was dependably there in the war years. And Untermeyer, too, although his friendship with Frost was severely, almost fatally strained by the latter's continued refusal to take a public stand against Germany, though he did say he was opposed to Nazism. Untermeyer, outraged by Nazi crimes against European Jews, was by 1944 openly hostile to Frost. The matter was defused when Frost composed a poem in apology, feckless at it may have seemed to a harder, less forgiving heart than Untermeyer's. Among others in the staff, Marquand came once, Stegner and Catherine Drinker Bowen twice, Mirrielees thrice; Walter E. Havighurst, novelist and mainstay of Ohio's Miami University English Department, was announced twice but made it once; representing the commercial side of publishing as agents or publishers, there were the dependable Alan Collins and Raymond and Helen Everitt, to be joined in 1945 by William Sloane of Holt; as his publishing career led him a-wandering, Bill Sloane would be at every subsequent session through 1971.

Among the thirteen holders of fellowships between 1942 and 1945, there was the Rhode Island poet and book columnist Winfield Townley Scott, who was nominated in 1942 by Robert Hillyer. His first book, *Biography for Traman,* had appeared in 1937. Untermeyer, who sooner or later reviewed everybody, criticized it in the *American Mercury.* It was, he said, "Excellent as writing, but bewildering in its echoes; the tone, as well as the technique, is alternately that of Aiken, Eliot, Putnam, and Robinson, sometimes a confusion of them all." But Untermeyer could be kind, also. "Under the shifting diction a personality begins to struggle," he judged. "It will be interesting to watch it—if it emerges." Scott's later work did show a growing originality, and beyond his second and third books there were his reviews and essays in the *Providence Journal.* They had a wider audience than what his little state could provide him, and for a while he floated a regular poetry column that published an eclectic list, such as its inaugural: William Carlos Williams, John Ciardi, John Russell McCarthy, and Rainer Maria Rilke. Scott paid between one and four dollars per poem and had no scarcity of good contributors. From the column came an anthology, *New Verse*, which Untermeyer obliged with a preface. Scott "belongs to no 'school,' he does not pit one tendency against another," he said. "A glance at the contents will show how skillfully he has maintained his course between the dangerous Charybdis of experiment and the alluring Scylla of tradition." Alas, the anthology was slain by the dragon of wartime paper rationing and never appeared.

Win Scott's poetry column, too, was slain, some years before it might have published young Donald Hall, who came to Bread Loaf in 1945 as a sixteen-year-old high school student. Hall, having begun to publish his verse in the littlest of the little magazines, made the pilgrimage to see Robert Frost on the Mountain. He had thrilled to Frost's "To Earthward," and he was transfixed in the Little Theatre at the first sight of the poet; Untermeyer's after-lunch manuscript clinics, however, were slightly more intimidating. "When Frost came we learned to tremble," Hall recorded. "Whatever poem was up for discussion that day, Frost was liable to be cutting, sarcastic, dismissive. The day when Untermeyer chose to read and discuss my poems was a day Frost didn't come. I was relieved." Hall and Frost built up a slight acquaintance on the veranda of the Inn, however, perhaps anticipating the pedagogical relationship they would soon have at Harvard. At Bread Loaf, Hall was surprised by Frost's unfathomable competitiveness, even with a sixteen-year-old, but the portrait Hall provides of the Frost he encountered at eighteen, in Cambridge, is refreshingly human—different from most pictures and worthy of reproducing here. "The only Americans more competitive than Harvard undergraduates are Harvard faculty members," said Hall in his memoir of a full life of writing and teaching, *Remembering Poets* (1978):

When I saw Frost at Harvard, it was among undergraduates and faculty, and he kept his elbows close to his sides, and he saw to it that he sat in a corner of the room, with his flanks covered. This was a sophisticated Robert Frost, suspicious, combative, happy, blessedly far from the benign farmer, capable of verses, one met in the news magazines. The great competitor appeared to enjoy the schoolyard of competition. If he made a slip it would never be forgotten. He made no slips.

Here sits Robert Frost in a corner, his eyes scanning the room for approaching enemies. Undergraduates ask questions about Yeats, Eliot, Pound. The corpses of Yeats, Eliot, and Pound litter the floor of the housemaster's living room. Someone mentions Robert Lowell's name. Frost says he guesses Lowell is pretty good. Of course he's a *convert,* he says, he lays the word out like a frog in a biology lab.

Another writer of quite a different stripe was also at Bread Loaf in 1945, a newspaperman from Lexington, Kentucky, named A. B. Guthrie, Jr., who answered to the name of "Bud" and who had won a Nieman fellowship to Harvard. Guthrie would only admit to friends that he had once published a cheap Western novel called *Murders at Moon Dance,* but he hungered to do something on a larger and more permanent canvas. With his Nieman time, he began work on a novel that had the American fur trade as its background. Ted Morrison had agreed to be his adviser. "All those first weeks with Ted as my tutor were hard," Guthrie recalled.

I would go home after a session and torture my brain. What was it he meant? What really was wrong, what really had he suggested? Like other beginners I was impatient with inexactitude in a critic and dejected by it. The course should be easy to chart. A guide shouldn't lose a man in a thicket. I didn't know then, though I surely learned later, that a teacher can only suggest, can at best reveal some of the tricks by which illusion is wrought. The rest is up to the student, to what there is in him, to his guts and his heart and his head, all working from the meager base camp that the teacher has managed to pitch.

Under Morrison's patient tutelage, Guthrie made great strides with the novel he would title *The Big Sky*. By the summer of 1945, when Morrison sponsored him for a fellowship to Bread Loaf, it was two-fifths completed. Guthrie arrived knowing that he would be in high literary company for a habitué of the newsroom. But he dreaded most his meeting Bernard DeVoto, who had as much as staked his claim to the very part of American history that Bud Guthrie was fictionalizing. DeVoto was reappearing on the Mountain after three years' absence—he had been gone as much in dismay over Robert Frost's ways as for his own weariness at what he called "the bloody membrane of personalities" at Treman, but Morrison had cajoled him back. DeVoto's *The Year of Decision* had succeeded beyond his wildest expectations, encouraging him to continue with narrative history; the new book, *Across the Wide Missouri,* was also to be about the trans-Missouri fur traders. Bud Guthrie's fears of unleashing a furious mountain lion of competition proved wrong. DeVoto had a growing but hard-won understanding that his gifts as a novelist were few. Moreover, he found sheer delight in research, in synthesizing a range of assorted human experience in the historical record into a synecdoche of an entire era. There would have been no juice left for a novel about the fur traders. So DeVoto "read *The Big Sky* in manuscript," remembered Guthrie, "and promptly beat all his drums to promote it."

Writing his novel and sending his mind back to the Montana in which he had been raised, Guthrie had been homesick in Cambridge but less so under the bigger sky of the Green Mountains. He reveled in the people he met—not only the writers on the faculty, whom he would join in a few years, but the literary hopefuls he encountered in the dining hall and on the lane between the Inn and the social center in the Barn. "The practice at meals, presumably aimed at the edification of the cash customers," he recalled,

> was to move us free-loading fellows about in the dining room, to assign each of us one table one day and another the next. So it came about that I sat next to a woman of sixty-five years, maybe seventy. She liked to write verse, she told me. Her manner suggested an old and amused sophistication. She not only liked to write it, she did write it. What was more, she sold it. She must have read my doubt. "Nothing to it," she said. "If I want to pick up five or ten dollars, I write a godgimme. It's a sure thing." I asked, "A godgimme?" "Of course," she said with a lovely and incredible cynicism. "You know, 'God give me a garden with a hollyhock in it.'"

A small thing, cherished in memory, as small things so often are.

The Big Sky would be very successful; the historian Allan Nevins would call it a "skillfully planned and beautifully finished novel," a sensitive evocation of the land and the people who settled on it.

Out of a taxi on August 17 stepped the evening's visiting lecturer, Richard Wright, tall, thirty-six, light-complected, celebrated, an object of politely veiled curiosity in the paler throngs at Bread Loaf, coming from a vacation in Quebec and dusty from a grim journey on a crowded and dirty train. His mesmerizing autobiography of his formative years, *Black Boy,* had recently appeared to greatly deserved attention and sales. Wright had grown up in Memphis, Tennessee, and Helena, Arkansas, an unruly product of a broken home. His mother, a onetime school-teacher, became totally paralyzed before he was ten, and the succession of relatives who then sheltered them could only despair at young Wright's willful hostility. Reading, though, began to transport him from his desperate circumstances and the structural racism that crushed him with every breath he took. During an idle moment in the eighth grade, he wrote a short story with a title and plot that would have made Fletcher Pratt proud: "The Voodoo of Hell's Half-Acre." A local African-American newspaper published it in three installments, and Wright began to dream of escaping the South and becoming a writer.

In time, working in Memphis, he found a diatribe in the *Memphis Commercial Appeal* about one H.L. Mencken of

Bernard DeVoto, 1940s

Baltimore. "I wondered what on earth this Mencken had done to call down upon him the scorn of the South," he remembered in *Black Boy,* and he convinced a white co-worker to lend him his library card so he could find out for himself. The book he pretended to check out for a white man was *A Book of Prefaces*; it became his literary bible. "I was jarred and shocked by the style, the clear, clean, sweeping sentences," he recalled.

Why did he write like that? And how did one write like that? I pictured the man as a raging demon, slashing with his pen, consumed with hate, denouncing everything American, extolling everything European or German, laughing at the weaknesses of people, mocking God, authority. What was this? I stood up, trying to realize what reality lay behind the meaning of the words. . . . Yes, this man was fighting, fighting with words. He was using words as a weapon, using them as one would use a club. Could words be weapons? Well, yes, for here they were. Then, maybe, perhaps, I could use them as a weapon? No. It frightened me. I read on and what amazed me was not what he said, but how on earth anybody had the courage to say it.

Occasionally I glanced up to reassure myself that I was alone in the room. Who were these men about whom Mencken was talking so passionately? Who was Anatole France? Joseph Conrad? Sinclair Lewis, Sherwood Anderson, Dostoevski, George Moore, Gustave Flaubert, Maupassant, Tolstoy, Frank Harris, Mark Twain, Thomas Hardy, Arnold Bennett, Stephen Crane, Zola, Norris, Gorky, Bergson, Ibsen, Balzac, Bernard Shaw, Dumas, Poe, Thomas Mann, O. Henry, Dreiser, H.G. Wells, Gogol, T.S. Eliot, Gide, Baudelaire, Edgar Lee Masters, Stendhal, Turgenev, Huneker, Nietzsche, and scores of others? Were these men real? Did they exist or had they existed? And how did one pronounce their names?

Finding out, he at once educated and prepared himself for the trip north to Chicago. He got a job in the post office there, began to publish a few poems in free verse, and in 1935 moved to work on the Works Progress Administration's Federal Writers' Project, first in Chicago and then in New York. Around 1937 Wright joined the Communist party, finding a steady outlet for his poetry in *The New Masses*. (He would dramatically resign from the party in 1944, when he published an essay called "The God That Failed.") For a novelette, *Uncle Tom's Children,* Wright won a $500 prize from *Story* magazine for the best story written by a worker on the Federal Writers' Project. With three other long stories, his first book was published in 1938.

Then, on Guggenheim money, Wright went to work on the novel that would establish him, *Native Son.* The book was a harrowing account of a racial murder and its social underpinnings. It was modeled after Dreiser's *An American Tragedy* and partly based on the much-publicized Chicago case of Robert Nixon, who was executed in Chicago in 1938 for killing a white woman. Living in New York, desperate for information about court testimony and police reports, Wright depended on a friend from his Chicago WPA circle for research—the friend was young Margaret Walker, still fresh from Northwestern and determined to become a poet and novelist (her first volume of poetry

would be in the Yale Series of Younger Poets in 1942, and her best-selling novel, *Jubilee,* would be published with a Houghton Mifflin Literary Fellowship in 1966). For more than a year, as Walker collected and sent off the press clippings necessary for Wright's inspiration, their easygoing friendship was cemented by literary correspondence about each of their projects. But a year before *Native Son* was to be published, becoming an instant best-seller and a Book-of-the-Month Club selection, their friendship went down in flames. Described with pathos and immediacy in Walker's *Richard Wright: Daemonic Genius* (1988), the lost friendship, with all its rich literary associations, was a victim of Walker's naive crush and Wright's uncertain sexuality; the book goes further than any other biography in uncovering the more obscure motivations of Wright's genius.

That, of course, was all history by August 1945, when Wright was launching a lecture tour "to enlighten his fellow citizens on the 'so-called Negro Problem,'" with his first stop being at Bread Loaf. Sixteen-year-old Donald Hall had read all of Wright's work and, he recalled, "I expected someone fierce. Years later I saw him—I'm not sure I ever spoke to him—in Paris, and he seemed a proud and strong fellow." But at Bread Loaf Wright was weary and not altogether himself. FBI agents had been dogging his heels, as J. Edgar Hoover was convinced that the now-apolitical Wright was still a Communist subversive and, one imagines, a dangerous, influential black man who by then had married a white woman. He was even scheduled to share a program at Howard University with Eleanor Roosevelt on "The Unfinished Task of Democracy," something that Hoover would not have wanted explored under such circumstances. Wright no longer felt at ease, even in the North. In a matter of months he would flee with his wife and daughter for an expatriate life in Paris. "He seemed obsequious" at Bread Loaf, remembered Hall; he seemed eager to please his hosts and the audience, in social gatherings laughing with a false heartiness and even bobbing his head—perhaps slipping slightly, unconsciously, into the protective affect about which he had written so poignantly in his autobiography. After delivering his talk, "The American Negro Discovers Himself," and after a night's rest, Richard Wright sought more reassuring surroundings. On the way to a Connecticut teachers' convention on Afro-American literature, he wrote to his agent, Paul Reynolds: "I found [Bread Loaf] to be a rather elaborate place, much larger than I had supposed it would be. . . . They were rather a middle-class and blasé lot, but I suppose I've got to get used to that. I find that people dislike the Negro problem intensely but they still want to hear about it."

Edith Mirrielees and Ted Morrison outside Treman cottage, 1947

POSTWAR—WITCH-HUNTING DAYS

I n the aftermath of the war, Ted Morrison struggled, not always successfully, to inject the Writers' Conference with new vitality. First, he was hampered by a tight operating budget from Middlebury College, out of which he had to pay the faculty and the administrative staff. The budget had not been raised since Morrison took over as director in 1932—throughout the Great Depression and the war and the session of 1946, he had paid his full-term faculty members $200 apiece for two weeks' work. After the 1946 session he persuaded the new college president, Samuel S. Stratton, to give them raises, but the new amount, $300, was still not much for what was expected of them, even with lodging thrown in. Morrison's own salary jumped from $350 to $500 for both teaching and seeing to the conference business in the nonsummer months.

There was much work to be done for almost everyone, and allegiance to the cause could carry staff members only so far. Walter Havighurst recalled arriving at his upstairs room at Treman Cottage on the first day of the 1945 session and being "confronted by a desk piled with typescripts of various bulk and disorder. Despite a conspicuous memo stating that some help would be available in sorting and summarizing the scripts, I foresaw late and early hours hunched over that desk while some of my colleagues merely awaited the cheerful call, 'Tennis, anyone,' at the foot of the stairs." Havighurst turned down Morrison's plea to "help out" by joining Wallace Stegner in fiction in the 1946 session, perhaps because he dreaded the work load.

Most of the faculty in any given year were assigned large piles of manuscripts. But beyond that, Morrison had said, there was the long-term problem: "We need a reserve of good staff members, new ones and younger ones to bring along."

Whatever staff he would assemble would contend with an enlarged body of students. Beginning in 1946 Bread Loaf was besieged by applications—as, indeed, were most educational institutions. The national emergency with its rationing was over, so travel was easier; returned veterans were hungry to resume their lives. In 1946 Ted Morrison reported that he had received nearly three hundred applications. It was unprecedented. From these he accepted 130 and later confided to President Stratton that the ideal number should go no higher. After three years, though, applications fell off sharply—probably owing to competition, as the idea of holding writers' conferences grew popular. The decline underscored the need for attention to staffing.

As Morrison foresaw, the core staff upon which he had relied for more than a decade was beginning to succumb to time—Raymond Everitt, for example, died in 1947—and to outside pressures from the "real world" off the Mountain. There would be outright dropouts, regretted as they might have been. Wallace Stegner's post at Harvard ended in 1945; he moved to become professor of English and director of the creative writing center at Stanford, and for some years he served as West Coast editor for Houghton Mifflin. Additionally, he was building on the success of his novel of 1943, *The Big Rock Candy Mountain,* about a fortune-hunter's family in the early twentieth-century West, drawn partially from his own youth. Even with the Vermont farm bought with his first literary success, Stegner's time as teacher at Bread Loaf would be over after 1946, with one brief visit in 1953. Edith Mirrielees, who retired from Stanford in 1943, retired from Bread Loaf in 1948. The widowed Helen Everitt went back to work at Houghton Mifflin, then the *Ladies' Home Journal,* and read her last Bread Loaf manuscript in 1949.

Louis Untermeyer, whose wit and gentle encouragement of beginners' verse had made his presence at Bread Loaf seem immutable, stopped coming after 1948. That was the year he married his fourth wife, Bryna Ivens, whom he had met at Bread Loaf. This wedding would, in two years, precipitate a tangled marital situation when his third wife, the lawyer and former municipal judge Esther Antin, tried to secure her grip on Untermeyer's vast literary properties by having herself declared his legal wife. (But the courts would surprisingly hold for Jean Starr Untermeyer, his second wife, from whom he was divorced in 1926. It is said that when the court verdict was handed down, making him a temporary bigamist, the irrepressible Louis Untermeyer turned to embrace Jean Starr, exclaiming, "Darling!" They amicably divorced for a second time soon thereafter.) It is likely that Untermeyer decided to forgo any more temptations or complications at Bread Loaf in favor of his quiet farm in Elizabethtown, New York.

These depletions left Morrison a small core staff that had to be increased. Of course there would be Robert Frost, who now divided his time between Cambridge, Ripton, and Florida; he published two biblical masques, or verse plays—*The Masque of Reason* (1945) and *The Masque of Mercy* (1947). On the opposite literary pole there would be Fletcher Pratt, still doing what he did. There would be the publishing people. Periodically, Alan Collins of the Curtis Brown Agency would serve. More permanent was William Sloane, who was to take an increasing stature in the conference even as his professional life roller-coastered. Sloane left Holt in 1946 to form his own imprint, William Sloane Associates, but he was an inferior businessman and the failed company was taken over by Morrow in 1952; in 1955 he would lodge as director of the Rutgers University Press.

Another mainstay of Bread Loaf, Bernard DeVoto, was not so steady a presence as in former years. Each new meeting with Robert Frost after the stormy session of 1938 had persuaded him that Frost had all but destroyed his cherished little community of friends and with it the shared endeavor they had taken on as their true mission. DeVoto had confided to a friend, with all the hurt and rage and paranoia of a spurning son, that Frost "has hated me

with an appalling violence as a man whom he could not consume and whom in the process of trying to consume he has opened himself to far more than the demon in him could ever bear to remember."

After his appearance in 1945, when the glacial air between him and Frost had been so obvious to so many, the Mountain exerted its magnetic pull and DeVoto was persuaded to return in 1947. There, he swallowed his pride—a choking gulp for him—for the sake of the community. On August 13, as Frost entered the Little Theatre to deliver his first lecture, DeVoto leaped out of his seat in the first row. "Robert, you've been a damn fool and I've been a damn fool," he whispered in Frost's ear as the audience continued to applaud the appearance of their bard. "Let's forget it and be friends." He led Frost over to the empty seat he had saved him next to his own. The poet then turned to see Kay Morrison seated behind them. "Now," he whispered, "wasn't that nice of him?" If a public equilibrium was struck for the moment, in private it would not last. It may have been during the next session that John Ciardi saw Frost toss a quip in DeVoto's direction. "DeVoto picked it up," he recalled, "I thought very deftly, without malice, and dumped it back on Frost's lap so that the honors were left with DeVoto. Frost hated that. The next day, as I was told later, he walked up and down the hillside attended by Kay Morrison, taking a stick and beating saplings to death while he cussed DeVoto."

But on the public face of things, the feud was ending in an uncertain truce. DeVoto was again able to be pleased with the work done on fiction. "It was team work that did it," he wrote to a colleague three weeks after the 1947 conference. "We demonstrated the superiority of the T-formation to the single wingback, and I got an aesthetic satisfaction from the running plays. It was a cooperative endeavor that teaching ought to be and damn seldom is." Bread Loaf was, he continued, "the damnedest place. My own hangover has persisted up to now. The bloody membrane of personalities . . . oppressed me there and does still. I went only under duress and it about used up my margin of safety. At the same time, the experience of working with friends at a common job is damn near inestimable . . . I suppose that's why so uncomfortable, vexatious, and emotionally exhausting a place as BL becomes so memorable to us as experience looked back on."

Indeed, the experience rekindled the old warmth to the extent that DeVoto enthusiastically devoted his November "Easy Chair" column in *Harper's,* some three thousand words, to Bread Loaf. In it one would find absolutely no clue that anything untoward had ever happened between any members of the Bread Loaf faculty. "No misunderstanding can last very long," DeVoto wrote, because every staff member pitches in to help clear it up.

No mistake in teaching has serious results for the staff are, so to speak, so used to backing up throws from the outfield that nothing can get through them. What makes this co-operation the more impressive is one's startled awareness that writers, normally the most antagonistic of men, are doing it. It may be that some of them are prima donnas or exhibitionists but if so they don't act naturally at Bread Loaf. A strong common acidity would take care of them if they did, but the true explanation is different and important: they are so interested in the job they are doing that they subordinate themselves to it. So they work without the antagonism, envy, and jealousy which most college administrators regard as institutional aberrations but which the wiser ones know are an integral function of academic institutions. The result is effective teaching. I say soberly that it is the most effective teaching I have ever seen. No college English department works anywhere near so well.

A measure of wishful thinking was in it, but the column was wonderful publicity for the conference, although Ted Morrison recalled that there was no sudden swell in applications during the next several months.

Morrison would not be able to persuade DeVoto to return after the 1948 conference, which again underscored the need to find, as he had written to Walter Havighurst in 1946, "new ones and younger ones to bring along." Wisely, Morrison turned to scrutinize his roster of past fellows.

One he chose was Mark Saxton, rugged looking and genial, and well known to many on the Mountain. He was a former Harvard writing student of DeVoto's and the son of the longtime chief of the book division of Harper Brothers, Eugene F. Saxton. Mark, a novelist, had been an editor at Farrar and Rinehart and had moved over to work at Bill Sloane's new house; when that enterprise failed he moved to Harvard University Press where he would stay for nearly twenty years. Saxton held a nebulous sort of fellowship in 1947 as a teaching assistant while Morrison tried him out; he taught again in 1948 and again in 1950 and 1951, the one year of absence due to the thirty-four-year-old's sudden and unexpected embolism a month before the 1949 session. Another new recruit would be A.B. Guthrie, Jr., who arrived in 1948 after finishing his second novel, *The Way West,* and after quitting his Kentucky job in the *Lexington Leader* newsroom ("I had the shaky hope," he said, "after *The Big Sky,* that maybe I wouldn't have to ride a payroll"). *The Way West* would win a Pulitzer in 1949.

Still another recruit to the Bread Loaf staff would be frail and kind Rachel MacKenzie, who when she won a fiction fellowship in 1948 was an English instructor at Radcliffe with several stories in *Harper's* and *The New Yorker.* She joined the Bread Loaf faculty in 1951, staying through 1955. It would be in 1956 that MacKenzie would join *The New Yorker* as a fiction editor, succeeding Katherine White. She remained there for twenty-five years and developed a loyal following among writers all over the world—including Saul Bellow, Isaac Bashevis Singer, Philip Roth, Bernard Malamud, and Edna O'Brien. "Her genius," a colleague would write, "was a combination of absolute friendship and a shared love for the work in progress. Even a young writer submitting his first story at once knew instinctively that here was someone dedicated only to making his story succeed as well as it possibly could. She had an immense gift for participating in other people's curiosity and delight, and many writers spoke of learning 'with' Rachel MacKenzie rather than 'from' her. But whether with or from, learn they did." And so it was on the Mountain.

In terms of the future of Bread Loaf, the most carrying choice Morrison was to make was to appoint his poetry fellow of 1940, John Ciardi, to the staff. A gunner in an Army Air Corps B-29, Ciardi had flown some fifteen missions from Saipan and had used his combat experiences to illuminate the poems of *Other Skies* (1947). The starkness of these poems, which would be compared to those of Wilfred Owen, won him a number of prizes. He was also named to the Bread Loaf faculty in 1947.

If they were paying attention, conference members in the late 1940s and early 1950s could have looked at those sessions and perceived a new locus of energy as Ciardi made himself the conference's anchor in teaching poetry as surely as his deep baritone found a place in the evening sing-alongs; they could have noted his utter (sometimes dismaying) lack of modesty and felt the physical and literary self-assurance radiating from him. Truly, leaping from a B-29 into a civilian life of letters, he hit the ground running. Ciardi followed *Other Skies* with one book, more or less, every other year. In 1946 he began the five-year Briggs-Copeland teaching post at Harvard, the seat formerly occupied by DeVoto and Stegner. In 1949, Ciardi became poetry editor for Twayne Publishers; backed by the enthusiasm of owner Jacob Steinberg, Ciardi promised to publish eight new books of poetry each year—more of a commitment to the genre than larger houses were willing to make—and the little imprint and its poetry editor took on a formidable presence in literary circles.

Then, in 1950, Ciardi published an anthology, *Mid-Century American Poets,* that was important—even seminal—for the time. It served as a multivoiced manifesto of a new generation of poets who had distanced themselves from the generation of the 1920s; each of the fifteen poets had come of age either just before or during the Second World War; each was given the opportunity to select work for *Mid-Century American Poets* and write an introductory note for it. Even today the list—cronies and all—holds up surprisingly well for a period anthology, and it is to the editor's credit that he recognized so many of his contemporaries well before they attained their later standings: Richard Wilbur, Robert Lowell, Muriel Rukeyser, Theodore Roethke, Randall Jarrell, Elizabeth Bishop, Karl Shapiro, John Frederick Nims, Delmore Schwartz, Richard Eberhart, Winfield Townley Scott, John Holmes, Peter Viereck, E.L. Mayo, and Ciardi himself. The collection became a popular college textbook, greatly influencing the next generation of poets. Ted Morrison would affectionately remember Ciardi in those years as "impressive in figure, possessed of a fine voice both in depth and resonance, inexhaustibly fertile as a speaker in wit and metaphor, a poet of widely recognized resourcefulness and vigor."

In those postwar years several other writers at the beginning of their careers came to the conference. One of great promise served as a teaching assistant in nonfiction in 1947—the forty-one-year-old Joseph Kinsey Howard, a journalist, historian, and activist, whose *Montana—High, Wide and Handsome* (1943) had attacked the copper, cattle, and railroad corporations, and many of his fellow Montanans as well, for allowing the state's great natural resources to be devastated. It was, said *The New Yorker,* "superior history . . . by an indigenous editor who understands ecology, as well as gun-play, and who is tearing mad about what a mistaken land policy, monopoly practices, dust storms, and two wars have done to his native earth." Howard was to die, at forty-five, before finishing his second book, *Strange Empire,* a compelling account of the Canadian métis revolt. It was finished by Bernard DeVoto, who also contributed a moving preface. "With his death," DeVoto wrote, "the West lost one of its few writers of the first rank and one of its most valuable citizens." As Wallace Stegner pointed out, DeVoto "in a characteristic gesture" sent his fee to Howard's mother.

Three fellows in the late forties bear some scrutiny. There was, for instance, a young Austrian refugee named Frederick Morton, who had come to the United States in 1940 and who held a Bread Loaf fellowship in 1947, the year his first novel came out. Morton would go on to publish many distinguished works of prose, a number of them about his native Vienna. There was also a former Stanford student of Wallace Stegner's, Eugene Burdick, at work on a novel when at Bread Loaf in 1946. Burdick met another fellow, William Lederer, at that year's conference. Out of the resulting friendship came a writing partnership that resulted in the novel of folly in Southeast Asia, *The*

Ugly American. But one cannot move on without mentioning someone in attendance that year who would barely have fit the category of "emerging writer." He was just twenty-one, a college senior from Virginia by the name of William Styron.

Styron's first literary effort, at thirteen, had been a bad imitation of Joseph Conrad; he had called it "Typhoon and the Tor Bay." "You know," he told Peter Matthiessen and George Plimpton in 1954, "a ship's hold swarming with crazy Chinks. I think I had some sharks in there too. I gave it the full treatment." But Styron did not give writing any further thought until after a short noncombative hitch in the U.S. Marines at the close of the war, notable only for the frequency with which the rebellious, authority-hating Styron got himself on report. Then, when he studied Elizabethan drama and poetry under William Blackburn at Duke University, he began to develop an interest in writing. He read omnivorously—Fitzgerald, Hemingway, Huxley, Wolfe, and Orwell. He also published some stories in the college magazine that he would later wish to disavow.

In August 1946 Styron was still a year away from his disastrous, brief editorial internship in the McGraw-Hill division of Whittlesey House—where he would be fired for blowing bubbles in the hallway and for not wearing a hat, but not for rejecting Thor Heyerdahl's *Kon Tiki* and giving another publisher the opportunity to make millions on it. Styron was also a year or so away from beginning his magnificent first novel, *Lie Down in Darkness* (1951). He had not yet read anything by William Faulkner. At the suggestion of his professor he went north in that August to Vermont, where it rained for thirteen days, to sit attentively in fiction classes conducted by Wallace Stegner, Helen Everitt, and Grame Lorimer.

It was a session characterized by some discontent, "turning largely," as Ted Morrison reported, "on the old controversy, which has agitated the conference before, between writing for art or social purpose and writing for money." Largely because of his difficulty in finding teachers of fiction, the emphasis that year leaned heavily—in fact, much more than usual at Bread Loaf—to the commercial side. Lectures bore punchy result-getting titles like "Tricks of the Trade," "Plotting the Short Story," "Setting Up Your Production Line," and "Writing as a Job." One merely had to look at the schedule for the back-to-back classes on August 15, as young Styron must have. At nine, Mr. Stegner taught "The Architecture of the Novel, Part One." And at ten-fifteen, Mr. Pratt lectured on the topic "Four Out of Five Don't Have It." Art versus commerce, one supposes. And reactions could be heated when such sticks of advice and wisdom were rubbed together. There were, Morrison recalled, some young hotheads in the short story discussions who caused quite an amount of trouble. It is not known whether any Duke seniors were among this group—but one hopes, no, *expects* so.

I t was in October 1948 that the term "Cold War" was coined by the wealthy businessman and elder statesman Bernard M. Baruch in a Washington speech on Soviet-American relations before the Senate War Investigating Committee. The term reflected a state of mind that had predominated since the close of the Second World War, not just in foreign affairs, but also in domestic matters—an institutionalized paranoia that would grow to shadow all levels of American life, particularly intellectual and artistic life.

Politically, the pendulum had swung over into a time of reaction against thirteen years of Roosevelt liberalism and the New Deal, and its apparent successor, the beneficent Fair Deal of President Truman's early administration. The war was over but times had not improved much; serious inflation crippled the economy. The postwar Communist consolidation of Eastern Europe was viewed with an alarm equal to that over the "loss" of China. On the ascendancy were conservatives of both parties, joined by the far right fringe, and their tactics were similar and complementary. In the late 1940s and early 1950s, the best way to build political capital or to maintain power was to hurl a reckless charge of "communism" at an opponent. Successful careers were thus built—less on rooting out actual "card-carrying" members of the American Communist party, of whom there were not very many—nor were they much of a threat—but on smearing and wreaking revenge on liberals with connections to Roosevelt's New Deal. Also a target were progressives, active and inactive, most of whom had flirted with the Left in the intellectually and politically faddish 1920s and 1930s. In a grandiose and cynical sweep, they were all labeled "Communists," "reds," "fellow travelers," or "sympathizers"—this, most of the time, for fighting against the depression, supporting organized labor, opposing the fascist revolution in Spain (as "premature antifascists," a disgraceful term), or working for amity with Russia at the time when it was a war ally against Germany.

Ambition and orchestrated paranoia infiltrated public life as it assaulted artistic and intellectual liberty in those years. Investigations of two million federal employees yielded only a paltry number of resignations and firings and a crisis of governmental confidence. There was the most public trial of all, that of former State Department official Alger Hiss. There was the Senate probe of Communist infiltration in the film industry, the naming of ten screenwriters as "reds," and the tragedy of the industry's

self-policed blacklist, which destroyed careers as it stifled free expression.

This exposition is necessary to illustrate how writers and the process of writing was affected during the witch-hunting days of the House Un-American Activities Committee and of Senator Joseph McCarthy of Wisconsin. A chill similar to that in Hollywood swept over all but a very few book publishers. And, behind the scenes, there were the governmental intrusions into the lives of writers, into their very minds—the secret war of J. Edgar Hoover's FBI, as documented in Herbert Mitgang's angry, eloquent book, *Dangerous Dossiers* (1988). Mitgang found that the bureau, fueled by Hoover's empire-building and far-right paranoia, investigated and maintained files on many revered authors, including Sinclair Lewis, Pearl S. Buck, William Faulkner, Ernest Hemingway, John Steinbeck, Carl Sandburg, Theodore Dreiser, John Dos Passos, Thomas Wolfe, Dorothy Parker, Dashiell Hammett, Thornton Wilder, Lillian Hellman, Edmund Wilson, and H.L. Mencken. The FBI infiltrated writers' guilds, investigated magazine subscription lists, brought pressure against noncompliant publishers, and waged a smear campaign against its "enemies" through friendly columnists and so-called patriotic organizations.

Though the bureau maintains it kept no file on the Bread Loaf Writers' Conference, one inevitably wonders. With Hoover's deep distrust of creative types, other writers' enclaves or groups were certainly investigated. But the fact remains that many writers connected to the conference, representing a wide range of political persuasion, were on their own considered "enemies" of the United States government and the nation's way of life. Their lives were affected in various ways by this air of suspicion, and some were no doubt put under surveillance. It was characteristic of the bureau that its files showed no familiarity with writers' actual words or views. As has been said, Richard Wright was one of those judged a "security risk"; when he lectured at Bread Loaf in 1945 he had been hounded his whole trip by federal agents. Archibald MacLeish was also subject to governmental surveillance and interference. So were Louis Untermeyer, Dorothy Canfield Fisher, W. H. Auden, Elmer Rice, and Howard Fast. Incredibly, so was Robert Frost. And so was Bernard DeVoto.

"We are dividing into the hunted and the hunters," DeVoto wrote in his October 1949 "Easy Chair" column in *Harper's* entitled "Due Notice to the F.B.I." "There is loose in the United States today the same evil that once split Salem Village between the bewitched and the accused and stole men's reason quite away. We are informers to the secret police. Honest men are spying on their neighbors for patriotism's sake. We may be sure that for every honest man two dishonest ones are spying for personal advancement today and ten will be spying for pay next year. . . . I like a country where it's nobody's damned business what magazines anyone reads, what he thinks, whom he has cocktails with. . . . We had that kind of country only a little while ago and I'm for getting it back." DeVoto had been criticizing the Communists for twenty years—but still, he would be denounced as a Communist sympathizer by Senator Joe McCarthy in a nationwide telecast during the presidential campaign of 1952.

At Bread Loaf in 1950, the issues that had inflamed DeVoto so eloquently in *Harper's* came home to the Mountain in an incident that involved an old Cambridge friend of the Morrisons and the DeVotos, Owen Lattimore. Lattimore, a frequent guest at the Writers' Conference in the thirties, had spent much of his youth and young adulthood in China, although he was educated in Switzerland and England. In the late 1920s, as a businessman in Shanghai and then as a freelance writer, Lattimore focused on China's frontier and the lands of Turkestan, Manchuria, Tibet, and, prominently, Mongolia. He contributed articles to Edward Weeks's *The Atlantic Monthly, The New Republic,* and many newspapers.

His first book, *The Desert Road to Turkestan* (1929), was a riveting account of the rough journey he took with his new wife, the writer Eleanor Holgate Lattimore, in those bleak environs—a honeymoon on camelback and sled. A succession of fellowships allowed him further travel and study of Asian languages and political affairs, which led to a number of other books, which ranged from high adventure to even higher scholarship. Mild mannered, square jawed, and moustachioed, Lattimore left China at the Japanese Occupation and was named director of the Walter Hines Page School of International Relations at Johns Hopkins University. During the war he was a consultant to President Roosevelt, a deputy director of the Office of War Information, and an adviser to Generalissimo Chiang Kai-Shek. By the end of the war he was one of the nation's most knowledgeable experts on China and the Far East, an anti-Communist whose advice was consistently ignored by the government.

Lattimore was in Afghanistan in March 1950 with a United Nations technical assistance mission when he learned that he had been called "the top Russian espionage agent in the United States" by Senator McCarthy, then engaged in a "loyalty campaign" against the State Department for its "failed" China policy. Lattimore immediately returned home to find himself in a firestorm of publicity. He denied the charges and called McCarthy "base and despicable." McCarthy would later amend his charge to "one of the top espionage agents." But the senator promised to retire if he could not make the accusation stick and

to resign if he failed to repeat the accusation in a forum exposing him to suit for libel. The result, even after McCarthy's four-hour Senate speech against Lattimore, was none of the above.

In early May a Senate committee found no truth to McCarthy's accusations. But the controversy was almost immediately rekindled when a seedy ex-Communist writer and lecturer named Louis Budenz came forward to echo the Wisconsin senator's story. Although the matter was ultimately dropped, along with all charges against him, the shadow would hang over Lattimore for five years.

Outside of his congressional testimony, Lattimore's reply would come in an angry, persuasive book he wrote over nineteen days in May 1950. *Ordeal by Slander* was an immediate best-seller. It was published in June by Little, Brown, went through two subsequent printings by August, and in that month was serialized in *Harper's* and the *New York Daily Compass*; a paperback edition hit the stands in December. "Fear and suspicion now run wild in our country," Lattimore wrote. "The McCarthy demagogues who are working to destroy our traditional liberties have already made great gaps in the tradition of freedom which has made this country unique. They have been working to strengthen and to exploit politically a dark tide of unreasoning, hysterical fear. McCarthyism insists constantly, emotionally, and menacingly that the man who thinks independently thinks dangerously and for an evil, disloyal purpose." It was fascism in an American cloak.

On Monday, August 28, Owen and Eleanor Lattimore and their son David, a Harvard student, pulled up in front of the Bread Loaf Inn. Observers said that they looked tired, sad, and a little hunted. Lattimore was still the object of great controversy, though large numbers had rallied to his support and to applaud his indictment of witch-hunting. The evening before, however, a speaking engagement in New Hampshire had been canceled because Lattimore was a "controversial" character. Some conference members began grumbling about the subversive lecturer, though not in Ted Morrison's hearing; still, he worried about how his friend would be received at Bread Loaf: "[W]ould the air be thick with conflicting emotions, among them hostility and suspicion? Would anyone try to bait him from the floor?" That evening, in the Little Theatre, Ted Morrison stood to make an unusually long introduction. "I am not a judge of the rightness or wrongness of his views," said Morrison.

Has anyone been right in the world of the atomic bomb? But I believe that we need on our team a few people who have knowledge about the remote and vast realm of Asia with which we are entangled in the human chaos. Is it a prejudice against knowledge that has got Owen Lattimore into some part of his recent ordeal? Is it, could it be, even a prejudice against the stylist, the magnificent writer in an age when public affairs are settled so often by gobbledegook and the leprous soothing-syrup of official cliches?

Owen Lattimore once used in conversation a phrase I never forgot. I dare say it was a phrase with a degree of fine exaggeration about it. He was telling us about crossing a high pass in the Pamirs, and not in an airplane. This was many years ago. He said that he and Mrs. Lattimore and their pack train slept at a height from which they looked down on the Himalayas. The elevation from which Mr. Lattimore now looks down on his political slanderers seems to me at the same time both loftier and more arduous. To see him up there is a spectacle of awe and of deep concern, for his ability to cling to his perch means everything to that right to be heard without which neither free society nor honest writing can exist.

As Lattimore got up to deliver his address the entire Bread Loaf audience rose with him. By all accounts the thunderous ovation, the feeling that by being there and welcoming him they were also speaking truth to power, was magnificent, and for those moments there were no politics, no differences, only pure fellowship.

It was also on that day—which had started with a fiction clinic run by Bill Sloane and ended with Lattimore's speech—that a review in the book trade magazine *Publishers Weekly* was placed on the desk of J. Edgar Hoover in Washington. It was for a book published by William Sloane Associates, a history of the FBI by Max Lowenthal, a former congressional aide who had researched the book for more than a decade. *The Federal Bureau of Investigation* was a scouring critique of Hoover and his organization, and it sent the director into the stratosphere. He immediately launched a campaign to discredit the author and the publisher.

Within days FBI agents and staff members of the House Un-American Activities Committee (HUAC) were paying separate visits to Lowenthal and to Sloane's New York office. Within weeks the author was hauled before an executive session of HUAC where he was questioned about past "subversive" contacts; at the same time FBI agents were reporting to Hoover on the bookselling calls of William Sloane's salesmen. They later followed up with attempts to discourage stores from stocking the book. The bureau helped write a speech against Lowenthal for a friendly congressman, leaked derogatory information about the author and William Sloane, and prepared critical reviews that were planted with compliant reporters and columnists—the list included the influential Walter Winchell, Fulton Lewis, Jr., and George Sokolsky. A year later Hoover was still at it, urging the newly created Senate Internal Security Subcommittee to investigate "the matter of Communist infiltration into the book publishing business," with particular attention toward "the left-wing element" in the house of William Sloane. Nothing came of the request. Apparently the Senate subcommittee did not follow Hoover's lead, and in any case by then Bill Sloane was trying to stave off bankruptcy. He may have been a bad businessman—but his situation could only have been worsened by the pressure from Hoover's FBI.

One more story involved Louis Untermeyer. It has its light side but there is a dark core to it, just as in the cases of Owen Lattimore, William Sloane, and many others. Untermeyer had found an ideal place for his verbal agility—as a cast member of the popular Sunday evening television quiz show "What's My Line." Untermeyer found himself being repeatedly stopped on the street, a degree of celebrity not previously enjoyed. Once, when he was lunching with Robert Frost, three teenaged women approached their table to ask Untermeyer for his autograph. "Of course," he replied, "but I'm sure you'd prefer my guest's. He's one of our country's most important writers . . . Robert Frost, the poet." "Oh, thanks," one replied, "but we only collect celebrities." Frost said nothing until they were gone, and then only, "They're pretty girls, aren't they."

All this ended when American Legionnaires began writing the show's sponsors in droves, calling Untermeyer a pinko, a Communist party dupe, a dangerous stooge. Thirty and more years before, he had been a friend of John Reed and Max Eastman. He had also recently supported the presidential candidacy of the progressive Henry Wallace. Such actions were too much for the Legionnaires, and to whatever person or persons who had initiated the campaign. Typically, the show's producers suggested that Untermeyer perform some "patriotic" act to "clear his name."

Instead, Louis Untermeyer resigned.

Theodore Morrison and John Ciardi, 1955

1951 Staff: (rear) Richard Brown, Lincoln Barnett, Rachel MacKenzie, {unknown}, William Sloane; (center) Inga Pratt, Fletcher Pratt, Theodore Morrison, Wallace Stegner, Mary Stegner; (front) Mark Saxton, May Sarton, Kay Morrison, John Ciardi, Judith Ciardi, Julie Sloane

MORRISON'S TWILIGHT

In August 1950, in his cottage overlooking the Bread Loaf campus where he customarily spent his summers, Donald Davidson entertained a former student from Vanderbilt, Elizabeth Spencer, and her friend, Mary Elizabeth Witherspoon, who both held fellowships for their first novels. The conservative Davidson warned the two young women against "the politics of Treman cottage." "It was the year of Joe McCarthy's Wheeling, West Virginia, speech, the decade of the Silent Generation," recalled Witherspoon,

> but Bread Loaf wasn't silent. Neither was it radical, however; it was simply open—that is, within the bounds of moderation. When Malcolm Ross, a visiting radical with a genial, weathered face and a booming voice, began a protest song about man's basic right to overthrow his government, I glanced at Mr. Morrison's face and found him looking thoughtful and amused. When the protest song was finished, one of us began an old Methodist hymn, the other followed suit, the group joined in, and the subject was changed.

When she received a Bread Loaf fellowship to the twenty-fifth annual conference Elizabeth Spencer had published *Fire in the Morning* (1948), to considerable acclaim. Just twenty-nine, she was then teaching creative writing part-time at the University of Mississippi and at work on *This Crooked Way.* It would appear in 1952 to consolidate her standing as a gifted writer of finely crafted and plotted novels and short stories set mostly in the South.

Spencer had been a sickly child in Mississippi; her parents had kept her spirits up by reading to her—Bible stories, myths, Arthurian romance, and tales from the Civil War. Later, she recalled, her taste ran exclusively to the adventure novels of Edgar Rice Burroughs, creator of Tarzan. But she moved into more solid literary territory at a small denominational school in Jackson, Mississippi. There she edited the school newspaper, wrote poetry and short stories, won some awards, and met Jackson's Eudora Welty. Despite their age difference they became good friends, and Welty aided Spencer's career in a number of ways. After college, Spencer won a scholarship to Vanderbilt, where she studied under Donald Davidson for a year. He, too, became a valuable friend and ally, encouraging her after she began teaching at small schools in Mississippi and Tennessee, and after she left teaching for a reporter's job on the *Nashville Tennesseean.* "This kind of writing was still not what I wanted," she remembered. "I had earlier, during my senior year in college, started a novel, never titled, never finished, and mercifully never published. Poor and inept as it was, certain characters from it did not forsake me. I at last shut my eyes and jumped: resigned from the paper, cleaned my portable, and bought a ream of paper." She had, by then, begun collecting friendly rejection slips for her short stories. A year later she had enough of *Fire in the Morning* done to show to a publisher; Donald Davidson introduced her to an editor at Dodd, Mead, who eventually bought it—and, after he published it, nominated her for a Bread Loaf fellowship.

Spencer was overjoyed at seeing New England for the first time as her train rolled north toward Middlebury. She drank in the countryside up on the Bread Loaf plateau; in between classes the Davidsons took her for long drives up in the hills, and there were, of course, long walks with other conference members. "Along the pasture fences," she recalled many years later with undiminished fondness, "walking in the mountains, you could walk up and pat the horses on the nose." Associations, too, were memorable. Davidson soon introduced her to Robert Frost. "In fact," she recalled, "he asked us both to dinner at the Middlebury Inn. Frost talked a good deal. I was glad of the chance for a closer acquaintance, though being shy in those days I was almost tongue-tied. Everyone around the conference was in awe of him." Spencer attended some of the poetry workshops run by John Ciardi and showed some of her poems to him. He gave her some kind attention, she said, "though I believe he thought I should stick to prose."

Another person Elizabeth Spencer met at Bread Loaf, whose friendship would extend for many years, was Richard Wilbur, also twenty-nine, a young Harvard instructor who backed up Ciardi in the poetry clinics. His intellectual and formal poetry, both witty and musical, had appeared in two books by 1950; his first, in fact—*The Beautiful Changes* (1947) had been marked by unusual maturity for an emerging poet.

Richard Wilbur had spent a pleasant boyhood in the still-rural New Jersey suburbs. He wrote his first poem when he was eight, titling it "That's When the Nightingales Wake." "There are, of course, no nightingales in New Jersey," he remembered, "and the poem was a pure verbal and rhythmic exercise, drawing not at all upon my eight years' experience." For some time Wilbur aimed at a career in journalism, editing the Amherst College newspaper. He spent his summers in vagrancy, hopping freights over most of the forty-eight states. Most of his poetic attempts, he said, were "diversions with other people's nightingales." After graduation, the army took him. "It was not until World War II took me to Cassino, Anzio, and the Siegfried Line that I began to versify in earnest. One does not use poetry for its major purposes, as a means of organizing oneself and the world, until one's world somehow gets out of hand. A general cataclysm is not required; the disorder must be personal and may be wholly so, but poetry, to be vital, does seem to need a periodic acquaintance with the threat of Chaos." After the war, while he was studying for his master's degree at Harvard, a friend sent a packet of his poems to Reynal and Hitchcock. That long-gone publisher issued *The Beautiful Changes*.

Wilbur was, in the eyes of his Harvard and Bread Loaf colleague Ted Morrison, a superb staff member in the classroom as well as out of it. "His personal elegance, with just a touch of raffishness about it, matched his style as a speaker," wrote Morrison. "His tall, athletically proportioned figure and baritone voice, adept at ballads, made additional resources in his presentation of poetry. Of an evening at Treman he could wield one of the best guitars heard in a place where a succession of more than ordinary good performers had plied their skill, and he could team with Ciardi in impromptu vaudeville routines that dissolved sense and sensibility in the ridiculous."

Once, Wilbur went on a picnic with Mary Elizabeth Witherspoon and John Fischer of *Harper's*; the editor had his wife and children with him and thought that the two Bread Loafers would be missing their own families. Witherspoon was two years older than Wilbur, a Tennessee housewife with two children who lived in total literary isolation; but she very likely overwhelmed the sensitive Wilbur with her assertive temperament—she was outspoken and peppery and enjoyed popping bubbles wherever they rose, even at Bread Loaf. For her, the outing with the Fischers "was life-saving. There had been too much intensity, too much pressure all week long, and suddenly I was relieved of it, out in the wilds on a stream much like those I was used to in the Smoky Mountains." She and Wilbur went rock-hopping in the stream. "Almost immediately," she recalled, "he stooped to his haunches to study a fault in the rock. Then he made some remark I thought too academic, and I teased him about it." Ears reddening, Wilbur could only reply, "One must always verbalize, I think." But Witherspoon could only think rebelliously: "Must one? Like Eliza Doolittle, I had had nothing but 'words, words, words' for a week and was desperately in need of a little silent communion with the natural." Later on she wrote a poem about that interchange, knowing that the young introspective intellectual in Richard Wilbur would not recognize himself in it if indeed he ever saw it. "But I am grateful to him," she wrote, "for the inspiration."

Morrison had grown to depend on the Harvard and Radcliffe faculty for staffing at Bread Loaf in those years. It would be at the next session, 1951, that May Sarton, a thirty-nine-year-old Briggs-Copeland instructor in composition, would join the staff, taking on a mammoth share of faculty work in the short story and novel and in poetry. "I had to give three lectures a week and read seven or eight novels and try to give helpful criticism," she recalled, "so I did not stay up drinking till four A.M. in the faculty house! I prepared my lectures carefully and they were effective and greeted with much applause." This caused a certain amount of jealousy among some of the staff, as will be seen.

May Sarton was even more of a renaissance person than Richard Wilbur. She had spent the Second World War writing propaganda film scripts at the Office of War Information in Washington. Her family had fled Belgium in the earlier war, at the Kaiser's onslaught, when she was barely two; her father was George Sarton, the eminent scientific historian who later lodged at Harvard. She had taken no interest in education beyond high school; for eight years after graduation she was an actress with Eva Le Gallienne's Civic Repertory Theatre and the Associated Actors Theatre. The young actress also became a prolific writer. She published her first collection of lyrics, *Encounter in April,* in 1937, a novel, *The Single Hound,* the following year, and another book of poetry, *Inner Landscape,* in 1939. Much of her early work drew inspiration from the homeland she had never really known, imagining it as it was and as it might have been. After the war, she rolled right on with three more novels, a play, and another poetry collection. In 1951 at Bread Loaf, she was at work on a novel inspired by the suicide of Harvard literature professor F. O. Matthiessen; the fictional counterpart, like Matthiessen, was an idealist whose life rebounded between a love of literature and a passion for radical causes, and whose death was spurred at least in part by the witch hunt.

Despite a distinguished and critically praised publishing record that would have humbled many, Sarton appreciated Ted Morrison's faith in her when she was named to the Bread Loaf faculty. "I was not famous at the time," she wrote. At least, though, at Bread Loaf in the early fifties, she was—not always to the approval of less diligent and often less talented members of the staff, some of whom were men who could not countenance assertive women. One day she delivered a lecture to thundering applause. "I remember walking into the faculty house," she recalled, "and being greeted by Bill Sloane in these words: 'You would do a really good job if you were not so intense.'" Undeniably it was, as she felt, "a mean crack"— the sort of male chauvinist remark that became for many women of her spirit and attainment an all-too-common, always enraging dismissal.

Unpleasant as that interchange had been, Sarton's other associations were long and rewarding. She shared many sympathies with Rachel MacKenzie and they became fast friends, greatly enjoying the sessions through 1955 when their appointments coincided. (In a time when other ground was remaining undisturbed, their respective lectures were welcomed for their rigor and for breaking new ground at Bread Loaf. In 1951, for instance, Sarton talked about a writer's duties toward her imagined audience in a lecture entitled "The Woman at the Sink," while MacKenzie lectured on "Women as Writers.") When May Sarton's editor at *The New Yorker,* Katherine White, was ready to retire, Sarton was instrumental in getting Rachel

Rachel MacKenzie, mid-1950s

MacKenzie named to the job. And in fellow faculty member Eric Swenson she eventually found a new publisher; he would issue all of Sarton's books over the Norton imprint for many years to come.

As the fifties went on toward the mid-mark, Ted Morrison could not ignore something central about Bread Loaf: he felt himself going stale and feared that the conference was, too. "Over twenty times I had stood up at the opening session to give conference members advice on how to take the program in order to make the most of it," he recalled. "My ideas on this head or on the teaching and learning of the craft of writing were not changing or growing fresher. I was saying the same things year after year, struggling to give them a new frame or a new turn of phrase."

Moreover, he had failed to develop a new core of faculty members in the postwar years who could give the conference continuity. He had made a number of distinguished appointments. Saul Bellow, whose third novel, *The Adventures of Augie March,* had received a National Book Award for 1953 and considerably enlarged his audience, came in 1954 to teach fiction and lecture about the writers' profession. Catherine Drinker Bowen appeared twice as a visiting lecturer and as a full-term teacher, as did the sparkling Irish storyteller and poet Frank O'Connor and a staff writer for *Life,* Lincoln Barnett, who was known for his profiles of the celebrated, from Albert Einstein to Fred Astaire. DeVoto's onetime student Arthur Schlesinger, Jr., whose history, *The Age of Jackson,* had won a Pulitzer in 1945, came up from Harvard to lecture on the relation of writing to its social background. Jessamyn West, the red-haired and freckled Quaker author of *The Friendly Persuasion* (1945), appeared in 1952, the year before her charming stories about the adolescent Cress Delahanty, which had appeared in *The New Yorker,* were collected into book form. And, in 1955, twenty-four-year-old Adrienne Rich came to teach poetry with May Sarton and John Ciardi. She was four years out of Radcliffe and about to issue her second book of poetry; still under the influence of Auden and Yeats, she was, nonetheless, already showing a concern for women's issues. This interest would develop over time into the politicized work for which she would later find a large audience. Another presence that year was the brilliant political journalist Richard Rovere, whose "Letter from Washington" column in *The New Yorker* helped make sense of events in the capital in the fifties and sixties.

These and a number of other writers came to Bread Loaf, did their work, and departed. But connections to the conference, inheritance and bequest of tradition, and acknowledgment of the ghosts who had begun to populate the verandas, the classrooms, and the lecture hall could not be forged to a faculty cottage full of passersby, no matter how distinguished. Continuity was simply missing. In frequent fits of pessimism, Morrison even wondered if the whole project ought to be abandoned. "It was a time," recalled Ted Morrison, "for a regime which had enjoyed its successes and weathered its disappointments to consider seriously whether it hadn't played out its usefulness."

A personal tragedy could only have pushed him toward the inevitable conclusion. The Morrisons had raised two children, Anne and Bobby, who were born in the thirties and who had spent their summers in idyllic Bread Loaf isolation—roaming the woods around the Homer Noble Farm, playing with the domestic animals, balancing on Robert Frost's knees, attending—when they were old enough—the readings and lectures, as many children of staff would do on the Mountain, and maturing under the eyes of the conclave of writers. Then, in the winter of 1954, Bobby Morrison was driving to a ski slope on the state highway that ran through the Bread Loaf campus. He stopped to remove a broken tire chain on the driver's side of his car. While tugging it, he was killed by a passing car. Such a crushing loss, occurring right on the Bread Loaf plateau, had to have helped Ted Morrison feel almost that the choice was being made for him. So he tendered his resignation during the 1954 conference, to be effective the following year.

But who should succeed him? He waited to be consulted about his successor, but during the interim year, college officials seemed unable to suggest anyone at all suitable. Morrison privately spent many nights weighing the respective qualifications of writers on and off the Mountain without coming to any conclusion that seemed right the next morning. Then, the 1955 conference opened, still there was no one named, and Morrison decided to take matters into his own hands. He only had to look across the living room at Treman Cottage, where his faculty was gathered, to know whom to pick. "The obvious successor," he remembered, "was right at hand in the person of John Ciardi."

At first Ciardi refused the post, wanting nothing of administration. But old-timers loved the idea and began to press him. For a full week Ciardi resisted—putting the veteran Bread Loafers into a funk; it was hard enough to think of the conference without Ted Morrison at the helm, but if it was going to be so difficult to get a willing successor, why bother? Perhaps 1955 should be the last conference—let it go down with memories of its golden past. Finally the mood of his confreres got to Ciardi. He relented. The announcement of the changing of one regime for another was made during the conference. Proceeding under the assumption that besides reestablishing a semblance of staff continuity, the entire program might have to be reapproached, Morrison and Ciardi huddled during the free periods talking with various members of the staff. One who was especially helpful was Bernard DeVoto— who had returned to Bread Loaf after an absence of seven years. DeVoto's last volume in his trilogy on the American continental experience had appeared in 1952. *The Course of Empire* was a brilliant historical narrative about the procession of discoverers who had edged their way around the unknown margins of North America from the sixteenth to the nineteenth centuries. He followed it with his third

1955 Staff: (rear) Bernard DeVoto, Richard Rovere, John Ciardi, A. B. Guthrie, Jr.; (center) Rachel MacKenzie, Fletcher Pratt, Ted Morrison, Robert Frost, Inga Pratt; (front) Judith Ciardi, Lincoln Barnett, Mrs. Barnett, Kay Morrison, May Sarton

collection of *Harper's* essays, *The Easy Chair* (1955). In discussions with Morrison and Ciardi, Bernard DeVoto pledged his fullest support in rethinking the Bread Loaf program, although he had no intention of doing what Morrison had been urging him to do for years—to return to the Mountain to do for nonfiction what he had done for fiction. He said he simply hadn't the heart or the energy to do it—and besides, he was too aware of the passage of time as he walked around the campus. "In Treman's crowded parlor," wrote Wallace Stegner in *The Uneasy Chair,*

> there were too many strange faces; in the cold mountain dusk he could smell the oncoming of winter. He gave his lecture, aware that many of the audience had come

to hear the volcano erupt and the ogre roar. But he couldn't erupt and roar for them. He gave them a talk that he himself thought lame, though Bill Sloane remembers it as a splendid exposition of the techniques of synecdoche—how one might write a social history of New England through consideration of a single town—and Ted Morrison recalls it as "impressive to the point of brilliance." But DeVoto thought it lame, and went lamely off toward Maine.

Eleven weeks later he was dead of a heart attack, at fifty-eight. Fletcher Pratt, advertised to appear on the 1956 faculty, would follow him in a matter of months. The loss of the two made it all the more clear that there would be much work to do to revitalize the conference.

Robert Frost chats with conferees as John Ciardi looks on, 1960

CIARDI RAMPANT

If anything, John Ciardi's visibility had increased of recent years. His books of prose and poetry appeared to consistently respectful attention. His translation of Dante's *Inferno* came out in 1954 to wide acclaim. In 1955 he became the poetry editor and a regular columnist for *The Saturday Review*. These, and Ciardi's wide contacts in the literary world, were seen as being of incalculable benefit to Bread Loaf. But he did not want to rush into things; in his mind, and in those of the Middlebury administrators, the 1956 session was to be thought of as experimental. The new director wrote to Stephen Freeman, director of the Middlebury summer schools, to say that at first he would do his best to keep it simple, but that if they were able to raise the number of participants substantially, "it is going to be necessary to increase the staff. The burden of reading is already a monstrous one."

In another letter he urged his new assistant director, Paul Cubeta, a young English professor at Middlebury and a Shakespearean scholar, to look up Bernard DeVoto's "Easy Chair" essay about Bread Loaf—it should be reprinted and distributed. "It's much too good a piece of artillery," wrote Ciardi, "to be standing muzzled in the back shed." They reprinted it. He then wrote his own essay on Bread Loaf in *The Saturday Review*; it sent applications soaring and prompted A.B. Guthrie, Jr., to call Ciardi long distance one night. He said he had a case of Bread Loaf fever and wanted to be with them in August. He wanted no fee. Ciardi told him to come ahead.

Just as easily, Ciardi secured other holdovers from Ted Morrison's regime: Catherine Drinker Bowen, Rachel MacKenzie, editors Bill Sloane and Bill Raney, and William Hazlett Upson. There was never any question but that Robert Frost, his largest drawing card, would participate, but for Ciardi the connection was tied up with two strong poets' egos and the whole issue of his acceptance by Frost. Frost was "a man who was punctilious in his ritual," recalled Ciardi some years later of the months following his succeeding Ted Morrison.

He liked to decide when a door was to be opened, and nothing would get his back up sooner than to have somebody push in against a door he would rather keep closed. For many years at Bread Loaf I kept my distance. I didn't want to thrust myself upon him. We had little conversations now and then, but always I was an extremely junior member of whatever was going. There were many people around who had known him longer and much better. But when I was appointed director of the conference some 15 or 16 years later, I got a letter from him. I suspect that Kay Morrison prompted the letter. As nearly as I recall it, he began with "Dear John, You read my poems, I read yours, what's this about your asking if"—I had a poem in which I said "Does God believe in me?"—and Frost said, "There you are, the fair-haired boy, director, professor, publisher, poet, asking questions like that." He's half kidding. He's being playful, friendly, but the real occasion of the letter was the fact that he signed it "Robert," which was his way of saying, "All right, you may now call me Robert, instead of Mr. Frost."

So Frost was on and they were to be friends.

To round out the faculty, Ciardi introduced some new-comers to the Mountain. Among them there would be the energetic Kay Boyle, whose twelve novels, six collections of short stories, and two books of poetry had shown an astonishing range of subject matter and mood. There would be the quiet lyric poet Leonie Adams, who had served as consultant to the Library of Congress in 1948 and 1949 and who had shared the 1955 Bollingen Prize with Louise Bogan; Adams, fifty-six, with a Dutch-boy haircut, was then teaching at Columbia. And there would be Merle Miller—the earlier Merle Miller, two decades before his best-selling oral biographies of Harry S Truman and Lyndon Johnson appeared—whose first novel, *That Winter* (1948), dealing with veterans' difficulties in adjusting to postwar America, was one of the better novels to emerge from the Second World War.

It was assumed that Ciardi, with all of his energy and contacts, would be good at expanding the fellowship fund. Early in the year he began by persuading Henry Holt to sponsor a Robert Frost fellowship in poetry and Houghton Mifflin to foot one in Bernard DeVoto's memory. "Each will be $150," Ciardi noted, "the best figure I could pin to the negotiations." He hoped for better, later.

Then, it was Paul Cubeta's idea to expand the conference scholarship aid—to nominate needy members for working scholarships in the dining room. For a number of years the procedure had been for the Middlebury College business manager to hire all conference waiters "as best they could," often from their pool of working Middlebury students. The practice had become engraved with tradition and academic territoriality, that poisonous destroyer, not always to the benefit of those marooned on the Mountain for two weeks. When luck was with them, the waiters arrived with an interest in literature and writing—as occurred with Richard Ellmann and Peter Stanlis, for instance—and their contributions to the little community spread far beyond the dining hall. Otherwise, at best the conference could hope for competence at keeping the coffee cups filled. With the new system in development, the concentration of committed writers in the Bread Loaf community was to be that much higher. And the arrangement would ultimately open the way to other ways of encouraging talented emerging writers by offering them a place and some recognition.

Four new writers came up to Bread Loaf on fellowships during Ciardi's first year as director, among them a North Carolinian journalist and novelist, Paxton Davis, and a New England journalist and poet, Herbert Kenny. The latter attended the conference with his wife and discovered that as published writers the fellows were expected to do more than simply enjoy their two-week introduction to the literary world. They were also expected to take turns making the martinis in the faculty lounge. This convenience, haphazardly observed since the early fifties, was institutionalized when Fletcher Pratt's death deprived the staff of its regular drinkmeister; it is remembered as having in conception the William Sloane touch. Convenience or not, it was a reinforcement of hierarchy that by today's standards is embarrassing. Almost immediately, with the Kennys, the service backfired. Martinis were quite foreign to them. "As a newspaperman, whisky and water, or a whisky followed by a beer was customary," Herb Kenny recalled.

> My wife, a sherry drinker, was putting the vermouth and gin together while I set up chairs, tables, glasses, napkins, and such hors d'oeuvres as might be around.
> "What are the proportions again?" she asked.
> "Three to one," I said.
> "Three vermouth?"
> "Yeah, that sounds right."

And so it was mixed. And so it was drunk. The next day, rather early, the fellows' social guru was overheard directing Wilbur Cross, another fellow whose turn to serve had come about.

> "Whatever brand of vermouth we had yesterday—get something else today. It was terrible." I never confessed at the time. I consoled myself that stout drinkers though they were, they were greater talkers because the bowl was emptied before we all went across for lunch, there were no indignant outcries, and the conversation that day was as Olympian as always.

The practice of fellows serving as bartenders survived the Kennys' misunderstanding of the hallowed proportions of the sacred martini. Convenience won out. It would become institutionalized. So would the order, which had its genesis in 1956, that the closet-sized Bread Loaf bookstore would no longer stock the books of fellows, apparently because they crowded out the faculty's; instead, *The Crumb* would announce in subsequent years that the local Vermont Book Shop twelve miles away in Middlebury, owned by the wise and genial bookman Dike Blair, would stock their books should the conference participants wish to buy them. Another change from the Morrison years was announced—abandoned was the practice of rotating conference participants' seating during the midday meal so that each would have an opportunity to break bread with the director and a number of his staff members. From Wednesday, August 15, 1956, in *The Crumb*: "Mr. and Mrs. Ciardi are sorry to announce that the physical limitations of the dining room facilities make it impossible to continue this year the traditional Director's Luncheon Table which has been so pleasant a feature of past conferences. A series of informal coffee hours will be announced later." From *The*

Crumb of Friday, August 17: "Informal coffee hours will be held by invitation on Tuesday, the 21st, Thursday, the 23rd, and Monday, the 27th, from four until five in the barn. Object: to meet the staff. Problem: not everyone can come at once. Urgent request: please (apologies) do not come to the barn during those hours unless you have received an invitation. (More apologies.)" Beginning in a subsequent year (according to several accounts, although photographic evidence from at least some sessions seems to belie this), the faculty table was turned at an angle from the rest of those in the dining hall. And it was raised on a dais.

The 1956 conference, in which some apparently innocuous and experimental changes occurred, was by all accounts congenial. The teaching met the highest Bread Loaf standards. Robert Frost appeared more than members had even hoped for; Kay Boyle dilated brilliantly on the novel; Catherine Drinker Bowen dispensed wisdom on the importance of narrative in biography, drawing on her own work and on the teachings of Bernard DeVoto; Merle Miller lectured on the relationship between fiction and the writer's times and renewed dialogues on the postwar novel in the lecture hall and under the maples; John Ciardi read his poetry. The traditional square dances brought everyone out on Saturday nights, to much hilarity. Members wondered if any of their female number would brave the frigid Bread Loaf streams and social scrutiny to sunbathe in the new bikini bathing suits. One entrenched social regulation began to erode that year as male participants rebelled against the coat-and-tie regulations in the dining room. And there were no recorded complaints about a new rigidity of hierarchy in 1956. But nonetheless, invisible to all who gathered there, the seeds for dissension were sown, although they would not bring forth fruit for another decade.

The Ciardi regime was still fresh when another dissonance was sounded over Bread Loaf; when the American Academy of Arts and Letters awarded John Ciardi a fellowship to the American Academy in Rome, it was an honor that he had no thought of refusing—few writers would. Four months before the director's first Bread Loaf session in 1956, he informed Middlebury that he would be in Rome with his family from September 1956 to August 1957, returning home just in time for the Writers' Conference. In his stead Ciardi asked William Sloane to help select a faculty, find lecturers, and dispense fellowships. Sloane would require no fee for the multitude of letters and phone calls necessary. Still, college officials were disappointed, saying that Bread Loaf should not be a "hydra-headed conference." Ciardi's terse reply was that with airmail he would be in touch with everyone just as before. But there was another complication upsetting Mid-

dlebury officials: Paul Cubeta would have to perform his Bread Loaf administrative duties from Harvard, where he was to work under a Carnegie grant. It was probably the most scattered circumstances—light-years less than ideal. So Ciardi went to Europe, Cubeta went to Cambridge, and Sloane went to work.

Somehow, with little evident confusion or ill-feelings, everything fell together. By May 1957 the faculty roster was complete, though several accepted after the catalogue went to press. Welty had declined, Stegner had declined, but no one was disappointed with the final choices for the fiction team. Bud Guthrie volunteered. Kay Boyle agreed to return. Mildred Walker, author of ten novels including a Hopwood Award winner, accepted. Steward Holbrook, journalist and stolid popularizer of history, came aboard. And most agreeably, Nancy Hale signed on. She would return to Bread Loaf for eight sessions to teach the novel and short story. At forty-nine, a Bostonian granddaughter of Edward Everett Hale, Nancy Hale could legitimately boast that she could sell more stories to *The New Yorker* in a single year than any other writer. She had begun contributing "casuals" to the magazine in 1929 after working for a short time as a junior editor at *Vogue* (where she occasionally pinch-hit as a model) and then as a reporter for *The New York Times*. In her short stories and numerous novels, Hale explored the emotional territory of women's relationships: "I specialize in women," she had once told an interviewer, "because they are so mysterious to me. I feel that I know men quite thoroughly, that I know how, in a given situation, a man is apt to react. But women puzzle me."

For poetry there would be Ciardi, Leonie Adams, and David McCord, writer of light and children's verse. Robert Frost, of course, would come over from his farm for visits, voluble over his successful campaign to get Ezra Pound freed from Saint Elizabeths Hospital where he had been incarcerated in lieu of being prosecuted for treason for making profascist radio broadcasts in wartime Italy. Friends diplomatically refrained from mentioning how Archibald MacLeish had instigated Frost's actions; in the long view, Pound was out and everyone was reconciled after long years of public and private acrimony. Another poet returning to Bread Loaf was Richard Wilbur, whose lithe and handsome presence had proved to be a cause for heartthrobs at Wellesley, where he was currently teaching. His writing career had certainly continued its steady upward climb. Wilbur had delightfully translated Molière's *Misanthrope* and had just completed his collaboration with Lillian Hellman on the comic opera taken from Voltaire's *Candide,* for which he had contributed the lyrics. His last volume of poetry had won a National Book Award in 1956, and his next would win a Pulitzer.

William Sloane, serving as dean of fellows, was quite explicit in a letter to Ciardi about the kinds of writers he wanted to invite. "For many years the service we get from fellows has been deficient," he complained, "and necessitate a great deal of barkeeping and dish washing from your humble servant. I therefore hope and trust [Paul Cubeta] will select someone with a neat wrist and strong instinct for hospitality and housekeeping. Such people are often found in juvenile ranks." This less-than-literary chore defined, with no dissent noted from the director, the fellowships were dispensed to eight emerging writers. One was thirty-year-old Utah-born May Swenson, daughter of Swedish immigrants, graduate of Utah State Agriculture College, and former reporter for a Salt Lake City newspaper. Her first book, *Another Animal,* had appeared in 1954 and showed her talent for oracular rhythms and experimental techniques, the latter of which would grow more pronounced over time. Swenson certainly could not have been selected under the Sloane rule. Luckily though for William Sloane, Treman Cottage had an experienced and conscientious bartender in the twenty-five-year-old Dan Wakefield. Born in Indianapolis and educated at Columbia, a veteran freedom-rider and now a denizen of Greenwich Village, Wakefield had just published his first book of journalism, *Island in the City,* which scrutinized New York's Puerto Rican community. He would follow it up with a number of other nonfiction books but in later years would turn to fiction—at which he would find great commercial success—and even be seduced by Hollywood. In 1957 at Bread Loaf, young Wakefield was jaunty and irreverent, his willingness to be at the center of any good times not obscuring his commitment to good writing. Both Swenson and Wakefield would ascend the Mountain again—Wakefield for some seven sessions between 1961 and 1986, Swenson for the 1976 conference.

After returning to the United States just before the conference began, if the director detected an occasional icy stare among the participants when he walked through the crowded, wicker-chaired lobby of the Bread Loaf Inn, he would not have been surprised. Earlier in the year, after Ciardi had turned his sight on Anne Morrow Lindbergh's *The Unicorn and Other Poems* in *The Saturday Review,* his salvo detonated an unanticipated explosion of reader protest. Irritated that her publisher was exploiting the Lindbergh name (and, it was implied, all its associations with her aviator husband and their kidnapped and murdered child of twenty-five years before) to sell bad poetry by Anne Morrow, and infuriated that receptive public taste was buying hundreds of thousands of copies of her books, Ciardi went after a literary moth with a howitzer. *The Unicorn* was "an offensively bad book," he wrote, "inept, jingling, slovenly, illiterate even, and puffed up with the foolish afflatus of a stereotyped high-seriousness, that species of esthetic and human failure that will accept any shriek as a true high-C."

The column was pure and delightful bombast, utterly devastating an easy target, and it unleashed the biggest storm of reader protest in the thirty-three-year history of *The Saturday Review.* Letters all but called for his lynching—hundreds decried Ciardi's "cruelty" and "arrogance," his brutality to "beautiful," "meaningful" poetry and his "personal attack" upon a fragile author. One letter noted that "Mr. Ciardi's favorite word 'I' [was] used thirty-six times" in his review, a telling fact in the reader's mind. Only four came to his defense. At the 1957 conference when talking about the affair, and indeed for the rest of his life, Ciardi suspected that many of the protesters were some of the genteel versifiers whose work had been accepted by his predecessor as editor of the poetry column, Amy Loveman, who upon her death had given him a backlog of several years' worth of unpublished and unpublishable poems; a year before the notorious review had appeared, he had summarily returned all the manuscripts to their authors; how else to explain the furor in the wake of his Lindbergh review but in terms of insulted, unrequited contributors?

Editor of *The Saturday Review* Norman Cousins exploited the letter-writing campaign for all it was worth, printing many of the more colorful protests. But, eyeing his subscription rolls, he put some daylight between his magazine and his poetry editor: "We don't see anything inconsistent between good criticism and good taste," he wrote in an editorial. "Strength doesn't always depend on violence." From his villa in Rome Ciardi wrote another column to answer his detractors with customary hauteur. "I am not yet persuaded," he said, ". . . that the avalanches of indignation are an intellectual measure I can respect." (Howls around the country and rummaging for a pencil and a stamped envelope.) Then, in case anyone had missed his points about *The Unicorn,* Ciardi reloaded and fired again. It was an example of genteel poetry at its worst, just as "mushy and mindless," "pretty, vague, and easily effusive" as any poetry of the genteel tradition.

The matter simmered on in the editorial columns for some time, and although Ciardi never said as much, Paul Cubeta thought his director was worried that "the rhubarb stewed up over Anne Morrow Lindbergh," in addition to his eleven-month residency in Rome, would hurt the attendance of the 1957 session. Nonetheless, Bread Loaf attendance surpassed final figures for all but four conferences in thirty-one years, registering 173 participants. The controversy didn't seem to have an effect. And on the veranda of Treman Cottage there could be a chorus of guffaws, audible even on the other side of the screening

1957 Staff: (rear) {?}, {?}, William Sloane, John Frederick Nims, Stewart Holbrook, {?}, {?}, Paul Cubeta; (front) Eunice Blake, Nancy Hale, Robert Frost, Leonie Adams, Kay Boyle, John Ciardi

hedge where the unelected literary dwelt, at someone's suggestion of selling *The Unicorn and Other Poems* in the Bread Loaf bookstore, or bringing Anne Morrow Lindbergh up as a visiting lecturer. With her steel, she probably would have come.

James E. Cronin, a teacher of writing at St. Louis University, provided a remarkably full discussion of the 1957 Bread Loaf in all of its aspects for the *St. Louis Post-Dispatch* in an article that gives a more detailed picture of a working conference in the fifties than is usually available. Cronin arrived at the conference convinced that "the teaching of writing, insofar as it can be taught, must be a longtime process in which the talented young writer's growing acquaintance with technique must be synthesized with his expanding knowledge and experience." It was, he thought, "the intellectual approach, a slow, systematic developing of the writer to the degree that his inborn abilities permit." Professor Cronin found the Bread Loaf idea "quite different without being fundamentally contra-

dictory. It is a kind of crash program. Intellectualism is there, but the fluid in which it works is intense excitement, both physical and intellectual." He noted the "sheer beauty" of the surroundings and the novelty of encountering "real live authors" and finding them to be human, "sometimes nervous and ill at ease like anybody else." The whole operation, he wrote for his hometown paper, "was extremely deft, carefully conceived and smoothly operated, promotionally impeccable."

At the first evening's program, he heard the director discuss the Bread Loaf ethos. "No great writer ever became one in isolation," Ciardi intoned. "Somewhere and some time, if only at the beginning, he had to experience the excitement and intellectual ferment of a group something like this." Ciardi's lecture on poetry "was one of the best that I have heard"; the "elegant, hawk-faced" Kay Boyle taught fiction though convinced that "of course, the short story is dead, completely dead, anyhow"; Nancy Hale disagreed, saying that the possibilities of the psychological short story had hardly been explored; Kitty Bowen and Bud Guthrie provided living proof that, when artists cooperated, emerging writers could be helped along in their careers.

Staff members attended each other's talks and applauded vigorously—not simple uplift, in Cronin's eyes, but reactions to good people who talked well. And there were the amusing moments of revelation. "Nearly everybody showed a deepseated conviction, interesting in would-be writers, that one picture was worth ten thousand words," he recorded. "Everybody photographed everybody. Not infrequently, people photographing people photographing people." Wandering about, Cronin "caught snatches of many conversations among the amateurs, always about the problems of writing." But, he said, "it was not until I broke into a conversation between two nationally known professionals that I heard a discussion of the chief problem of the writer—something of interest to professionals from Shakespeare through Dr. Johnson to the present—they, of course, were talking about money."

Almost immediately after any conference, the director must begin staffing for the following year. Ciardi set a high goal for 1958—and probably set a record for strikeouts. He invited John Steinbeck, Wallace Stegner, and Edwin O'Connor. They declined. He asked Frank O'Connor, but the Irish writer's wife was due to deliver a child in the summer. He invited John Cheever, whose episodic novel, *The Wapshot Chronicle,* would win a National Book Award for 1957, and for a while it seemed almost as if Cheever would come. Then no. Kay Boyle could not return to teach the short story. Bruce Catton, prize-winning Civil War historian, sent his regrets. "All I do is run up phone bills," Ciardi complained to Paul Cubeta, who needed names for the catalogue, "only to be told people are going to Europe. Why don't we move the conference to Europe? It will be easy to staff there." Even by mid-June, the roster was far from complete and Cubeta was still trying to round up emerging writers for their twelve-day coming-out party. "Scratch Phil Roth as a candidate," he wrote Ciardi of a twenty-five-year-old short story writer from New Jersey whose *Goodbye, Columbus* was a year away from publication. "He changed his plans and like everyone else is now heading for Europe."

So the staff was largely familiar, Bread Loaf's core professional faculty of the late fifties—Adams, Bowen, Hale, Sloane, et al. However, two new faces who had not heeded Europe's siren call but instead Ciardi's were the gifted science writer for *The New Yorker,* Berton Roueché, who had managed to transform reportage on epidemiology into

work with all the drama of a good detective yarn (he stayed only for one session), and the poet John Frederick Nims (who would go for fourteen). Forty-four and teaching at Notre Dame, Nims came highly recommended by his publisher, William Sloane, and was well known to Ciardi as an editor of *Poetry* magazine between 1945 and 1948. Moreover, Ciardi had included him in his *Mid-Century American Poets* anthology. He had been born in Michigan and educated at Notre Dame and the University of Chicago. Nims's witty and lyrical poetry had appeared in two books since 1947; he was then preparing skillful translations of *Poems of St. John of the Cross* and of several Greek tragedies, but his highly praised and unforgettable translation of Sappho was still a number of years off.

It may have been in this year that Robert Frost endured what Ciardi later remembered as "the dumbest question ever asked a distinguished speaker following a lecture." One afternoon he came over from his farm to deliver his customary program of speaking extemporaneously about whatever came to mind, interrupting himself from time to time to "say" one of his poems. As always, he held his Bread Loaf audience in his thrall. Afterward, during a brief question-and-answer period, a woman rose to speak. She had been in the bookstore and had seen a shelf full of various volumes of Frost's—with titles like *Selected Poems, Collected Poems, Complete Poems,* each building upon the poet's previous work and adding his latest. And she did not want to spend her money foolishly in buying a book that would become outdated.

"Mr. Frost," she said, "is it safe to buy the *Complete Poems* NOW?" The words seemed to hang in the air between the lectern and the audience. Ciardi never saw Frost so nonplussed. "He shook his head as if someone had just belted him," he recalled. "He didn't lose his composure, but I guess he was expressing disgust more than amazement. I guess he had had enough experience in not being really stunned by human stupidity. He shook his head and leaned into the microphone and said, 'I don't give a damn whether you buy the book or not.'"

Intriguing juxtapositions in certain Bread Loaf years, such as 1959, fairly leap out to command one's attention. Not unlike skilled cooks concocting recipes out of thin air with an adventurous flair—"what would happen if you added garlic and *cinnamon* to the browned, ground lamb?"—one ponders: Take a pinch of Wilbur and one teaspoon each of Ciardi and William Meredith, to which add a half-cup of Anne Sexton. Stir. Whatever was the resulting flavor of such a mixture is hard to know today for those who were not present at the table; little documentation survives.

Robert Frost poses with 1959 Fellows: Elizabeth Baker, Irene Orgel, Anne Sexton, George Lea.

In the spring of 1959, Anne Sexton was nominated for a Robert Frost fellowship in poetry at Bread Loaf, for her first book. She was instantly accepted. The poems collected in *To Bedlam and Part Way Back* (1960) were original, finely crafted, lyrical, and so frank as to be emotionally challenging to the reader.

Sexton had taken the long and hard way around to being a poet. Born in Wellesley in 1928, the daughter of a salesman, she had been groomed for a conventional life of marriage and motherhood—she had married a salesman two months after finishing two years at a junior college in Boston and prepared herself for a conventional, uncreative life. But she had problems that could not be buried. "All I wanted was a little piece of life," she once told an interviewer, "to be married, to have children. I thought the nightmares, the visions, the demons would go away if there was enough love to put them down." For two years Sexton worked as a fashion model in Boston—a business that could only have done violence to her self-image. She had a daughter, then another daughter, and it was after the second birth that she suffered a psychotic breakdown and tried to kill herself. The poems of *To Bedlam and Part Way Back* were begun as therapy.

Sexton had composed poetry in high school but had been easily disparaged out of writing by her mother, who said

she was only plagiarizing Sara Teasdale. It was not until ten years later, when her psychiatrist recommended that she lift her spirits and her ambition by watching educational television, that Sexton saw a program in which the important critic I. A. Richards of Harvard read a sonnet and explained its form. "I thought to myself, 'I could do that, maybe; I could try,' " she recalled. "So I sat down and wrote a sonnet. The next day I wrote another one, and so forth. My doctor encouraged me to write more. 'Don't kill yourself,' he said. 'Your poems might mean something to someone else someday.' That gave me a feeling of purpose, a little cause, something to *do* with my life, no matter how rotten I was." Three months later she enrolled in a poetry class at the Boston Center for Adult Education. Her teacher was John Holmes—the same teacher who had inspired and encouraged John Ciardi twenty years earlier, still moonlighting from Tufts because of his stingy salary. "The most important aspect of that class," she said, "was that I felt I belonged somewhere."

For two years Sexton wrote her poems for the class—frank and frightening glimpses of the madness and despair, the rage and the self-loathing, that lurked beneath her lovely surface; they found few sympathetic ears then, with some notable exceptions. In the workshop she struck up a durable friendship with Maxine Kumin, whose voice was also emerging, though Holmes tried to warn Kumin off. He told her Sexton was evil and that what was divulged in the confessional wasn't fit for poetry. Then Sexton picked up a copy of *The New Poets of England and America* and discovered W.D. Snodgrass and his poem "Heart's Needle." She then made what she recalled as a "pilgrimage" to the Antioch Writers' Conference to meet him. Snodgrass was the first established poet to like her work; she began working harder, sold a few poems to good magazines like *The New Yorker*, and took Snodgrass's suggestion to approach Robert Lowell, then teaching a graduate course at Boston University. He accepted her into his class. There she met George Starbuck and Sylvia Plath; after class the three would go off to drink at the Ritz where Plath and Sexton would compare their demons and their suicide techniques.

Cal Lowell was a hard taskmaster. His workshops were often painful. "He worked with a cold chisel," she recalled, "with no more mercy than a dentist. He got out the decay, but if he was never kind to the poem, he was kind to the poet." He urged her to throw out half of her book-length collection and Sexton did. He "helped me to distrust the easy musical phrase and to look for the frankness of ordinary speech. . . . [H]e didn't teach me what to put into a poem, but what to leave out." Not too long after, the manuscript, accepted by Houghton Mifflin, was readied for publication, and Sexton was given a fellowship to Bread Loaf.

"How silly it all is," she wrote to Snodgrass after Houghton Mifflin had urged her to get herself published by an impressive number of poetry magazines because it would look good on the book jacket. "I am beginning to think poetry is some sort of racket. . . . I guess you are supposed to add credits like some sort of badge to wear." She told him that to her surprise she had been granted the Bread Loaf fellowship. "Maybe I'll go there," she said. "No one interests me to study with . . . I mean so few poets really fire me with enthusiasm." After seeing the announcement of who would be teaching on the Mountain that August, she wrote to Carolyn Kizer: "I am going to study with Roethke this summer. . . . [H]e probably won't like my work. And there we'll be (you and me) with our Cal and our Ted, not liking our work enough (sobbing in our own private caves of womanhood and kicking at the door of fame that men run and own and won't give us the password for)."

But Theodore Roethke would not be able to keep his date. In the years since his first book and his Bread Loaf fellowship, in 1941, his career had shown all of the success predicted by those who knew him at the beginning. His work had deepened in psychic intensity and personal insight, earning him two Guggenheim fellowships, a Pulitzer in 1953, a Bollingen Prize in 1958, and a National Book Award in 1959, and Ciardi keenly wanted him back at Bread Loaf to close a circle begun in 1941 and to renew their long, affectionate baiting of each other. Roethke, particularly, loved to kid Ciardi (though he was half, sometimes all serious) about his ethnic background—certainly, with a name like Ciardi the poet had to have ties with the Boston mafia. Then, in May, word reached Ciardi that Roethke, a manic-depressive who had been hospitalized after an embarrassing incident in his classroom at the University of Washington, was still barely recuperating. He had arrived at school late, muttering and soaked from having run across town, and smashed himself against the blackboard almost in a crucifixion pose. For his own protection (and others'—Roethke was ever bearlike) he was restrained and taken away for treatment. "Letter just received," Ciardi wrote on May 8 to Sloane and Cubeta. "Roethke is ill again and simply cannot make it to B.L. I join you in regretting but I know Roethke is not just dodging. Matters beyond his control."

How to replace him? Three months before, Paul Cubeta had suggested inviting thirty-nine-year-old William Meredith, who had served on the faculty of the Bread Loaf School of English in 1958. In fact, that year Meredith had been offered a poetry fellowship to the Writers' Conference, but the offer had been inappropriate; Meredith's first book, in the Yale Series of Younger Poets and introduced by Archibald MacLeish, had been published fourteen years before, in 1944; two other volumes had appeared in 1948 and 1958. A fellowship would have been, as Cubeta later admitted, "something of a comedown" after those books and after being on the faculty of the English School. But "he has turned out to be a first-rate lecturer," Cubeta had written Ciardi in February 1959, and he was someone well worth considering.

A native New Yorker, William Meredith flew in the Army Air Force and in the Naval Aviation corps during the Pacific War and in the Navy Reserves over Korea. Graduated magna cum laude from Princeton in 1940, Meredith briefly worked as a copy boy on *The New York Times* before being promoted to reporter; the war interrupted his promising journalism career and delayed the publication of his undergraduate poems by Yale. He was always a slow worker, but the individual voice emerged over time with succeeding books. By 1959 he had taught at Princeton, the University of Hawaii, and finally at Connecticut College and had acquired a handful of poetry prizes and fellowships. With Roethke incapacitated with mania, Ciardi tapped Meredith to step into his place and join himself and the British poet George Barker as full-term faculty for poetry.

Another new face appeared at the conference in 1959:

Ralph Ellison, whose extraordinary and enduring novel *Invisible Man* had been published seven years before, made his first and only visit to Bread Loaf. Even in his Oklahoma youth Ellison had defined himself as an artist, though his original career plan was not to be a writer but to be a composer and musician. But at Tuskegee Institute in the thirties, he discovered Eliot's *The Waste Land,* and it fundamentally changed his life. "I was intrigued by its power to move me while eluding my understanding," he recalled. "Somehow its rhythms were often closer to those of jazz than were those of the Negro poets, and even though I could not understand then, its range of allusion was as mixed and varied as that of Louis Armstrong." He set out to discover the answers to his questions about *The Waste Land,* tracing Eliot's footnotes to his sources. Readings in mythology, folklore, and history led him to twentieth-century writers, notably Hemingway, Pound, and Gertrude Stein, and then back to Melville and Twain. When his Tuskegee scholarship money dried up, he moved to New York where he found a job on the Federal Writers' Project and where, in Harlem, he was encouraged by Langston Hughes and Richard Wright. They led him to read Joyce, Dostoyevski, André Malraux, Conrad, and Henry James. He began to publish his essays and stories, many in *The New Masses.* During the war, serving in the Merchant Marines, Ellison started a war novel, which he later abandoned in favor of the impressionistic, apocalyptic, uniquely American novel *Invisible Man,* which took seven years to complete. It won a National Book Award in 1953, with other prizes and fellowships to follow.

In 1959 when asked to Bread Loaf, Ellison was teaching American and Russian literature at Bard College. Through some mutual error he arrived at the Inn with no advance knowledge of what was expected of him, and in the words of administrator Paul Cubeta, who absorbed the brunt of his dissatisfaction, he "howled like hell." Ruffled sensibilities were smoothed, however, and Ellison went on to deliver several lectures on the novel and to read participants' manuscripts. He met and befriended a young New Jersey undergraduate from Rutgers, Alan Cheuse—years away from the novels and criticism for which he would become known, then just a vaguely Bohemian kid who was an associate editor for his college literary magazine. Cheuse had been invited by Bill Sloane to wait on Bread Loaf tables in exchange for room and board. Racial matters of the day were on the minds of many—earlier in the year the state of Virginia had desegregated its schools under court order, and similar legal measures had been brought to bear against Arkansas governor Orval Faubus, who had closed public schools rather than submit to desegregation. One night a group of Bread Loafers threw a party, an off-campus beer blast at the lodge of Middlebury College's ski area. A

number of faculty members, including Ellison, attended. "A mountain of cans piled up in the large trash barrel in the middle of the room," recalled Cheuse. "Someone started singing folk songs. Pretty soon someone started up 'Old Black Joe.' I became incensed that someone would sing such a song in Ralph's presence and I leaped up and knocked over the huge trash bin full of beer cans, effectively ending the party. Big conscience, big drunk!"

It was a most public conference—*Life* magazine sent reporter and photographer Alfred Eisenstaedt to examine Bread Loaf and trail Robert Frost around the campus. At night the crowd in Treman Cottage swelled to the point that the faculty party could be likened to a New York subway at rush hour. Many of the newer faces were freeloaders. "Who the hell *are* all these people," in Ciardi's carrying voice, could occasionally be heard over the din. Alan Cheuse was at the edge of a group that invaded Bread Loaf that year, many of them on waiters' scholarships but also others among the regular clientele. Mirroring the times, and to the bemusement and even chagrin of many, they derided authority, smoked marijuana, held impromptu readings, and boldly became fixtures at the restricted, nightly faculty parties. They caused quite a stir: beatniks at Bread Loaf! "Please," implored one notice in *The Crumb,* "do not slam, clatter, bang, shout, and/or guffaw between 10:30 P.M. and 7:00 A.M. If you want to whoop it up, head for the woods. Have fun—but quietly please." After the conference, letters between Sloane, Ciardi, and Raney railed at the unwashed and unwholesome aspect of the "bums" and "beats" and discussed ways to keep them off the Mountain. Only the milder voice of Paul Cubeta offered any dissent, partly to defend his consciously admitting them to the session. "I never had met one in the flesh and blood before," he wrote to George Starbuck at Houghton Mifflin. "I wonder if hindsight would allow me to be so daring again. I hope so. If Bread Loaf is to thrive, the only criterion for admission must be the quality of writing. Those beatniks who submitted manuscripts can write. In any case, they surely broadened all our horizons and gave the entire conference plenty to talk about for a year. I think that it was rather extraordinary the way in which only a handful of them so completely dominated some two hundred squares."

To prevent such irritating breaches of discipline and propriety in future conferences, Ciardi decided to appoint someone to run Treman Cottage and to enforce the guest policy. He appointed Avis DeVoto, veteran of many sessions of Bread Loaf with her husband. She had frequently visited the conference in the years since Benny DeVoto's death, and her combination of firmness and diplomacy would mark Treman sociabilities for more than a decade. Nevertheless, there would be many memories of high

1959 Staff: (rear) Richard Gehmann, William Sloane, Hollis Summers, William Raney, {?}, Ralph Ellison, {?}, William Meredith, Paul Cubeta; (front) {?}, Nancy Hale, Robert Frost, John Ciardi, {?}.

times to take away from the conference—like those of Anne Sexton, who met Wilbur and Meredith; who sat at Frost's feet for a *Life* photograph; who renewed a friendship started at Antioch with novelist Hollis Summers; who enjoyed her recognition and her freedom from family and home; and whose remarkable poems captivated her listeners and readers in 1959, seven months before her first book was to be issued. A few days after returning to the suburbs to her husband, children, psychiatrist, and typewriter, she wrote to Hollis Summers to apologize for sweeping off the Mountain without saying goodbye—she did not like goodbyes. "I am beginning to feel and speak like a human living woman that I am," she wrote. "My voice, as it descended from Bread Loaf, had a terrifying whiskey tone (gin I guess—but the same bloodstream voice). . . . My doctor said that I'd been on a binge. I mean, he knew I hadn't—but I certainly attended one and did indeed partake thereof." She enclosed a new poem, for after six days of recovery she had already resumed writing.

I f, in the first three Bread Loaf sessions of the sixties, John Ciardi continued to find it hard to fill his staff positions with his primary choices of "name" writers, he did not do badly when it came to selecting emerging writers for fellowships and scholarships.

With all of his connections in the literary world, and they were vast, he simply found it impossible to persuade people to give up their vacations to work up on the Mountain, as vacation-like as the setting was. Moreover, in the autumn, winter, and spring months, Ciardi had much more occupying his mind than picking staff for what he now liked to call the "land-locked summer cruise" at Bread Loaf, and perhaps these distractions were more than partly to blame for the staffing difficulties. He was a husband and the father of three spirited children, and the owner of an imposing suburban New Jersey house. He was still a prolific writer; the stirring love poems of *I Marry You* had appeared in 1958; a year later there was another collection, *39 Poems,* and a best-selling textbook, *How Does a Poem Mean?* He had also begun writing children's books. Not only was he writing but he was teaching at Rutgers and editing at *The Saturday Review* and at Twayne. Even more demanding was his role as an extremely well-paid mainstay of the literary lecture circuit. "Chance to putter in the garden," he retorted to Paul Cubeta's remark on the coming spring in 1960.

You'd best be looking for a conference director. At the rate I'm going, I'm about to kill myself with running. I've got to learn to slow down but the end is not yet. I'll be home this next week, then gone for twelve days, then home a few days, then gone three days, then home about twelve days, then gone for two weeks, *et seq.* And I'm truly swamped to the point of psychic distraction. ANYTHING you can do to cut down the number of fellowship and scholarship MS. will be toward the salvation of my psychic balance, if any.

"I wish you would try and take it a little easier, John," Cubeta replied. "I think we're all very worried about the pace at which you're pushing yourself. Perhaps what you need is a crate of fellowship manuscripts just to help you relax. Unfortunately this year most of the stuff is fiction and long."

The process of selecting winners from the field of candidates (which each year grew wider), still a haphazard affair and at least partly dependent on the random scoutings of Ciardi and Sloane and a few others with seniority, fell largely upon Paul Cubeta's beanpole shoulders. There were some years when he made final choices because his director was too busy to be distracted. In February 1962, for instance, Cubeta wrote to Bill Raney: "Ciardi leaves for the Caribbean and then the lecture tour in Haiti and after that the West Coast, and after that, Europe, so Happy Valentine's Day." It fell to Raney to fill in the blanks in the faculty roster. Nonetheless, between 1960 and 1962 a number of emerging writers, later of note, came up to mark their first book publication. These included the gifted poets X. J. Kennedy, John Engels, Miller Williams, Lewis Turco, and A. R. Ammons. Among the novelists there were Richard Yates, an "angry young man"—or close enough to it for balance, in Ciardi's approving words—and author of the well-received *Revolutionary Road* (Yates, a noted carouser who sometimes found it difficult to adapt to Bread Loaf's particular kind of stress, would return twice to Bread Loaf on the faculty but suffered something like a nervous collapse in mid-conference in 1962); John A. Williams, definer of the ugly realities of racism in American culture in a number of compelling novels, the first of which was *The Angry Ones* (1960), about the lives of black jazz musicians in Greenwich Village; and Edward Wallant, author of four novels about haunted, anguished Jews—beginning with *The Human Season* (1960) and *The Pawnbroker* (1961)—who died at only thirty-six in 1962.

For the 1960 session a particular Boston College senior with literary aspirations accepted a Bread Loaf scholarship in exchange for working in the dining room—George V. Higgins. This was more than a decade before the manuscript of his first novel about the Boston underworld, *The Friends of Eddie Coyle,* was unearthed from the slush pile at Knopf by editor Ashbel Green to launch his successful career. It was also in 1960 that Allen Drury, a student of Edith Mirrielees at Stanford in the thirties, appeared to

lecture on the novel. The year before, building upon years as a Washington journalist, his sprawling, turgid, sensational political novel *Advise and Consent* had appeared and climbed the best-seller lists. Drury's evening talk, as was common in those days, touched less on literature than it did on contemporary culture and political events—specifically, on the July presidential conventions, which had nominated Richard M. Nixon and John F. Kennedy: "Twelve Characters in Search of an Administration: A Foolhardy Guide to the Election of 1960." Less than a year later, in July 1961, Drury was to put John Ciardi and Bread Loaf in a difficult fix when he suddenly gave notice that he would not be teaching at the 1961 session in favor of taking up some more lucrative Hollywood work; coincidentally, that was the same month in which another highly anticipated new faculty member, Ray Bradbury, delivered an identical excuse for not being able to keep his word and teach on the Mountain.

Drury's defection caused some unpleasant last-minute scrambling; he had also caused a stir of excitement in that Camelot spring by offering to invite his old pal Jack Kennedy and his missus up to Bread Loaf. Cubeta, in particular, was beside himself in stumping for such a glamorous event. Kennedy could talk about *Profiles in Courage*—and think of the publicity it would garner! "Getting Kennedy there—no," responded Ciardi. "Even if he would come, the necessary intrusions of Secret Service men and retinue would be such that it would destroy too much of what the conferees have come for." It was the same conclusion Ciardi had come to a few years earlier, when he had briefly entertained the idea of inviting *his* pal Arthur Miller and *his* missus up to Bread Loaf—though undoubtedly, it was admitted, a photograph of Marilyn Monroe lounging on the margin of Johnson Pond would have done wonders for attendance.

One writer who came to Bread Loaf in 1961 had been a friend of Avis DeVoto's since the early 1950s when, from France, she had written a fan letter to Bernard DeVoto about his column in *The Easy Chair* on the inadequacy of American kitchen knives. She had sent him a new carbon steel knife, following up their subsequent correspondence with a visit to the DeVoto's home in Cambridge. The woman did such wonders in their kitchen that Avis DeVoto suggested that she write a cookbook and helped arrange an option with Houghton Mifflin. The first installment did not thrill her editors when it arrived a year later—American women would never be so interested in French-style sauces nor so enamored of fish. They declined it. Knowing that Alfred Knopf was a frequent visitor to Europe, an astute businessman, and a noted gourmet, Avis DeVoto sold it to him, and Julia Child began her illustrious career of publishing witty and eloquent books on

Julia Child outside the Little Theatre, early 1960s

cooking. For the 1961 conference, Avis successfully campaigned to bring her friend up to work in the tiny Bread Loaf administrative office. As Julia Child typed memos and address lists, her imposing physical presence filled the room; her husband, Paul Child, became the official conference photographer, and they returned for several sessions in the sixties.

John Ciardi himself was having a good year. He tendered his resignation at Rutgers to devote more time to writing and family and to lecturing on the road. His translation of the *Purgatorio* was published with an enthusiastic reception similar to that accorded the *Paradiso* in 1954. And he began a weekly television show, "Accent"—roaming, quirky, intellectual fare that, sadly, was replaced by CBS two years later in favor of "Mister Ed." It was also in 1961 that Ciardi hired Howard Nemerov to join him, Dudley Fitts, and John Frederick Nims in teaching poetry. Nemerov, a tall and handsome forty-one-year-old New Yorker, then taught at Bennington, and by dint of his wartime experience he was eligible for the Bread Loaf corps of combat-decorated aviator poets (which included Ciardi, the de facto founder, and William Meredith). Nemerov had enlisted in the Royal Canadian Air Force after gradu-

ating from Harvard in 1941, had spent much of the war attacking German shipping in the North Sea, and later served with the U.S. Army Air Force. After the war, in New York, Nemerov wrote his first book of poetry, *The Image and the Law* (1947), beginning a prolific writing career in poetry and prose that, if not universally well received at first, gradually won over the critics and the reading public—who finally caught up with his pointed wit and stylish, satiric dexterity. By 1961 Nemerov's credits included five collections of poetry, one of short stories, and three novels as well as numerous prizes, awards, and fellowships, and he was finishing up a fifteen-year term as an editor of *Furioso,* a literary journal. Nemerov had a sly and epigrammatic way of teaching and even conversing, as if every utterance had quotation marks around it and, devious in its simplicity, demanded concentrated thought before being replied to. Once, in 1961, the poetry fellow Lewis Turco confessed that he was baffled how Nemerov or anyone could write both poetry and novels. Nemerov's eyes wrinkled up as his hollow voice replied, "All you need . . . is a novel idea!"

Turco had another conversation with Dudley Fitts, who had been assigned to read Turco's poetry manuscript. Fitts, the noted translator of Aristophanes, Euripedes, and Sophocles and the editor of the Yale Series of Younger Poets, told Turco that when he was teaching at Cheshire Academy he used to read the *Morning Record* of Meriden, Connecticut. "I told him that was my home town paper," Turco recalled, "and I'd first published my poems in Lydia Atkinson's poetry column, 'Pennons of Pegasus,' when I was a high school student. He laughed and said, 'My wife and I used to read that column aloud every Wednesday morning and begin the day with a hearty laugh.' I told him I had no idea I'd had such a distinguished audience, and I was pleased he'd been familiar with my work for so long."

Turco provides an affecting portrait of Robert Frost, who was by then truly in his twilight years. With every succeeding year there were fewer familiar faces for Frost at Bread Loaf. In 1962 Frost stood out in front of Treman Cottage, shaking his head in disgust as he looked across the road to where the stately three-story Victorian "cottage," named after a birch tree, had been stripped of its ornate steamboat-style wraparound porches by Middlebury College, which did not want to spend the money to renovate them. It was such a waste—not cherishing but ignoring an important heritage, though it was ravaged by time. Frost, too, was growing frailer—more obviously dependent on the watchful ministrations of Kay and Ted Morrison—and his age and stature occasionally drew a hurtful line between himself and other Bread Loafers, even at Treman Cottage. One evening in 1961, Lew Turco noticed that everyone was ignoring their poet laureate, who sat alone in an easy chair with a shawl across his lap. "It was a form of fright," recalled Turco. Even after Ciardi urged him to go over to Frost and talk with him, the young poet quailed. "I continued standing," he wrote, "until I heard Frost mutter, 'Won't someone talk to me?'" Turco summoned his courage, went over, saved the evening for both of them, and they spent the rest of the evening in happy, inconsequential talk.

Frail as he was, Frost still possessed remarkable spirit and was still capable of riveting respectful audiences in the Bread Loaf lecture hall. After 1960, when off-the-Mountain people from around the county filled the theatre for Frost's recital and crowded out many enrolled participants and staff, Ciardi instituted a conference-only pass system for Frost evenings. And there were other changes. "At the end," John Ciardi once told an interviewer, "Frost began to go deaf." It was, Ciardi said, a little odd and rather endearing.

But he was too proud to wear a hearing aid. He didn't like to wear glasses though he needed them to read. When you're in your eighties, you begin to be in your eighties. Nevertheless, he had his sense of pride, and he wasn't going to wear a hearing aid. Therefore, at the end of a lecture, at Bread Loaf, I would sneak up behind him, field the questions from the floor, and shout them into his right ear, which was his good one. And he accepted this without any objections. Somehow this arrangement was less obvious than a hearing aid. And it soothed his pride. But . . . unless you have these little quirks and cantankers, what have you got to go on when you get that old? I never knew Frost in his prime, but from what I've read and from photos I've seen, he was an extraordinarily powerful man. We hate to give up our stubbornness and identity. Who wants to decline into old age without railing against it a bit?

Railing against old age, Frost put in time as consultant to the Library of Congress, as inaugural poet for John F. Kennedy, as goodwill ambassador for the State Department during a tour of Israel, Greece, and England, and as a similar cultural diplomat on a visit to Russia—where he became gravely ill from a schedule that would have seemed demanding even to a much younger individual. The year 1962 was his last time at the Bread Loaf Writers' Conference, his thirtieth session, a record that would be surpassed only by Theodore Morrison and William Hazlett Upson. Robert Frost, the great and gifted poet—the preternaturally complex man with his brilliance, his boorishness, his extraordinary generosity and his sometimes embarrassing competitiveness, his way of lighting up his surroundings and his way of darkening them, all responses to his inner light and darkness—died at eighty-eight on January 29, 1963, leaving an emptiness at the conference that could never be filled. In the Little Theatre, on the west lawn, and at certain places on the state highway, where his night-owl walks took him over Bread Loaf's west-running brooks, his presence can often be felt.

Between lectures, mid-1960s.

Robert Frost, 1962

ROLLER COASTER

It takes only a bit of stretching to see the ironic symmetry between John Ciardi's roller coaster Bread Loaf era, from August 1963 to August 1972, and events occurring off the Mountain—beginnings and endings, mirroring one another.

For Ciardi, the thirty-eighth annual session in 1963 was a cause to celebrate success and future promise, and there was a sense of having hit one's stride; by 1972 his long love affair with Bread Loaf was over and he was left bitter and resentful, not understanding why it had gone bad. Off the Mountain and in the "real world" in August 1963, a page turned in American political and cultural history: Two hundred thousand civil rights demonstrators occupied the capital, and half a world away, U.S. diplomats and intelligence agents pointedly told South Vietnamese military officers that Washington would have no objection if a coup removed President Ngo Dinh Diem from office. This exchange brought the country greatly closer to an inexorable, nearly inevitable war. Diem would be assassinated (coincidentally the month in which President John F. Kennedy also was murdered) in November 1963—and twelve thousand American advisers were already in South Vietnam. Nine years later, in August 1972, nearly fifty-eight thousand American soldiers were dead, conscription was over and the charade of "Vietnamization" was in place, and the final troop pullout was only seven months away; the arrest records of five unprofessional Watergate burglars were less than two months old, and a presidential administration had begun to self-destruct through coverup.

Juxtapositions, reflections in a funhouse mirror. Outside, the screams and screeches, the thumps and bumps of a roller-coaster ride.

News that John Ciardi's friend of more than twenty years, Theodore Roethke, had died on August 1, 1963, partially dimmed anticipation of the thirty-eighth annual session, as did the knowledge that this would be the first Bread Loaf conference without Robert Frost since 1934—which was before some of the conferees were even born. In remarks prepared for the spring announcement bulletin, Ciardi wrote of Frost's first principle, which had "always been the center of the Bread Loaf idea: let them come together; let the writers, and the teachers, and the would-be writers, the hopeful and the hopeless come together; let good writers lead their discussion and set the terms of it; and let the talk be of writing from inside the writing process." The opening day of the conference, he continued, "will be a day strangely balanced between the pleasures of anticipation and the sadness of knowing he will not be among us. But his memory will be there, the memory of the man and of the thousands of insights he gave us over the years. And his idea will be there, given into our custody now, and held in great memory to honor and to share."

There *was* much to anticipate, and the air of Treman Cottage, where the faculty gathered on the day before the conference began, was infused with a certain freshness.

With some luck and a little arm-twisting, the director had enticed several writers new to the Mountain. First there was the fifty-four-year-old novelist Nelson Algren, once deemed "the poet of the Chicago slums" by Malcolm Cowley. Algren, son of a machinist, grew up in a Chicago working-class neighborhood and studied journalism at the University of Illinois. No jobs being available when he graduated in 1931, he drifted around the South and the Southwest; as a somewhat seedy door-to-door salesman in New Orleans, he sold coffee and worthless beauty parlor discount certificates. Later, he went to tiny Rio Hondo, Texas, to manage a filling station with a man who was later found to be secretly siphoning off the gasoline. Algren abandoned Rio Hondo in favor of a freight train to El Paso, but he was arrested for vagrancy and thrown in jail. After he was freed, he moved to Alpine, Texas, decided that he had seen and done things that could be set down on paper, and began sneaking into the sleepy Alpine Teachers College to use a vacant typewriter. He sent his first short story, "So Help Me," to Whit Burnett of *Story* magazine, who published it. Thus encouraged, Algren stole the typewriter, intending to head toward Chicago, but he was arrested and spent four months in jail.

Algren's first novel, an angry story of hobo life published as *Somebody in Boots* in 1935, was almost entirely overlooked. The Works Progress Administration employed him briefly, and he also coedited an experimental magazine with a leftist bent, *The Anvil*, until 1940 when he took up a new novel. *Never Come Morning* (1942), about crime and poverty in a Chicago slum, caused critics to stand up and compare him to Richard Wright and James T. Farrell. His reputation made, Algren served as a medical corpsman during the war. Later he published a strong collection of short stories, *The Neon Wilderness* (1947). Algren's gritty, best-selling novel about drug addiction, *The Man with the Golden Arm*, won the first National Book Award in 1949. He followed this up with a long prose poem (originally assigned by *Holiday* magazine for a theme issue), *Chicago: City on the Make* (1951). Then there was his 1956 novel, *A Walk on the Wild Side*, a raunchy story set during the Great Depression in New Orleans.

When he appeared at Bread Loaf in 1963, Algren's triumphs were partly forgotten and he had lately turned to nonfiction. But he had many misgivings about the conference even before he arrived; he was certain that he would find the faculty full of effete establishment types. To his rough and iconoclastic sensibility, he did, although others on the faculty would have grunted their disagreement with Algren had they seen enough of him for the subject to come up. But after he arrived, Algren befriended a twenty-three-year-old New Hampshire pipefitter, Russell Banks, who fiercely admired the older writer's work. Since Banks

owned a car, after Algren had read his novel manuscript and pointed out the few paragraphs that worked, the two began leaving the conference for longer and longer periods. When Ciardi complained that other aspiring writers weren't getting their money's worth, Algren's reply was a simple shake of his head. His evening talk was by all accounts jazzy and brilliant—but only its title has survived: "American Literature from Rimbaud to Shulman: An Agonizing Reappraisal, or, There's Been a Terrible Accident on Route 66."

Even with all of his absences, Algren did the minimum of what he was paid to do, and his natural gifts as a writer and even a teacher benefited more Bread Loafers than just young Russell Banks. Still, he was part of a particularly strong teaching team of fiction writers. Another member of the team, John Hawkes, was tanned from living for a year in the West Indies, where he had written a novel. An English teacher at Brown, Hawkes was the author of a number of sardonic and surreal novels, beginning with *The Cannibal* (1949) and including the work just completed, *Second Skin*, about the path to renewal taken by a tired, aging, melancholy man haunted by his past. Joining Algren and Hawkes from San Francisco was Mark Harris, forty-one, author of several novels about army life and a series about a fictional baseball team, the New York Mammoths. In the most famous of these, the affecting *Bang the Drum Slowly* (1956), the team's catcher is dying of Hodgkin's disease, an event that transforms the lives of his fellow players.

On the literary playing field of Bread Loaf in 1963, the fiction team was not as close-knit as the New York Mammoths. In an article prepared for the Middlebury College alumni magazine, John Ciardi reported that "this year John Hawkes and Nelson Algren had the happiest of times sniping at each other's theories." To say the least, this description put a gloss on things. Algren took an instant dislike to Hawkes, who was Connecticut-born and Harvard-educated and to Algren represented everything that was effete and precious and intellectual about American literature. "Hawkes, of course," recalled one writer, "wanted nothing to do with getting into any public altercation with Algren. But Algren loved baiting and making innuendoes about him. And once he lost all sense of decorum and consideration for John Hawkes—in public, Algren suddenly wisecracked, 'Only a *fag* could write a book like that.' It was an ugly and shocking incident and left everybody speechless."

Not only was Algren's outburst ugly and shocking—it was inaccurate, and anyone who had spent more time on the Mountain than Algren could have known that. The torrid romance of 1963 was between John Hawkes and a tiny twenty-eight-year-old first novelist by the name of

John Hawkes, John Frederick Nims, Nelson Algren, 1963

Joan Didion, who had come to Bread Loaf on a fellowship. "They were like tragic teenagers," observed one Bread Loafer. "*'Two weeks left to live!'*—before they had to go back to their respective lives! It was very touching; they were both basically very shy people and for a short time they found each other."

Didion came up to Vermont from New York City where she was an editor at *Vogue* magazine. Born in Sacramento, California, Didion had written stories since she was a little girl. Part of this earliest work involved furtively following adults around the neighborhood and scribbling down their dialogue into a notebook. But she wanted to be an actress, not a writer: "I didn't realize then that it's the same impulse. It's make-believe. It's performance. The only difference being that a writer can do it all alone." As a student at Berkeley she took a course from the novelist and short story writer Mark Schorer, who was also author of a massive biography of Sinclair Lewis. By his example Didion got "a sense of what writing was about, what it was for."

Then, in her last year at Berkeley, Didion wrote a profile of the architect William Wilson Wurster. It won the 1956 Prix de Paris award given by *Vogue* to college seniors. The magazine also gave her a job after she graduated. She wrote her first novel over a number of years, working at the magazine during the day and writing at night. Didion had seen a little wire-service story in *The New York Times* about a Carolina murder trial of a farm worker charged with killing the foreman on his farm. With this central incident fictionalized and greatly enlarged, she set the novel in her native Sacramento, California, because she was homesick. "I wanted," she recalled, "to remember the weather and the rivers. . . . There's a lot of landscape which I never would have described if I hadn't been homesick. If I hadn't wanted to remember. The impulse was nostalgia. It's not an uncommon impulse among writers."

What she did was to simply write scenes, in no particular order. "When I finished a scene," she would recall, "I would tape the pages together and pin the long strips of pages on the wall of my apartment. Maybe I wouldn't touch it for a month or two, then I'd pick a scene off the wall and rewrite it." When she started to write, Didion observed that male novelists could operate in a certain tradition—"hard drinkers, bad livers. Wives, wars, big fish, Africa, Paris, no second acts. A man who wrote novels had a role in the world, and he could play that role and do whatever he wanted behind it." However, women did not have anything like that role—in fact, they had "no particular role. Women who wrote novels were quite often perceived as invalids. Carson McCullers, Jane Bowles. Flannery O'Connor of course. Novels by women tended to be described, even by their publishers, as sensitive." Didion wanted no part of such pigeonholing. She put in her time during the day in stylish and sedate surroundings, editing service pieces and writing captions at *Vogue,* and then she went home to occupy a very different world, telling few people about it. "I just tended my own garden, didn't pay much attention, behaved—I suppose—deviously." After completing 150 pages Didion sent the manuscript, which she had titled *Harvest Home,* off to a publisher. He rejected it. So did eleven others. The thirteenth was Ivan Obolensky, heading his own now long-vanished firm, who accepted the novel and gave Didion about a thousand dollars to finish it. She took a two-month leave of absence and completed the novel. It was published in 1963 as *Run River* and received very respectful attention. It would be a long time before her next novel. In 1964 she would marry John Gregory Dunne (then a *Time* magazine writer, later the author of several nonfiction books and novels, including the magnificent *True Confessions,* and collaborator with Didion on many screenplays) and they would move to California. Years of Didion's finely wrought essays would be collected in *Slouching Towards Bethlehem* (1968); her best-selling novel, *A Book of Common Prayer,* appeared in 1977 to reaffirm her mastery of both prose genres.

John Ciardi hired another new face for the 1963 session, a thirty-four-year-old, baby-faced, Bronx-born poet whose trip to Bread Loaf would utterly change the course of his life—and who would inherit the helm of Bread Loaf's land-locked cruise after 1972: Robert Pack.

An English professor and literary magazine editor, Pack had answered the telephone at his Barnard College office a few months before to hear an invitation from John Ciardi of *The Saturday Review* to teach at a place called Bread Loaf. He didn't know anything about the conference and the older poet filled him in. Ciardi had reviewed his first book of poems, *The Irony of Joy* (1955), and knew the anthology *New Poets of England and America,* which Pack had edited with Donald Hall and Louis Simpson, and for which Robert Frost had written an introduction. Pack had also

Robert Pack, 1964

Howard Nemerov had graduated in 1937—he developed a frenzied interest in sports. He was on the swimming, baseball, and football teams, but all this was not enough to slow him down. Accordingly, to keep him manageable, the administrators created "the Pack Rule," which applied only to Robert Pack: Between every class he was required to run a mile on the track and do one hundred push-ups. "The teachers knew very well that there was no way that I could sit still through a whole class if I didn't burn off some energy," he remembered. "It served me well in later years."

During his high school years Pack had another interest, which he concealed from his friends on the athletic teams. He composed poems, enjoying the rhyming and the working within rhythmic forms. One early poem, of which only the title has survived ("The World of Protoplasm," which he composed after he discovered the word "protoplasm" in his science readings and loved its sound and shape), presaged his later interest in bringing poetry and science together. His teachers encouraged him, occasionally allowing him to turn in poems instead of term papers. Then, at Dartmouth, the college reading list and a modern poetry class with Professor Thomas Vance pushed him along in the same direction. But it was a cursive path. After marrying his high school sweetheart, then at Vassar, he graduated in 1951 and went to work as a copywriter for the C. J. LaRoche advertising agency in New York. Among his accounts were Hiram Walker's liquors and Warner's brassieres. Pack did not mind the work; what he minded was taking it seriously, which did not endear him to careerists in the firm. He soon realized that he couldn't live with city life; he felt out of touch with nature. The idea of teaching and of finding a job in a place like New England took hold, though his family still had keen memories of the Great Depression and disapproved of his taking up such a nonlucrative profession. So he kept his advertising job and enrolled in night classes at the Columbia University graduate school.

Back in an environment that nurtured rather than murdered the English language and that revered literature, Pack knew it was the path he had to take. Around 1953 he picked up some teaching slots at The New School—and two poems were accepted by Vance Bourjaily's little magazine, *Discovery*. "Vance invited me down to his office to meet him, and when I did he offered me a job as his poetry editor," Pack recalled.

After I had been doing that for awhile, showing Vance my own work as it was written, he picked up a stack of my poems and asked me if I'd ever thought of putting together a book. I said no, and he asked me if I minded if he took my poems down to John Hall Wheelock at Scribner's—they had just published Vance's novel. In

published a trenchant examination of the poetry of Wallace Stevens, had cotranslated the librettos of Mozart, and had issued three other volumes of his own verse.

It had been while at Dartmouth in the late 1940s and early 1950s that Robert Pack had fixed the New England light and terrain in his mind, never wanting to lose it. Like many other lifelong writers, he had originally wanted to do something else—to either be a baseball player or a naturalist or somehow a combination of the two, maybe coming home from practice and playing with marmosets. The son of a New York State assemblyman representing the Bronx (later a state senator) who annually gave his family a summer in the country, Pack always intended to live in the country and be close to nature. So he brought nature inside. In the winters, the family inhabited a large house in the Bronx with an extra kitchen and spare rooms. The whole downstairs was given over to young Pack's zoo and laboratory—he had an aquarium, and turtles, alligators, guinea pigs, dwarf goats, and a monkey. The boy wanted to travel the world discovering rare animals. Later, after Pack was enrolled in the exclusive Fieldston School run by the Society for Ethical Culture—from which

those days young people didn't even think about publishing that early—it seemed like only grownups did that; *real* writers published. Well, he took that manuscript down to Scribner's and, by Lord, John Hall Wheelock offered to publish it in his new series, "Poetry of Today."

Pack had been growing more and more impatient with his daytime office work at the advertising agency. "One day a very grouchy executive came to me," he recalled, "saying, where was the copy? I said to him spontaneously, quoting some lines from Hamlet, 'If it is to come, it is not now. If it is not now, it is to come. If it is not now, yet it will come. The readiness is all'—*I quit, you bastard!* And in that moment of glory I walked out of the advertising world, never to return." Then Pack's nighttime literary career asserted itself; almost immediately, he left on a Fulbright grant for Italy, and while there he received an invitation from Barnard College to teach, beginning in the fall of 1957. In the classroom he met Patricia Powell, whom he would marry in 1961.

Pack went to Bread Loaf from Barnard in that first Frostless summer of 1963—but he had had enough encounters with Robert Frost to appreciate what Ciardi and others were talking about when they talked about Frost's Bread Loaf "idea." Frost had been a favorite poet from the time Pack had begun reading poetry; his poetry library had begun with a copy of Frost's collected poems, presented to him by an aunt. Then, in the late forties while at Dartmouth, he had met Frost. Frost made regular visits to the college to talk about literature and writing with young writers in a relaxed atmosphere out of the classroom. "It was charming and wonderful, and we all had in our minds that this was what it was like to be a poet!" Pack recalled.

Either in my freshman or sophomore year I had gotten to know him a little bit, and I had boasted to my girlfriend that I was a pal of Robert Frost. She was immensely impressed by this. Not only that, I said, but I could arrange for you to meet him. She came up for Spring Weekend. Robert Frost was staying at the Hanover Inn; he would meet with people in a little sitting room. When my date arrived on campus she was very nervous. So I took her to my fraternity house and asked if she wanted a drink. She did not drink—so I persuaded her to have just a little vodka with grapefruit juice. Not being a drinker, she had two of these, tasting only the juice and not realizing how much vodka she was having. Afterwards we began walking over to the Hanover Inn and she began to feel a little woozy. 'Don't worry about it,' I said. 'Just sit down and Robert Frost will come over and talk to you.' We got up to the sitting room, and Frost was sitting in an easy chair and we were sitting

opposite him on a divan. He began holding forth, and we were talking about some great poetic issue, and my date leaned over to me and said, 'Bob, I'm not feeling well.' I said, 'Just hang in there.' Shortly after, she just passed out, pitched forward off the couch, and went tumbling onto the floor. Without a moment's delay Frost was out of his chair and the two of us lifted her up. He insisted that she take his arm, and then she took my arm, and Frost insisted we walk her around. We went out into the New England night and we must have taken a half hour walk, the two of us talking about high poetic matters—and between us, my date, taking in the sublimity of the occasion.

At his first Bread Loaf session, Pack made long-lasting friendships with John Frederick Nims and Brock Brower, a nonfiction writer and an editor at *Esquire*. Brower had more room than he needed in the off-campus house he occupied and suggested that Bob Pack send for his wife, Patty, and their infant son, Erik, for a few days. Then, after everyone had made their way down the Mountain and back to their regular lives—Ciardi to the lecture circuit, Algren to more travel pieces, Banks to his pipefitting and then tardily to college, Harris and Hawkes to new novels, Didion to Manhattan and a greater longing for California light—Bob Pack was offered a teaching job at Middlebury College beginning with the next academic year. It would be a return to the New England landscape and to Robert Frost country, which as a younger man he had grown to love.

On August 12, 1964, an automobile driven by Howard Nemerov pulled up in front of the Bennington, Vermont, house of Shirley Jackson to transport her to Bread Loaf. For Jackson, what she faced for the next twelve days was at once a professional responsibility and a psychic nightmare. California-born, Syracuse-educated, and married to the critic Stanley Edgar Hyman, Shirley Jackson's fame as a writer had begun early in her career with the publication of a macabre short story in *The New Yorker* entitled "The Lottery," about which Brendan Gill has written, "from time to time, a new and unexpected talent is seen to leap Roman-candle-like straight off the pages of the magazine." The story is about a rural community that each year selects a scapegoat to be stoned to death. "Hundreds of letters came in from troubled and excited readers," Gill recalled, "causing a furor not to be equalled until the publication of Salinger's 'Franny.'" Nearly all of Jackson's stories and novels were populated by disturbed people, fanatics, poisoners, and ghosts—*The Haunting of Hill House* (1959) and the best-selling *We Have Always*

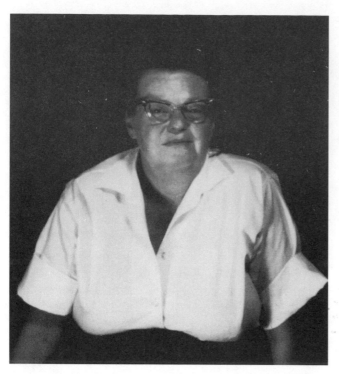

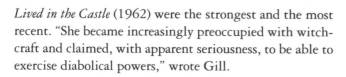
Shirley Jackson at Bread Loaf, 1964 (PC)

Lived in the Castle (1962) were the strongest and the most recent. "She became increasingly preoccupied with witchcraft and claimed, with apparent seriousness, to be able to exercise diabolical powers," wrote Gill.

Once, when for some reason she was angry with her publisher, Alfred Knopf, she learned that he was journeying up to Vermont to ski. The Hymans had then recently moved to Bennington, so Knopf was unwittingly putting himself within close range of Shirley's evil eye. She made an image of wax and stuck a pin in one leg of the image, and, sure enough, Knopf broke a leg skiing—broke it, indeed, in three places. Shirley would hint darkly that she had enjoyed a good many other triumphs of that nature.

In 1964, Jackson was aged forty-four (and size forty-four, she could have joked); a heavy drinker and smoker, she suffered from obesity, asthma, arthritis in the ends of her fingers, periodic anxiety attacks, nervousness, depression, and writer's block. She was dependent on tranquilizers and amphetamines. She was afraid to go out in large groups or even to shop. What better place to go for therapy than the Bread Loaf Writers' Conference? That is what her therapist urged her to do when she received a teaching invitation from John Ciardi. She would not have followed his advice but for the affirmation of her husband and his Bennington colleague, Howard Nemerov, who had been to Bread Loaf before and would be a reassuring

presence. On the pleasant drive up State Route 7 to East Middlebury, Nemerov tried to calm her nervousness by talking about her most vexing of afflictions—writer's block, to which Nemerov was also occasionally prone. With his characteristic deftness he posed her a deceptively simple question that echoed in her mind for weeks: "Why do you *not* write?"

At Bread Loaf, between manuscript clinics and lectures, Jackson chain-smoked and drank and was alternately subdued and gaily shrill; Robert Pack recalled her stationed every evening at the big round table in the Treman Cottage living room, ashtray overfilling and ice cubes melting in a cocktail glass, her grip solidly on the table and the table solidly between her and the rest of the staff.

I t was not immediately apparent to most of the conferees gathered in Treman, but friction was developing inside Bread Loaf just as surely as it was beginning politically and culturally in "the real world" off the Mountain. Civil rights in 1964 was becoming an even greater issue than before, and race riots were breaking out in American cities. A hot presidential campaign was under way between Lyndon B. Johnson and Barry Goldwater, with strategists likening the political struggle to the apocalypse. Ten days before Bread Loaf opened, North Vietnamese patrol boats allegedly attacked an American destroyer, the *Maddox,* in the Tonkin Gulf, and the retaliatory aircraft bombing of

North Vietnam—for the first time—began later in the month. Culturally, enormous changes were just beginning to be felt in the United States, Britain, and other Western nations. The youth counterculture was beginning to manifest itself; the car radios of younger conferees on their way to Bread Loaf would have bombarded the quiet Ripton forests with the percussive guitar chords of a group that had meteorically appeared earlier in the year—the Beatles—and though, as always, radios and record players were banned from the campus, during Saturday night dances the "Fab Four" were played incessantly. Hair was creeping down over collars. There was something new in the air, and it was not simply marijuana smoke.

Events in the "real world" piled up, action and reaction, and to many of those writers going to Bread Loaf in the sixties, these events had relevance to their professional lives and aspirations—no matter what their political persuasion—and resonated with events every August under the shadow of the Mountain. There was, in 1965, Lyndon Johnson's presidency, the sustained bombing of North Vietnam, called Operation Rolling Thunder, the first combat troops' landing on Vietnamese soil, the student demonstrations at colleges and universities, the Watts race riots in Los Angeles, and, by year's end, nearly 200,000 United States troops in Vietnam. In 1966 there were more protests against United States policy and nearly 400,000 in Vietnam; the new slogan, "Black Power," split the civil rights movement. In 1967, with Hanoi bombed and American generals saying they were optimistic, 70,000 prowar demonstrators marched in New York, 50,000 antiwar protesters massed at Washington's Lincoln Memorial, Martin Luther King led an antiwar march in New York as another was held in San Francisco, and race riots charred poor neighborhoods in Detroit, Newark, and Cleveland. The year 1968 was still new when the Tet Offensive of North Vietnamese and Vietcong troops attacked many cities and towns and General William Westmoreland responded with a call for 206,000 more troops; instead of getting them, he was removed—for a tide was turning. The upstart Senator Eugene McCarthy, a poet, nearly defeated President Johnson in the New Hampshire primary. Robert F. Kennedy entered the race only to be assassinated in June, two months after Martin Luther King had met that fate. In August 1968, while Bread Loaf was ending its session, the Chicago Police Force rioted against demonstrators and innocent civilians alike during the Democratic National Convention.

Bread Loaf was not Hue and it was not Hanoi, and it certainly was not Harlem; it was blessedly removed from the problems of those places but not unaffected by them. John Ciardi was no LBJ and he was no Richard Daley; he had been progressive enough in the 1940s to get on an FBI enemies' list for playing a role in the presidential campaign of Henry Wallace, and he still counted himself as a political liberal, although moderate wealth and fame and a socially conservative nature had hardened some of his attitudes. But authority and hierarchy were going to come into question everywhere. It would take years from that Tonkin Gulf month in 1964 for criticism and controversy to climb to a point where it would tower and totter over him. At Bread Loaf in 1964, the tip publicly surfaced in *The Crumb* with an anonymous bit of doggerel found by the editor on his cluttered desk and published on August 16:

> The staff at Bread Loaf dwell apart;
> With us they do not bother.
> But still I note
> They always dote
> On hearing one another.

It opened a Pandora's box of debate. Ciardi's reply came a few days later:

> The conferees they like to breeze
> About the staff's seclusion.
> "This conference just makes no sense
> Unless there's more collusion."
> The conferees with sullen stares
> Concluded their own conclusion.
>
> In confidence I question whence
> This wrath the wroth are feeding.
> If the staff's shut away just what
> Do you suppose it's reading?

His was the better poem and there was a measure of truth to it—all staff members were expected to carry on prodigious amounts of manuscript readings in preparation for classes and individual conferences—but it ducked the social question of exclusivity and hierarchy, a question that had begun to surface as the conference grew and that would not go away.

Not just in 1964 but all during the sixties, even as events were transforming social matters (at least on the face of things), faculty members took their meals apart from students, arriving just before the dining room door was closed and occupying reserved tables. Except for breakfast and on weekends, conferees took assigned seating; experimenting in 1967, the management tried a daily lottery to assign seats, with the exception of the faculty table. Beyond the dining room, the classroom, and the lecture hall, there was Treman Cottage. Not many faculty ventured to public gatherings beyond the usually twice-annual official "teas." Moreover, there were lines drawn not only between faculty and tuition-paying conferees but between faculty and the published younger writers brought up on fellowship or

Faculty table, late 1960s: Seymour Epstein requests decaf

scholarship. Though scheduled for a few years to deliver public readings of their work, as was not the case in the Morrison era, no longer were these emerging writers' books sold in the hole-in-the-wall bookstore lest they crowd those of the staff off the shelves. "The Bread Loaf Bookstore is not permitted to carry works by Bread Loaf Fellows and Scholars," reported *The Crumb* in August 1966. "However, works by these people are carried by The Vermont Book Shop, Main Street, Middlebury. The Bookstore Manager cannot explain this injunction other than to say that it remains inexplicable, or at least unexplained to him. He has one remaining copy of [scholarship holder] Hal Bennett's *A Wilderness of Vines,* which he will sell contraband and under the counter to anyone who is interested."

Trouble brewing in the bookstore, mutterings in the dining room, people on tiptoes trying to peer over the hedge around Treman—hearing laughter and the clink of cocktail glasses. And dissension in the classroom: Why

were the public gatherings in which conferees' manuscripts were discussed called "clinics"? "It treated the student poetry," recalled a young poetry fellow in 1966, Diane Wakoski, "as if it were a disease which had to be diagnosed." *The Crumb* editor was instructed to quell complaints, which he did with a detectable irony:

CLINICS: Clinic: "a class meeting devoted to the analysis and treatment of cases in some special field" (*Webster's New Collegiate Dictionary*). The "cases" at Bread Loaf are manuscripts submitted by contributors. The "class meeting" consists of those whose interest and illness lead them to the clinic, and of those who analyze and treat. These latter may be the conference staff, fellows, and conference members, contributors and auditors alike, according to their skills and interests as diagnosticians and prognosticians. The manuscripts to be discussed in each clinic will be selected by the staff member(s) whose name(s) is (are) identified with the clinic. This has not been read out loud.

To counter any stigma perceived in the official attitude, Diane Wakoski organized a Sunday morning poetry reading on the lawn in front of the Tea Cabin. "Any conference member—auditor or contributor, fellow or scholar," she informed *The Crumb,* "who is interested in reading his poetry," was welcome. Wakoski later recalled that she gave "informal workshops on the lawn, discussing the students' poetry and giving them a forum to more or less present their own ideas about what they were trying to do." When invited back for later sessions, Wakoski continued the ad hoc practice—but it would take years before the term of "workshop," with its presumed more democratic attitudes, was officially adopted. Still, the programs continued with occasional fluctuations of dissension, protest, and sometimes simple discourtesy on both sides of the lectern. In 1968, for instance, two former holders of poetry fellowships (both in 1961), Miller Williams and Lewis Turco, now on the faculty, conducted their scheduled manuscript clinic. "It's slightly embarrassing," recalled Turco, but "when Miller and I gave our clinic together, John Ciardi, who was sitting in the audience, kept interrupting to make comments. Finally, one of the conferees raised a hand. I acknowledged him and he said to me, 'I wonder if you can get Mr. Ciardi to shut up. We came to hear you and Williams this afternoon.'" However well the moment was handled, Turco did not get an invitation to return to Bread Loaf.

And so the sixties tension gathered toward what might have been called John Ciardi's Excedrin Headache Number '71. Still, it can be argued that in choosing faculty for Bread Loaf, John Ciardi had hit his stride. The teaching at Bread Loaf began to emerge as more sophisticated and more coordinated, and the faculty picked up on the sense of mission that had inspired earlier gatherings. The job of anchoring the year-round administrative matters at Middlebury passed from Paul Cubeta, who was promoted to more demanding duties with the Bread Loaf School of English, to Edward "Sandy" Martin, an English professor at Middlebury with a scholarly interest in H.L. Mencken. In 1964 Howard Nemerov and Robert Pack returned to the Mountain, as did Nancy Hale, Dudley Fitts, and the 1957 fellow in nonfiction, Dan Wakefield. Also hired—to teach fiction alongside Shirley Jackson, making quite a pair—was the wisecracking, thirty-four-year-old Stanley Elkin, whose first novel, *Boswell,* a comic story of a modern-day James Boswell who is a celebrity-hunting strongman, appeared that year. Elkin had been

Stanley Elkin at Bread Loaf, 1964 (PC)

born in New York and raised in Chicago; he took three degrees at the University of Illinois, during which time he studied creative writing with Randall Jarrell and worked on the staff of *Accent* magazine, which published one of his first short stories in 1959. In 1961, teaching and working on the footnotes of his Ph.D thesis and growing despondent of ever doing more creative work, Elkin received "a mother's grant"—his mother offered to finance a year away from teaching. "I went off to Rome and to London and wrote *Boswell,*" he recalled. "I guess that's what made me a writer. Otherwise I would have been a kind of Sunday writer." *Boswell,* with its rich, complex, colloquial use of language and its exquisite satire quickly made Elkin's reputation. Ahead of him there would be grants and fellowships, a string of marvelous novels and novellas, and a steadily growing audience. He would not return to the Mountain for a dozen years—but, returning, Elkin would plant his feet for a while.

In 1965, while at a party in New York, Ciardi met a novelist and short story writer, Seymour Epstein, whose work the poet had read and liked. They had a pleasant conversation, ending with Ciardi saying, "We'll have to have you up on the hill next summer." Epstein smiled, thinking he was hearing a vague dinner invitation. When Ciardi had moved on, the poet Grace Schulman came over and whispered, "I suppose you realize you were being invited to the Bread Loaf Writers' Conference." Indeed, Epstein went for a total of ten sessions ending in 1980, making many friends, discovering that he could teach, and making a contact that resulted in an eighteen-year-long appointment at the University of Denver—"I who hadn't even taken an undergraduate degree! Another Bread Loaf miracle!" He was among the first on the faculty to arrive in 1965, as was another fiction writer, Charles Jackson—whose most famous work was the alcoholic nightmare *The Lost Weekend* (1944), later made into a film starring Ray Milland. As Ciardi drove them down the Mountain in a pink Cadillac to dinner at the Middlebury Inn, he told them that he had wanted to be the first poet in the United States to own a pink Cadillac. (The following year, poet and populist Diane Wakoski eyed the pink Cadillac, explainable if not by taste then by Ciardi's many lecture fees, and then she looked at John Frederick Nims's Mercedes—but could not understand how a college professor could afford a Mercedes.) Young Epstein sat at dinner with Ciardi and Jackson certain that he "would never fully absorb the wonder of that evening. That first occasion has secured for itself a timeless corner in my head."

Not everyone found the Mountain convivial. Not knowing, or forgetting, that they hated one another, Ciardi had invited both John Frederick Nims and Henry Rago of *Poetry* magazine to serve on the 1965 staff. Robert Pack recalled being in the audience during a program involving the two when they began sarcastically sniping at one another from opposite sides of the lectern. The wrangling escalated steadily, though Pack noted that Nims was trying to hold himself back, given the public forum. But Rago finally burst a valve and began shouting at Nims, who contained himself against the onslaught for a time but finally succumbed. Furious invective hurled over the lectern as each accused the other of needing a psychiatrist.

In succeeding years Nims returned—but not Henry Rago, who had "lost it" at the lectern. Instead, in 1966, there was David Wagoner, forty-year-old lyric poet of the Pacific Northwest and prolific novelist, and X.J. Kennedy of Tufts, poetry fellow in 1961. In the next session there was another returning poetry fellow of 1961, Miller Williams, also a noted translator of Hispanic poetry, who with his beard and glowing eyes beneath a shiny scalp looked as much like a poet as he did a necromancer, as well as young, raunchy Judson Jerome, poetry editor of *Antioch Review.* Both were well published, they were effective teachers, and both would be invited back to the Mountain—and there the resemblance ends. Williams, who had published a critical work entitled *The Achievement of John Ciardi,* became like a son to the Bread Loaf director; for a time it seemed to some as if Williams might succeed Ciardi when the director retired. Jerome, in contrast, took advantage of the sixties' sexual freedoms to the detriment of his neighbors' sleep. He did not respond well to complaints nor to Ciardi's admonition to "cool it a little." "Once, in 1968, I asked John for permission to bring a woman student into

Judson Jerome, late 1960s

Treman, from which students were excluded," recalled Jerome. "He was in the midst of one of his eternal gin rummy games with his good friend the staff doctor, and he refused me curtly. Later I told him I didn't mind the refusal so much—but, I asked, why the tone? I thought we were by then old friends. 'Don't get too near a psychic buzz saw,' he said. All of us learned to be wary of a volatile and unpredictable personality."

Jerome did not fully heed the warning. In a subsequent exchange with the director, he was a little drunk, and incautious, and got across that he was no longer in awe of Ciardi but rather felt as if they were now brothers—and that he was expecting Ciardi to promote him from son to brother, too. "Later in the evening he was carrying on, as he often did, about how much money he had earned," Jerome recalled. "Coming from a poor immigrant family, he had provided security, he said, for himself and his family for as long as they would live—or something to that effect. Still feeling too cocky for my own good, I said, 'I think that's wonderful, John. Now you can stop thinking about money and get back to work.' It was stupid and rude, but several on the staff later told me they were glad I said it. We were all getting a bit sick of hearing about Ciardi's money." Jerome would never return to Bread Loaf, although his career would continue to expand his horizons beyond poetry into fiction; his poetry column in *Writer's Digest* would continue for more than twenty-five years. But many years after the 1968 unpleasantness he reconciled with Ciardi, whose comments about their last evening at Treman must be quoted here:

> We can all make horse's ass of ourselves, and I have certainly worked at it at times. I'd hate, for instance, to become known as a guy who kept talking about nothing but how much money he was making. Especially since I never really made a lot—an immense amount as measured by my first impoverished expectations, but not much as measured by our present economy, in which I look forward to a pensionless lower middle class old age—and the Hell with it. I want to believe I was drunk when I spoke that way at Treman. At 2:00 A.M. in the bourbon maunders, anything might come out, and usually with no definitive connection with the truth.

The 1967 session brought not only Archibald MacLeish, Bread Loaf's old friend, but also Norman Mailer—who, twenty-six years earlier, had been a student in Ted Morrison's advanced composition course at Harvard. He had been an A-minus student. Mailer, novelist and journalist, celebrated for *The Naked and the Dead* (1948) and *An American Dream* (1965), was publishing a new novel entitled *Why Are We in Vietnam?*, an absurdist, scatalogical story that contained only two mentions of the war—both on the last page. He had dashed it off in four months in 1966 to fulfill a stale, thousand-dollar contract with Putnam's. When it was published in September 1967 it received furiously negative reviews. One writer would call it "possibly the most obscene book of American fiction ever published." Writing in *The New York Times Book Review,* Anatole Broyard said that it "may be a third-rate work of art, but it's a first-rate outrage to our sensibilities."

Mailer arrived the evening before his scheduled appearance and found his way over to Treman Cottage. There he turned to Dave Etter, a poetry fellow, who upon recognizing Mailer thought, "My God, it's the man himself." The two stood in the kitchen having a relaxed conversation about the current situation in the heavyweight boxing division—talking of Joe Frazier, Jimmy Ellis, Thad Spencer, and others. "Some other people," Etter recalled, "realizing that Mailer had arrived started to push into the kitchen area. Someone asked him a question, something about how he liked John Updike or had he read such and such book by some guy from Chile." Etter began to excuse himself. Mailer smiled and mumbled something to his literary interrogator, looking as if he'd rather continue talking about the fights.

His evening talk on August 25 was announced in *The Crumb* as "Obscenity in Literature." Largely, it would be a reading from his new novel, with commentary. Beforehand, as Etter recorded, Mailer talked briefly on language and said that the four-letter words in the book were necessary, as the characters would use those words. He warned the audience that "I will say some words that will no doubt offend some of you and I will wait for anyone who does not want to hear these words and would like to leave." "Everyone more or less glanced around to see who, if anyone, would get up and depart the little theatre," wrote Etter. "I saw two nuns leave and perhaps one or two elderly folks." Seymour Epstein, sitting elsewhere in the theatre, watched several nuns who elected to stay, and after the reading commenced they seemed to pay polite attention, with the exception of one nun, who tended to nod off. "Some of those fantastic dirty words," recalled Etter, "made a lot of people twitch a bit, all of whom were trying to remain emancipated and casual as sliced tomatoes at a businessmen's lunch. It was a hell of an electric reading."

Several weeks after Mailer left his hearers quivering on the Mountain, he would be invited by his friend Mitch Goodman to attend an October protest march on the Pentagon. Mailer would go with Robert Lowell, Dwight MacDonald, and Paul Goodman and deliver a drunken, obscene ramble in front of a microphone. Almost as an afterthought, seeing it as good narrative, he got himself arrested and spent a night in jail. The resulting reportage—some of the most brilliant stateside journalism to emerge during the war years—was published in the spring in *Harper's* and *Commentary* and in book form as *Armies of the Night*. It would win a Pulitzer Prize.

It would also be in the spring of 1968 that relations between John Ciardi and the administration of Middlebury College began to seriously go sour. Already a gulf had opened between Ciardi and his year-round assistant, Middlebury English professor Sandy Martin. Repeatedly, Martin had sent off memos to Ciardi with suggestions for how Ciardi could alter the curriculum and the schedule to loosen up relations between the faculty and conferees and to add variety. Martin and many others saw no harm in according fellows and scholars more participation. Ciardi did. They saw it as healthy to have more than one point of view. Ciardi believed in one doctrine. Martin and others saw value in allowing ad hoc readings and gatherings to occur. Ciardi wanted them banned. One year he went so far as to direct Martin to admit no conferees under the age of twenty-five. This the assistant director refused to do— and Ciardi would not forget that. Each suggestion was refused with no indication that even healthy debate was welcomed. These were problems internal to the Bread Loaf structure—although presumably Martin informed his year-round superiors that he was not making progress. But then, in that spring of 1968, the problems went external.

An article published in the *St. Louis Post Dispatch* was clipped and forwarded to Stephen A. Freeman, director of the Middlebury language schools and nominal overseer of Bread Loaf. Professor Freeman was a teetotaler and had often complained that too much drinking went on at the Writers' Conference; Ciardi always replied that one could not govern adults when they gathered—they were not undergraduates and would not come if treated like such. But the article, by a Houston woman named Beatrice Levin, was another matter. For some reason Levin had waited nearly four years after attending the 1964 session to air her complaints. She said that she had gone to Bread Loaf "as a girl," probably in the thirties, and had been enchanted by the place and by Robert Frost and Louis Untermeyer. By contrast, at her later visit, "a young staff member recited to mild, middle-aged ladies some of the most pornographic poetry I've ever heard in my life. A chapter of a conferee's book was read aloud in public, and members of the staff criticized it so cruelly and savagely that the author promptly declared her intention of committing suicide." As bad as was the "intolerant and even hostile" atmosphere (in which she singled out William Sloane), Levin had worse to say about the "separate but equal" segregation of staff and conferees—the assigned seating at meals and the separate staff dining table, the "cliques," and the policies in the bookstore. "If you buy a book," she complained, "and want it autographed, you pay for it and leave it on a shelf with written instructions on how it should be signed."

Professor Freeman immediately wrote to Ciardi. Even making allowances for the probable frustrations of the author, he said,

> who was probably not lionized as much as she thought she ought to be by the staff, this still is not the kind of publicity that we like to see spread about the writers' conference. The staff of the conference have of course the right to their own privacy and should not feel that they are on duty to carry on smiling conversation twenty hours a day with the paying guests. On the other hand, perhaps some greater effort should be made toward mixing them up at tables, as we do in all the other schools. Perhaps some of the staff could be urged to tone down a little their public sarcasms.

Ciardi's reply came immediately. He said he understood the administration's unhappiness at the bad publicity, and that "Hers is in fact a standard and continuing complaint." Moreover, he wrote that "I have, therefore, had many occasions to think about it, but I have not found good reason to change things." The mingling policy might work at the slower-paced Bread Loaf School of English, he continued, but it would not work for the conference, which was "intense, rapid, informal, and more ego-driven, in most cases, than scholarly. Throw a faculty member to one of the dining room tables with conference members and he would be devoured. Insist on such a policy and half the staff would refuse to come back." The long, separate table was also necessary "because staff members are finishing their drinks" at Treman and "they tend to go to the dining room not when the doors open but as they close. It is convenient for such a late arriving group to have a single table waiting. I think, I may say, that I know your sentiments about drinking, but the cocktail remains a fact of life, and it is simply impossible to gather writers, editors, agents, etc. without alcohol." He said that he repeatedly recommended to staff "that it would be good of them to go to the barn for an hour or so in the evening to chin with the customers, and most of them have been generous about their hours there. I think that is all we can do." Finally, Ciardi addressed the problem of Beatrice Levin and other literary yearners, noting that the current Bread Loaf bulletin contained a disclaimer reminding conferees that acceptance into the program was not a sure step toward discovery.

> The Bread Loaf problem [he wrote to Freeman] in such cases is usually simple and arises from the fact that too many conference members say they come to Bread Loaf to learn but are really coming in the burning hope that they will be "discovered." When the conference goes by without brass bands, signed contracts, and a ticker tape parade of shredded mss., these secret dreamers are upset. I know of nothing in the conference management that could turn the rage of their ego in such cases. It's a built in casualty list.

As with his retort in verse published in *The Crumb* in 1964, when an anonymous poet complained of staff segregation, there was more than simply a measure of truth to his rationale. But only one side of the truth. And complainers like Levin were in the minority. However, giving just a little might have saved Ciardi much grief in the future. But that was not the way it was written.

The poet Vassar Miller attended the 1968 session as a tuition-paying conferee, and her experiences offer a contrast to the foregoing; she called them "among the most pleasant I have ever had." Miller was grateful that Bread Loafers were as helpful and sensitive about her crippling cerebral palsy and her special needs as they were about her poetry; she made several lasting friends there, including Judson Jerome, whose book, *The Poet and the Poem*, she greatly admired. There were a number of other emerging writers there that year with fellowships and scholarships—Ciardi's fundraising efforts, in fact, had allowed him to double the number of scholarships, and the scholars secured official sanction for their public readings, which stretched into the wee hours of the night. In 1968 there were thirteen fellows and nine scholars, among them novelists Robert Cormier and William Kotzwinkle, whom Cormier recalled as getting married during the conference in a setting out in the woods, and wild, energetic Harry Crews, up from a Fort Lauderdale junior college where he taught, with one published novel and another scheduled for the next year. He impressed Ciardi to the point that he would be back on the Bread Loaf faculty in 1969. Crews was "magnetic, hell-raising," in Cormier's words, "playing the guitar, singing country songs, yet you sensed an underlying and brooding sensitivity."

In August 1968 Reverend Martin Luther King and Bobby Kennedy were dead, the body count of Americans and Vietnamese was up, and Richard Nixon and Spiro Agnew had received the nod of the Republican party assembled in Miami. Bread Loaf, beyond the confusion of rushing off-Mountain events, had an evening's counterpoint to them—John Ciardi's old classmate from his Bates College days, Senator Edmund Muskie (whose own presidential bid had ended earlier in New Hampshire) stood at the lectern to talk about politics. He was on his way to Chicago and Hubert Humphrey's nomination at the most violent presidential convention in history; the debate over the Vietnam War would be all but kept off the official agenda as police rioted in the streets outside of the convention hall.

When Maxine Kumin was a freshman at Radcliffe in 1942, she turned in a batch of poems to an instructor for his comments. It is possible that they were improvements on her high school compositions, which she recalled as "very bad late adolescent romantic poetry." But her professor disagreed. "Say it with flowers," he wrote on the manuscript, "but for God's sake don't try to write poems." She did not try to write another poem for years. Kumin graduated from Radcliffe, got married, took an M.A. in comparative literature, freelanced as a medical writer, and began to have children. Living in a Boston suburb, programmed to lead a life as housewife, mother, and community volunteer, Kumin began to feel rootless and unfulfilled. On impulse, deciding to ignore her noble professor's exhortation, she sent away for a little handbook on writing light verse—the kind advertised in the back pages of *The Writer* magazine—and took the magazine's

advice on how to sell it. In early 1953 she sold her first quatrain to *The Christian Science Monitor*. Her "filler verse" began appearing regularly in *The Monitor*, and in *The Saturday Evening Post*, *Good Housekeeping*, *The Wall Street Journal*, and the *New York Herald Tribune*. "By the end of the year," she wrote, "I had set up a card file of markets and established a cottage industry that netted me twelve hundred dollars, all without *neglecting*—the buzzword of the fifties—husband and children."

Still she was discontented—she wanted to write real poems, but lacked focus and direction. She read the postwar poetry anthologies without fully realizing how few women were collected in them. By 1957 she knew she needed either a mentor or a fellow-struggler and enrolled in an adult education class taught by John Holmes—the one in which she met Anne Sexton. Their friendship sustained them as they each found their individual literary voices; Kumin and Sexton talked almost daily about their work, one never imposing her views on the other but remaining faithful to the central ideas and moods of the poems. They also began collaborating on children's books. Kumin's impeccably crafted poems—about her childhood outside Philadelphia, her Jewish identity, her feelings about nature, loss, and the tenuousness of life—were first collected in *Halfway* (1961), and she continued these themes in *The Privilege* (1965), published the same year as her first novel, *Through Dooms of Love*. John Holmes had continued to encourage her. It was through his intercession that she was hired to teach composition at Tufts, and later, when she moved to Radcliffe, Holmes's most famous former student hired Kumin to teach poetry and fiction at Bread Loaf, beginning with the 1969 session.

With her affinity with nature Kumin adapted instantly to the Bread Loaf plateau, in the interstices of the busy schedule taking long walks into the woods to discover wild mushrooms; indeed, over the seven sessions in which she would participate, Kumin would become known, as Ciardi dubbed her, as "the witch of fungi." "I can still hear John," she wrote, "who punctuated most lunches with a call for silence in the dining hall in order to make his announcement: 'the Witch of Fungi will lead a mushroom walk at three o'clock.' It became our custom to fry these comestibles in the staff kitchen to accompany the cocktail hour." More hip than housewife, in one Bread Loafer's admiring view, Kumin usually wore shades inside, even at the lectern, and delivered illuminating talks on the craft of both poetry and fiction. "A poem," she once said, "should give me goose bumps. I am hungry for something elusive that moves me." Distributing their own goose bumps, her poems would win her a number of grants, awards, and fellowships, including the Pulitzer Prize and the Borestone Mountain Award.

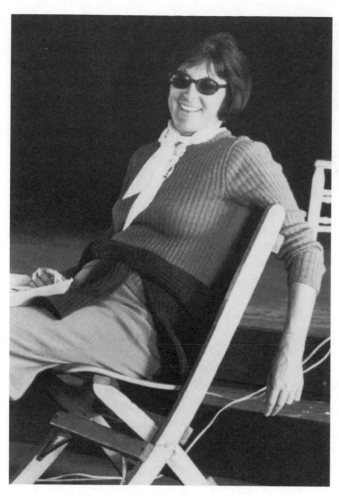

Maxine Kumin leads a discussion group, 1969

Having jumped from fiction fellow to Bread Loaf faculty member in one year, Harry Crews arrived from his new job at the University Florida at Gainesville. *The Gospel Singer* (1968), his first novel, had established his gleeful familiarity with the southern gothic tradition. Set in his home territory of Georgia, it was the story of an itinerant singing preacher who goes home to find himself embroiled in the aftermath of a murder; the novel was populated with mean-spirited yokels and sideshow freaks and ended in a wild burst of violence. His second novel, *Naked in Garden Hills,* would appear that year and continue his preoccupations with decadence and monstrosities; its central character was a six-hundred-pound man who undergoes a psychic reduction from the most powerful citizen in a Georgia town to a sideshow freak. Crews, with his close-cropped hair, squinty eyes, razor-trimmed muttonchop sideburns, and infectious and flamboyant manner, developed an instant following at Bread Loaf. In one presentation in the lecture hall with veteran Bread Loafer John Williams (author of *Stoner* and *Butcher's Crossing*), Crews eschewed a microphone and seemed to blow up like

a balloon on the proscenium stage, so overpowering was his presence and so wild were his physical contortions as he spoke. A twenty-year-old student poet in the audience, Julia Alvarez, recalled that when Crews lectured and read from his work, "he punctuated his sentences with a little Elvis Presley hip-wiggle and thrust." Coming from an extremely sheltered upbringing and from the staid Connecticut College where she was a sophomore, Alvarez could only wonder what the nuns sitting in the front row were thinking as they took notes. She thought she could guess. She had been billeted in a women's corridor in the Annex dormitory, with a nun next door on one side and an unknown woman on her other side, from whose room at night there would be howls and moans and thumps. One morning Julia Alvarez went down the hall to brush her teeth in the communal bathroom and bumped into a grinning, naked Harry Crews as he came out.

It was not, she told her mentor from Connecticut College, William Meredith, like any other place she'd been. The licentiousness of others aside, Alvarez was falling in love with the idea of being in a community of writers. Her delight was even unaffected by John Frederick Nims, who read her poems and began his discouraging critique by saying, "I don't know what Meredith has been telling you, but. . . ." He might have silenced a less determined student writer. Years later, after she had begun publishing and receiving awards, he remembered their first conference at Bread Loaf and wrote a begrudging congratulation. Meredith was quite a different kind of teacher in Alvarez's experience. He was a cultivator of talent within his students, offering quiet and gentle encouragement that made them want to stretch their own boundaries. "He had," she recalled, "a way of letting the class just *happen*—and yet you sensed he had control." In the decade since he had last attended the Writers' Conference, Meredith had edited Shelley, translated Apollinaire's poems, and published a new collection of his own verse, *The Wreck of the Thresher,* with another expected in 1970.

As with every other year, literary seriousness could take up only so much of the day. During the first four or five days of the 1969 conference, another gathering was taking place in upstate New York—larger by perhaps some three or four hundred thousand people—but elements of the Woodstock culture were certainly present at Bread Loaf. The director's spirited daughter, Myra Ciardi, convinced her father to allow a rock band to play for a dance in the Barn—a first for Bread Loaf. "The band showed up two hours late," recalled 1967 poetry fellow Dave Etter, who returned for a few sessions as a conferee, "and there were some heavy sounds bouncing off the mountains way after midnight . . . lots of sweaty fun." Another famous element of Woodstock manifested itself late at night with skinny-dipping in Johnson Pond, although Etter remembered a more public, sunlit occasion that sent conservative conferees scurrying: One day a young man walked out of the Larch dormitory in the altogether and sat down to sun himself in a lawn chair next to the lane leading to the Barn. "Never did find out what happened to him," wrote Etter. "We were so casual in those days. Nothing was a big deal."

Except, of course, for the war, which was still a presence at Bread Loaf, even though some 25,000 American troops were supposedly to be pulled out of Vietnam by the summer's end. A large public trial of radicals, including Abbie Hoffman and Bobby Seale, was set to open in Chicago in September; for believers, Woodstock consciousness called for peace and there was no peace. Interestingly enough, a twenty-nine-year-old native of Iowa who had served in a hospital support unit in Vietnam between 1965 and 1967 was at Bread Loaf in 1969. Currently he was a feature writer for the *New Haven Register,* and he published a notice in *The Crumb* calling for anyone with Connecticut ties to assemble to be interviewed for a feature article on Bread Loaf. He was at the conference on scholarship, and as it happened there were more readings than ever in 1969; Ciardi was allowing scholars and waiters to deliver public readings (though, some complained, at very late and inconvenient hours), and others organized what were called "ad hoc, vox populi" open readings on lawns and in the Inn's Blue Parlor. The young reporter was also a playwright, but since Bread Loaf no longer recognized drama as currency on the Mountain, David Rabe did not read from any of his scripts. Two years later his two short Vietnam plays, *Sticks and Bones* and *The Basic Training of Pavlo Hummel,* would be discovered and produced by Joseph Papp in New York to much acclaim, winning Tony, Obie, *Variety,* Drama Guild, Outer Circle, and Drama Desk awards. But in 1969 he told Bread Loafers that he was trying to convince his paper, or anyone else, to let him go back to Vietnam as a war correspondent so that he could educate those at home about what the war was doing to its soldiers. Failing that, Rabe would go back to school and then teach and write about the war in his own way.

Longtime Bread Loafers detected a difference between the Writers' Conferences of 1969 and 1970—as if a hidden thermostat had been turned up several notches until the temperature was on the verge of being uncomfortable. As had come to be the case in that era, the political and cultural scene off the Mountain in 1970 informed and affected Bread Loaf even in its sylvan surroundings: Anger and frustration was discernibly higher; the draft was still

an issue despite the Nixon administration's measured withdrawal from Vietnam, and people were still being killed at a tragic rate. In May, when huge demonstrations rose up all over the nation to protest the sudden widening of the war into Cambodia, students were killed at Ohio's Kent State University by National Guardsmen and at Mississippi's Jackson State College by police, touching off unprecedented unrest. Moreover, the heavy but relatively benign drug use of the Woodstock generation was getting out of hand, turning more complex and dangerous—reflected in more cases turning up in hospital emergency rooms and a greater demand upon drug hotlines and walk-in centers.

Every year since he had begun as director, Ciardi had found it necessary to call for "the men in the white coats" when a conferee could not take the Bread Loaf pace or the psychic strain—one case even had involved a faculty member who, when recovering in the hospital but still profoundly shaken, said, "God did not intend for all those writers to gather in one place at one time." People appeared at the conference and then wandered away; once Sandy Martin found a waif who had made her pilgrimage up the Mountain barefoot, in the rain, and had been so intimidated by all the other writers that she moved into the woods where she stayed like a sixties forest sprite, playing with the Martin children who brought her sandwiches and apples and who were sworn to secrecy. A gathering of some two hundred "artistic types" would naturally have casualties, with so many egos on the line—and as far back as the twenties, administrators from John Farrar to Ted Morrison had dealt with them.

But this phenomenon was getting worse. Ciardi and Martin were making more calls to remove people to emotionally safer surroundings than ever before. Once Ciardi had to talk someone down from a tree. Another conferee shinnied up an eight-by-eight support post in the Barn and went scampering around on the open beams of the former hayloft, twenty feet above the floor, then did something involving matches that could have set the old structure on fire. The same person arrived at his manuscript conference with a faculty member and produced an unloaded pistol, which he laid on the table between them. He was taken off the Mountain—and luckily there were no other outwardly ugly situations. But emotions still seemed rawer, nerves a little more fragile, than before. According to *The Crumb,* there was an outbreak of incivility: Repeatedly, it published waspish little notices about not littering, not removing tableware from the dining room or blankets from the rooms, or not carrying on so loud at night when people needed to sleep. Nearly everybody remembered 1970 as a year in which people would barge in and out of readings in the Little

Theatre, banging the screen doors and scraping chairs and creaking over the risers in the rear of the hall. Thirty years before, a young Truman Capote could scandalize an entire conference by ostentatiously and noisily leaving a Frost presentation. Now there were thirty Truman Capotes, and a hundred glares and shushing.

It would have been a hard time for any figure of authority, teacher or administrator, but especially for someone like John Ciardi who had come to consider Bread Loaf as an extension of his family—an Italian family, it must be added, modern but still old world, with Ciardi as the increasingly firm *patrone*. And schisms were opening up within his family. He had children of his own who expected to be accorded all of the rights of modern-day youth ("but none of the *responsibilities,*" he and countless other fathers would rail). He had faculty members who identified with the new cultural pluralism, though inevitably there were others who did not. "Looking back," the Denver novelist and editor John Williams wrote, "I begin to realize how difficult those years were, the middle and late sixties; anyone who could afford a ballpoint pen or a typewriter was allowed to think of himself as a poet or a novelist; talent and craft were suspect, more often than not described as 'elitist,' a curse-word of the period; and literacy was thought by many to be a species of corruption, a loss of innocence or a kind of damnation." At the time there were some who would not have been so cynical.

One of these had a particular affinity for the young and restless and a way of affirming their political concerns— Galway Kinnell. He became an object of some controversy among more socially conservative faculty at Treman. A product of Rhode Island, Princeton, and the University of Rochester, at forty-three Kinnell was the author of seven books of poetry, was a translator of Villon, and had lived a poet's gypsy life on visiting professorships, grants and fellowships, and year-long writing residencies at various schools, most recently at Iowa. Already well known and rewarded for his Whitmanesque free verse that celebrated or explored nature, common people, and the bonds between life and death, he would receive even wider recognition in a decade or so. At Bread Loaf, exuding vitality, Kinnell conducted manuscript clinics with a certain populist air, coming around from behind the safety of the lectern to pace the stage or sit down on its apron, almost—but not totally—on the same level as his students. In readings he hunched over the lectern, gripping it, and seldom referred to his poetry texts but rather said them from memory.

Kinnell's overriding concern in public forums was the war still being carried on in Southeast Asia. He had been a contributor to an anthology, *Where Is Vietnam?: American Poets Respond,* published in the early protest days of 1967.

Galway Kinnell, 1970

"His deepfelt comments stirred much discussion," recalled a visiting journalist,

> and he was most truly obsessed with the viciousness of the Vietnam war—at times appearing to say that America *needs* a war as an expression of some national flaw of character. I say "appearing" because one could listen to the poet with rapt attention and still find him more allusive than direct. Always, there was the irony of watching him take the platform looking like a boxer past his prime, warming up the crowd for the main event. Then he would begin to speak in a blue-white whisper and with such naked sincerity that, during one late evening reading, he literally broke off in mid-sentence and could go no further with the poem at hand.

Taking a much more extreme side was a rough young self-taught novelist named Shane Stevens, who had been at Bread Loaf on fellowship in 1967 and in whom Ciardi took a fatherly interest. He would be a faculty member in 1970 and 1971. Stevens had, in a journalist's mind, "a Marlon Brando kind of sex appeal and the dubious distinction of having signs appear around the Bread Loaf area that read, 'Shane is sweet.'" Stevens had an active social life at the conference with enough energy left over to be an active and committed teacher. He had, the journalist said, "the look of a street gang leader and is very much a part of today's revolutionary scene, yet, when he lectured, his street argot held the scholar's suppleness of phrase and meaning." He had friends whom the FBI considered dangerous but saw himself as an activist whose function was to write, not bomb. "History is on our side," he said darkly. "Your scribblings will outlast the enemy."

Probably there was no one on the faculty that year who was actually prowar. But opinions differed on the relationship between politics and art and the responsibilities of an artist during an unjust and illegal war. Dan Wakefield, who had been looking with a gimlet eye at the establishment for thirteen years, brought the debate back to the literary table by stressing that writers should not preach or tell the reader what to think. "Let the story permit the reader to make up his own mind," he said. One could still communicate the horror.

Most of the rest of the faculty could agree with Wakefield, who by that time had published a first novel, *Going All the Way,* which had made the best-seller lists. Maxine Kumin came with a new poetry collection and most of a new novel completed. William Meredith and Miller Williams struck newcomers with their expertise, Meredith particularly with his humility and his ability to put nervous conferees at ease and reconcile them, almost with eagerness, to the prospect of more hard work. Harry Crews was back with a new novel, as energetic as earlier, showing—in the eyes of scholarship holder Hilma Wolitzer—a remarkable sensitivity and enthusiasm to an unknown writer who knew *nobody.* "He gave me a feeling of not just doing his job for the twelve allotted days," she recalled, "but of having made a commitment to the writer he was working with." After the summer she received a letter from Crews in which he explained why she would publish the novel she later published, and they stayed in touch. Wolitzer did not get to know anyone else on the faculty, nor any of the fellows; though she was invited to one cocktail hour at Treman Cottage she spent the hour alone, "drinking too much and feeding little bits of cheese to a dog on the porch. In retrospect, I was projecting an aloofness onto them out of my own shyness: they didn't seem to be on Bread Loaf Mountain. They seemed to be on Mount Olympus."

Hilma Wolitzer was new on the Mountain and did not see that there was trouble on Mount Olympus. Though Ciardi felt benevolent and forgiving toward Shane Stevens's "rabble-rousing," he was apoplectic toward Galway Kinnell, whose exhortations were doing, mostly in

"Every lecture a performance":
Harry Crews, late 1960s

Ciardi's eyes, inestimable damage to the Bread Loaf "family." Plain competition has to be considered in the equation. In any case, the *patrone* would not invite Kinnell back. But the clamor that so irritated Ciardi's sensibility would not go away. There was a gathering dissatisfaction among even Ciardi's friendly associates on the Mountain. Relations between the director and his chief Middlebury contact, Sandy Martin, were cooling; doggedly Martin had continued to press for reforms in the structure and the curriculum, and he was not without support among senior Bread Loafers. And there was a building tension between Ciardi and college administrators who saw social matters at the conference getting out of hand. Being a moral magistrate, he told his friends, was never to his liking and he would not start now. And as for changes—well, they had some years to go and could take their time about instituting, perhaps, some of them, while remaining true to their stewardship.

T he bulletin and poster for Bread Loaf's 1971 session carried a photograph taken during the previous year's angry conference: It was of a verbal confrontation between the bulky, graying Ciardi and a long-haired youth, Ciardi making one of his incontrovertible points and the boy, seeming to listen but probably not, looking flushed and resentful. They were surrounded by other people, none of whom looked happy. There is no way of interpreting the scene happily. It was a curious choice for advertising but a prophetic one.

On opening night some two hundred conferees assembled in the Little Theatre. On the faculty, there was graceful, tough Maxine Kumin; chubby William Meredith with his ironic smile and love beads; Seymour Epstein, looking more like Franklin Roosevelt every year; wan, ghostlike but genial Bill Sloane; brooding Shane Stevens; gnomish John Williams; and intense Miller Williams. The 1966 Robert Frost poetry fellow, Diane Wakoski, returned, her sixth poetry collection about to appear. Grinning limericist Isaac Asimov, Ciardi's friend of twenty years, was there, on about his hundredth book. And so was puckish Robert Pack, who had last taught at Bread Loaf in 1967, and who was readying a new collection to follow his well-received *Home from the Cemetery* (1969). Also present in the room was a *Washington Post* feature writer, who would turn in the sort of innocuous feature story that one saw every year in one paper or another and that would touch all the obvious points, and the talented fiction editor of *Esquire,* Rust Hills. The latter, whose encouragement of emergent writers over a long career would be hard to match, initially appeared incognito as a student; his subsequent piece in *Audience* magazine would

William Sloane, 1971

be extremely partial—yet the breezy, often amusing account would be replete with accurate observations. (When, later, Wallace Stegner wrote about Hills and his *Audience* story, he was also speaking about others who appeared from time to time to partake of the sociabilities at Bread Loaf and write lurid stories: "It has been fairly easy," Stegner noted in *The Uneasy Chair,* "for a certain kind of journalist to strike the body and count coup on it." Of course, it is easier for reporters to write about cocktail parties and social relations than it is to illuminate how teaching gets done.) In addition to these two journalists, a seven-person crew from Vermont educational television would take up a distracting residency during a single day in mid-conference.

Ciardi's welcoming remarks strayed for a few moments to what a mistake it had been to hire Galway Kinnell at Bread Loaf in 1970. This comment only puzzled the majority of the audience, who had not been present in 1970, and struck those who had been as negative and gratuitous, setting a bad tone for the session. But then the conference got under way and everyone did the best they could under the circumstances.

They were not good. Hurricane Doria rolled up the East Coast into New England, giving Bread Loaf five days of miserably cold and rainy weather. Somehow the wires in the fire-alarm system were drenched and they short-circuited, which produced a false alarm that sent people running in all directions. Denied the balancing and healing recreation of nature hikes, tennis, volleyball, and swimming, tempers began to fray. Bad colds began making the rounds, with Ciardi's so bad that he disappeared for several days. His presence, however, was still felt, and resentment began to build. The problem was not about politics off the Mountain or Vietnam; most of the political anger among conferees and staff alike had dissipated in a year's time, as indeed it had largely done in the outside world. Undeniably it was still generational and ego-driven, but a more supple hand might have turned it. Even a posture of willingness to listen to the other side might have made a difference. There had been some small changes, enacted only with great struggle. The traditional long faculty dining table, a fixture for forty years or more, was gone. In its place, however, were several smaller faculty tables; occasionally staff members, though not the director, sat down to eat with conferees—a gesture apparently much appreciated. (On the first morning of the conference, however, Ciardi walked into the dining room, repented of his liberalization, and ordered the faculty tables joined again; Martin held him to his word, not without difficulty.) In the late evenings, a few staff members attended the long, impromptu waiters' and scholars' readings held in the Barn, though not the director. One night the waiters threw a dance party in the third-floor loft of the Barn—loud and dark and raunchy with rock music—again, a number of staff members visited, but not the director. Judith Ciardi, who did look in, remarked candidly to someone that "the kids would appreciate it so if he at least made an appearance." But the small gestures that might have meant something would not have been genuine—and Ciardi was not the kind of man to make them if they weren't.

A particular kind of atmospheric inversion had settled over the conference, in which petty and significant dissatisfactions alike rose in the way that they always had and always would in such a unique gathering—but they rose to an invisible ceiling and became trapped, and then amplified. By the last formal day of the conference, morale among the staff had plummeted; not since 1955, after Ted Morrison had resigned but before John Ciardi had accepted his draft, had morale been so low.

On the afternoon of August 31, conferees gathered in the Little Theatre for the final clinic—a traditionally wide-open session for the staff to consider questions not yet raised or answered. It began quietly; Sandy Martin, the moderator, was a man who valued consensus. But it grew acrimonious as John Ciardi took over to deflect, not address, complaints and suggestions from the audience. Much of the subject matter was petty—tinkering with the

schedule, making different use of various facilities, selling beer in the Barn snack bar—but then, after giving the audience reasons why they could not tinker, Ciardi began taking larger questions, and each was like a little detonating device hurled in his direction that set off his larger explosion.

Why could not auditors (who had not paid for private staff conferences) slip their manuscripts to teachers? "They shouldn't do that!" responded Ciardi. "I've made it a firm rule that no student may give a staff member a manuscript directly. They must all go through the office." The questioner did not want to get anyone in trouble, but he wondered: "What if they like you and *want* to read it?"

"You are trying to swindle the conference," said Ciardi. His usual commanding baritone took on a more imperious air. "Not of the money, I don't mean that. But of the teacher's time, which someone else has paid for." He paused, having made a valid point, and then went on. "I'm sorry, but it's necessary for me to growl a little. I must protect my staff from the *arm-grabbers.*" He pantomimed what arm-grabbers looked like and the audience did not enjoy seeing themselves portrayed that way. "They grab at you to read their manuscripts. They insist that you come to their readings." He went on, but his anger and frustration were losing him sympathy every second. A young long-haired waiter got up and quietly began to criticize the hierarchy. "It seems to me that nothing very worthwhile will ever happen here until you recognize that you have just as much to learn from me as I do from you." The young man had meant his point experientially, was expressing one of the most common tenets of sixties counterculture—but Ciardi took it in its narrowest sense. He was calm and quiet, but it was the calm and quiet of a man in a bar who, as he gets off his stool, is saying, 'What are *you* looking at?'

"You mean . . . that you know just as much about writing as I do?" The self-made poet who had risen all that way from the tough Medford streets of the Great Depression, whose family was now questioning his authority and his right to sit at the head of the Bread Loaf table, unpent his frustrations and launched into a tirade about the privileged and overencouraged generation. An astute observer would have seen it as symbolically directed at his own children, with whom he felt uneasy. It went on for some time. And then in front of the audience some of his staff members began to say that perhaps the young man was right in a way.

"At this point," recorded Rust Hills, whose account of this particular gathering jibes with others present, including the director (recalling it more than a decade later), "Ciardi waved the boy aside impatiently and indicated he should go back to his seat, which he did. Ciardi took full possession of the lectern, hunched forward over it, and

William Meredith discusses a conferee's poetry, early 1970s

began to speak seriously. 'What we have to teach you and you have to learn from us is technique,'" he said.

> I believe in the maestro system. To learn to write poetry you must learn to move easily in harness, to use Frost's metaphor. You must learn the discipline of the harness. Before you can fly a plane you need to know how to use the controls. Before you can play the piano you must practice the scales. This emphasis on learning the craft of writing has always been part of the Bread Loaf tradition. This conference has been going on for many years: it doesn't chop itself down and grow anew every year. Any apparent hierarchy at Bread Loaf is to some extent a sense of trusteeship. I feel I am trustee for a number of ghosts—Frost, Theodore Morrison, Bernard DeVoto, Fletcher Pratt, Joe Green, and there are others, but you won't have known them.

There was a long silence. A bearded student in a straw hat got up. "This is really just therapy for us, isn't it? All this letting us sound off? Nothing is going to change, is it?" Shane Stevens answered him: "It may be therapy for you,

but it's punishment for us. I move we adjourn."

And so they did.

That evening, nearly all of the staff drifted into Treman Cottage after their director delivered a reading of his own poetry. Everyone was sick, emotionally exhausted, and demoralized. Even Ciardi's closest friends recognized that something fundamental was wrong—but no one knew what could be done. When Ciardi came in to take his customary place at the window seat he was still in an angry mood. Before the others, he began to dress down Sandy Martin for a number of lapses, all mostly having to do with overencouragement of the overencouraged: "Goddamn kids with their over-positive assertions." After an argument, Martin left the cottage. Years of struggle with Ciardi had taken their toll. He resigned as assistant director. Independently, out of a sense of their own philosophical disagreement, William Meredith and Maxine Kumin also resigned.

In the aftermath, Middlebury College administrators tried to make sense of the resulting letters and reports on the 1971 session from many of those concerned. One conciliatory letter sent by Ciardi to President James Armstrong on September 1 praised Sandy Martin "for his superb handling of a vast number of details" but noted a "mutually respectful disagreement" that seemed to point to a parting; in Ciardi's mind, however, it was Martin who would go. Nonetheless, during the discussions, John Ciardi typed up a resignation letter that he left undated. "When you want it to be time," he said, "just fill in the date and I'll be gone."

Ironically, for almost as many years as he had been director he had been, in effect, protecting the conference in a time of changing social and political values so that Bread Loafers would be free to express themselves socially and politically; most administrations of any sort were slower to adapt to cultural changes and Middlebury was no exception. But—at the same time, Ciardi had absorbed the pressure from the same people he was protecting, who had no way of knowing that, on one level (perhaps just one), he was with them spiritually. But the times were complicated, and the conference was complicated, and the director was complicated. And rigid, especially in the sense of the times. Moreover, his was an absentee directorship for fifty weeks of the year, he had been abroad or on the lecture trail at inopportune times, and this had caused administrative problems. Ciardi did not expect his resignation to be accepted. But it was—an official flew down to New Jersey to deliver the letter and the news. There would be no possibility of completing, say, a three-year term, "to get things right." Ciardi would have the 1972 conference, his twenty-seventh, and then he would be replaced with a younger and more flexible administrator with a solid literary career and an address closer to Middlebury's Old Chapel: Robert Pack.

T he bitterness, however, would never go away, and shortly before the 1972 conference opened, Ciardi learned that his successor had reappointed Sandy Martin to be his assistant beginning in 1973. "When Sandy resisted my plans and did his best to take the conference in directions I thought would defeat its purpose," Ciardi wrote to Middlebury president James Armstrong on August 2,

I resisted him, explained the reasons for my resistance to you, and thought I had your understanding and approval. Your answer was to pick up my open resignation despite the fact that I had asked for a year or two in which to reset the switches Sandy had thrown open, and to put the conference back on what I thought was the right track. I made myself approve your decision, telling myself you had to keep in mind a college-wide range of

problems invisible to me. Now I learn—and from a news release—that Sandy has been reappointed to the conference as administrative director. I am left with a sense of having played a stupidly amateur role among professional politicians.

Hoping that Bob Pack would nonetheless remain true to the Bread Loaf mission, but anticipating in horror that "undergraduate types will have their soul sessions and their chance to pound a podium half the night," Ciardi made it clear he wanted "no ceremonial gestures in honor of my services to Bread Loaf."

And in many ways the 1972 conference was denouement to the foregoing drama. Probably as a measure of respect for the director, none of the changes he had resisted were enacted. William Sloane was dead, but John Ciardi had other friends with him: Miller Williams, Isaac Asimov, John Frederick Nims, Bill Lederer. Diane Wakoski returned, and Harry Crews, John Williams, and Robert Pack, whose sixth collection, *Nothing But Light,* was being published. In addition there was James Whitehead, poetry fellow in 1967; Robert Hayden, poet and editor of a collection of black American poetry; and Joy Anderson, an author of children's books. Replacing Sandy Martin as assistant director for the one session was Jonathan Aldrich. Among the fellows was novelist David Madden, writer-in-residence at Louisiana State University.

John Ciardi, near the end of his reign, early 1970s

With all of John Ciardi's feelings of nostalgia during that final conference being obvious to those around him, people expected a nostalgic reading of his poems on the evening of August 26—his elegies to Bernard DeVoto and Fletcher Pratt, his love poems to his wife Judith, his limericks, and new work, of course, from his autobiographical *Lives of X* (some of his greatest poems and, unaccountably, when published in 1972, ignored by critics). However, with all the sweep of his work, Ciardi could not resist showing his gall. He delivered one angry poem after another that seemed to float out to the uncomfortable audience and hang there, accusingly. Betrayal, after all, was not to be forgotten, nor betrayers forgiven.

The next day, however, *The Crumb* carried an announcement that had not been run in several years. Ted and Kay Morrison—who had been summer neighbors at the Homer Noble Farm during all the years since 1955, making friendly visits to various conference functions—were opening the Robert Frost cabin for visitors. A shuttle bus was to run continuously from the Inn's porch up to the farm. Such had been planned for days, but it came at a symbolic time; if indeed it was a reopening, then it was also a reaffirmation of the ghosts for whom Ciardi counted himself a steward. And when he stood at the Bread Loaf lectern for the last time, two days later, to deliver his farewell remarks, it was the expected nostalgic farewell, in which he invoked the names of Frost and DeVoto and Pratt and Mirrielees and recalled the golden times. For a number of years he had been working at a small poem that he could have offered. The title was "Exit Line":

> Love should intend
> realities. Goodbye.

Privately, to Robert Pack, he said: "I have nothing but high regard and friendship for you. It's your show now—I'll not be back." In a final letter to President Armstrong, Ciardi did not mince words when he piled the blame on his former assistant for plotting behind his back and "ousting me." But he was now satisfied that Pack, at least, would be a good guardian of the Bread Loaf ghosts. "It's in Bob Pack's hands now," he ended, "which is to say in good hands. Let time be joy when good men guard it."

THE PACK ERA BEGINS

Robert Pack had a habit of putting his hand on the shoulder of whomever he was talking to and an infectious cheeriness that put people at ease. The difference in personal style between him and his predecessor was remarkable, with Pack's seeming more in keeping with the times. When he was not among only his closest, most trusted friends, Ciardi had been ill-at-ease in small groups, holding forth rather than communicating, and there was a noticeable wall between him and strangers; behind a lectern he seemed most natural, addressing the sea of anonymous faces with the sight of a few reassuring islands of friends to touch upon. In contrast, Pack had a way of turning his entire attention to people and reaching out reassuringly, whether he was talking with a single person or addressing a throng. Both men had dramatic speaking voices—Ciardi's was imperious, Medford by way of Harvard, whereas Pack's rich and dark-toned voice with its tinges of New York sounded like one of the actors from Orson Welles's Mercury Theatre radio troupe.

Pack was the first Bread Loaf director to take up the reins joyfully since John Farrar had agreed to direct the conference in 1926. However, he knew there was a difficult transition ahead. To help in that transition he appointed Sandy Martin as his assistant director.

The faculty makeup and structure would have to be reappraised. Pack was determined to be more rigorous than his predecessor in choosing the Bread Loaf faculty; no longer would just friendship be the criterion for appointments—mandatory would be teaching ability, attainment

in the publishing world, and demonstrated respect for the less-accomplished writers, unpublished as well as published, whom Ciardi had always called "arm-grabbers." In the previous administration, problems had cropped up when standards were relaxed. William Sloane, who stayed at Bread Loaf for twenty-seven sessions because of his friendship with Ciardi, had dragged down the administrative machinery for years with last-minute scheduling demands and surprise visitors who needed accommodations. More serious still, he had alienated a number of valuable Bread Loaf teachers and used his access to Ciardi's ear to discourage other reappointments; also, though once a good teacher, Sloane's lectures began to fall into a rut as his utterances in manuscript clinics became more doctrinal. Knowing all this, however, Ciardi had refused to recognize it out of loyalty to his first publisher. As long as Sloane was alive, Ciardi would say, he had a place at Bread Loaf. But beyond this one example were others—teachers who were invited and reinvited but who could not teach, writers who had stopped actively publishing but continued to reappear on the Mountain, professionals who had nothing but scorn for amateurs and made no attempt to hide it—in each session they had been overshadowed by the talented and the committed, but they had, in some measure, held Bread Loaf down.

The conference Pack inherited went through a dramatic change that could be seen immediately in the 1973 session. Still in place was the hierarchy, or meritocracy, beginning with unpublished beginners and rising through the ranks of reward, recognition, and attainment—the system had developed through the Farrar, Gay, Morrison, and Ciardi years, and it was the Bread Loaf system. But it could be made palatable to those uncomfortable with lines drawn around them. Immediately, the dining hall was desegregated; faculty and fellows usually ate with one another, having personal and professional connections, but seldom *only* with one another. Arriving late to lunch or dinner from manuscript conferences or from the Treman cocktail hour, and with no reserved table for congregating, the staff members would filter osmotically through the crowded hall, finding empty places, reserving chairs for tardy friends, introducing themselves to those conferees already seated and talking with them. More all-conference social gatherings dotted the twelve-day schedule, and the once-annual tea or cocktail party gave way to events almost every other day. "The famous are friendly and grow modest," wrote tuition-paying poet Hilda Gregory. "They spread among us their cocktail stories. They read from their works, published and in progress, and gather us around them." (Later she would come as a scholar, still later as a fellow, and now Hilda Gregory is Hilda Raz of *Prairie Schooner*.) Readings of fellows took place during regular daylight hours; their books stood on the little bookstore's shelves. *The Crumb* announced open readings, which were held in "Quaker-style format"; a late-night women's workshop, featuring tapes of Doris Lessing speaking and Marge Piercy, Robin Morgan, Erica Jong, and others reading their poetry; and noted that a suggestion box had been put out by Pack and Martin for comments about curriculum, extracurricular activities, and organization, "or lack of it."

Harry Crews returned from Florida by way of the Appalachian Trail, having walked for two months from Georgia to Vermont. He told Bread Loafers that he had been chided by some critics for the bizarre characters and ridiculous or base events depicted in his novels. Deciding to get back in touch with the "real" America on his hike, Crews went looking for normal people. He encountered them in beautiful national parkland, people who watched television in their Winnebagos. He found a place where townspeople had lynched a circus elephant by a crane because it had stomped a child. On the Skyline Drive, Crews went to fill a water jug.

I heard this man say, "Son, git the club." I turned around real quick, and there was this man and this boy and this Japanese station wagon and the boy was getting a three-iron or whatever they call them out of the trunk. And that boy set a little golf ball on the edge of the stone wall of the scenic overlook there, the one where you see five bends of the Shenandoah River, and that boy hit that ball about, oh five thousand feet. He said they were

going to drive the full length of that highway in the sky, and they'd stop at every scenic overlook and take turns hitting balls off the edge.

After two months with all those normal people, Crews said, "it's kind of a nice change to get to Bread Loaf." "He looked very much the pirate that summer," recalled Dan Johnson, a waiter, "and arrived tan and lean for volleyball with earring and moustaches intact." His novel *The Hawk Is Dying* appeared that year.

The Morrisons and the Cubetas paid visits, which gave the conference a feeling of support and continuity. Maxine Kumin returned for more readings and workshops and mushrooms and could be seen scribbling her poems on the backs of directives and old copies of *The Crumb*. Seymour Epstein also returned. Anne Sexton appeared for several days, her voice "gravelly and bewitching and dramatic" in her reading (according to fellow Katie Lyle), although to an old friend, poet Anthony Hecht, "she seemed very remote, and a trifle haughty, and seemed to regard herself as a rather fragile superstar who had to be handled with kid gloves." Of course, to her closer friend and confidante Maxine Kumin, Sexton was not cool; it was the last time Hecht would see Anne Sexton alive. She would commit suicide in 1974.

Inevitably there would be new faces on the faculty, and Anthony Hecht, forty-year-old author of four collections of formal and philosophical poems, translator of Aeschylus, and winner of many awards, including a Pulitzer, was not alone in his newness. There was Mark Strand, thirty-nine, of Princeton, also with four collections—his of dramatic and surreal poetry that critics did not always understand but had to admire—and some translations of Mexican poetry. Blessed (or cursed) with strikingly good, Charlton Heston looks, he was always "surrounded by thin girls with swinging blonde hair," wrote fellow Katie Lyle. "He smiles without a break." The elegant prose writer Lore Segal, with her grinning Viennese ways, was there; and the bearded, affable George P. Elliott, novelist and poet; journalist Walter Goodman, who had written about the fifties' witch hunts; and novelist Vance Bourjaily, who had managed, book by book, to speak to each succeeding chapter of American cultural history—from the Second World War to the nuclear age, from the Kennedy administration to the swinging sixties. His most recent book was *Brill Among the Ruins* (1970), about the sixties' effect on a middle-aged man. Bourjaily at Bread Loaf provided a nice symmetry for Bob Pack; his old friend had published his first verse in *Discovery* and arranged for Pack's first book to appear. He was currently working on an updated Americanized version of *The Canterbury Tales*. Of his talk, Hilda Gregory recorded: "We sit still as Vance Bourjaily tells us of the fall of Biafra, he and Vonnegut escaping by plane over the black men who die helping them."

Finally, there was the poet Marvin Bell—a wispy-bearded, hip cherub in a feed cap. Actually, he did not arrive with a Blue Seal Feeds cap, but during a Bread Loaf doubles tennis match in 1973, his partner, poet Peter Sears, lent him his to ward off the sun; it looked so good on Bell that he was allowed to keep it. He became so identified with Blue Seal over the years that he could have charged the company a fee, or at least a bag of oats every once in a while. At thirty-six, Marvin Bell defied categorizing, so different were his three collections of witty, deceptively simple free verse, *Things We Dreamt We Died For* (1966), *A Probable Volume of Dreams* (1969), and *The Escape into You* (1971); his next work, *Residue of Song,* was due to be published in 1974. His development over a relatively short period of time, though, had been noted by critics who appreciated his restless need to strike out for new poetic territory and his willingness to build himself anew in the process. Bell's influence on poets, particularly the emergent, would be wide—through his teaching, his many essays appearing in *The American Poetry Review,* and his many readings and lectures around the nation. Awards, grants, prizes, and fellowships would be his for the taking.

Having heard about Bread Loaf since he was a young man on the south shore of Long Island, Bell had driven over from Goddard College, where he was teaching while on leave from the Iowa Writers' Workshop, for a half-day in 1972 to look the place over; he met Bob Pack, they were familiar with each other's work, and over the winter Pack invited him back to Bread Loaf. When he arrived, he was immediately struck by the change in atmosphere: It was freer and in his eyes seemed more rife with possibility. But he tried to go to every reading and lecture and party, got worn down, and caught a virus from Harry Crews, who had brought the illness up from somewhere along the Appalachian Trail. After Bell had been bedridden at Maple Cottage for two or three days, Pack sent him off to the community hospital in Middlebury. It was the summer of the Watergate hearings—and Bell, as he was being bundled off the Mountain, yelled out in Nixonian tones, "You won't have Marvin Bell to kick around anymore!" He spent two nights getting his strength back—it was his first time in a hospital. In his absence, Bell's classes were conducted by poetry fellows Calvin Forbes, Karen Swenson, and Lawrence Raab (a former Middlebury student of Bob Pack's). With these emerging writers' help, thirty orphan poetry students had been given their tuitions' worth and the Bread Loaf mechanism had gone on working. Perhaps this was the birth of the idea of a new tier of faculty—a new wrinkle in the meritocracy: Using the younger published writers to better effect would make it possible to

John Gardner, 1975 (EB)

expand the conference while making the inhumane work load of reading and commenting on individual manuscripts a little less exhausting.

The conference of 1974 opened on Tuesday, August 13, without the presence of new faculty addition John Gardner, forty-one-year-old novelist and phenomenon. Several days went by with no word, and no one at his home at Carbondale, Illinois, had any idea where he could be reached. General panic: What to do with empty time slots for lectures, workshops, and readings, and with orphaned student fiction writers? When Gardner did appear, it was at the wheel of a new Mercedes, his long white hair streaming out the window as he eased the car to a stop in front of the Inn. He had just earned a fortune on a new contract or subsidiary rights deal and had bought the luxury car to convey his wife, Joan, and children from Southern Illinois by way of Canada. Anthony Hecht, who had returned for the session, recalled what happened next. "Only a few days after his arrival, he all but totalled the car one night when driving drunkenly with his wife." Despite the adventure, Gardner immediately fit into the Bread Loaf scene. It seemed like he had always been there, that he had been *born* on the Mountain.

Actually from Batavia, New York, Gardner was the son of a dairy farmer and a former schoolteacher—two learned and restless characters who preached, quoted Shakespeare, sang spirituals, and made up stories that they told to their farmer-neighbors at regular grange meetings. Young John

Gardner also grew to be a storyteller; in between chores he wrote poems about farm life and read his melodramatic tales to his bedridden grandmother, to his brothers, and to the numbers of foster children whom the Gardners took in. When he went off to school at DePauw University in Indiana it was to study chemistry. But he fell in with a bohemian crowd and got interested in literature and philosophy. Shortly he transferred to Washington University in St. Louis, where he continued to write fiction and developed a strong interest in Nietzsche. An essay on the philosopher won Gardner a fellowship to study at the newly formed Iowa Writers' Workshop. However, he didn't like the work of his fellow students and dropped out of the workshop and into the Ph.D. program to study medieval literature.

After receiving his Ph.D., he taught for one year at Oberlin and for three at Chico State College in California. One of his favorite writing students was Raymond Carver. "Gardner had a crewcut, dressed like a minister or an FBI man, and went to church on Sundays," wrote Carver.

But he was unconventional in other ways. He started breaking the *rules* on the first day of class; he was a chain smoker and he smoked continuously in the classroom, using a metal wastebasket for an ashtray. In those days, nobody smoked in a classroom. When another faculty member who used the same room reported on him, Gardner merely remarked to us on the man's pettiness and narrow-mindedness, opened windows, and went on smoking.

In Gardner's class students were expected to write one short story or one chapter of a novel—but then they were to revise it about ten times. "It was a basic tenet of his that a writer found what he wanted to say in the ongoing process of *seeing* what he said," recalled Carver. "And this seeing, or seeing more clearly, came about through revision." He referred so much to writers whom his students had never heard of that they were forced to go out and discover those whom Gardner liked. He published a number of these writers in a little magazine he founded called *MSS*. Still unpublished himself, he had completed a number of novels that piled up in his college office.

Not until 1970 did the floodgates begin to open as books he had already completed, long gathering dust, began to find homes. Gardner was teaching at Southern Illinois University when he published his first book, *The Wreckage of Agathon*, set in ancient Greece. In 1971 there was *Grendel*—the Beowulf poem told from the monster's viewpoint, a tour de force about the struggle between good and evil, which firmly established the author's reputation; it was named one of the year's best novels by *Time* and *Newsweek*. The next year saw the publication of *The Sunlight Dialogues*, a sprawling, magical story set in Gardner's hometown, which made the best-seller lists. After his next book, the unsuccessful epic verse *Jason and Medeia*, Gardner recovered his standing with a pastoral novel, *Nickel Mountain* (1973) and a short story collection, *The King's Indian* (1974).

At Bread Loaf Gardner seemed to sleep almost not at all; instead he stayed up most of the night in deep, almost ecstatic literary chatter with Bill Gass and Sy Epstein and with any number of enchanted fellows. He took on more manuscripts from conferees than assigned—and could be seen huddled over them in the Barn, the air murky with his pipe smoke. His reading was universally well received—and although some of those in his lecture audience found it unfocused and impromptu, others scribbled madly, trying to keep up with him, and wandered off in little groups to chew over what he had said. In short, Gardner did what he would become famous for at Bread Loaf for the next eight years.

Two other new Bread Loafers rounded out a faculty of returnees from the previous year: Rosellen Brown, prose and poetry writer, and Mona Van Duyn, who was then already author of five poetry collections and winner of the Bollingen Prize and the National Book Award. Van Duyn came to Bread Loaf not knowing what to expect from it, and during her evening reading on August 21, she got a shock. After she started, a bat flew into the Little Theatre and began swooping over the audience in its effort to escape. Entire rows began ducking, men and women alike covering their heads. Van Duyn saw and heard the clamor and, as she continued to read her poetry, tried to look past the glare of the spotlight to see what was going on. All she could see was ducking and veering heads. She obviously thought that people were registering disapproval with her reading. Finally, from the back of the hall, Mark Strand called out: "Mona, it's a *bat!*" Mona thought that she was being called a bat, and she glared. As the tumult continued, Anthony Hecht called for someone to open the doors and turn out the lights. Despite many objections from those who did not want to sit in a darkened theatre with a swooping bat, the lights were turned off and Mona forged ahead in the darkness. With the bat either quietly listening in the gloom of rafters or departed for other territory, the rest of her reading was, in the words of several who were there, "magical."

Two writers of the eleven holding fellowships bear scrutiny here because of the deep friendship that developed between them and because of their subsequent Bread Loaf longevity: novelist Hilma Wolitzer and poet Linda Pastan. In the four years since her scholarship and her uncomfortable, unapproached hour at Treman Cottage, Hilma Wolitzer had published a number of stories and completed

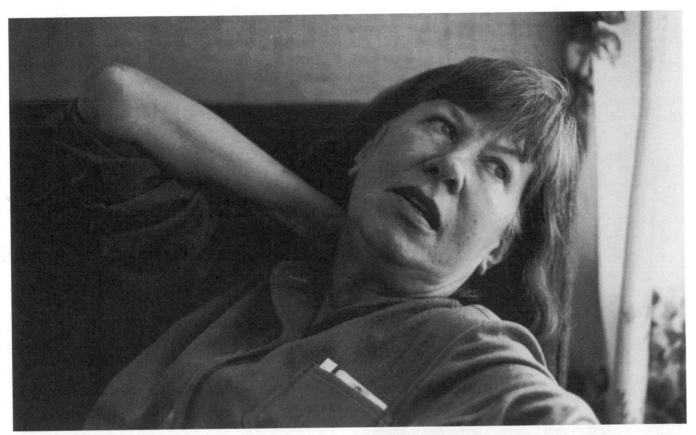

Mona Van Duyn, 1974 (EB)

Linda Pastan, 1975 (EB)

her first novel, *Endings,* which was published just before she arrived at Bread Loaf in 1974. Her hallmate in the gabled Cherry Cottage turned out to be poetry fellow Linda Pastan, whose *A Perfect Circle of Happiness* appeared that year. Pastan had been a high school student at the Fieldston School three years behind Robert Pack; she had only known him as a distant football star. Later a student of May Sarton's at Radcliffe, Pastan won the 1955 *Mademoiselle* college poetry contest (edging out Sylvia Plath). She married while in school, and after graduation she stopped writing for more than ten years, not wanting to deflect her attention from her scientist husband and children. Not until she was in her thirties did Pastan return to her poetry and begin publishing it. A small press in Chicago, Swallow, kept her book-length collection for two years. When she went up to Chicago for a wedding, Pastan went over to the office and asked for her manuscript. The editor said, "Give me six more months and I'll let you know if we can publish it." She said no, she just wanted it back—and he replied, "Okay, okay, we'll publish it."

At Bread Loaf, Wolitzer and Pastan found that they had much in common beyond being some years older than the other fellows: They had started writing late, after their families were well under way, and they had both found their independence and identities from their work; like Wolitzer in 1970, Pastan had her first "room of one's own" under the eaves at Bread Loaf. Also, the two would, with Robert Pack's active encouragement, continue to publish and continue to return to Bread Loaf in a steady rise through the ranks: For three years they would serve in the new junior faculty tier, afterward becoming steady presences in Bread Loaf's senior faculty.

Readings bloomed in 1974 like never before. Faculty read. Fellows read. Scholars read. Waiters read. Conferees read. The official day began just after breakfast and went to past midnight. It was exhausting—but the multiplicity of voices and points of view was also exhilarating. No one wanted to miss anything. During the past administration, John Ciardi had liked to quip that you had to have the constitution of a water buffalo to try to attend all of Bread Loaf's functions. He strongly recommended that no one try. Now, with Pack and Martin, even a water buffalo would have been thoroughly exhausted.

I n 1974 Robert Pack gave a reading at the University of Iowa and afterward attended a party in his honor at Marvin and Dorothy Bell's home. There Bell introduced him to two Iowa colleagues whom Pack would subsequently invite to teach at Bread Loaf beginning in 1975—poet Donald Justice and novelist John Irving. They would return to the Mountain again and again. From Miami, soft-spoken Donald Justice had studied at the universities of Miami, North Carolina, and Iowa and also at Stanford with Yvor Winters, Karl Shapiro, John Berryman, and Robert Lowell. He had produced five collections of elegant, pared-down verse and won a number of awards and fellowships, many more of which (including a Pulitzer) would come his way in due time.

In 1975 John Irving, rugged, compact, and thirty-three, was a largely unknown author of three good novels. He had enjoyed respectful critical attention but very sparse sales, had received a couple of good-sized grants, and would likely have been consigned to the publishing purgatory of the "mid-list," where books are allowed to live or die with no aid or encouragement from their publishers, and where the future is usually ever-declining sales and royalty advances, were it not for the novel he had started two years before. He had titled it *The World According to Garp.* Its subsequent rocketing success in 1978, with sales of well over three million in hardcover and paperback, would change the way the world perceived John Irving.

Born in Exeter, New Hampshire, the son of a teacher, Irving grew up at and graduated from Phillips Exeter Academy. In succession he attended the University of

Donald Justice, 1975 (EB)

Pittsburgh, the University of Vienna, the Institute of European Studies (Vienna), and the University of New Hampshire—from which he finally graduated cum laude. In between his studies, Irving worked as an orchardman, a bartender, a translator, and a referee of collegiate wrestling matches—a fitting variety for an aspiring writer. Then he did graduate work in writing at the University of Iowa, followed by teaching posts at tiny Windham College in Vermont and at Mount Holyoke in Massachusetts, then did a writing residency at Iowa. During these early years of his career he published *Setting Free the Bears* (1969), *The Water-Method Man* (1972), and The 158-Pound Marriage (1974), all funny, picaresque, language-loving novels with a macabre edge to them.

So, when he arrived at Bread Loaf with a relatively small part of his new manuscript completed, Irving knew that *The World According to Garp* would be longer and more complicated than anything he'd previously tried, and he was not really sure how it was going to fit together or indeed if it ever would. "It was a big undertaking what with full-time teaching and coaching responsibilities,"

Irving said. "It was put together piece-meal over a long period of time in every which way, all out of order," with many false starts and narrative culs-de-sac that were discarded after much consideration. At Bread Loaf over a period of three years, 1975–1977, Irving discovered his first real audience—"I don't mean the audience in the little theatre, clapping, but the other writers, the faculty, fellows, and scholars. It was on a level with getting my first novel published. In those years the obvious excitement from the people at Treman to that work-in-progress was central, a real confidence giver—especially from Bob Pack, whose support of my work I took very personally." Other Bread Loafers present during the period recalled Irving's readings from *Garp* and also his lectures—in which he often used portions of the developing manuscript to make points about the problems a writer faces—and they reported a similar excitement of discovery as they heard the novel progress over those years as it moved toward what everyone hoped would be success.

A strikingly similar story also began in 1975 with the appearance of a twenty-eight-year-old fellow in fiction, Tim O'Brien. Born in Minnesota and educated at Macalester College, O'Brien had enlisted in the U.S. Army in the summer of 1968, though he was anything but gung-ho soldier material; in fact, he was against the war, but after much soul-searching he could not accept any alternative to going. So he went to Vietnam. His experiences as a foot soldier in that horrifying war informed all of his subsequent work. After the war, while working as a national affairs reporter for the *Washington Post,* O'Brien began writing several nonfiction sketches about his experiences, piling them up without thinking of publishing them. Then, he sent them off to Knopf, but that publisher had just signed up a journalist named Michael Herr to do a series of nonfiction sketches about covering the war, and it did not want to go too far out on a limb with another book on the same subject. War books were being routinely refused in those days by most publishers; no one could determine how to publish them successfully. Knopf suggested that the independent-minded Seymour Lawrence might be interested, as well he was. The sketches of *If I Die in a Combat Zone* were published in 1973; his first novel, *Northern Lights* (1974), about a returned Vietnam veteran and his relationship with his brother, followed. By then O'Brien had studied government in the Harvard graduate program. By the time he reached Bread Loaf in 1975, O'Brien had begun a similarly new and agonizing work that, like Irving's, was taking him in unfamiliar literary directions. The novel would be called *Going After Cacciato,* a magical narrative of a Vietnam platoon and the lengths to which the soldiers must go to psychically survive—probably the best novel to emerge from the Vietnam

War. Until its publication in 1978, O'Brien would feel his way along, trying much and discarding many pages, all the while sharing a sense of discovery and progress with his annual audience of fellow writers. As with Irving, O'Brien would feel sustained as he followed his own solitary path toward completion and would draw inspiration from his colleagues. The first reading he attended in 1975 was William Meredith's—"it was magical and dignified," he recalled, "it showed the infinite possibilities of literature," and it implicitly connected O'Brien, as listener and as writer, with literature's traditions. Despite doubtlessly well-meaning but misplaced advice from his first manuscript reader, George P. Elliott, to "drop the fantasy parts" in *Cacciato,* John Gardner and Seymour Epstein urged O'Brien to continue. Gardner took him under his wing at Treman Cottage, holding forth for hours on subjects with which O'Brien was marginally familiar. There were times in the bleary early hours of the morning when he wondered if Gardner himself knew quite what he was saying—but it didn't matter. Standing at a lectern to read his prose to the

Tim O'Brien, 1975 (EB)

assembly, feeling it necessary to take chances with work he was still polishing and considering, O'Brien found that time vanished as he was buoyed upward by the feeling of community. "It was a generosity of spirit," he recalled, "that went beyond the goodness or badness of what I was reading." Bread Loafers were celebrating the *process* of writing. At Pack's invitation O'Brien would return in 1976 as a teaching assistant to serve alongside Pastan, Wolitzer, and Raab; half a year before *Going After Cacciato* won a National Book Award in 1979 and proved to a fainthearted and jaded New York publishing community that books about Vietnam could succeed, Pack presciently invited him back as a senior faculty member

In retrospect, one of the striking qualities of the conference in the first seven years of Pack's directorship, through 1979, was the prescience of his administration in selecting faculty and in awarding fellowships and scholarships to emerging writers. John Irving and Tim O'Brien, young and little-known writers when they found the encouragement of a community of their peers at Bread Loaf, are only two of many examples, especially in terms of writers being on the brink of breaking through into new literary territory and, at the same time, commercial success. Not all of the others returned for other conferences, but a number did.

One was Toni Morrison, a faculty member in 1976 and 1977. When she first went up to the Mountain, Morrison was an editor at Random House and the author of two critically well-regarded novels, *The Bluest Eye* (1970), published when she was thirty-nine, and *Sula* (1974), which had been nominated for the National Book Award. She had just completed her third, *Song of Solomon,* which would be her breakthrough; released in the fall of 1977, it would win the fiction awards of the National Book Critics' Circle and the American Academy and Institute of Arts and Letters and would secure her a large and devoted reading audience. It has been said that after her two sessions at Bread Loaf, Morrison came away wishing for a more racially and ethnically diverse population among the conferees—a wish echoed over the years by many other conferees and by the Pack administration itself, although no large strides were made until more than a decade later. But the impression left behind by Toni Morrison as a teacher and a reader was overwhelmingly positive: She was a well-prepared and eloquent lecturer and, on the reading platform, a dramatic performer of *Song of Solomon.* "She whispered, she shouted," recalled Hilma Wolitzer. "It was a stunning performance which, when it ended, left us in awed silence for a few seconds—before everyone leaped up for a standing ovation."

Another was Geoffrey Wolff, thirty-nine, who taught in 1976 for the first of five sessions. A former book editor for the *Washington Post* and *Newsweek,* Wolff was the author of two well-regarded but commercially overlooked novels and one other to be released to much the same attention the following year. August 1976 saw the publication of his engrossing biography of a tragic but very minor literary figure of the 1920s, *Black Sun: The Brief Transit and Violent Eclipse of Harry Crosby.* For his readings between 1976 and 1979, Wolff turned to the manuscript of a memoir of his con-artist father, "a bad man and a good father," *The Duke of Deception* (1979). It was a work of courage and intelligence, beautifully rendered, and when published it found him a vast audience. In Marvin Bell's recollection, Wolff's first reading from *The Duke of Deception* was terribly moving, and not just because it involved powerful material from the author's emotional attic. Wolff was encumbered with a stutter that, under the right stress, could paralyze his words right in his mouth. But, as Bell recalled, Wolff delivered his reading with a forthright acknowledgment that there might be slow going ahead. His wife and sons were sitting in the audience. What ensued was indeed slow and even painful at times, but it was an affirmation of the author's considerable strengths and of the feeling of support he derived from family, friends, and colleagues in a new situation, entering new literary territory.

There was another time at the lectern, Wolff recalled, that was memorable in a different way:

> Performing at Bread Loaf with graphic passion from a novel that explores, among other ailments, gangrene ("Fistulas had been attached to the dying man's legs . . . and peccant humor trickled through these glass elbow-pipes and dripped into white ceramic troughs. . . . The juice that drained from his wounds was dark, like molasses, or"—as I added in an intimate aside to the audience—"*Vermont maple syrup*"), I saw people stand, indeed, to "drip" away. One, just clear of the auditorium, threw noisily up.

The list of fellows and scholars who appeared in the mid- to late 1970s is hard to condense. There was Richard Ford, whose tough, absorbing first novel, *A Piece of My Heart,* was published the year he had a fellowship, in 1976; by the time the Mississippian's second novel was published (*The Ultimate Good Luck,* 1981), Ford was gone from the Mountain, but he served on the Bread Loaf junior faculty in 1977 and 1978 and left good memories of his teaching and collegiality. A friend of Ford's from the 1976 fellows roster was Terrence Des Pres, a rigorous critic and author of a book on survivors of the Holocaust, who also moved up to the junior faculty, where he served between 1977 and 1979 and sporadically into the eighties until his untimely death.

Terrence Des Pres, 1977 (EB)

With his shades and neatly trimmed beard and motorcycle jockey ways, Des Pres was "a philosopher in a black leather jacket," in Marvin Bell's memory. During his tenure he lent an intellectual rigor and a political urgency to the nonfiction sections at Bread Loaf, as well as a loose, iconoclastic presence on a faculty that, as always, tried not to take itself too seriously but occasionally strayed. Often Des Pres and John Gardner could be seen monkeying with their respective high-powered motorcycles, their conversation easily bouncing back and forth from RPMs to literature and philosophy. It was with Des Pres that Linda Pastan took her only hundred-mile-an-hour motorcycle ride on a back-country road somewhere on the Bread Loaf plateau. Another fellow in 1976, and subsequently a close friend of Des Pres, was the gifted, intense poet Carolyn Forché, who had risen through the Bread Loaf ranks from waiting on the Ciardi-era faculty dining table. She would later return in the eighties to teach on the junior faculty. Forché, whose later poetry would limn the climate of brutality in El Salvador and our nation's complicity in making it possible,

is chiefly remembered by 1976 conferees by her long absences. It was there that she met poetry fellow David St. John, who was also rarely seen during the proceedings. At least one faculty member received a giggling phone call from the pair shortly after the conference was over; they announced with great certitude that they had run away together—but that particular relationship did not, in fact, last long.

Other emerging poets who appeared in the late 1970s and returned for some years thereafter were Sydney Lea, Tess Gallagher, Carol Frost (married to 1961 poetry fellow Richard Frost), Carole Oles, Pamela Hadas, and Julia Alvarez. Prose writers included Larry Heinemann, James Atlas, Susan Shreve, and four others who would become regular faculty members during the following decade: David Huddle, Ron Hansen, Robert Houston, and Ron Powers.

During this same period the faculty became almost semipermanent. Meanwhile, their own off-the-Mountain careers seemed quite expansive. John Gardner won a 1976 National Book Critics' Circle Award for his novel *October Light*; he published the opinion-laden treatise *On Moral Fiction* (1978), which castigated most of his contemporaries (including friends and colleagues) for not writing enough morality into their novels, a charge that made him the target of much of the literary establishment's ire; and he released a critical biography of Chaucer, the reception of which was dimmed by complaints that not all of his scholarship was original. Stanley Elkin returned to Bread Loaf in 1976 after a dozen years' absence, with three brilliant novels to show for his time: *A Bad Man* (1967); the surreal, hilarious novel about talk radio, *The Dick Gibson Show* (1971); and *The Franchiser,* about a wheeler-dealer businessman. Elkin would teach at Bread Loaf through 1978 and return for four sessions in the 1980s. Over the years in Treman Cottage, he found himself carrying on a delightfully contentious dialogue with John Gardner that somehow combined respect for each other's individualism and disdain for each other's work. To younger writers sitting literally at their feet, their conversations were Olympian as they hurled thunderbolts at each other with sardonic grins on their faces.

Among the oft-returning poets was Marvin Bell, marathon runner in Honolulu and Boston, who published three praised collections in the 1970s; Maxine Kumin, mushroom maven, who followed her Pulitzer Prize–winning *Up Country: Poems of New England* (1972) with two other collections and a novel; Mark Strand, tennis player during colleagues' readings and lectures, who published five collections of poetry during the decade; Linda Pastan, with three, including the award-winning *The Five Stages of Grief* (1978); Howard Nemerov, back in 1978 after fourteen years but thereafter planted on the faculty for six sessions, with three volumes of essays, four new poetry collections, and one-half of the Bollingen Prize; returning 1957 poetry fellow May Swenson, with the other half of the Bollingen, working on her sixth book; Donald Justice, with two more collections and a Pulitzer; William Meredith, with two new volumes; and of course Robert Pack, with two new books and another on the way. To this roster in 1978 came drawling, loose-limbed Stanley Plumly, author of four collections and winner of a number of awards.

It was a solid, distinguished corps neatly augmenting the prose writers, Gardner, Elkin, O'Brien, Segal, and Elliott. To that group came Gail Godwin; former fiction fellow David Madden; and the prolific, pacific, wide-ranging Nancy Willard, writer of novels, short stories, poems, and children's stories, all of which drew upon magic and mythology. Willard, with her flowing blond hair and fairy's eyes, always clad in almost medieval costume, lent a certain ethereal air to Bread Loaf. She sparkled—from glittering jewelry in which unicorns and moons figured prominently. Once Marvin Bell encountered her in the hall of Maple Cottage and paused to admire her tiny antique perfume flagon hanging on a gold necklace. Smiling slyly, Willard unscrewed the cap. She had drilled a minuscule hole in the end of the perfume dipper. The flagon was filled with water and soap, not perfume, and in the hallway of Maple she blew tiny bubbles all around Marvin Bell.

One of the hallmarks of the 1970s, from the perspective of many returning faculty, was the presence of children on the Mountain; all previous directors had actively discouraged faculty members from bringing their children, although of course the young Morrisons and Ciardis were in attendance. Pack, though, made it a point to extend his invitations to as many family members as could be accommodated. Fortunately, in the 1970s Middlebury College began to acquire additional properties on the Bread Loaf plateau, making housing less of a limitation than previously. As a result the children of the Packs, the Martins, the Hechts, Gardners, Irvings, Elkins, Pastans, and Wolffs added their voices to the din in the dining room, and their own anecdotes to the annals of Bread Loaf.

A few will suffice. For several years Bernie Elkin cornered the market in five-cent-deposit aluminum cans, going so far as to pay younger children three cents for the ones they found and pocketing his commission. His younger sister Molly volunteered to help the social staff during a Barn dance; helpfully, she began setting up new drinks by retrieving almost-empty plastic cups from around the Barn and pouring the flat, forgotten beer into new cups—which the sweaty dancers downed without noticing or missing a beat. Once, little Brendan Irving

disappeared from the dining room at dinner and could not be found in the usual postprandial gathering places—on the front porch of the Inn or on the meadow side of the old stone wall across the road. Finally, as time drew near for the evening's reading (it would be John Irving's), search parties began to form. Then, someone discovered young Brendan—sitting quietly alone in the first row of the dim and empty theatre, waiting for his father's reading to begin. Another year, Nancy Willard's young son, James Lindbloom, decided he was going to be a writer like his mother. But where to begin? He decided to copy a phrase out of one of her books, at the beginning, in fact, and showed his first line to his mother and to Hilma Wolitzer. It was this: "All rights reserved."

Anecdotes and vignettes from the 1970s rise like the little yeast bubbles in bread dough: John Irving and Marvin Bell doing as credibly as runners ten or fifteen years their junior in the annual Robert Frost runners' marathon (a contest conceived by Bell and Gary Margolis), cruelly held on the Sunday morning after a late-night Barn dance; in contrast, the nonrunners, such as unathletic John Gardner, with his capacious belly and pipe smoker's lungs, or Stanley Elkin, leaning on the canes or the walker that multiple sclerosis forced him to rely on, joking about his "manuscript disease," MS; John Gardner, staying up late for the brilliant Treman conversation and afterward even later to read his students' manuscripts. He could usually be found around 2:00 or 3:00 A.M. sitting on a straight-backed chair out in the hall of Maple Cottage so he would not wake up his wife by turning on a reading light in their room. Once, as a preface to an evening reading, he enlisted Nancy Willard and Hilma Wolitzer to join him in singing a rousing Irish nuisance song. Another time, not being in the mood to read from one of his books, he composed a radio play with parts for a good proportion of the faculty. Children were to sit on the stage apron and perform the sound effects. Beforehand, Hilma Wolitzer asked Gardner what she should wear for her part. "Hilma," he replied, "this is a *radio play*!" So she appeared in jeans and a hooded sweatshirt, her curly hair standing up in an Afro. But when the radio dialogue between Gardner and Wolitzer called for him to exclaim, "Madame, your hair . . . your gown!" the audience drowned his words with their laughter.

Once Marvin Bell was addressing the assembly when the Martins' Irish setter somehow wandered through an open door into the dim backstage area, where risers had been piled up so that they pressed against the drawn curtains. The dog ascended them—and curiously poked his head between the curtains. The audience, watching Bell as he read and talked, suddenly saw a disembodied dog's head poke out between the curtains about six feet above the stage. They instantly dissolved into hysterical laughter. Bell looked up fast from his notes, at first not understanding what was going on, but when he saw where people were looking he whirled around to see who was behind him. But the dog was too fast for him and had vanished. Shrugging, Bell tried to carry on. But the dog looked out again, disappearing just as Bell whirled around.

And there was one of many Bread Loafer jokes of the late seventies: "How many Bread Loafers does it take to change a flat tire?" "Two hundred and twenty—two hundred and nineteen to fix its place in the cosmos, and one to call a gas station."

It would be in 1978 that Robert Pack announced an important change in his staff. After serving two three-year terms as his Bread Loaf assistant, his Middlebury colleague Sandy Martin would be replaced. Undeniably, philosophical differences had arisen over that period with regard to staffing and scheduling, but the differences (as opposed to those during the previous administration) had been aired openly and without much apparent acrimony. In the director's mind, it was simply time for a change, for consolidation, for a different kind of energy in the Bread Loaf office. His choice for a new assistant director would be the congenial Californian Stanley Bates, a philosophy professor at Middlebury who was also well-versed in contemporary American literature. The replacement, which took effect beginning with the 1979 conference, did not go down easy with at least two longtime Bread Loafers—Maxine Kumin and William Meredith—who announced that they would retire from the Mountain rather than see Bread Loaf without their friend of ten years. In total, Martin had managed the administrative side for fifteen years, some of the most difficult and some of the most exhilarating sessions in Bread Loaf's history. It is a measure of how well a conference is run when the business and the administration of admitting conferees, collecting their money, scheduling activities, and dealing with the multitude of problems recede to the point almost of invisibility; to most Bread Loafers, the smoothly running Sandy Martin years would be replaced by the smoothly running Stanley Bates years—in no small part due to the diligence of secretary Carol Knauss, who worked for both. But the loss of Maxine Kumin and William Meredith as the inspiring teachers and readers they were was more public, and keener, and it was lastingly felt.

In the first seven years of his directorship, Robert Pack presided over a Bread Loaf that had steadily enlarged in size and scope. The new tier of associate teachers swelled the faculty to about twenty-five and made it possible for the conference to handle twice as many conferees' manuscripts. For some five decades, each director and his staff had wished to admit more writers carrying manuscripts with them but could not, then felt obliged to fill vacancies with auditors up for a vacation, no matter how literary their interests. Now, with an expanded faculty, it became possible to alter the proportions within the student body. When the number of auditors was thus allowed to sharply decline, it could truly be said that *everyone* on the Mountain was a writer. The new faculty tier also deepened the impression of talent encouraged and merit recognized—again and again, situations could be found in which, over time and through publication, waiters had returned as administrative scholars, conferees as scholars, scholars as fellows, fellows as staff associates, staff associates as faculty, and faculty as, well, senior faculty.

The change in atmosphere was noticeable to anyone who had been present in earlier administrations, as if the air was richer in oxygen and in more highly charged ions. Also perceptible was a more even level of excellence among those receiving aid. Beginning in 1973, in place of a few people making decisions about awarding aid and bestowing recognition upon emerging writers (sometimes to war buddies, former students, children of friends, lovers), there developed a committee system of judges to select from a greatly enlarged pool of applicants. Even under such a system, favoritism and inside tracking could not be eliminated, but it was greatly diluted. Moreover, Pack's assiduous fundraising made financial aid more widely available, raising the average number of fellowships and scholarships to thirty-two, which augmented the thirty-five working scholarships that already existed.

Bread Loaf was still the oldest writers' conference in the country, and sometimes it seemed like the largest, though personal attention was still highly prized—but one of its secret strengths from the 1970s on was that almost half of its two hundred and more attendees were published writers or (in the case of the working scholars) by dint of talent clearly destined for it. The experience and the dialogue made possible under such circumstances could be duplicated nowhere else in the world.

1980 Fellows: (rear) James Bowden, William Davis, David Martin, Paul Mariani, Stephen Tapscott; (center) Nancy Thayer, Susan Wood, Marcia Southwick, Deborah Clifford, Suzanne Berger, Stephanie Tolan, Patricia Baehr; (seated) Michael Blumenthal, Judy Mearian, Mary Morris, David Bain (EB)

FIRST PERSON

In the late spring of 1980, I was going over the galleys of my first book in my dim New York apartment when I received a call from Carol Knauss, secretary of the Bread Loaf Writers' Conference in Vermont. My agent, Ellen Levine, had nominated me for a fellowship several months before; I'd sent in the requested manuscript and backup material and thought nothing more about it until Carol's call.

Of course, I'd heard of the conference. My English teacher in junior high school had been a great admirer of Robert Frost, and he often talked about Frost and Bread Loaf that year, 1962–1963, during half of which Robert Frost was still alive. I don't think my teacher had ever attended the conference, but his enthusiasm for the depth and the music of Frost's poetry allowed him to overlook our horrid memorized renditions of "Stopping by Woods" and "The Road Not Taken." Any place where the poet had camped out for thirty years of his life had to be hallowed ground.

Ten years later, when toiling away in the lower editorial echelons of Alfred A. Knopf, I seized every opportunity to write jacket flap copy and author notes for Knopf books; often, as I wrote I noticed that many of the authors I admired had connections of one sort or another with the Bread Loaf Writers' Conference: "So and so was at such and such at the Bread Loaf Writers' Conference," I would write, knowing only that Bread Loaf was some kind of mountain in Vermont and that the conference seemed to have a lot of good people going for it. It was only after another space of years that I got to find out about Bread Loaf for myself,

when Carol Knauss telephoned to say that I had received a nonfiction fellowship to attend the 1980 conference.

If the warm and musical voice on the other end of the telephone line was any indication, I was going to find the Mountain a congenial place. But over the following weeks, despite a succession of friendly, encouraging letters from the Bread Loaf office, I began to dread the oncoming middle weeks of August. Two years of full-time writing had turned me into a recluse. What kind of reception would a nonfiction writer have at a conference primarily of poets and fiction writers? And my only previous experience with literary gatherings had been of the Manhattan variety—crowded apartments or bookstores or hotel function rooms where the ambition and envy seemed as thick as cigarette smoke. A dozen times I decided not to go, and a dozen times Mary, the woman who would become my wife, convinced me that, at the very least, getting out of my three-room New York apartment and getting a little sun would be therapeutic.

So I went. All during the overnight ride on the Amtrak Montrealer I looked at the other passengers, wondering if any of them were similarly bound. At Essex Junction at dawn, several other Bread Loafers did alight—although we shared a thirty-mile ride in a taxi-van to Ripton, I kept silent. All I remember of the ride is the horrifying view I had from the front passenger seat of the furious roilings of the Middlebury River as our driver lurched and swayed through the hairpin turns of the Ripton Gorge. Now I realize that, sitting on the passenger side, my shoulder was to the mountainside during the most alarming stretch on the trip up from East Middlebury; there's no way I could have looked out and down into the torrent, terrified that the garrulous, inattentive driver was going to plunge us to destruction. But that's what I remember seeing—rapids boiling up to engulf me—and it's only an indication of how unwillingly I was being conveyed to Bread Loaf.

Pleasant people—Dick and Hilde Ross at the front desk, and Carol Knauss supervising a stack of conferees' folders in the Blue Parlor—told me I was to bunk in an upstairs room at Treman Cottage. But I was to have a roommate! Not for twelve years had I been forced to share quarters with a stranger. I was too old to want to change. When I found my room, being the first to arrive, I began rearranging the beds, desks, and chairs so that my half of the room was physically and psychically separated from *his* half by a bookcase and a desk. Then I called home to say that I didn't much like things at Bread Loaf. When was the next train leaving?

Twenty-four hours later my second phone call reported the light-years of progress I'd made. My roommate, a fiction fellow, was almost instantly upon meeting one of my closest friends—it was the grinning, wild-haired Bob Reiss, a former reporter for the *Chicago Sun-Times* and then a Washington-based writer of political thrillers; later he would turn to gritty and effective books of political journalism. We stayed up all night excitedly talking with several of the other fellows. Some of them, like Reiss, were to become treasured friends, notably the poet Paul Mariani and the novelist and essayist Elizabeth Arthur, both of whose first books were published in 1980.

The atmosphere at Bread Loaf, I found—at least for me—was *not* competitive. It was supportive and reassuring and seemed to affirm the highest of our individual aspirations as writers. And in the first-floor lounge at Treman, directly under my room (from which cigarette smoke filtered up through some mysterious process of osmosis through an inch of plaster and lathe, a hardwood floor, and a beaten-up old carpet), I found the same feeling of welcome as I began to meet the writers on the faculty. There was Bob Pack, with his crushing handshake; John Gardner, with his flowing white hair, whom I'd seen periodically around the offices at Knopf when *Nickel Mountain* and *The King's Indian* were published; Tim O'Brien, whose National Book Award for *Going After Cacciato* had sparked publishers' interests in Vietnam and made an elusive book contract possible, I was and am convinced, for my first book; and Stanley Elkin, whose novel about talk radio host Dick Gibson had astonished me with its brilliant language and loony low comedy. There was also Michael Arlen, staff writer for *The New Yorker,* whose essays on politics and culture, on foibles committed by Washington and Hollywood and all of the landmarks in between, had thrilled me

for years. Two of Arlen's books had for me set high standards for literary nonfiction: *Exiles,* about his parents and boyhood, and *Passage to Ararat,* about a journey of self-discovery to Armenia. As a nonfiction fellow I was to be teamed with Arlen and with his staff assistant, a tall, grizzled, mannerly journalist who'd won a Pulitzer for media criticism at the *Chicago Sun-Times,* Ron Powers. Powers, author of a novel as well as a book about what passes for news on television, had held a Bread Loaf fellowship in 1979; he had been added to the staff at the last moment when Terrence Des Pres could not come. Bringing Powers back was a fortunate choice for the conference, for in succeeding years, as senior staff member in nonfiction, he would imbue his audience in the lecture hall with a sense of fellowship and mission as he described the writer's duty in a monolithic mass culture of television and disposable values. Repeatedly during the twelve days of the conference, Ron and I tried to assist Michael Arlen with his teaching, as was our duty, but he kept politely, most politely, shrugging us off. Meanwhile, he conducted the nonfiction discussion groups and workshops with insight and skill. Being shut out, no matter how agreeably, forged a bond between Ron and me; many of the lesson plans we concocted for succeeding Bread Loaf years had their genesis in our huddles over ways to not feel so superfluous in the classrooms of 1980, where Arlen was the entire A-Team of nonfiction, and Powers and Bain were the guest walk-ons. Our opportunity awaited us.

I remember the panic among many of the fellows at the prospect of delivering public readings of our own work, and how Bob Reiss and I dragged two forest-green Adirondack lounge chairs out into the middle of a field where we could try out our deliveries on each other. Bob's reading came and went quickly, but mine, scheduled for the second Wednesday, loomed. Paul Mariani, with his immense supportiveness, tried to reassure me, but what did he know of Bread Loaf fear? He was a *poet.* I was to be preceded and followed by poets—Suzanne Berger (former student of Anne Sexton) and Marcia Southwick. I still fretted about my nonfictionist's place in a conference dominated by poets. Moreover, the chapter I planned to read was from a journalistic account of a post–Vietnam War murder case; I'd heard that in 1979 someone had read from what was described as a gratuitously gory account of the murder and dismemberment of a woman and a child, and it had spurred a walkout during the reading and any number of furious artistic and political debates in the days afterward; a fatuous and dismissive article about Bread Loaf in a recent issue of *Harper's* had, in fact, showcased the dispute. My book was neither gratuitous nor gory, but it was gritty. And Vietnam was still a dicey subject five years after the fall of Saigon.

Jam session in the Barn: Stanley Elkin, Steven Bauer, John Gardner, and Bob Reiss (all standing) spur the musicians on; David Bain is at the piano (MSD)

It was fortunate that I found a way to alleviate my stage fright—and the opportunity came early in the conference when I confessed to three friends—Reiss, poet Steven Bauer, and children's book writer Mally Cox-Chapman—that I had once, and still occasionally, played piano for money in public places. Some of my fondest memories of my early twenties were of backing blues legends like John Lee Hooker and T-Bone Walker when they came to Boston for week-long gigs and formed pickup bands of local musicians, or of sitting in for a set with Muddy Waters, James Cotton, or Junior Wells and Buddy Guy when they played at Boston's Jazz Workshop. I had played with a popular New England band led by one James Montgomery, had known Bonnie Raitt when she was still at Radcliffe, and had joined Montgomery in playing behind her at a celebration party when her first album was released. For a while, I had been the "blue-eyed soul brother," as it was called, in an otherwise all-black rhythm and blues band from Roxbury. And I had partially financed the writing of my first book by playing and singing in a wine and cheese cafe out on Long Island. If anything, in 1980 I felt more at home entertaining people with raucous and silly music than I did in reading prose to them. It felt daring to expose that literary side of me on the Mountain, and I needed my friends' encouragement to do so. One night when the smoke and the talk at Treman got a little too thick, we took our restlessness out into the night and headed for the Barn and a much-abused Steinway grand piano. I did not know then that we were joining a tradition of Bread Loaf musicales that went back all the way to Joseph Battell's imported Boston minstrels, through the glee-clubbing Ted Morrison and Louis Untermeyer, the square dances, the cowboy guitar-singing Wallace Stegner, the folk-singing Myra Ciardi, and the twangy yodeling country boy, Harry Crews.

But the music became a tradition in itself over the next decade, helping conferees to blow off some of the steamy tensions (intellectual and otherwise) that naturally build up at Bread Loaf—putting aside the canons of contemporary literature for the earthier, sillier, more arcane lyrics of Big Joe Turner, Louis Jordan, Ray Charles, Willie Dixon, and the Falcons, the Crests, Buddy Holly, and Jerry Lee Lewis. To many of the writers who gathered around the Steinway, some of those lyrics were as deserving of *footnotes,* for heaven's sake, as anything by a modernist poet—but to their credit, Bread Loafers eagerly committed them to memory and faithfully belted them back at me as I played, my eyes taking in the wonder of them all and then straying up into the gloom of rafters high above us where our racket must have disturbed any number of ghosts keeping watch over the place. Especially in the earlier years, Treman would empty out around midnight and even the most diehard window-seat-sitters would find their way up to the Barn. It made for a nice egalitarian touch: Literature brought us together in daylight, in the classrooms and lecture hall, and around midnight music would do the same in the cavernous old Barn.

One could not get up and leave such an eager audience. Sometimes more than half of the conference would be there, with headwaiter-poets Steve Bauer or Carl Stach leading the prizewinning chorus of novelists and poets. On the far side of the Barn, dancers would do the Lindy and cast giant shadows on the walls from a fire in the enormous fieldstone fireplace, Bob Reiss outdoing them all by seeming to swing his partner *over* his head. Always on the fringe, watching and swaying and drinking in the energy and sometimes even singing, would be Tim O'Brien with his ubiquitous Red Sox baseball cap. And always, Paul Mariani would wander over, intent in a deep literary conversation with Bill Matthews or Mark Jarman or Wyatt Prunty until a silly, vocalized R & B lyric would jolt him onto another plane, causing a wide Mariani grin. Once I played for five and a half hours without leaving the piano stool, and I left blood on the keys from ravaged cuticles. I still carry the scars on my fingers from the time an inebriated young Middlebury scholar for some reason dropped a sharp-rimmed wooden potato chip bowl on my left hand from what felt like a great height; some people swear I finished the song, but I doubt it. Once I remember looking up from the keyboard to see Stanley Elkin leaning on his cane beside me, singing backup to Louis Jordan's silly call-and-response tune, "I Want You to Be My Baby." Later, he sat next to me on the stool resting his legs and singing, "Shake, Baby, Shake" to a Jerry Lee Lewis song. Another night, while leading people in what became a Bread Loaf anthem, Sam Cooke's immortal "Bring It on Home to Me," I felt John Gardner's hands upon my shoulders—and later he made the first of his many promises to pack his French horn the next year (he never did). Once during that first session in 1980, the piano was trucked into the Little Theatre for a Sunday afternoon chamber music recital. As there were no plans to move it back to the Barn, we enlisted volunteers to *carry* the grand some one hundred yards back up the driveway; we all must have looked like a huge, strange centipede with twenty legs. Someone climbed a tree and took pictures. I'd love to see them.

A decade of these sessions has in my mind now dissolved into one big long hoot—in which poet-saxophonist-flautist-harmonica-playing Terry Hummer wails, and poet-editor-talkshow host George Murphy knows even more lyrics than I, and poet-chanteuse Carolyn Forché belts out an old blues tune, and poet-iron-pumper Sidney Lea composes as he sings a hilarious "Bread Loaf Blues," and novelist-actor Robert Houston delivers a raucous, Bible-thumping parody of a southern foot-washing radio preacher, and novelist-visionary Robert Stone catches the spirit, sings in tongues, and has to be restrained from clambering atop the wobbly piano, and kinetic poet Marvin Bell pulls his Blue Seal Feeds cap over his eyes and sings "Ain't Misbehavin'" in Louis Armstrong's voice, and the trio of Nancy Willard, Hilma Wolitzer, and Linda Pastan seem to be singing "Route 66," and the suddenly melancholy John Gardner clutches a beer can with both hands as we all do "Amazing Grace," and then the big screen doors fly open and grinning, cowboy-booted Bob Pack clomps in to deign to listen to something far afield from his beloved Mozart. And the next morning at breakfast my bleary eyes light on Howard Nemerov, who delivers the line he usually reserves for esteemed faculty colleagues who have just lectured or read: "I didn't go to hear you last night but I'm *sure* it was wonderful." Sometimes when I am playing I have what might nearly be called an out-of-body experience, and for a second I am above us all in the rafters with the ghosts, looking down on the happiness and the energy and the utter lack of pretension, or I am up on a hillside in the Widow's Clearing, looking down upon the porch and window lights of Bread Loaf as people murmur on the darkened paths, and from the huge open doors of the Barn floats music, thumping piano and honking saxophone, and laughter.

P erhaps it was the music during that first session in 1980. Or perhaps it was my willingness one evening to crawl through a transom and somersault down into the Bread Loaf administrative office—not to know what a manuscript feels like but only to unlock the door for Carol Knauss, who had left her keys on her desk. Perhaps it was Michael Arlen's recommendation to Bob Pack that Powers and Bain seemed to want to do something with nonfiction teaching at Bread Loaf, and perhaps they might be given a chance. But not many weeks had elapsed before Pack was calling to invite me for the 1981 session. By then the lessons of Bread Loaf, the multiplicity of voices that cut across genres, the willingness to try something new and different and a little more taxing, had begun to sort themselves out—and my own writing was undergoing a certain metamorphosis. With the words of poets and novelists still in my ears, with the advice and example of Michael Arlen, my straightforward nonfiction history was developing into something more complex and ambitious, and I felt as if I was leaping toward something unknown but strongly enticing. Sure—I'd go back to Bread Loaf.

During the 1981 session, for the second weekend, I brought up my wife of two months, Mary Duffy, who is an artist. She found the Bread Loaf climate so agreeable that (thanks to Bob Pack's willingness to accommodate families of faculty whenever possible) she has accompanied me for every subsequent session. Attending the lectures and readings, filling her sketchbooks with watercolors, seeing old friends again and again, and singing harmony in the Barn has been more than enough recompense for her managing the gala second-weekend, all-conference cocktail party on the Treman lawn. When, in 1987, we decided to flee the gathering miseries of life in New York City for a more humane life in a rural setting, it took no time to decide to move to the Champlain Valley of Vermont, within sight of Bread Loaf Mountain, where many of our friends had already settled. We now live in a 150-year-old farmhouse and we write, paint, teach, and raise sheep; from the top of our hilly pasture one can see the Mountain that brought us to this new life of ours. And when our daughter was born in 1988, Mimi Aitken Duffy Bain joined the current crop of young faculty children who after dinner play on the edge of the meadow across from the Inn while their parents divide their attention between the children and the sunset; in 1992 her five-month-old brother, David, saw what he could of Bread Loaf while ensconced in a backpack carrier. Mimi took her first steps—not one, not two, but twelve!—outside the Little Theatre, at ten months, in August 1989. During that conference, young Dean Paul Powers attended his first readings without fidgeting or complaining, and Nancy Willard's son, James Lindbloom, was back from college to work in the bookstore. But the pang of realizing how quickly they grow up was evenly balanced—as for all parents—with the joy of watching it happen.

I have found, as have many others who have returned to the Mountain repeatedly, that the sessions tend to blend together. Thirteen years times twelve days makes 156 days, only twenty-two weeks out of that baker's dozen of Bread Loafs. But the vividness, no matter how blended, has not diminished. In that twenty-two-week-long Bread Loaf Writers' Conference of the mind, with a musician's ear, I hear the sublime aural qualities of certain readers, much as how Maxine Kumin reported being alerted to the dramatic possibilities of the public reading by John Ciardi's unforgettable voice. I hear resonant Robert Pack sounding as if he had studied under Orson Welles as he reads from his nature poems, his cycle of monologues in *Faces in a Single Tree,* and his booming narrative *Clayfield Rejoices, Clayfield Laments.* There is Tim O'Brien with his Minnesota accent and his tight, intense, explosive delivery, holding pages from *The Things They Carried,* with their rhythmic, short sentences and irresistible power. Hilma Wolitzer appears, reading with a New Yorker's delightfully dry irony from *In the Palomar Arms* and *Silver.* Here comes John Irving, a real dramatist, conveying from deep inside his iron voicebox the raspy old-guy platitudes of the grandfather in *The Hotel New Hampshire* and the appalling fury of Melony in *The Cider House Rules,* making the audience jump in their seats though they've been sitting in them for two hours. There is well-modulated Ron Powers with his soothing announcer's voice as he reads from his elegiac memoir of boyhood in Hannibal, Missouri, *White Town Drowsing,* or breaking into an uncanny take on the voice of sports announcer Harry Carey from his tragicomic novel *Toot Toot Tootsie, Good-bye!* or doing a perfect Kermit the Frog from his affecting Jim Henson biography. Now it is the pulpit-pounding oracular thunder of Paul Mariani, reading from his hilarious family poems or his harrowing account of the life and death of John Berryman. Or Marvin Bell, with his dry, witty Long Island voice (punctuated with glottal chuckles) and his extraordinary ear for language, his sublime playfulness. There is John Gardner reading the opening from *Freddy's Book* or the eerie ghost-scenes from *Mickelsson's Ghosts,* his voice having the dark, low, throaty quality of the actor Martin Sheen. Stanley Elkin lowers himself with difficulty into a chair, the only sitdown reader, his Chicago cadences and dazzlingly complex sentences giving the audience something like a trapeze to swing from as they listen to *George Mills* and *The Magic Kingdom* and *The Rabbi of Lud*; he does not step upon their laughter. Here comes Nancy Willard with her palpable aura extending beyond her golden hair, reading fables, bringing out the awestruck children in all of us. Then Linda Pastan appears, her voice like an alto saxophone, rilling along familiar charts, making this listener think of beatnik jazz clubs, murky smoke, and black leotards. Francine Prose, too, could be a saxophone, though of the playful rhythm and blues variety; her satire makes one giddy. She is followed by Robert Houston, in a brass-buttoned blue cavalryman's shirt, who draws on his acting past to do all five characters' monologues in his story in five completely different voices, and then by poet Pamela White Hadas, who draws upon similar reserves as her monologues from *Designing Women* transform her from purring Marilyn Monroe to drunken Martha Mitchell to loopy Carrie Nation. There is the deep hollow tone of Howard Nemerov, the nasal Detroit delivery of Philip Levine, the chanting of Galway Kinnell, the honeyed smoothness of Nicholas DelBanco, the melodious drawl of Ellen Bryant Voigt, the Hispanic cadence of Judith Ortiz Cofer, the Mississippian music of Larry Brown and T. R. Hummer, the quiet matter-of-factness of Joyce Johnson recalling being young and in love with Jack Kerouac, the soft Virginian cadence of David Huddle. There is a wide variety of voices, a range of rhythms, a multiplicity of accents—the last reminding one that Bread Loaf has always been the most national of writers' conferences. Above the aural effects of the readers, of course, there is the *work*. As a musician I comment on these writers' tones, their rhythms, their melodies, for a reading is another kind of public performance. As a writer, I place them here for another purpose, too, and it must be simply put: I draw inspiration and gain insight from the extraordinary alchemy of their words on the page; their example is enrichment itself.

In 1981 the conference took on, for that session, a decidedly prosperous air because of the commercial success enjoyed by some members of the faculty—and the prospects entertained by others. After skipping a session, John Irving returned, a new novel about to be published and its status as a best-seller already established. It was *The Hotel New Hampshire,* Irving's saga of the Berry family, hoteliers of a singularly, hilariously inept breed. Hollywood was already at work at filming it, and Irving drove up to the Mountain from the set on a First World War–vintage German motorcycle, complete with sidecar, which he borrowed from the producers. Stanley Elkin was sliding into the home stretch of what he and his publisher hoped would be his commercial breakthrough novel, *George Mills,* an episodic, reincarnate biography, spanning centuries, of one of the great losers of our time. There was not one empty seat in the theatre on the evenings when Irving and Elkin read from their novels, nor were there any fewer standees when John Gardner read two long, intense passages from *his* forthcoming novel (for which he also had great hopes), *Mickelsson's Ghosts,* about a college professor who unknowingly moves into a haunted house even as he becomes mired in difficulties of a more corporeal nature.

John Irving, for one, had reservations about the celebrity that had broken over him with the publication of *Garp* and now promised to inundate him again. He would be shadowed during the 1981 session by a cover-story-writing team from *Time* magazine (the issue would appear on the last day of August) and by a clamoring retinue of female admirers. As one who cherished his privacy, though it pained him he had suffered the former for the good of the publicity value for the conference and for his colleagues, who were mentioned and pictured in the article, but the latter had completely exhausted his patience. Undergoing his own marital difficulties at the time, Irving had no interest in being treated like a rock star; irritated by the lack of dignity of people dazzled by his ever-growing celebrity, he left Bread Loaf early, and although he accepted an invitation to return in 1982, he had to bow out after catalogues were already printed and advertisements placed. It was time to be a recluse—to turn away from the glare of

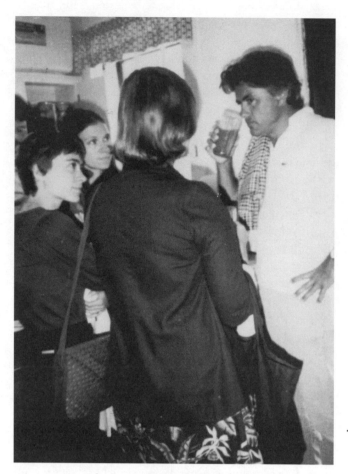

John Irving chats with Lisa Steinman, Susan Thornton, and Devon Jersild, 1981 (DHB)

publicity in favor of the reading light over his typewriter. He felt as if he was letting down Bob Pack, but there was no alternative. Irving would come back in 1983, for the most part uneasy and a trifle paranoid, with good reason, but he was not to return to the Mountain until 1990, after the excitement accorded *The Cider House Rules* and *A Prayer for Owen Meany* had dissipated and when, he hoped, he could be himself again, and teach.

One newcomer to the Bread Loaf staff, whose commercial success and personal celebrity at that time had equaled or possibly outdone the wildest dreams (or nightmares) of any Bread Loafer in recent memory, was Erica Jong. She was the author of several volumes of poetry and three novels, the first of which, the outspokenly sexy *Fear of Flying,* had gained her all of the attention. She drove in behind the wheel of a large Mercedes, alighted from it in mauve harem pants, and for the duration of the conference it must be admitted that she was a trifle ill-at-ease, partly (one learned) because of the august reputation of Bread Loaf and partly because she was one of a very few newcomers to join the semi-permanent senior teaching staff. (That year, the poets William Matthews and William Stafford also joined the faculty, the former to return cheerfully for many years, the latter to decide the pace was not his.) Some staff members did not fail to notice her discomfort and tried to make her feel at ease, but still it was hard going. Jong's twenty-minute lecture, about how she came to write her historical novel, *Fanny,* would perhaps have satisfied a suburban public library audience but left her Bread Loaf audience wishing not just for more length but for more depth and rigor. In fairness, she has had (I've seen) splendid hours at the lectern elsewhere.

In contrast, there was the rich and well-organized lecture of John Gardner, "How Does One Know If One's a Writer?" The ideas he presented would later appear in one of the best handbooks on the creative process, *On Becoming a Novelist* (1983). In it he spoke eloquently of the special compact between writer and reader (in which the writer's generosity is the most valuable component), the elemental requirement of verbal sensitivity, the need for evoking a "vivid, continuous dream" in the mind of the reader. "We read five words on the first page of a really good novel," he said,

Ron Hansen and Ron Powers, 1983 (BA)

and we begin to see images—a dog hunting through garbage cans, a plane circling above Alaskan mountains, an old lady furtively licking her napkin at a party. We slip into a dream, forgetting the room we're sitting in, forgetting it's lunchtime or time to go to work. We recreate, with minor and for the most part unimportant changes, the vivid and continuous dream the writer worked out in his mind (revising and revising until he got it right) and captured in language so that other human beings, whenever they feel like it, may open his book and dream that dream again. If the dream is to be *vivid,* the writer's "language signals"—his words, rhythms, metaphors, and so on—must be sharp and sufficient: if they're vague, careless, blurry, or if there aren't enough of them to let us see clearly what it is that's being said, then the dream as we dream it will be cloudy, confusing, ultimately annoying and boring. And if the dream is to be *continuous,* we must not be roughly jerked from the dream back to the words on the page by language that's distracting.

At a place where the level of discourse on the craft of writing is, with very few exceptions, consistently high, Gardner's talk in 1981 was on an even higher plane. The excitement of the audience as it filed outside the theatre was so great that it was only with difficulty that they could be persuaded to go back inside for a panel discussion on little magazines.

In many ways, throughout the eighties the presence of Ron Powers as senior faculty member in nonfiction did more than bring a new literary legitimacy to a genre that had not always enjoyed that status at Bread Loaf in the past. Nonfiction practitioners, defined by what they are *not,* can find it difficult to strike common cause because their work and aims can vary so widely. In his well-attended lectures, Powers helped to anchor the conference in the realities that *all* writers have to face. Television was making even greater inroads into leisure time than before, its self-referential and value-free nature affecting all other forms of communication, colonizing mass culture into a tyranny of the familiar. At the same time, on Publishers Row in the eighties, merger-mania and foreign acquisition had their own effects on what was being published. More and more, writers were retreating into the groves of the academy. It was a time in which the greatest danger, Powers said, was the idea of writers talking and writing only to each other. It was a theme that all poets and fiction writers and nonfictionists needed to take with them as they left the reassuring isolation of the Bread Loaf plateau for the harsher and more complex realities awaiting them at home.

There were years in the 1980s in which the directness of Powers's message dovetailed with a heightened awareness of the duties of the artist in society. Many sessions emerge with particular themes, and one such occasion was in 1982. Separately, faculty members such as John Gardner, Tim O'Brien, Terrence Des Pres, and Carolyn Forché came to the conference prepared to lecture on or discuss the need for artists to speak truth to power no matter what the consequences. Writers had to look beyond themselves and address larger human—and inhuman—conditions. The resulting electricity in the air—not anger, but a feeling of urgency, informed by deteriorating situations in Central America and by the "Evil Empire" relations between Washington and Moscow—was both unavoidable and unforgettable. It palpably increased on each succeeding day—especially after O'Brien's and Gardner's lectures, Forché's afternoon reading of her poems about death squads in America's client-state, El Salvador, nonfiction fellow Howard Kohn's selection from his book on the mysterious death of a plutonium worker, *The Killing of Karen Silkwood,* and Robert Houston's multivoiced reading from his galvanizing historical novel on an *earlier* American imperial adventure in Nicaragua, that of the nineteenth-century freebooter William Walker, *The Nation Thief.* This was also a year in which I had just returned from an expedition through Ferdinand Marcos's Philippines; at Bread Loaf I read from my account of our nations' postcolonial relationship. The ink seemed hardly dry on the pages of my manuscript, and it is never easy to read still-developing work in front of so distinguished an audience. But most people read new work at Bread Loaf. Besides, I felt the urgency as much as anyone else.

I may be wrong, but it seems that 1982 was one of the years that Tim O'Brien read from his powerful novel *The Nuclear Age.* Tim was wrestling with demons over the novel—striving to get it right and in his fervor throwing away, as Ron Powers once quipped in class, "entire chapters about which anyone else of us would give a right arm to be able to say we'd written." The story had its roots in young Timmy O'Brien's night-fears about looming nuclear destruction, and to the author's mind, the narrative kept galloping away of its own volition with him clinging on by his fingertips. That night, in the midst of a crisis of confidence about the material he was reading, he finished—and walked out of the theatre without acknowledging the thunder of applause of an audience that had been held spellbound for an hour. Instead of tarrying to talk with well-wishers in the tradition of many churches and of Bread Loaf, he stalked away into the night. We watched that book grow over several years and worried at the toll it seemed to take from Tim's peace of mind, each of us taking inspiration from one of the hardest-working writers in contemporary literature; around that time in 1982, unfortunately, it seemed as if he could take nothing back from us, such was Tim's own intense style of authorial isolation. Mercifully, his friends would note in subsequent years, Tim seemed to stride onto surer psychic ground

when the extraordinary tales from *The Things They Carried* began to appear; we would revel in their success.

Themes, of course, are never straightforward in real life, nor are they all-encompassing. The 1982 session was also John Gardner's last time at Bread Loaf—for he was killed in a motorcycle accident only weeks after the end of the conference, and days before he was to marry his student Susan Thornton, who would have been his third wife. In turns at his last conference he had seemed melancholy, stoic, and even guardedly hopeful about the future. Gardner had been besieged by the Internal Revenue Service and creditors and had entertained many hopes for his haunting, sprawling mystery novel, *Mickelsson's Ghosts.* In that summer of 1982 it had not been well received. As in prior years, Gardner talked late into the night and read manuscripts until early in the morning. I remember seeing him huddled in the Barn over a short story with its author, Blue Argo, both of them in a haze of pipe and cigarette smoke fixed by bright beams of sunlight from the high windows; I remember hearing from a puzzled Karen Andes that he had told his discussion group that "I don't have to write any more novels—you write them for me," and also I remember seeing Gardner leading acolytes Ron Hansen and Bob Houston on a talking and walking expedition out of noisy Treman Cottage and into the dark meadows. To Marvin Bell and several others (including myself), it seemed as if Gardner went out of his way in 1982 to build, or reaffirm, bridges with his Bread Loaf colleagues—picking random private moments to step up the intimacy of their friendship. In retrospect, it was as if he had—on some level—a foreknowledge that he would not return to the Mountain again.

His death took the form of a spinout on a gravel-littered mountain highway curve between his Pennsylvania home and his college seminar at SUNY–Binghamton. He could have walked away had his handlebar not punched him in an old surgical scar, causing internal mayhem. Afterward there was some bargain-basement psychoanalyzing nonsense written about the accident being on some level suicidal. No one at Bread Loaf—including some of Gardner's deepest and most perceptive friends—saw any hint of this. What they did see was a man with fewer, perhaps, illusions about himself and about what life would return to him but who remained steadfast in his generosity and in his capacity to discover all the joy and the surprise he could in the time left to him. Phone records of Bread Loafers all over the country would show, on the night that Gardner's death was reported, how strong was his effect on their lives; ultimately, in their own writing and their own teaching they show ample testimony of his own superior gifts as teacher and writer.

During the conference's sixtieth annual session in 1985, Theodore Morrison returned to Bread Loaf for the first time in many years. In a spirit of celebration, Bob Pack had invited both Ted Morrison and John Ciardi to come up for a short visit, perhaps a brief talk, a cake-cutting, nothing fancy or disruptive of the annual teaching mission.

Ciardi declined. He said that during the conference he would be delivering literary talks on a cruise. In fact, he would be at his home in Metuchen, New Jersey. It had been thirteen years since Ciardi had set foot on the porch of Treman, but he could not bear to do so again. Earlier in the year, during an agreeable, three-day interview session at his place on Key West, he had seemed open to a reconciliation, and I had begun to try to make that happen. His note in late January buoyed my hopes. "Our talks (good) brought my long absent thoughts to Bread Loaf," he wrote, "and I'm still not sure how I feel. The Conference was a beautiful marriage once and went sour but now I can hardly remember the wench's name." Nice bravado, John, one could have retorted—but hardly convincing. And despite the fleeting sense that some demons were laid to rest by talking over the old controversies of the late sixties and early seventies, he could have nothing of the conference ever again. After his death in April 1986, at a memorial service at Rutgers, there was much talk of Bread Loaf by his wife Judith and children Myra, Benn, and John L. and by his close friends Miller Williams and John Stone. But not even then, with warm acknowledgment of what the Mountain had meant to the poet and the family man, could Ciardi's sense of loss and betrayal be laid to rest. And so it will not.

But Ted Morrison had no such barriers keeping him from ascending through the Ripton Gorge once again. The Morrison summer place, the Homer Noble Farm bought by Robert Frost in 1939, had passed into the hands of the college. Kay Morrison, unfortunately, had been institutionalized with Alzheimer's disease, but Ted—retired to Amherst, Massachusetts, and in proximity to grandchildren, enjoying his health in this, his eighty-fourth year, drove up to the Bread Loaf Inn with his daughter Anne. Characteristically, Ted wanted no special mention of his appearance—just a place to stand on the Treman porch and a few old friends, like perennial Bread Loafer Jack Bridgman, with whom to reminisce. (Jack's grandfather, a friend of Joseph Battell, had built Bridgman Cottage down the road from Treman). Ted would be happy with just

lunch at the director's table, a conversation with biographer Paul Mariani about Ted's former student John Berryman, a walk between the Inn and the Barn with the Bread Loaf historian, a pause to fix the moment on film as Ted posed in front of the Bread Loaf Inn, as a few conferees paused on the marble sidewalk to stay out of the picture and wonder who the old gentleman was standing in the middle of the highway having his portrait taken. "Probably," Morrison could have remarked, "just a tourist."

Several other long-absent Bread Loafers returned to the Mountain to teach in the mid- to late 1980s. In the interim they had been busy. Francine Prose returned beginning in 1984, eleven years after receiving a fellowship for the first of her string of funny, mordant novels. Dan Wakefield, who had turned with such commercial success to fiction, had begun to write nonfiction books again when he came back to Bread Loaf to teach in 1986. And the former pipefitter Russell Banks, who had gone to Bread Loaf in 1963 to become a drinking buddy and devotee of Nelson Algren, returned in 1987 to serve as a "mystery guest reader" and in 1988 to join the full-term faculty. Banks had recently married the poet Chase Twichell, herself no stranger to the conference. By then he was enjoying considerable success as the author of the taut, best-selling novel *Continental Drift,* and he had just issued his ninth work of fiction, *Success Stories,* to strong critical acclaim. It was good to see someone wearing his own success so naturally—especially knowing how long and hard he had worked for it, and how long he had endured being buried in publishers' midlists despite an enviable literary reputation. Anonymity was behind him and the work still came out as strongly. And one afternoon, the literary agent Ellen Levine arrived to deliver a talk. Ellen, a frequent Bread Loaf guest whose client list (and list of friends) includes Banks and, on a lower remunerative plane, myself, is an indefatigable champion of the writer's cause; she had done much for us over the years and there is no limit to our gratitude. It felt good on that sunny Bread Loaf afternoon—Russell and Chase, and Ellen and her husband Ivan Strauss, and Mary and me—to raise our glasses to toast our friendship, our being together on the Mountain.

Indeed it can be difficult to differentiate the separate sessions within my thirteen-year, twenty-two-week-long Bread Loaf of the mind. What year was it that the faculty decided, at Marvin Bell's suggestion, to take over waiting on tables for one dinner and then for the rest of the

George Murphy, Paul Mariani, Bob Reiss, {?}, Jim Simmerman, 1983 (DHB)

session showed effusive gratitude to the hardworking waiters who did it for thirty-six meals? When did John
Gardner's first ex-wife, Joan, hire a plane to bomb the
conference with fliers denouncing his alleged noncompli-
ance with alimony agreements? What year was it that the
corniest skit in a long line of corny dining room skits
merged the summer season's most popular film, *Ghostbusters,* with our resident ghost of Robert Frost? Novelist Ron
Hansen—decked out in a bed sheet, carrying a copy of
Frost's *Collected Poems*—materialized at dinnertime to roam
through the dining hall reading from "Stopping by Woods
on a Snowy Evening." Almost immediately the public
address system erupted with the pulsing movie theme
music just as George Murphy, Bob Reiss, and Doug
Woodsum appeared dressed somewhat like ghostbusters,
fire extinguishers strapped on their backs, to chase the poor
apparition from the room. What year did the annual
Marvin Bell Look-alike Contest begin? When will it end?
(Marvin wants to know.) When did Ron Powers, with the
contest semi-finals all but closed, suddenly scoop up a
handful of chocolate pudding and smear his year-old son's
face to approximate what Marvin Bell's beard looked like,
thereby winning the contest but thoroughly confusing
Dean Paul Powers, who had been told it was not proper to
make messes with one's food? When did a quartet of
waitresses emerge from the kitchen in high-cut bathing
suits to serenade novelist Jerome Charyn and children's
book writer Nicki Weiss with "Hey, Big Spender," an
unveiled attempt to solicit tips from the conferees? When
did some idiotic participants decide to set a large round
hay bale on fire in the meadow across from the Inn, making
it necessary for groundsman Leo Hotte, along with Carl
Stach, Phil Gerard, myself, and some others to connect our
old Bread Loaf horsedrawn pumper (drawn this time by a
golf cart) to the high-pressure hydrant system? The Bread
Loaf plateau was beset by a thermal inversion and we lived
in a pall of smoke for days after the fire was put out. Was
that the same year that some conferees stole a golf cart for
a midnight joyride only to be yanked out of it as they passed
Stach and Gerard? When did city slicker Ron Powers
empty the fireplace ashes at the Homer Noble farmhouse
into a rubber wastebasket, later to discover a charred patch
on the wall and floorboards where the ashes had been?
When did Linda Pastan faint during a long and grueling
John Irving reading from *The Cider House Rules*? When did
the sparks first fly between Bob Reiss and Ann Hood,
leading to a long Bread Loaf friendship that was unspoiled
by their short Bread Loaf marriage? When did the friends
of Rick Jackson, poet and editor of *Poetry Miscellany,* set
him up during a talk about little magazines by getting
someone in the audience to ask if he accepted unsolicited
manuscripts? When he said "Yes," twenty poets jumped

up with huge sheaves of manuscripts and knocked each other down depositing them on the lectern in front of Jackson, who soon could no longer be seen behind the pile. When was Hilma Wolitzer conveyed out of the kitchen on a big dining tray? Would she do it again? When did Howard Nemerov advise a conferee to take her poem, tear it in half, and throw away both halves? When did we discover one Ophelia carrying on a conversation with John Gardner's dog, Teddy (renamed by some as Moral Fiction)? When did the fiction-teaching team of Tim O'Brien and Mary Morris dissolve into bickering over technique in front of a bemused class, stopping only when Morris stalked out and slammed the door? When did a fellow read beyond her allotted twenty minutes in the Little Theatre— for *an hour and ten minutes*? Where is she now? When did pilot Don Axinn buzz Bread Loaf so low that the window-clutching white knuckles of his passenger, Paul Mariani, were visible to the naked eye? For which costume dance did three enterprising male waiters outfit themselves with dormitory curtains to become a three-headed, dress-wearing, curtsying entity labeled, "the Bronte Sis-

ters"? During which two or three conferences did Joyce Johnson break a foot or sprain an ankle? When did courtly, mild-mannered poet Wyatt Prunty knock down wise-cracking poet Richard Tillinghast? When was the worst mosquito plague—when one could sit in the theatre at night and watch the clouds of mosquitos hovering above us in the spotlight, when the smell and taste of repellant ruined every gin and tonic, and when one late-night waiters' reading in a Barn classroom became known as the "Thursday Night Massacre"? When did we have an eclipse? A double rainbow teamed with a sunset? Snow flurries? An entire week of rain? When did all those children of faculty get so big?

For those who have returned year after year there is much to be said for the continuity of tracking one another's progress (or commiserating at one's lack of it). Each year, as one's solitary toil comes to an end, the faculty gathers at Treman Cottage on opening day with the latest crop of fellows for the only official staff meeting of the

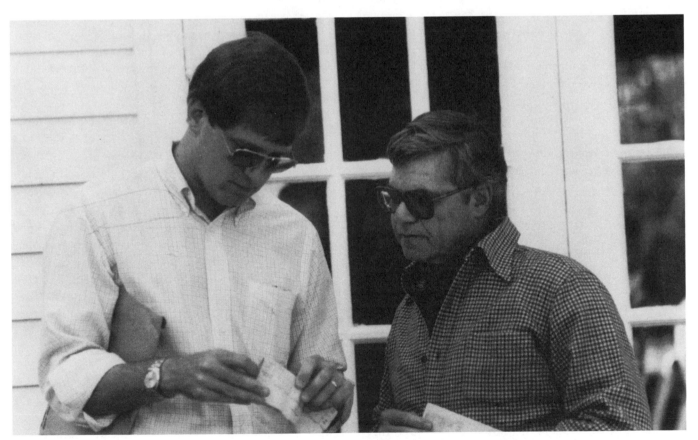

Wyatt Prunty and Robert Pack outside the Little Theatre, 1983 (DHB)

Howard Nemerov, Hilma Wolitzer, Mary Duffy, 1983 (DHB)

conference. There is always a delicious sense of anticipation in the air. Vermont sun streams in through the windows along with Green Mountain air and Bread Loaf excitement. Everyone is well-rested (that will change within twenty-four hours), relieved to have an excuse not to write for two weeks, and in the mood to be worked to the outer limits of mental and physical strength. Above all, there is that palpable friendship in the room—the intensity bedazzles or intimidates newcomers, who share the returning staff's incessant smiles but not yet their family-style physical ease with one another. "Returning to Bread Loaf and receiving those welcoming hugs," Hilma Wolitzer once said, "replenishes my spirit and realigns the bones of my spine." I can hardly disagree after thirteen sessions of what has come to feel like an annual family picnic with mostly one's *favorite* cousins and aunts and uncles in attendance, along with a goodly crop of intriguing newcomers. There are certainly any number of replenishing hugs—although whenever I spot bearlike Paul Mariani approaching I must wince, guard my right floating rib, and warn him to have care.

As the Treman congregants once, more than a decade ago, scrutinized newly hatched me and Mariani and Reiss and Arthur—first-timers who would later return as faculty—and our confreres, we do the same, welcoming the fellows and telling them how envious we are of their position. A fellow's duty is only *to be*—to read one's work aloud and otherwise enjoy the conference. No foot-high pile of manuscripts awaits their attention, nor need they concern themselves with cramming hour-long conferences,

eight, ten, or twelve of them, into an already tightly packed twelve-day schedule; in those empty hours they may nap, swim in Johnson Pond or Lake Pleiad, walk the Long Trail, play tennis, read books. They may even write. Most of all, they may enjoy, we hope, the sense of being welcome members of a community that will last far longer than our allotted twelve days on the Mountain.

I think of the fellows who appeared, impressed Bread Loafers with their work, intrigued the administration with their teaching potential, and returned to get their share of bear hugs. Many of them, before their first books and their fellowships, were at Bread Loaf on scholarship in recognition of the poems or stories or essays they had written but not yet published. I think particularly of ebullient poet and novelist Steve Bauer, wielder of perhaps the most infectious laughter in the hemisphere, waiter in 1979, headwaiter in 1980, fellow in 1981, and staff associate thereafter, whose marriage came out of Bread Loaf when he met novelist Elizabeth Arthur; the talented poet/essayist Deborah Digges, waiter in 1980 and later a fellow and staff associate, whose marriage to poet Stanley Plumly seemed to be a foregone conclusion after Plumly swept up to her in the dining hall and declared himself; and Sharon Sheehe Stark, who began writing at forty when her children could take care of themselves, paid her Bread Loaf tuition two years later, returned the following session as a scholar when her stories began to be published, met a book editor, and returned the next year as a fellow. I think of Joyce Johnson, Thomas Gavin, Mary Morris, Larry Brown, Robert Finch, Wyatt Prunty, Richard Tillinghast, Judith Ortiz Cofer, Edward Hirsch, T.R. Hummer, Richard Jackson, Jim Shepard, Jay Parini, Julia Alvarez, Richard Hawley, Mark Jarman, Don Mitchell, Ann Hood, Michael Collier, Reginald McKnight, Andrea Barrett, and Carol Frost. Their teaching and their writing are inspiration itself.

But there are many more former fellows and scholars about whose work we all shared a feeling of discovery, whose careers have deservedly risen over the past decade (some also began as scholarship holders or as conferees), and this is certainly not an all-inclusive list: Christopher Merrill, Mary Pope Osborne, Judson Mitcham, Sue Ellen Thompson, Gjertrud Schnackenberg, Meg Wolitzer, Mary Hood, Nancy Mairs, Cornelius Eady, Sherod Santos, Agha Shahid Ali, Amy Hempel, Bob Shacochis, Faye Moskowitz, William Hathaway, Ron Carlson, Michael Cunningham, Chase Twichell, Robin Behn, Alan Weisman, Kathleen Lawrence, Mark Hertsgaard, John Hildebrand, Garrett Hongo, Antonya Nelson, Hilda Raz, and David Baker. The appendix includes all of the names of those so honored—but alas, not of those holding waiters' scholarships. Records are woefully incomplete; each of the listed years should include another twenty or

1987 Fellows: (rear) Philip Gerard, Sue Ellen Thompson, Samuel Pickering, Walter Mead, Mark Hertsgaard, {?}, {?}, {?}; (center) {?}, George Murphy, Marianne Gingher, Ann Hood, {?}, Jean Nordhaus; (front) Judith Ortiz Cofer, Agha Shahid Ali (DHB)

1988 Faculty: (rear) Paul Mariani, Philip Levine, Francine Prose, Donald Justice, Mark Jarman, Ron Powers, Wyatt Prunty, David Huddle, Nicholas Delbanco, Jay Parini, {?}, Thomas Gavin, Carole Oles, Hilma Wolitzer; (center) Richard Jackson, Carol Frost, Linda Pastan, Julia Alvarez, Ann Hood, Joyce Johnson, Bob Reiss; (front) David Bain, Robert Pack, Lynn Sharon Schwartz (MSD)

1989 Faculty: (rear) Carole Oles, William Matthews, Wyatt Prunty, Donald Justice, Hilma Wolitzer, Nicholas Delbanco, Robert Houston, Richard Hawley, David Huddle; (center) ?--?, Tim O'Brien, Robert Pack, Marvin Bell, Linda Pastan, Nancy Willard; (front) Ann Hood, Ron Powers, Carol Frost, Margot Livesey, Don Mitchell (DHB)

twenty-five names—many of whom, I am sure, have done as well as former Bread Loaf waiters George V. Higgins, Alan Cheuse, Jonathan Galassi, Carolyn Forché, Rick Jackson, Leon Stokesbury, Joy Williams, and Tama Janowitz. One of the great problems of looking at all of these contemporary writers who have attended Bread Loaf in the past decade is not the obvious one of applying a long view to writers still writing and developing; rather, it is that in recent years the Bread Loaf selection process for encouraging new writers has raised the level of excellence high enough to make it difficult to select one or two from each year for the purpose of this narrative; history has seemed to have done that for Bread Loaf's first half-century, give or take a few years, but it will have a more difficult time choosing from this pack. That is my prediction.

The year 1990 was also the year in which Bread Loaf became eligible for Social Security. A cake was planned—though not an engraved gold watch, since the conference showed no sign of being ready to retire.

But there was a blemish on the session in 1990, at least for the faculty and support staff and the high proportion of returning conferees—poet, prose writer, and teacher Carl Stach, who had a passion for flying and had hoped to achieve his pilot's license, had been killed in a small plane crash only weeks earlier. For years he had served as head-waiter and paterfamilias of the annual crop of twenty-five emerging writers who traded their sleep and their sanity to wait on tables in exchange for their places at Bread Loaf. His gifts as an administrator were legion and his efforts to help the conference run smoothly far surpassed his mere job description. He had come to Bread Loaf originally as a poet, but as he began to see intriguing possibilities in nonfiction writing, he conceived of an idea for a meditative book about the Pacific War, his father's part in it, and the postcolonial atomic legacy of the islands, which had gone from battlegrounds to testing sites in a few short Cold War years. He had become an adherent of one of the many, many (sometimes contradictory) unwritten doctrines at Bread Loaf: Write your poem, story, or essay with the passionate certitude that you are the only one who can write it exactly the way it *should* be written, and use that passion like the rocket fuel it can be; don't be swayed, and never be afraid to take risks to get it down on paper as it *demands* you to do. Carl Stach had taken risks and had mortgaged himself to the hilt in order to follow his passion and certitude to the South Pacific. He returned home full of notes and plans, the future landscape of the book as clear to him as his Illinois countryside could be from the cockpit of a small plane. When, inexplicably, the plane and the man went down, the book went with him. He would be sorely missed. And the book would have been a great one.

Carl would have been pleased to note that the 1990 session started off with three very nice stories making the rounds, in his own dining hall, that say much about the reasons we all congregate at Bread Loaf. That each year there are variations on these stories gives everyone hope, solidifies purpose, purifies fellowship. Somewhere between the kitchen and his station of tables toiled waiter Bruce Murphy, who had just learned that his first collection of poems would be published later that year by New York University Press. Elsewhere, one longtime conferee, a fiction writer named Herb Brown who in real life was a supreme court justice in his home state, had appeared at Bread Loaf with exciting news. He had received word on the day before he arrived that his novel had been bought by the New York publisher Donald Fine. I sat at dinner talking about it with Tim O'Brien, who had worked with him on the manuscript every year for *years.* "It started off pretty rough," Tim said, "pretty rough, but each year Herb came back with the same novel and it was *incrementally* better than before, year by year a little bit better, and now look at him." Herb was one of the most preternaturally genial men one could ever hope to encounter, but as he sat a few tables away, seeing that Tim was talking about him and his forthcoming book, Herb became luminous. "Here's another example right here," Tim said, elbowing a Bread Loaf scholar sitting next to him. It was Jenny Egan, from New York, who had come up a few years earlier, unpublished, on a dining room scholarship. I remembered her as someone who had managed to make a waiter's smock look jaunty and fashionable, and whose work during the late-night waiters' reading had shown real promise. Her manuscript had been assigned to O'Brien, and their conference ended with Jenny in tears. Tim is no sadist; he is tough and direct but also fair and compassionate, and he likes to imbue his students with a zeal for even more work than they thought was needed or indeed thought themselves capable of achieving. Jenny Egan was simply overwhelmed with the hard work ahead of her. But by August 1990, her stories were being published in places like *The New Yorker,* and further successes were simply a matter of time and faith and patience—qualities that can often be replenished on the Mountain.

Bob Pack opened the 1990 conference looking better than he had in years. Several years before he had undergone a quadruple-bypass coronary operation, and recuperation had been long and sometimes painful, with several frustrating setbacks. But now, as Stanley Bates introduced him and Bob stepped into the spotlight with his trademark cowboy boots and boyish grin to open his eighteenth

Stanley Bates and Robert Pack, 1991 (Elisabeth Bates)

session as director, he had his color and his boxer's physique back, and he had new poetry and essay collections under way to follow his latest sequence, *Before It Vanishes* (1989). Pack had other projects that lent, rather than borrowed, energy; he relished new challenges. He felt confident about the coming revitalization of the quarterly he helped sponsor, *New England Review/Bread Loaf Quarterly,* which under its new editor, Terry Hummer, was to be renamed *New England Review* (Middlebury Series), redesigned, and more widely distributed. And there was a proposal on the table at Middlebury College to start a graduate writing program that could draw from the strength of the Writers' Conference and of the summer English School (on the table, alas, it would stay, when members of the college English department would later block its passage; Pack, though, would remain optimistic of eventual success). Also, Pack was satisfied by the success of a copublishing arrangement with the University Press of New England: Bread Loaf anthologies of contemporary poetry, fiction, and nonfiction were enthusiastically received by critics and were finding a wide trade and scholastic audience, with royalties increasing the conference endowment; a new series of readers (by writers such as Donald Justice, Nancy Willard,

Rosellen Brown, and George P. Elliott) was in the works, as well as an anthology, *Writers on Writing.* Finally, a Pack-initiated annual springtime weekend program held on the Mountain for aspiring high school writers, the Bread Loaf Young Writers' Conference, had taken on a successful life of its own under Sandy Martin's direction, assisted by shepherd/prose writer Don Mitchell.

This sixty-fifth Bread Loaf session would open and close with readings from two novelists who were themselves Bread Loaf success stories: Hilma Wolitzer and John Irving. Wolitzer—former scholarship holder and invisible dog-feeder of cheese in Ciardi's Treman Cottage—had published her fifth novel, *Silver,* and at Bread Loaf read from her newest story. John Irving, onetime all but unread denizen of the midlist, was scheduled for the last reading of the conference; he had returned for the first time since 1983, as much to acknowledge his debt to Robert Pack as to show Bread Loaf to his radiant wife of three years, Janet Turnbull. In his lecture he incorporated a reading from *A Prayer for Owen Meany* (1989), but for the last night he concentrated on his new novel, set in India. Marvin Bell read from a new cycle of poems, "At the Writers' Conference," written specifically to be part of his 1990 lecture; as

I heard the cycle, I resolved to include poems from it in this book. With high drama and emotion, the poet and onetime Bread Loaf teacher William Meredith returned to the conference as a welcome and long-missed guest; in the dining hall, after Tim O'Brien delivered moving words about what Meredith had meant to him and to the conference during all his years of service and read from the first poem he heard Meredith read in his first Bread Loaf conference, the entire conference gave Meredith a standing ovation. And there was a rightness and a symmetry in the moment.

For many returning Bread Loafers—especially those on the staff—the sixty-sixth session in 1991 will be recalled in several aspects of negativity. Certainly there were things to celebrate: Old friends Ron Hansen, Amy Hempel, and Phil Levine returned on the faculty, and for several days other long-missed friends, Joyce Johnson and Walter Goodman, visited; several books by staff members were currently enjoying attention in the "real world," including Jay Parini's *The Last Station,* Ron Powers's *Far from Home,* Julia Alvarez's *How the Garcia Girls Lost Their Accents,* Marvin Bell's *Iris of Creation,* Ron Hansen's *Mariette in Ecstasy,* and Judy Cofer's *Silent Dancing*; the indefatigable Jud Mitcham's first poetry collection, *Somewhere in Ecclesiastes,* was soon due to appear. Moreover, a strong and gifted group of fellows, scholars, and dining room scholars appeared.

But many of us would recall of that session that Howard Nemerov was dead. (His moving poem, "During a Solar Eclipse," would be read before the assembly on the night of August 13, in memoriam; in the next eleven days I heard many affectionate anecdotes about Howard on the Mountain.) And that for a few days we could not ignore events in the outside world, as a rightist coup in the Soviet Union (Gorbachev locked up; Yeltsin defying Soviet tanks) sent shock waves of anxiety from Moscow across the world. And that another attempted coup—it seemed to many of us— began to unfold, first behind the scenes, then before our eyes, at the Bread Loaf Writers' Conference.

At issue was not just who would direct the conference— Robert Pack's retirement was somewhere on the horizon, set by then for 1994—but whether the institution should continue to exist in recognizable form. For one day—the session's last—the threat would seem to be greater than any previously faced in nearly seven decades. On that Saturday, Pack learned that Middlebury College President Timothy Light (a Chinese language scholar from Kalamazoo College who had assumed office only a year earlier, and who had no direct knowledge of the conference or its traditions) had secretly created a committee, composed mostly of non–Bread Loafers and even non–creative writers, to "reexamine Bread Loaf's mission." This development caused most of the faculty to conjure up images of our hallowed and successful institution being turned over to, possibly, critics, political academics, even deconstructionists, and it raised our fighting blood. During the last cocktail party, hearing that Pack had refused to cooperate in any such reappraisal, President Light stormed up from Middlebury to bend him to his will, a move opposed by Light's underlings who knew Pack's willpower and energy well. And Robert Pack ordered the college president off the Mountain. Everyone on hand prepared to mount a letter-writing protest campaign upon their return home— but within weeks, due to other serious deficits in his management of the college, Light was removed by the trustees. He was replaced by longtime professor of history at Middlebury John McCardell, an author in his own right (of a book on southern nationalism) and one who had (and has) shown every indication of respect for the teaching mission at the Bread Loaf Writers' Conference. Short as this public episode seemed, it underscored how fragile the venerable conference could be and how carefully it must be guarded, especially in charged political times.

Twelve months later, during the opening of the sixty-seventh session, it was clear that the distance traveled since that nervous, siege-mentality afternoon and evening in 1991 had been dramatic—and this success, one hopes, presaged a good future. The 1992 conference, Robert Pack's twentieth as director, was a time for celebration of two decades of steady growth (of enrollment, endowment, and scholarship distribution), of enhanced teaching, and of spirited encouragement of emergent writers. Instead of tension, which had pervaded the conference the year before as conferees had watched the conference director facing down the top college administrator—and fear that the future mission of Bread Loaf was suddenly open to question—there was encouragement. In 1992 the new young Middlebury President, John McCardell, welcomed conferees on the opening night's reading and hosted a reception marking Robert Pack's two decades of service. McCardell attended a number of other functions and readings, as did his second-in-command, Provost Nicholas Clifford, historian and author of a book on the foreign community in 1920s Shanghai and a forthcoming novel, *House of Memory,* linking the period with recent events in Tiananmen Square. (The provost was also the husband of historian Deborah Pickman Clifford, who had held the other nonfiction fellowship at Bread Loaf in 1980, my first year.) The presence of these officials was reassuring. Indeed, their participation represented more high-level administrative interest in Bread Loaf (which during the school year had not always been affectionately acknowledged by the regular faculty or administration) than the sum of what I had seen in twelve previous summers. One can only hope, then, that such outward signals of support will be matched by what must necessarily go on behind the scenes and off the Mountain in the years to come.

Undeniably, the conference could have done with less rain; it showered and drizzled, in fact, more times than it did not. ("Here's today's weather forecast," Ron Powers intoned in his announcer's voice one day in a lunch line. "Rain today, high winds and showers tonight, chance of suicide tomorrow.") When the sky finally cleared after more than five days of unrelenting wetness, Bill Matthews looked out over the damp but sunny meadow and said, "The submarine has come up."

Nonetheless it was a good year. The list of fellows was impressive and included a number of returnees, such as poets Teresa Cader and Nicholas Samaras and fiction writers Antonya Nelson and Pam Houston; others, such as essayist James Kilgo and novelist Jeff Danziger (also a syndicated newspaper political cartoonist), left strong impressions on those who met them or heard their work.

In addition, it was splendid to see several former faculty members returning after time away—William Matthews, Mark Strand, Jay Parini, Don Mitchell, Helen Schulman, and Michael Collier, all of whom had much to acknowledge as far as accomplishment, most of whom with new books. And not for a number of years had a Bread Loafer enjoyed the sort of satisfaction that Rosellen Brown had when her eagerly anticipated new novel, *Before and After,* received an enthusiastic front-page review in *The New York Times Book Review* while Bread Loaf was in session. But for many Bread Loafers—on and off the faculty, returnees and newcomers alike—one of the more welcome faces was that of Richard Wilbur, up from Massachusetts looking tan and fit and easily twenty years shy of his calendar age, who came for several days and delivered a marvelous afternoon reading that somehow managed to span all the years and the great breadth of his work.

Finally, however, although sooner than most would have liked, it was the second Sunday morning, the conference was over, and the great dispersal had begun. But what better place to see it than from the old highbacked green plank bench on the front veranda of the Bread Loaf Inn, five hours, more or less, after the last dancers stumbled out of the old Barn and groaned at the thought of leaving. By breakfast, the hug-a-thon would commence in front of the Inn as the cars with out-of-state license plates and the big

passenger taxi vans lined up there on the margin of the old Ripton highway, where once horses and carriages stood under the shade of the now-vanished maples and tamaracks. Conference secretary Carol Knauss would stand there indefatigably until the end, informing one and all that only 353 days remained until the next session. Luggage bulging with laundry and weighted down with newly purchased Bread Loaf books would be wrestled down the walk and stowed along with an undiminished passion for good writing and good reading and good talking. Most people had gotten their fill.

And to that next Bread Loaf, and to all the ones thereafter, would appear the newcomers as well as the returnees, all to be conscientiously guided and encouraged to explore their passions for writing and literature by a gifted staff, who, in nurturing the incremental advances as well as the stellar leaps, would in the process contribute more, even, than their individual writings to our national literature and to the culture that embraces it. To the next and future Bread Loafs would be added the thousands of books, who knows how many poems and stories, and a million anecdotes, and all of it somehow unhampered by a goodly number of hangovers, complexes, indulgences, bittersweet memories, neuroses, grudges, fevers, infatuations, eating disorders, eyestrains, tennis elbows, and writers' cramps.

There will be the words and the fellowship. There will be Joseph Battell's splendid isolating forests. There will be the rickety yellow and green Victoriana of the Bread Loaf Inn. There will be fewer mosquitoes and, in these soberer times, fewer hangovers. There will be children, and acknowledgment of other children who grew up under the summer's shadow of the Mountain. There will be the Milky Way overhead. There will be, as occasionally happens on that plateau, a simultaneous sunset and double rainbow. There will be spectacular northern lights, and meteor showers. And there will be—I hope—another magical moment, for me, of sitting in the crowded Little Theatre as someone reads from the lectern down off the stage on the level of the audience. And for a brief time it will seem as if the other congregation of Bread Loafers are there, standing on the stage in a group and just beyond the edge of corporeality—not only absent friends Carl Stach, John Gardner, and Terrence Des Pres but also Frost and DeVoto and the Morrisons and Ciardi and all the others. And a line of Robert Frost's will slide into my mind:

For why have we wings if not to seek friends at an elevation?

DOCUMENTARY

Don't you wish you were now among those Vermont mountains, where a manly heart grows nourished by the cold vigor of winter winds and the dark foliage of giant hemlocks? Wouldn't you be better there, among those scenes of healthy purity, than here at Paris, where there is no purity; where all the young men you meet, be they from America, from England, or from France, talk of mistresses as they would of popped corn, and help drag such girls as Louise to the dreadful torture of a harlot's death?

   —*Joseph Battell,*
     THE YANKEE BOY FROM HOME (1863)

This is the great fault I find with this [Scottish] Highland scenery, and why it can never equal kindred landscapes in America. There's a magnificence in our original forests that nothing I have seen in Europe can supply. The snow or greatness of the Alps won't do it, nor the beauty of the Pyrenees, nor now again the heather-covered and fern-waving hills of Scotland. Would that the day might never come when our mountains shall lose their greenness, or America her woods and forests

   —*Joseph Battell,*
     THE YANKEE BOY FROM HOME (1863)

Joseph Battell, aged 10. (Courtesy Sheldon Museum)

Joseph Battell, Paris, 1865. (Courtesy Sheldon Museum)

The Bread Loaf Inn, c. 1875, showing original farmhouse and rear extention. (University of Vermont)

From *The Middlebury Register:*

Having succeeded in securing competent help for every department of the Hotel, we no longer hesitate to recommend the Bread Loaf Inn to all who seek a place for recreation, amusement, health or enjoyment. Mr. Caleb Ticknor, now of Great Barrington, Mass., but formerly of the Addison House, and so well known as one of the most successful and accomplished landlords of our state, said lately of a dinner at the Bread Loaf Inn, that it was the best that he had ever sat down to at a country hotel.

Although so high a compliment from such authority was unexpected to us, we believe that the Bread Loaf Inn will maintain its reputation, and in its culinary department henceforth rank with Hyde's Hotel as one of the best in the country.

The situation of the Bread Loaf Inn is peculiarly adapted to enjoyment. One finds himself removed here to a higher atmosphere of entirely different life from that which he has been accustomed to. The novelty charms, the freshness fascinates, the decided character pleases, the walks delight, the mountains impress, and their air cool, clear, bracing, invigorates.

Near the Bread Loaf Inn, is the Bread Loaf Mountain, constantly urging the adventurous spirit to explore its wilds, or the man of action to conquer its distance. After this might be mentioned the drive from Ripton along the fern-lined, brook-crossed roads, and through the wilderness to the exquisite valley in which Lincoln lies; and the scarcely less strongly marked but more easily traveled route over the Hancock Mountain to the White River.

Within an afternoon's walk of the Inn is Burnt Hill, one of the finest points of view in the State, and Hancock Pond upon the top of the mountain. Within an hour's stroll is Bisby Hill, whence Lake Champlain is visible; the retired locality of Goshen river; the Lover's walk to the old mill. Trout streams everywhere.

A good livery is joined to the hotel, with saddle horses for ladies and gentlemen. Guests will find, too, at the hotel a superior spy-glass and field glass; different games of cards, chess, &c., croquet, foot-balls, quoits, fishing tackle, and facilities for target-shooting with rifle or revolver. In addition to these, there are daily, semi-weekly, weekly and monthly periodicals; a library; a piano, with several volumes of carefully chosen songs; and a very choice collection of photographic slides.

Dinners hereafter at the Bread Loaf Inn will be $1. Otherwise our terms will remain as hitherto advertised, $10 per week, $2 per day, although next year we shall intend to raise them somewhat as inadequate to the amount of entertainment offered. . . .

—*Joseph Battell,*
RIPTON, AUGUST 20, 1866

The Bread Loaf Inn and surroundings, 1870s (University of Vermont)

After three weeks of broiling city heat my brother and I sat nearly exhausted in the train jogging over the Rutland Railroad; when we heard "Middlebury, Middlebury!" We rejoiced that we still lived.

A massively built figure was standing on the station platform and as soon as he recognized us as the expected new guests he came forward holding out a firm, cordial hand. It was Mr. Battell, our host. During the long climb through Ripton Gorge when the young Morgan thoroughbreds that had raced the five miles between Middlebury and East Middlebury were allowed to take a quiet pace I had a chance to study the unusual man holding the reins in one huge hand. Big, was my first thought, everything about him on a big scale; the head with its firm jaw, the eyes flashing kindly humor or forked lightning, the wide mouth set and stern, but, as I came to know, tender in the presence of a little child or a friend in trouble. As we drove through that wonderful gorge—the stream glimmering far down below, cool, fragrant woods on either side—I felt that we were undergoing a test. Should we fail to respond to the beauty surrounding us, our doom would be swiftly pronounced. As we drove into the open, and the Bread Loaf mountains came into view, Mr. Battell became silent. . . .

. . . Our rooms were in the third story of what is now called "Bloomfield," and we made a hasty toilet, for a bugle call from the office porch was announcing supper and echoing the fact from the mountain side.

That supper! Never shall I forget it. Brook trout and fragrant, sweet wild strawberries, a combination fit for the gods! The next thing I noticed on the program was the general move to the Music Hall veranda to watch the sunset. As I sat there breathing the delicious mountain air and watching the departing glory as the sun sank behind Hurricane, casting a crimson glow over the Adirondacks, I said to myself, "This is a heavenly place."

As the air grew chill and the wind began to blow down from the summit of Bread Loaf Mountain we took refuge in the Hall where Prof. Chickering and his two daughters opened the evening's entertainment by singing a group of Negro Melodies which they had picked up at Hampton Institute. Then Mrs. Cornwall went to the piano and played for the young people to dance. "We always spend the evening in the Music Hall," said a cordial guest sitting beside me, "You see this inn is more like a big house-party than a summer hotel."

—*Clara K. Curtis,*
"THE OLD BREAD LOAF INN" (1933)

The Bread Loaf Inn has been very materially enlarged within the last two years by the raising of the old Inn, and the addition of French roofs and a tower. We have also built a Music Hall, forty-two by seventy-six feet, in which is a stage for theatrical entertainments. A new barn is well under way, and when completed the old one will be removed. This will give a fine view of meadow and wooded hillside in front of the house.

—*Joseph Battell,*
"THE BREAD LOAF INN" (1884), ADVERTISING BROCHURE

The Bread Loaf Inn following renovation by architect Clinton Smith, with two-storey east wing visible in the rear, 1885, The Annex (right) then flanked the turnpike

The Inn was topped, it was said, by the largest American flag in Vermont

The Bread Loaf Inn with 3-storey east wing, 1890s

He was above average height, massively built, big-boned; his head was set solidly on his strong neck, in keeping with the firm jaw, large mouth, and the keen blue eyes now flashing wrath, now kindly humor. One of his broad shoulders sagged perceptibly, owing to a siege of lung trouble in his college days. When he trod the veranda, one shoulder up, the boards trembled. So did any guest guilty of a possible infringement of the host's orders.

—*Clara K. Curtis,*
"JOSEPH BATTELL: AN APPRECIATION" (1939)

Joseph Battell, 1900 (Sheldon Museum)

Though a man of action, Mr. Battell was also a dreamer, often sitting for hours alone, his eyes fixed on the green hills, working out his plans for the next generation. Although he had a rare faculty for gathering about him at Bread Loaf men of ability and distinction, he lived much within himself, and one feels that at times he was subject to moods of loneliness and isolation. He never joined the guests in their gatherings in Music Hall, though he often went there alone and sitting at the piano sang to himself old favorites, the best loved being "Mary of Argyle." A prominent Philadelphia clergyman, a much beloved Bread Loaf guest, died without warning from a heart attack one night. An atmosphere of deep sorrow pervaded the Inn on the following day, a day of unusual beauty, Nature in the fullness of dazzling glory. Mr. Battell sat alone on the veranda, an expression of infinite sadness on his face. A guest touched with a feeling of sympathy, but not venturing to express it directly, called his attention to the wonderful beauty of the day. "Yes," he replied, "but the storms must come."

—*Clara K. Curtis,*
"JOSEPH BATTELL: AN APPRECIATION" (1939)

The Inn and attendant buildings, looking north, c. 1900

Treman Cottage, c. 1900

I began working for Mr. Battell in the summer of 1895, after resigning my position at Middlebury College . . . [and] I acted as a private secretary to Mr. Battell. In fact I did all kinds of work: surveyed, laid out the pipe line of the water system, also the extended sewer system, leveled for the cottages (the last three), looked over timberland, scaled logs, examined trespasses, and estimated damage, tumbled hay, drove teams for boarders, met them at trains, helped Mr. Battell look up horse pedigrees, spent several winters with him at Washington, D.C. While in Washington, we spent considerable time looking over the transactions of the Philosophical Societies of London, Ed-

inburgh and others. This was when Mr. B. was studying the theory of sound. John Houston and I built two lodges on Lincoln Mtn., also cut a trail between them over four miles. This was the beginning of the Long Trail. It took about four weeks to build each lodge with the road leading to the same. I used to help him take pictures, snapped the camera when he was to appear in a picture. . . . You see from the above that my work has been somewhat diversified.

—*Thomas E. Boyce,*
  "RE THE WORK OF T. E. BOYCE FOR
  JOSEPH BATTELL" (c. 1924)

His love extended to all forms of beauty; clouds and sunset, moon and stars, birds and flowers. "What's the name of that little grey bird that came and made faces at me?" he asked when the chickadees had greeted him after a night spent in the cabin on Lincoln Mountain. The little chipmunks running free and unafraid on the verandas were especial favorites, and no dog or cat was allowed at the Inn to threaten their joyous existence. You may notice that there are no chipmunks on the verandas now. Aversions he possessed as well, chief of which was the automobile; this invention he regarded as a murdering monster destroying the peace of the forest with its thunder and bringing in crowds of people where he desired only a few chosen spirits. He could often be seen in front of the Inn warning off a luckless intruder and telling him there was no admittance at Bread Loaf for such as he.

"What do you suppose they think of us?" asked one of the assembled guests watching the show from the veranda.

"They probably think this is a lunatic asylum and suppose we are the patients," replied a woman from New York.

—*Clara K. Curtis,*
"JOSEPH BATTELL: AN APPRECIATION" (1939)

Joseph Battell and companions (c. 1900) relax at a nearby pond

Albert Fletcher recalled how the Inn catered to the guests. Each spring, on March 15th, his grandfather and two other men started planting flowers and vegetable seeds for the five acre garden. His grandpa was the head gardener there for twenty-three years. Albert worked for him in the garden for three seasons. The greenhouse at the Inn was about eighty feet long and thirty feet wide, with two box stoves in it. The temperature in there was kept at 80 degrees Fahrenheit. Albert worked the night shift, keeping the fires going by stoking the stoves at 8:00 p.m., then at 11:00 p.m., again at 1:00 or 2:00 a.m., and if it was really cold, at 3:00 or 4:00 a.m. His last trip out there would be at 5:30 a.m. so he could be in on time for breakfast at 6:00 a.m. After that he would go to bed and his grandfather would take over for the daytime.

On May first the third man came on and they transplanted all the plants, mostly into outdoor hotbeds. Albert's eyes twinkled and he sat up just a little straighter when he talked about the muskmelons. The Inn's farm used to raise them by the bushel. These were started in hotbeds covered with glass windows that slid back and forth. So that the June guests could have fresh melons, one bed was dug up and set inside the greenhouse for double heat. At night, his grandfather placed bed quilts over all the glass windows, and a kerosene lantern was put in each window under the quilt. Albert had to check these lamps to make sure they were all lit. The fresh muskmelons at the Inn were a novelty the guests cherished.

Throughout the summer, one woman did all the washing of the bedding, table cloths, and napkins. She worked six days a week, and made sure the dining room girls always had clean linens for the tables. All the washing was ironed in the mangling room, where boys turned the crank on the mangle iron.

After the dining room girls had finished setting up the tables, the porter went in and lit the chandeliers with the help of a step ladder. These three chandeliers were quite large; each held ten or twelve lamps. After the meal, the porter returned with a piece of pipe, crooked down on one end, to go into the chimney, and crooked up on the other end so he could blow in it and put out each light.

The Inn and the cottages were all lit by lamps. The first thing each morning, the chambermaids brought all the lamps down to the lamp-cleaning lady's room. The porter brought in five five-gallon cans of kerosene from which she filled each lamp. Next she had to trim each wick and clean each chimney. By 3:00 p.m. each day, she needed to have close to four-hundred lamps done so the chambermaids could distribute them around the halls, rooms, and cottages for the evening. At 7:00 the porter lit the lamps and at 11:00 he made the final rounds and extinguished them.

Albert leaned forward in his rocking chair and smiled. "Did I tell you about the entertainment?" he said. "One of the buildings Mr. Battell had put up was a music hall with a stage and a piano. The boarders would put on plays in there. But each summer, Mr. Battell had six black people come up from Boston on the train. They stayed for one night. That evening, these six people would sing for an hour and a half to two hours. People used to pack in there to hear them sing. They were wonderful singers . . . the best!"

—*Meg Werner,*
"MOUNTAIN TOP MEMORIES,"
FROM COUNTRY PATCHWORK (1977)

A guest walks past Maple Cottage, 1890s

The winds of the autumn blew fresh, and its deep colors stretched far and wide over our mountains, when Ellen came again.

She held her hat in her hand as she emerged from the forest, and the sunshine seemed to be comparing itself with her soft hair, to see if there was any difference in their color. Stepping lightly across the rocks, and addressing me, she said:

"Ellen has come back to continue her review of the Yale College geometry. The second book treats of circles, and she is awfully in hopes that it will appear better than the first did."

—*Joseph Battell*,
　ELLEN, OR, WHISPERINGS OF AN OLD PINE (1909)

The Bread Loaf Inn, showing the northern extentions: the "Ell" and the Music Hall

Mr. Battell was very fond of the woods and went with his surveyors a great deal, carrying the dinner basket. On one occasion the surveyors—Brainerd, Houston, Damon, and Stringham—were to measure across the third division of Ripton, going over Bread Loaf Mountain. Mr. Battell was to drive around to Granville and bring them home at night. After dinner he ordered his team on a two-seater. He remembered that he was to go to Granville to meet some one, but he had entirely forgotten the matter of the survey. He thought he would be lonesome going and coming alone, so he asked three ladies to ride with him, which they did. Result: only Mr. Brainerd rode home and the rest walked. They were pretty tired when they reached Bread Loaf.

At another time he took a load of ladies on a ride to Granville. He came back over the "Texas" road and stopped to see the falls and gorge on the "Branch." Not being hitched, the horses promptly started down the road. Someone stopped them down towards Hancock Village and parts of the surrey were scattered along the road. Mr. Battell got his horses, borrowed a wagon, and took his company back to the Inn; thus originated the name, "Runaway Falls."

—*Thomas E. Boyce,*
   "RE THE WORK OF T. E. BOYCE FOR
   JOSEPH BATTELL" (c. 1924)

Two turn-of-the-century girls pose at the Inn's flower garden, across from the Inn

. . . I think his first housekeeper was Miss Woodbury of Bethel, Vt. She was a good manager and I think stayed with him many years. She would get mad now and then and "quit." Then Mr. Battell would get John Houston to talk to her and get her to work again. On one occasion Mr. Battell "bid off" the keeping of a pauper for a year at fifty cents a week. The pauper was Bill Dalby who could do considerable in the chore line and Mr. Battell thought he would pay for his board in work. Miss Woodbury saw Bill at the table his first meal there and asked John Houston who he was. John said, "William Dalby." She said, "What does Mr. Battell get a week for his board?" John, "Fifty cents a week." She, "What a fool." She at once packed her satchel and started for Bethel. Soon someone told Mr. Battell and he found John and sent him after her. When John overtook her he said, "Where are you going?" She, "Going home. I will not disgrace myself by working for a man who will take a boarder for fifty cents a week." John said, "You will have a long walk. I am going part way. Get in and I will carry you." He talked to her and smoothed her ruffled plumage and when he found a convenient place, turned around and brought her back to the Inn.

—*Thomas E. Boyce,*
    "NOTES ON BREAD LOAF INN AND ITS
    FOUNDERS" (1930)

Summer guests pose on the lawn south of the Inn

Much of the work at the Inn was done by young girls from the neighboring farms, and for them Mr. Battell felt the responsibility of a father. Here his policy was adamant; any social intercourse with a male guest was strictly forbidden; no buggy drives, no moonlit walks were allowed on pain of immediate expulsion from Bread Loaf. There was one instance that became a matter of general discussion and caused considerable excitement among the guests. A certain young man from a family of considerable prominence in his New England town succumbed to the charms of one of the waitresses. No one could blame him; she was refined, gentle, very pretty, and not at all averse to accepting invitations from a guest whose manner toward her suggested admiration and respect. Evening drives took place and the storm-clouds began to gather around her head. Mr. Battell began to frown, the guests began to protest, accusing the young man of selfishly ruining the financial prospects of the girl, who was surely on the way to lose her position at Bread Loaf. Mr. Battell was rather fond of her and endeavored to convince her of the mistake she was making. The young man went to her parents and asked them if they objected to his attentions to their daughter. They promptly replied, "No," and he bearded Mr. Battell in his den and reported the friendly attitude of the parents. Did that influence Mr. Joseph Battell? Not for a moment; his rules for the waitresses were well understood; they

Laundry and laundresses (University of Vermont)

obeyed them or left the Inn. Tears were shed, but there was no reprieve from the verdict.

Within a comparatively short time the offending pair married, and the Bread Loaf waitress adapted herself with great skill to the demands of her new life. Her husband became increasingly prominent in public affairs and his wife proved an admirable helpmate. A few years after their marriage they spent the summer as guests of Bread Loaf Inn, where no one gave them a more cordial welcome than Mr. Battell.

—*Clara K. Curtis,*
   "JOSEPH BATTELL: AN APPRECIATION" (1939)

Maple Cottage around the turn of the century

Guests pull up their team before Cherry Cottage

The easternmost cottages, looking north, c. 1900

Early in January of 1915 I had a special delivery letter from Professor Boyce telling me that Mr. Battell had left very unexpectedly for Florida without telling anyone but the young boy he took with him. He was not at all well and Professor Boyce was anxious about him, so, knowing that he usually stopped in Washington on his way south, he asked me to telephone the hotel where he always stayed to see if he was all right. Mr. Battell answered the call and we had a pleasant chat, and then he said that he would like to come and call on us the following afternoon. We waited all afternoon but he did not appear. When I called the hotel, the clerk said that he had left for Florida the night before. I notified Professor Boyce at once.

Then a few weeks later Mrs. Pierce telephoned on a Sunday evening to tell me that there was an article in the evening paper saying that Mr. Battell had been arrested in our railway depot and then taken to our City Hospital for Charity Patients! Imagine my horror! It was cold and rainy but I got my uncle to go with me to that dreadful place next to the jail to see what we could do. There was his name on the book of the Institution, but in the meantime Senator Green had heard the news and had him removed to a hospital which could care for nervous cases. I wired Professor Boyce to come at once and he stayed at our house until after Mr. Battell's death.

It seems that he dismissed the boy from Middlebury soon after they reached Florida and stayed on there by himself for a few weeks. Then growing restless he started homeward and bought a through ticket to Middlebury which was later found in his pocket. When he reached Washington he went to the Capitol to see Senator Green who cashed a check of one hundred dollars for him. Then he returned to Union Station to buy a second ticket for Middlebury (he had forgotten the first), and while there he began to act dazed and confused and to talk strangely—due to a serious kidney ailment—and a detective, who was watching him, arrested him. Of course he was not used to such treatment and became violent when his watch, ruby stud and money were taken from him. He also had his check book and other papers of identification which the police were too stupid to look into until later. Everything was returned to Professor Boyce after his death.

Of course Professor Boyce arranged for the best medical care. Mr. Battell suspected everyone of trying to abuse him, and begged Professor Boyce to bring him to our house, saying that he knew he would get well there, but of course he was too ill to be moved. Once when a nurse went to his room with a breakfast tray, he had barricaded the door with the bureau and chairs. He refused to open it in spite of her pleading. Then he asked if I were there, and when she replied yes, immediately let her in. He seemed so glad when Professor Boyce took me to see him one afternoon and then said they were keeping him there against his will and he was going to get up and go home with us. So I had to leave rather hurriedly to keep him from getting excited and that was the last time I saw him, for it was necessary to perform an operation a few days later from which he never rallied. So passed a great and lonely man.

—*Elsa Rauer,*
"RECOLLECTIONS OF JOSEPH BATTELL" (N.D.)

Carriages assemble during the Bread Loaf School of English, early 1920s

Arnold Swift, manager of the Inn, calls guests to meals

TWENTIES

ROBERT FROST TO WILFRED DAVISON
[South Shaftsbury, December 19, 1920]

Dear Mr. Davidson: I have been a good deal interested in your new Summer School from afar off. I have been wondering if what is behind it may not be what has been troubling me lately, namely, the suspicion that we aren't getting enough American literature out of our colleges to pay for the hard teaching that goes into them. After getting a little American literature out of myself the one thing I have cared about in life is getting a lot out of our school system. I did what in me lay to incite to literature at Amherst. This school year I shall spend two weeks at each of two colleges talking in seminars on the same principles I talked on there. School days are the creative days and college and even high school undergraduates must be about making something before the evil days come when they will have to admit to themselves their minds are more critical than creative. I might fit into your summer plan with a course on the Responsibilities of Teachers of Composition—to their country to make what is sure to be the greatest nation in wealth the greatest in art also. I should particularly like to encounter the teachers who refuse to expect of human nature more than a correct business letter. I should have to cram what I did into two or at most three weeks. . . .

ROBERT FROST TO WILFRED DAVISON
[South Shaftsbury, December 27, 1920]

Dear Mr. Davison: We are agreed on everything but the money. I suppose you offer what you can. But I really couldn't give of my time and strength at that rate—particularly of my strength, which I find I have more and more to consider. It would be stretching a point to offer to come for a week and give five lectures for $150 and my expense. I am sorry if that seems too much, for I wanted the chance to show my belief in what you have undertaken in literature and teaching. . . .

ROBERT FROST TO GEORGE F. WHICHER
[Ann Arbor, February 8, 1922]

Dear George: It would give you some idea of what you would be in for at Bread Loaf, if I wrote out a few of the things I may have carelessly said up there last summer. I came pretty near going the whole length. I told them they wanted for teacher a writer with writing of his own on hand who would be willing to live for a while on terms of equality almost with a few younger writers. Almost I say. I wouldnt have him go so far as to carry his manuscript to them as they would be free to bring theirs to him. But I would have him stick at nothing short of that. He would assign them work no more than they would assign him work. He would expect to take as well as give in as fair exchange as possible if not ideas of form, then ideas and observations of life. He would stay mainly at the level of the material where he would show to not too much advantage. That is to say he would address himself mainly to the subject matter of the younger writer as in good polite conversation. He would refrain from fault finding except in the large. He would turn from correcting grammar in red ink to matching experience in black ink, experience of life and experience of art. There's the whole back side of every sheet of manuscript for his response. The proof of the writing is in what it elicits from him. He may not need to write it out. He can talk it out before the fire. The writing he has nothing to say to fails with him. The trouble with it is that it hasnt enough to it. Let the next piece have more to it—of Heaven Earth Hell and the young author. The strength of the teacher's position lies in his waiting till he is come after. His society and audience are a privilege—and that is no pose. On the rare occasion when he goes after the pupils it will be to show them up not for what they aren't but for what they are. He will invade them to show them how much more they contain than they can write down; to show them their subject matter is where they came from and what in the last twenty years they have been doing.

I kept repeating. No exercises. No writing for exercise. The writer's whole nature must be in every piece he sets his hand to and his whole nature includes his belief in the real value the writing will have when finished. Suppose it is a good bit of family tradition. It must be done once for all. It must be an achievement. And so on. You know how I get going and you know I mean it. . . .

. . . All this plan lacks is someone to carry it out. I wish I had nothing else to do.

Robert Frost at Bread Loaf, 1920s

John Farrar at Bread Loaf, c. 1930

Farrar is capable of changing his mind. He is not one of these one-track fellows. He is not always a Cato. There is no one, at times, who has more belief in and sympathy with youth, even gay and obstreperous youth. He has, probably, encouraged as much new talent among young men and women as any editor in America. He has a vast, an amazing fund of energy; and no little of it . . . is devoted without hope of reward or gratitude to the fostering and development of promising work among fledgling poets, novelists, short-story writers, essayists, and other artists. He has taken what was once a desueté and uninteresting house organ and made it a lively and interesting magazine, playing up to no clique or cult, fair, intelligent, well informed, steering a clear course between the radicals on the one side and the mossbacks on the other. He is at once a good editor and a good business man, having a regard both for the end and the means to that end of literary development. He has ideas; he is by nature something of an impresario. But, so great is his vital energy that his activities are incredibly numerous. It is difficult to imagine how Farrar finds time to do all the things he does, or, doing them, to carry them off so well.

—*John Farrar,*
  THE LITERARY SPOTLIGHT (1925)

The first faculty of the Bread Loaf Writers' Conference, 1926: (l-r, rear) John Farrar, Robert M. Gay, Edward Davison, Grant Overton; (front) {?}, Doris Halman, Harriet Monroe, {?}, {?}. (Courtesy Poetry Society of America)

The Conferences in Creative Writing at the Bread Loaf School of English proved a fascinating experiment, to me at least. The students, some thirty-five of them, were exceptionally brilliant for a class in the first season of any new educational scheme. . . . I am thoroughly convinced that it is only by direct contact with editors, publishers, critics, and writers that those who are trying to write will be able to diagnose their own cases and know whether or not they have any chance in their field. In looking over the work done in the Creative Writing classes conducted by Dr. Gay of Simmons and of Harvard, I found much that was interesting. This unique summer school, under the guidance of Wilfred E. Davison its dean and Paul D. Moody, president of Middlebury College, is establishing itself as one of the most intelligent and broadening influences in the teaching of English to English teachers and others in the country. Many interesting people were there. William McFee arrived in a whirl and left after delivering a positive and gay lecture. Honore Willsie Morrow told the story of her struggles to become a writer, of the preparation for her new Lincoln book. She was superb. Harriet Monroe, kindly and brilliant always, proved an able representative of American poetry. Edward Davison, Grant Overton, Arthur McKeogh, Robert Gay, Doris F.

Halman, Isabel Paterson, lent the rays of their personalities and wisdom to a series of talks and conferences which became violent with advice and opinions and drew out some of the most provocative theories on writing and publishing it has ever been my privilege to hear. The business of advising young writers is becoming this autumn next to impossible. No one has any idea how many of them put in an appearance in the editorial offices. What's wrong with America that every boy out of college wants to sharpen his pencil and tune his typewriter? Marcella Burns Hahner, that wizard of Marshall Field's, Chicago, who sells books by the millions and makes a friend a minute, took me to a delightful tea party given by the parents of young Mr. Cobbin, about to be married. The room was filled with talk, and with beauty you may be sure. Suddenly a young man was introduced. "How does one earn a living writing?" he asked, whereupon the clouds descended and the wind blew. I told him that our purpose at the Bread Loaf School had been to analyze specific cases in order to see, in the first place, whether the students wanted to make a living writing, and, in the second, whether by any chance they could.

—*John Farrar,*
THE BOOKMAN (NOVEMBER 1926)

John Farrar and Robert M. Gay, late 1920s

Harriet Monroe, Bread Loaf, 1926 (Poetry Society of America)

Walter Prichard Eaton, 1930

The people of America should learn that their poets cannot do their work alone. An artist must feel his neighbors behind him, pushing, urging, arousing him, if he is to achieve his utmost. The great epochs, in any department of human activity, come only when a strong creative impulse in the minds of the few meets an equal impulse of sympathy in the hearts of the many. A masterpiece is no isolated miracle, but a conspiracy between a man of genius and his epoch.

—*Harriet Monroe,*
 POETS AND THEIR ART (1926)

Louis Untermeyer conducts an outdoor poetry clinic, 1939

It was the less lovable side of Miss Monroe that I usually met. She did not seem either hard or bitter, but I must confess she seemed definitely astringent. I admired her purpose and her pertinacity; I respected the impulse that changed a society woman into an editor of poetry and a friend of poets. Yet I cannot claim that I was fond of her. A feud had developed between us. For one thing, I had lampooned her high-handed manner of handling manuscripts, scribbling suggestions and penciling annotations over the submitted sheets. For another, I had intimated that *Poetry: A Magazine of Verse* was helped, if not made, by the renaissance of poetry which began when the magazine was founded, whereas she implied that the excitement about the new poetry was caused by the magazine. I demurred; she never forgave me. I should have known better than to have belittled the small monthly, even by inference. It published some of the most famous poets and much of the best verse of the period. It was an important outlet and a focus. But my chief mistake was criticizing it because it was Miss Monroe's. It was her unassailably spotless ewe lamb, the virgin's belated child. We quarreled about it at long distance; we argued face to face.

I remember one of our more embarrassing encounters. We were having lunch at Le Petit Gourmet in the days when Mrs. Moody was supervising that excellent restaurant. Miss Monroe and I were trying to compromise our differences. She was more gracious than I had ever seen her; the food was delicious; I was practically won over.

"You know," Miss Monroe said, "perhaps our quarrel is not so personal. Perhaps it is only a matter of locale. East versus West. Athens and Sparta."

"Of course," I replied eagerly. "That explains it all. We in the East have taken too much of our culture for granted, while you in Sparta—"

"Sparta!" She froze immediately. "*We* are not Sparta! I assumed you knew that Chicago had become the Athens of America. Even your friend Mencken has been saying that the literary heart of the country is in the Middle West! It isn't just that you in the East lack our physical vitality; you lack—"

And the feud was on again.

—Louis Untermeyer,
FROM ANOTHER WORLD (1939)

Stephen Vincent Benét and Joseph Auslander, 1928.

[Benét] agreed to deliver some lectures Farrar had arranged and to go with him up to the Bread Loaf Writers' Conference in Vermont. He was leery, however, of their major publicity dream [regarding the impending release of *John Brown's Body*]. "I'd rather not arrive," he told Farrar, "on exactly the day the book comes out. It seems too pat." Benét was thoroughly skeptical of any magic that might accompany his presence. "There are some people whose personalities can arouse interest in their work," he said. "I am not one of them. My work is the best of me, and I would rather lie behind it, as *perdu* as possible."

"I gave a few conferences (God save the mark!)," Benét told Rosemary, "read, [and] talked foolishly before classes." His youth, which took most of the Conference members by surprise, as well as the aura of his extraordinary success and his modest willingness to help in whatever way he could, combined to make him as warmly regarded here as he had been at MacDowell.

"He tipped his head back and chanted," remembered [Robert M. Gay,] one of the staff, . . . "his voice having a volume surprising in so meager a man and a quality that sounded like a butcher sawing a bone. But it was oddly effective, probably because of his air of complete sincerity, and after the attitudinizing and affectations of some poets we had heard, was very refreshing."
—*Charles A. Fenton,*
STEPHEN VINCENT BENÉT (1958)

1928 Faculty: (rear) Sinclair Lewis, Stephen Vincent Benét, Grant Overton, Joseph Auslander, Wilfred Davison; (front) Robert M. Gay, Margaret Widdemer, John Farrar, Gorham Munson

John Farrar has a quaint and rather creepy capacity for undergoing a gradual but complete metamorphosis before your very eyes. You look, and while you look the lines of his thin, hungry face assume new relations among themselves: what was before an obtuse angle slowly closes to the acute, and the straight lines forming it bend at the unjoined ends with the sinuous undulations of an angle-worm that has been partially crushed. This metamorphosis is not that swift facility for assuming protective coloration with which we associate the salamander; for Farrar, though outwardly the most socially amenable of party-hounds, has actually a most meager faculty for identifying himself with the moods and manners of a group: it is rather a matter of painful sensitiveness to disturbing contacts. And most contacts to Farrar are disturbing. What we see, then, is the unconscious performance of a sort of quick-change artist, who foregoes the advantage of a momentary retirement behind a screen. One moment he is a pink-cheeked seraph with all three pairs of wings aflutter and at the end of the next moment he is a bent old man, disconsolate and agape at youth. One moment he appears a case of arrested development, with immaturity, even pubescence, soliciting your forbearance and kindly patronage; the next, he is an austere and censorious ascetic frowning his disapproval of gaucheries and frivolities. He is, in the course of a single evening, child and birchman, pupil and lecturer, defender and carper, Pierrot and pedant, monk and playboy.

. . . I have never known any man, woman, or child who so thoroughly as Farrar constitutes himself his brother's keeper. Farrar assumes a paternal protectorate over every friend he has or makes, watching after his friend's health, counseling him in money matters, advising him against the pitfalls of a big city, choosing his acquaintances, censoring his pleasures, defending him against criticism, tooting his horn, giving him a leg-up with people of influence, and worrying himself ill lest through some failure in his plans his friend will go to the dogs. I spoke of a paternal protectorate; but Farrar's solicitude is maternal rather, even grandmotherly or, perhaps even more accurate still, grand-auntly. He is always arranging love matches, furthering courtships, trying to straighten out marital difficulties, reconciling estranged couples, making young poets sign the pledge, trying to distract the sentimental attentions of ingenuous novelists and playwrights away from dangerous women, advising fresh air, wholesome amusements, and hard work against the claims of temptresses, the flesh and the devil.

—*John Farrar,*
THE LITERARY SPOTLIGHT (1925)

1929 Faculty: (rear) Edward Weeks, Robert Frost,
Robert M. Gay, Wilfred Davison, Hervey Allen,
Gorham Munson, Louis Untermeyer, Grant Overton;
(front) Elinor Frost, Edith Mirrielees, Margaret
Widdemer, Frederica Weeks, Jean Starr Untermeyer

Edward Weeks on the Inn veranda,
1929

In the summer of 1929, Dr. R.M. Gay, the director, invited me to give a course on the essay and the magazine article at the conference. To do so meant sacrificing the whole of my summer vacation, but the experience proved to be worth it (and was to bring me back as a lecturer for at least one weekend over the ensuing decade).

Fritzy and I shared the small cottage with Dr. and Mrs. Gay, their daughter and their wire-haired fox terrier, Judy. One of the remaining guest rooms was occupied by Gorham Munson, the critic, and the last by Joel Spingarn, the philosopher from Columbia. In such intimacy I soon came to admire Bob Gay, especially the gentle firmness with which he dealt with the literary temperament.

The faculty, of which I was the youngest member, was a versatile group. In addition to those I have already mentioned there were Edith Mirrielees, head of creative writing at Stanford and a gifted exponent of the short story; and Hervey Allen, that broad, hulking figure who still limped from the leg wounds he had received in the Argonne and who in his big, deliberate way reminded me of Doctor Johnson. Hervey was lecturing on the novel and at this point was halfway through a vast sprawling narrative of his own, from which he read us chapters in the evening sessions. He had been working on it for two years in Bermuda. The Guggenheim Foundation had turned down his request for a fellowship—they thought his book too involved—and John Farrar, his publisher, had advanced him $14,000, but he needed every penny he could pick up to keep the story going and his family fed. It was his first novel and it was to be called *Anthony Adverse*. We had the New York book critic Grant Overton; Sinclair Lewis might drive over the mountain to spend an evening; John Farrar arrived for weekends; and several of our evening sessions were enlivened by Robert and Mrs. Frost. I found Robert impressive, wry, and delightful: some of the gleaming asides he tucked into his recitals had surely been uttered before, but they were as true as what came forth spontaneously. He liked to watch our tennis, especially the doubles with the quick volleys and overhead smashes. He borrowed a racket and had me feed him lobs, which he missed or smashed into the backstop in great swings.

We lived on mountain air and almost uninterruptedly in the flow of words: the first class began at 8:45, when the clanging of a dinner bell called us away from our last bite of breakfast; the same bell summoned us at 2:00 for the afternoon session, and our early supper was immediately followed by a public lecture or a reading or a play. After three days of this, Fritzy, who had nervously audited my class and was attending some of the others, found the regime a little less than a holiday. "They don't even give you time to go to the john," she whispered as we hurried out of the dining room.

Not until the evening performance was over did I relax. Then, with the guest of honor in our midst, we stretched out before the open fire to talk. It was good talk, sparked by Robert Frost; there was never any problem in getting him started, the problem was to get him to stop. He was a nighthawk who loved the stars, and he and Hervey would go on and on until two or three in the morning unless Mrs. Frost put her foot down. A flare-up occurred when John Farrar in a rambling lecture remarked that he liked to read poems aloud to his children and that his five-year-old responded much more eagerly to the music of Shelley than she did to Frost. He said it facetiously but it was tactless and Robert was miffed—it took all of Bob Gay's diplomacy to bring about a temporary reconciliation. For two years thereafter Frost would not attend.

Some forty students were in attendance, ranging from undergraduates to a grandmother in a wheelchair—Queen Victoria I called her—whose reminiscences I tried to put in order. There was no star comparable to Catherine Drinker Bowen, who a few years later came up to work with Bernard DeVoto; my ablest were career women nearing retirement, a superintendent of nurses, an able teacher with a long experience in Harlem. I tried to help them be less reticent.

—*Edward Weeks,*
MY GREEN AGE (1973)

Louis Untermeyer, 1929

He is five feet seven inches in height, stocky, inclined to take on weight because of an uncontrollable lust for sweets; is equally worried about the state of the world and the thinning of his hair; puns as often (and as atrociously) as Christopher Morley, and is as fussy about his neckties as a Wall Street stockbroker. The absurd smallness of his ears is overcompensated by the prominence of his nose. He has a long slanting forehead, wears eye-glasses, and affects racy colloquialisms that are not suited to his temperament. The shape of his head is dolichocephalic.

. . . As a critic, he has had the dubious advantage of occupying a strategic position close to the center, thus receiving the direct fire from both the opposing camps. The members of the extreme left regard him as a damnable reactionary, while such defenders of the conservative traditions as Cale Young Rice and Stuart P. Sherman consider him a red-eyed Bolshevik. As a poet, he is similarly contradictory. His themes, figures and points of view are radical, but his form is, if not always orthodox, at least fairly regular in shape. He would rather, he has said, write one intense, concentrated quatrain than all the carloads of free verse shipped annually to the offices of "Poetry."

. . . A most aggravating and unreasonable combination. A poet, yet a practical business man; a passionate propagandist, yet a critic without any axes to grind; a reviewer who has made dozens of enemies, yet an anthologist with little prejudice or partisanship. . . . A creature mythical, fantastic, incredible—but nevertheless very much alive.
—*John Farrar,*
   THE LITERARY SPOTLIGHT (1925)

ROBERT FROST TO GEORGE F. WHICHER
[South Shaftsbury, c. June 1926]

. . . Louis has a new high school anthology of modern poetry out [*This Singing World for Younger Children*] with exactly two poems in it by his last wife and two by his next. That looks more dispassionate than I'm afraid it is. . . . Nevertheless I feel put in a hard position. Jean [Starr Untermeyer] has as good as forbidden us to receive Virginia [Moore]. That hangs Louis in limbo. . . .

Frost's body, which is sturdy and square, makes little impression on one who meets him for the first time. It is the eyes: bright blue, steady, gentle yet canny, two vivid lights in a face that is otherwise gray. There is the loose, coarse, now almost white hair, the full but finely cut lips, the nose that is a trifle too broad to allow the characterization "Greek" for the whole head, which is indeed a noble one. Physical movements are casual. In old age, they may become soft and shambling. Loose clothes become the poet. If he were to wear a snappy cut suit, it would take on the appearance of homespun. He is a dignified figure as he sits on the back porch of his stone farmhouse on a rise of the road near South Shaftsbury, Vermont.

. . . The only note of bitterness in his make-up is his attitude toward the writer who despoils his art, and the public which does not countenance comparative indigence in the artist. He feels, perhaps, that the leisure of poets is misunderstood, that periods of contemplation seem times of drought to the average intelligence. The sound of literary claques is annoying to him. If he is intolerant of anything, it is of a certain type of literary personage chiefly to be found in New York clubs.

—*John Farrar,*
THE LITERARY SPOTLIGHT (1925)

The breadth and quality of Frost's landscape were in the man's face. Carved out of native granite, the effect would have been cold had it not been for the pale blue but quizzical eyes, the quick bantering smile, and the sensual bee-stung underlip. It was a stubborn scholar's face masking the irrepressible poet's.

—*Louis Untermeyer,*
FROM ANOTHER WORLD (1939)

Robert Frost, 1929

Robert Malcolm Gay, 1930s (Courtesy Simmons College)

ROBERT M. GAY TO ROBERT FROST
[Boston, January 16, 1929]

I meant to have written you long since to tell you how delighted I was when Davy [Wilfred Davison] wrote me that you were to take charge of the Conference next summer. . . . The main thing seems to be to get rid of the commercial flavor of the Conference, and I do not think that it will be hard. . . . The morning meetings of the Conference have as a rule been profitable, I am sure, but the afternoon "discussions" have not. The latter too often became merely one more lecture . . . and the subject "discussed" was trivial or commercial. . . . To sit there for hours, as we did, and discuss how to sell MSS, the "taboos" of editors, and so forth, seemed quite literally a desecration. . . . Your presence and influence alone will do much.

THIRTIES

ROBERT FROST TO HERVEY ALLEN
[South Shaftsbury, June 7, 1930]

[In 1930 Hervey Allen invited Robert Frost to a "conclave" of writers, which differed from Bread Loaf in that no teaching was involved.]

Dear Hervey:

I commend your pains. I can commend your plans too for the most part. (It warms me to the heart to be assured that there will be no manifesto.) Only you couldn't have chosen the time more effectually to leave me out, if you had chosen the first ten days of September on purpose. That's when I'm a fugitive from hay-fever in the higher mountains. I havent been below the ragweed line for anybody or anything between August 20 and September 15th since the year 1905. It wasn't just that the fever was unendurable, but it left me in no condition to face the winter. I'm sorry. But I mustn't think I matter too much. There are one or two on your list who will be no unhappier for not having me of the party. I shall be anxious for the success of the experiment. It is a good idea. (If I remember rightly it was partly mine. At any rate I have long contemplated such an annual conclave on the side hill of my own farm—if I should ever feel executive enough to carry it out. It will amply satisfy me to see someone else carry it out. I shall want to hear all about it.) I wish you could visit me here before you go back to Bermuda this fall and report to me. I like your seriousness in your books and out of them and count some time on more converse with you.

Hervey Allen, 1930

1930 Faculty: (rear) Lee Simonson, Walter Prichard Eaton, Theodore Morrison, Gorham Munson; (front) Mrs. Eaton, Edith Mirrielees, Margaret Widdemer, Samuel Merwin, Robert Gay, Hervey Allen

ROBERT FROST TO LOUIS UNTERMEYER
[South Shaftsbury, July 14, 1930]

Dear Louis: I am left out of the Two Weeks Manuscript Sales Fair as I had reason to suppose I would be. I thought perhaps it would be less embarrassing all round if I simply forgot to go to the earlier educational session at Bread Loaf. But I have been come after by Pres. Moody and flatteringly written after by our friend Gay to be present and help them dedicate the Memorial Library to Wilfred Davison on Monday July 21st. Pres. Moody said frankly that he saw no way but for the second session to go on commercial as it had begun. I judge he thought the two sessions could be kept like the right and left hand each from knowing what the other was doing. He asked me to think of the two as separate. They can't be separate, of course, and in the end belonging to one will mean belonging to both. But I don't care if it does in the end. This year can make no difference in principle, and I hate to put on airs that will hurt either Moody's feelings or Gay's. I agreed to go on the understanding that they would give you your choice of sessions. I knew you said you came a good deal to be there when I was. But of course we are going to see each other here right off anyway, and maybe it would be too ostentatious for you to desert the Farrow [John Farrar] session because I was left out of it. You may be sure I don't mind your being with that gang for a visit if only as a spy and agent provocateur. You can't imagine how cleanly I have forgiven the Johnnie. The explanation is that I am at heart secretly tickled if I offended him unintentionally. I suppose it to have been unintentionally because to this hour I don't know what my offense was. I am too cowardly to offend anybody intentionally and usually too skillfull to do it unintentionally. So I am stuck. I can't hurt anybody no matter how much he deserves it. When I do it is a triumph of the divinity that shapes our ends. It gives me a funny feeling I must say I like. I suppose it's a manly feeling, but I'm such a stranger to it I hardly know. Yes I came off so well with the Johnnie that I shan't care if you do treat him as if nothing had ever happened. I even evened the score between him and Lesley. . . .

ROBERT FROST TO LESLEY FROST FRANCIS
[Coconut Grove, Florida, February 1942]

. . . I have seen more than usual of Hervey and listened to about a fifth of his big new novel [*The Forest and the Fort,* 1943]. It sounds all right. All about Indians and Fort Pitt in the seventeen fifties. He is a case study in his reduced circumstances. He is all tightened up with anxieties, real or imaginary I cant guess which. If it is as bad as he thinks it is, he is a tragedy of the income tax. He seems to spend part of his time every year going over his profits and losses with the income tax collectors. Thats really all thats been the matter with both Anne and Hervey—finding themselves poor when they and everybody else thought they were rich. They have come a swift fall from butlers chauffers and the Surf Club clear down to the possibility of having their proudest possession Bonfield taken to satisfy the commissioner of internal revenue. They may rent Bonfield if they dont have to have it sold. I take Herveys side against a system that puts such a heavy penalty on enterprise and creation. . . .

—FROM FAMILY LETTERS OF ROBERT AND ELINOR FROST, EDITED BY ARNOLD GRADE (1972)

The old Music Hall and "Ell," taken sometime before the 1931 fire

COLLEGE HEAD LEADS VOLUNTEERS
IN DASH TO BLAZING SCHOOL

Paul Dwight Moody Helps Save Bread Loaf Inn
At Ripton, Vt.

RACES 12 MILES IN BACCALAUREATE GARB

Antique Furniture and Rare Books Are
Carried To Safety

MIDDLEBURY, Vt. June 14—President Paul Dwight Moody, clad in the robes in which he delivered the baccalaureate address to 700 students and graduates at Middlebury College, today led a procession of cars which raced 12 miles over the Green Mountains to the blazing Bread Loaf school of the college at Ripton.

The college head and hundreds of alumni volunteers arrived in time to save antique furniture worth thousands of dollars, and several rare autographed book collections from the Davison Memorial library.

Despite the efforts of firemen, graduates and students, the adjoining buildings of the school were destroyed with a loss of $50,000. Two men, Dean Burt A. Haveltine of the men's college and Farm Manager Hubbel, were injured.

President Moody had completed his baccalaureate address and was greeting returning alumni on the chapel steps when he was told of the fire. He quickly told the 700 men and women that Bread Loaf school was in danger and announced his intention of going there at once.

In every form of conveyance, from luxurious limousine to rattletrap automobiles and bicycles, students and graduates followed the president. Students stood on running boards as the swaying cars raced perilously over the road. Scores of women, many of them graduates of Middlebury College, were included in the hundreds who joined in the dangerous mountain parade.

BUT ONE STEAM AUTOMOBILE

Despite a restraining order, issued to students as soon as it was seen that almost the entire senior class was heading for the cars, many of them, still in their caps and gowns, seized the chance to end their college days in a literal blaze of glory.

When President Moody and his volunteers arrived at the scene, after a hectic 12-mile drive, they found flames sweeping the school annexes, the school theater and the Davison Memorial Library.

Manager Arnold Swift and a score of school employees, who had just finished setting table for the annual commencement dinner, had organized a fire-fighting brigade. They were handicapped by lack of water. The Middlebury fire department sent a truck when an alarm was telephoned, but the 45 minutes spent in toiling over the mountain had given the fire great headway.

Only one stream of water was available, Fire Chief Caswell of Middlebury found, and this was pumped through a hoseline a mile long.

Running to Bread Loaf Inn, the original structure willed the college by Joseph Battell in 1915, President Moody began to carry out the antique furniture. He was assisted by the others as fast as they arrived.

Volunteers fighting a losing battle

Adjacent to the ruins, the Inn survived

Others hurried to the Davison Memorial Library, dedicated only last summer by Robert Frost, the poet, to Prof. Wilfred Davison, former dean of Middlebury College. This building was destroyed but priceless rare autographed book collections were saved from the flames. Scores of books were rescued from the fire by the volunteers and firemen, at great personal danger.

OTHER BUILDINGS BURNED

The theatre, which had a seating capacity of 200, and the electric power plant, the exhaust of which is believed to have started the fire, were razed by fire, as were several small farm buildings. Heat and smoke hampered the amateur fire-fighters.

Aid was called from every town within a 40-mile radius. Brandon and Vergennes were among those which responded. The Brandon was used to send a protecting blanket of water over the original inn structure by Chief Caswell and this saved the building from destruction. As it was, the inn was the only building standing when the flames were finally extinguished.

Burt A. Hazeltine, dean of the men's college, was one of the first to arrive from Middlebury. He sustained a foot injury when he jumped or fell from a first floor window in the inn. Ligaments in his foot were torn, and his ankle sprained. Farm Manager Hubbell was burned about the hands and feet as he tried to save farm property. Both were taken to the college hospital at Middlebury for treatment. Many of the fire-fighters suffered from smoke inhalation, but none of them needed treatment.

Included among those who made the wild ride with President Moody to Ripton were William Hazlett Upson, nationally known magazine writer, and his wife, who is a graduate of Middlebury College. They assisted in removing furniture, as did J. J. Fritz, business manager of the college.

SCHOOL WILL OPEN JUNE 30

After the flames had been put out, President Moody announced that the famous Bread Loaf School of English, conducted each summer by Middlebury College, would open as scheduled on June 30. Trustees of the school, a graduate institution, will meet tomorrow to make temporary arrangements.

Bread Loaf Inn, a three-story wooden structure which dates back to 1865, was bequeathed to the college by Joseph Battell, long known as "the connoisseur of mountains." In his grant to the college, which included 35,000 acres, are four mountains.

The school buildings were to be open today under Manager Swift for the commencement dinner, to follow the baccalaureate exercises.

Prominent writers and literary critics are among those who conduct courses at the school each summer, bringing the school a national reputation. No class distinctions are tolerated at the school during the season. Waitresses, all of whom are college girls, are invited to attend entertainments in which the faculty and students participate.

—*Boston Herald,* June 15, 1931

Theodore and Kathleen Morrison, 1932

[Robert Gay] wanted to be relieved of the Conference, and recommended to President Moody that I take over as his successor in 1932. I had plenty of diffidence about accepting the job, but I had what I suppose were presentable external qualifications. After some five years on the staff of the *Atlantic Monthly* and the Atlantic Monthly Press, I could be called an editor, though actually it had been made clear to me that successful editing and publishing were not my metier, and I had gone back to teaching at Harvard. I had literary aspirations of my own, and my first book, a narrative poem, had been published. Like most of the world's families at any time, and especially in America in 1932, my wife and I needed any income we could scrabble together. Salaries at the bottom academic ranks did not stretch far. I agreed to try directing the Writers' Conference, and as it turned out, I kept on doing so for twenty-four years.

— *Theodore Morrison,*
BREAD LOAF WRITERS' CONFERENCE: THE FIRST
THIRTY YEARS (1976)

Theodore Morrison, early 1930s

THEODORE MORRISON TO HARRY OWEN
[September 30, 1932]

Dear Harry:

I was glad to receive your note, and glad to hear that the Conference has been well spoken of. It seemed to me that we had a gratifying session in several respects. I felt that it passed on a more mature level than usual; that we had a much larger proportion of actually qualified and promising writers, indeed that the group as a whole was more advanced intellectually than usual; and I think that the lectures and round-tables were for the most part well-received, and with some exceptions livelier and more stimulating than in the two previous years I attended.

There is no denying that there were some failures and objectionable features also. We got off to a propitious start, but as the Conference went on, some of the members of the staff felt that the group was hard to get acquainted with, and that relations between staff and students were not as cordial as usual. At the same time, complaints of neglect by the staff, or aloofness, gathered head toward the end of the session. The reasons for this state of affairs I think I have got pretty clearly in mind by now. The chief cause was Mrs. Eudy. She came avid for flattery and social distinction; the staff held her off with frigid politeness, and some of the students wrote ridiculous rhymes about her behind her back. I felt badly for her, knowing how generous she had been to the Conference previously. But I give you my word that neither I myself nor any member of the staff could bow down and connive in that terrible woman's passion for flattery and advertising. The result was that she went about definitely trying to create dissatisfaction, and within limits, succeeding. I had a final attack from her in person, and know all about it. The consensus of everyone's opinion is that it would be extremely unwise for her to come again; we could not, in fact, permit it.

Another cause of dissatisfaction was Margaret Widdemer's attempts to heal some wounded and neurotic souls—attempts intensified this year by the state of her own health, and made the more injurious by the fact that several members of the Conference were ready to be hysterical on slight encouragement. The result of this is that I shall have to make a change in the staff; I've never been content with Margaret's work, and have always resented her emphasis on problems that seem to me out of our scope, such as marital difficulties. I tried last year to obtain the services of several nationally known novelists in her place, but was unsuccessful. She is on the point of resigning anyway, knowing that I am out of sympathy with her methods; and I shall have to give her the opportunity.

Despite these disturbances, I am still convinced that the Conference passed successfully. I have numerous plans for next summer. . . .

Bernard DeVoto (center) holds forth
before admirers, early 1930s (Rae Eastman)

DeVoto at the lectern: an
assured tour-de-force (Rae Eastman)

Last night DeVoto spoke on religious experiments in America, culminating with the Mormons, and he and the storm were a perfect orchestration. He began by reading a passage from Isaiah about the end of the world, accompanied by active lightning and thunder, but when he progressed to Revelation, the storm intensified. He said that the Mormons were insane, and a door slammed in punctuation, he said their attempt was hysterical and it slammed again. He said that they had failed, and the door banged shut, with a frightening crash. But the best part was at the beginning. After the Bible readings which began his talk, he closed the Scripture solemnly and said, "These are troubled times," and all the lights went out.

—*Frances Fox Sandmel,*
   JOURNAL (1938)

Bernard and Avis DeVoto, 1930s

Even at Bread Loaf, where his friends were most numerous and most tested, where his authority was most respected and submitted to, where he was no Johnny-come-lately trying to break in but one of the inner group of regulars, DeVoto's abrasive temperament sometimes offended people, and their resentment brought him back to the old, unsleeping suspicion that there were "DeVoto-haters" around. Edith Mirrielees could cut away literary gangrene, or put a deformed story out of its misery, so gently that the victim did not even know he bled, and kissed the knife that ventilated him. DeVoto in private, or in a letter, or to anyone about whom he felt protective, could do the same—could deal with the sad incongruity between ambition and talent with a surprising understanding and gentleness. The respect for him that many Fellows and Conference members carried away with them was close to reverence. But when he stood before an audience he had to impress it. As Kubie told him, he heard the bugles of his own rhetoric and sniffed dust and gunpowder. He could not resist making a phrase, and when he was warmed up there was no such phrasemaker in the United States unless perhaps Mencken. The implacable show-off in him stamped and thundered, he lacked the internal governor that would have told him when enough was enough. In chasing foolishness and pretension through Bread Loaf's auditorium with his bloody hatchet, he sometimes forgot that pretension and foolishness had people wrapped around them and that these people could bleed.

—*Wallace Stegner,*
   THE UNEASY CHAIR: A BIOGRAPHY OF
   BERNARD DEVOTO (1973)

Wallace and Mary Page Stegner, 1938 (BDV)

Louis Untermeyer charms a conferee, late 1930s

Then Lewis went alone to the Bread Loaf Writers' Conference at Middlebury College [1928]. He had been invited to give two special lectures to the general session, which consisted of an audience of the aspiring and idealistic young and of spinster schoolteachers, with Robert Gay, Edith Mirrielees, and Grant Overton in charge. Lewis was fantastically drunk. He smoked on the platform, swore, and made faces at his tumbler of water. He assured his listeners that they were wasting their time, that it was impossible to teach "creative writing," and that writers generally were a bastard lot of human beings. His major theme, however, was that too much attention had been given to Colonel Lindbergh and not enough to Willa Cather, and presently he was talking about the admirable work of Colonel Cather. When he finished, there was no applause whatever. He had been invited to a party afterward at Robert Gay's cottage, but he wisely chose to disappear for an hour and nap. Then he turned up. How to get rid of him? everyone wondered. But he was now quite sober and he completely charmed them. He was not, however, held to his second engagement, but made a hurried trip to New York.

—*Mark Schorer,*
SINCLAIR LEWIS: AN AMERICAN LIFE (1961)

DeVoto, in the recollection of Gorham Munson, persuaded Lewis to come to the final session of the Bread Loaf Writers' Conference, trustful because Lewis now was drinking only beer. Lewis agreed to serve as leader at the last afternoon round-table discussion and to attend the closing banquet, and he arrived at Bread Loaf with a large bottle of whisky, which he at once passed around. The discussion was not very lively because the students were in awe of the visitor and some of them, conceivably, remembered an earlier, disastrous occasion. At one point Lewis tried to provoke them into discussion by a fiery demand that they speak up, without conspicuous success. In the evening his spirits were even higher. At a considerable distance from the speakers' table, he indulged in mimicry of Arnold Bennett and other English writers, and he improvised at intervals a free-verse poem on "Bennie DeVoto from the Wasatch Mountains," a Sandburghian bit. DeVoto was writing his novel, *We Accept with Pleasure,* and he could not resist creating a character, Frank Archer, "a great revelist," in the image of Sinclair Lewis:

> It took her some moments to realize that Frank Archer wasn't drunk, that this appalling restlessness, this St. Vitus, this inundation of talk was his normal pressure . . . he was a kind of electrical disturbance. He wasn't actually spinning like a top or hanging by his toes from the ceiling but you had a dizzy impression that he must be.

The alteration of physical characteristics—short and round, black and gray-haired, bushy-browed—is no disguise, nor is the anticipation of a still-unenacted item in his matrimonial history:

> Two women had divorced Archer. In the purest self-protection, as one would flee from a falling cliff. . . . He had the mind of a cheer leader–Ploughboy gaping at the eternal dawn. Diurnal wonder of the tremendous platitude. Periodical discovery of the utterly apparent.

The appraisal, like the portrait, is nearly just; it is also cool.
—*Mark Schorer,*
SINCLAIR LEWIS: AN AMERICAN LIFE (1961)

Sinclair Lewis, 1930s

My wife and I were uncertain what the evening might produce. We had invited President and Mrs. Moody . . . to join the staff and our Nobel Laureate guest at dinner. We thought a protective interval of insulation might be in order between the Moodys and Lewis and accordingly put them at opposite ends of the table. In this we miscalculated. President Moody kept straining, at an inconvenient distance, to hear what Lewis was saying. Moody would have liked nothing better than to sit elbow to elbow with Lewis and engage him in direct talk without a row of frustrating intermediaries eating their dinner in between. Fortunately Lewis launched into a performance which became audible throughout the whole dining room. People put down their knives and forks or held them suspended, hunching closer to listen. Once he got started on his theme, Lewis took the bit in his teeth and galloped off with it like a runaway horse. His eyes grew bulbous with concentration, totally indifferent to the fascination of everyone within earshot. He produced an extraordinary *tour-de-force,* elaborating at surprising length, a kind of free-verse, Vachel Lindsay–like chant celebrating the hegira of Bernard DeVoto from Ogden, Utah, to the effete culture of the East. If DeVoto, listening close at hand, was in the least put out, he did not show it by a twitch. He appeared to be disinterestedly studying an unusual feat.

—*Theodore Morrison,*
BREAD LOAF WRITERS' CONFERENCE: THE FIRST
THIRTY YEARS (1976)

*Josephine Johnson admires a pitcher
of Fletcher Pratt's martinis, 1936 (BDV)*

*Josephine Johnson, in one of many
photos snapped by Bernard DeVoto, 1934*

Reclining on the lawn of Maple Cottage, 1934: Owen Lattimore, Hervey Allen, Theodore Morrison, Kathleen Morrison, Josephine Johnson (BDV)

1936 Faculty and Fellows: Dick Brown, Anthony Wrynn, George Stevens, Edward L. Crook, Theodore Morrison, Robert Hillyer, Gorham Munson, Robeson Bailey; (center) John Mason Brown, Raymond Everitt, Bernard DeVoto; (front) George Marion O'Donnell, Avis DeVoto, Helen Everitt, Eleanor Delamater, Janet Johl, Kathleen Morrison, Hope Sykes

Josephine Johnson, frail, pretty, poetic, and feminine, appeared at Bread Loaf as a Fellow . . . in the summer of 1934. She elicited from DeVoto a fury of admiration that lasted for several years. Her winning the Pulitzer Prize for *Now in November* was a triumph that he predicted and enjoyed fully. As editor of *The Saturday Review of Literature* he published a number of her poems. His admiration did not go unnoted. On one occasion, a staff artist at *The Saturday Review* produced a DeVoto Map of the United States, which showed only Cambridge, Bread Loaf, Utah, and the routes of Lewis and Clark, Mark Twain, and Josephine Johnson.

> —*Wallace Stegner,*
> THE UNEASY CHAIR: A BIOGRAPHY OF
> BERNARD DEVOTO (1973)

We begin by thinking that we're going to be Proust, and we end by being happy if we can achieve a few paragraphs we aren't ashamed to have our best friends read.

> —*Bernard DeVoto,*
> AN OFT-REPEATED REMARK AT BREAD LOAF

Wyman Parker, Julia Peterkin, William Harris, and Hervey Allen relax before the Inn, 1934 (BDV)

Julia Peterkin, 1936 (BDV)

I was unprepared for her extraordinary picturesqueness, for I had at that time seen no one who could describe her to me. She has, as is now generally known, an almost classical figure, quite magnificent red hair, and a head that Frances Newman once described as "a modern edition of an old Greek classic." And her voice and manner match her hair in warmth. Her unusual height, her supple erectness, unyielding to the current careless slouch, and her amazing quantity of hair which has never known shears, are in no sense modern. This special blend of periods in one personality made our meeting with her memorable. Life outside of Lang Syne Plantation was, for the first time, awaiting her then [1922], and she was eager and vibrant as a girl in her awareness of it.
—*Emily Clark,*
  INNOCENCE ABROAD (1931)

Julia Peterkin's story is one of the brilliant chapters of [*The Reviewer*'s] history. It is also one of the brilliant chapters of Southern literary history, for in spite of the strict limits of her own special field her name has become almost universal. She has given to a modern public the half-barbaric plantation Negro in a form quite new; a creature far removed from low comedy or from conventional romance; a courageous, inarticulate, heart-tearing creature to whom propaganda or race conflict is yet unknown; a creature in conflict, as she herself has said, single-handedly and rather majestically with Fate itself, more inescapable, uncompromising, and pitiless than any superior race or individual.
—*Emily Clark,*
  INNOCENCE ABROAD (1931)

*Owen Lattimore, Raymond
Everitt, unknown, mid-1930s*

*Hervey Allen, Margaret Farrar,
Avis DeVoto, Alexander Laing,
Owen Lattimore, 1934 (BDV)*

*Lauren Gilfillen and
Raymond Everitt, 1934 (BDV)*

1937 Faculty: (rear) Louis Untermeyer, Herbert Agar, Raymond Everitt, Theodore Morrison, Paul Green, Gorham Munson; (front) Kathleen Morrison, Helen Everitt, Eleanor Chilton, Edith Mirrielees, Bernard DeVoto, George Stevens

John Mason Brown, Isabel Wilder, Raymond Everitt, Cassie Brown, George Stevens, 1936 (BDV)

The Bread Loaf teaching was a how-to course—how to do, how to avoid. Inevitably it reflected [DeVoto's] personal attitudes, and it helped to establish Bread Loaf as a hard-headed, commonsensical, practical academy, anti-faddist, anti-modernist, anti-Bohemian, anti-Marxist, anti-coterie (or at least *non* all of these), closer to the middle class than to the proletariat either *lumpen* or intellectual, closer to America than to Europe, closer to *Harper's, Atlantic,* and *The Saturday Review of Literature* than to *The New Masses, New Republic,* or *The Nation,* more inclined to stress the traditional than the experimental or revolutionary. And, DeVoto might have added, more inclined to think than to throb, more inclined to consult fact and experience than wishful theory, more interested in communication than in self-expression, exhibitionism, or public confession.

—*Wallace Stegner,*
THE UNEASY CHAIR: A BIOGRAPHY OF
BERNARD DEVOTO (1974)

Relaxing on the Inn front porch, 1930s (BDV)

The dining room was not only an indispensable locus of nourishment but a center where social stratifications made themselves felt. Staff members sat together at their own table, while the general membership were rotated among smaller tables up and down the room. A good deal of eyeing of the staff table with its visiting celebrities took place, but an even more invidious distinction affected both staff and conferees alike. The Inn not only took in transients, but boarded an appreciable number of Bread Loaf cottage owners, some of them relics of the Battell era. This favored corps occupied tables along the south wall of the dining room, next to the tall windows overlooking the parterre of snapdragons, marigolds, and other annuals across the road from the Inn. Fingerbowl Alley, as it was called, not only preempted a superior position, but provided choices from a menu while Conference members and staff had to accept whatever fare they found set before them.

The cottage residents complicated the scene in other ways. Some of them felt a right of proprietorship in Bread Loaf and its doings. They wanted to attend lectures without registering as members of the Conference; sometimes they felt entitled to interviews with the staff about their own literary ventures. Bob Gay asked me once to read a manuscript novel by a lady for whose family one of the Bread Loaf cottages had been named. The novel proved no better than my worse fears, but when I tried to approach its defects by saying that I had some difficulty distinguishing its characters from each other, the author answered, "That's queer, because I played them all over on the piano before beginning to write." Traditionally all evening affairs at Bread Loaf have been open to the public gratis, and this rule still holds. To protect the daytime program, a system of fees was

Lula (Mrs. Robert) Gay, Marjorie Upson, Theodore Morrison, William Hazlett Upson approach the Little Theater for an evening program

worked out by hour, day, or week for transients or residents not registered at the Conference. The scheme was awkward and unenforceable, and the problem remained unsolved until the Inn gave up its hotel license, becoming simply the quarters of the School of English and the Conference.

Fingerbowl Alley was not the only vexation imposed by the dining room. Meals had to meet a rigidly enforced schedule. In very early years, a bugler took his stand on the porch of the Inn and summoned the indolent to breakfast with a relentless reveille. Later he was supplanted by a no less insistent bell ringer. Laggards at any meal encountered a firmly closed dining room door.

—*Theodore Morrison,*
BREAD LOAF WRITERS' CONFERENCE: THE FIRST THIRTY YEARS (1976)

Theodore Morrison and John Crowe Ransom stand outside the Little Theater, 1935 (BDV)

Ransom "always stood easily before the class" at Bread Loaf and taught "extemporaneously in a quiet voice" that just managed to "compete with the lawn mowers outside the window." When he read there was no rhetoric in his voice, none of what at that time was popularly called interpretative reading. "He had too much love for a poem," [Laurence N.] Barrett thought, "not to let it stand on its own, and too much regard for his students to come between us and the poem. He simply read with a quiet dignity, and beneath his restraint we could feel his affection for the thing." He never tried to interpret a poem or to make his students see the poem through him, but if his students chose they were "welcome to watch him encountering the verse, not as a *magister* but simply as another human reader, and not in order that we should imitate his responses but, one level beyond that, in order that we might work with them and against them." He taught the poem, then, as he read it, "almost anonymously."

—*Thomas Daniel Young,*
  GENTLEMAN IN A DUSTCOAT (1976)

1937 Faculty and Fellows: (rear) Louis Untermeyer, Herbert Agar, Raymond Everitt, Theodore Morrison, Bernard DeVoto, Paul Green, Gorham Munson, Richard Brown, James Still; (center) Fletcher Pratt, George Stephens; (front) {?}, {?}, Helen Everitt, Eleanor Chilton, Edith Mirrielees, {?}, Kathleen Morrison, {?}.

Though it was an obscure and happy-go-lucky life, I did not drop altogether out of sight. In August of 1937 I was given a fellowship to the Bread Loaf Writers' Conference in recognition of my first book of poems, *Stand With Me Here,* published the preceding fall. Bread Loaf, even thirty years ago, was prosperous enough to be able to offer seven such fellowships at a time, to four men and three women in 1937. Aside from a free two-weeks' vacation in the Green Mountains, the chief boon for me was having James Still as my roommate. Full of earthy tales of the Kentucky hills, he was wonderful company, once I had got to know him beneath his protective shell of shyness and taciturnity. He too had had a first book of poems the previous year, but at Bread Loaf he was working on short stories. These, the first he had ever written, were being taken by the *Atlantic,* the *Yale Review,* and the *Virginia Quarterly.* He was correcting proof on one or two of them while working on a new story.

It was my first experience of being with a fellow-writer at work. (And I can't offhand think of any I've had since.) In those years I used to start work on a poem with pencil or pen, and move to the typewriter when I began to feel anything permanent in what I was doing. But still, I think, composed at the typewriter. It was all very much a matter of sentence by sentence with him. He would work on a sentence or short group of sentences until it satisfied him, then tear off the strip of paper and add it to a little pile of sentences already written. Someone was writing prose with as much attention to detail as I was trying to write poetry. What was less obvious was how every detail in his stories was functional, no matter how casual it appeared. He had to point this out to me time and again. What was easiest to appreciate and relish was the delicious speech of his Kentucky mountain people.

—*Robert Francis,*
THE TROUBLE WITH FRANCIS: AN
AUTOBIOGRAPHY (1971)

Theodore Morrison and Edith Mirrielees during a picnic on the West Lawn, late 1930s (BDV)

James T. Farrell, 1937 (BDV)

James T. Farrell, 1937, parodying a Nazi goose-step

Writing is one of the cruelest of professions. The sense of possible failure in a literary career can torment one pitilessly. And failure in a literary career cannot be measured in dollars and cents. Poverty and the struggle for bread are not the only features of a literary career that can make it so cruel. There is the self-imposed loneliness. There is the endless struggle to perceive freshly and clearly, to realize and re-create on paper a sense of life. There is more than economic competition involved. The writer feels frequently that he is competing with time and with life itself. His hopes will sometimes ride high. His ambitions will soar until they have become so grandiose that they cannot be realized within the space of a single lifetime. The world opens up before the young writer as a grand and glorious adventure in feeling and in understanding. Nothing human is unimportant to him. Everything he sees is germane to his purpose. Every word that he hears uttered is of potential use to him. Every mood, every passing fancy, every trivial thought can have its meaning and its place in the store of experience he is accumulating. The opportunities for assimilation are enormous, endless. And there is only one single short life of struggle in which to assimilate. A melancholy sense of time becomes a torment. One's whole spirit rebels against a truism that all men must realize, because it applies to all men. One seethes in rebellion against the realization that the human being must accept limitations, that he can develop in one line of effort only at the cost of making many sacrifices in other

lines. Time becomes for the writer the most precious good in all the world. And how often will he not feel that he is squandering this precious good? His life then seems like a sieve through which his days are filtering, leaving behind only a few, a very few, miserable grains of experience. If he is wasting time today, what assurance can he give himself that he will not be doing likewise tomorrow? He is struggling with himself to attain self-discipline. He weighs every failure in his struggle. He begins to find a sense of death—death before he has fulfilled any of his potentialities—like a dark shadow cast constantly close to his awareness.

—*James T. Farrell,*
   "How Studs Lonigan was Written,"
   The Frightened Philistines (1945)

1938 Faculty: (rear) Raymond Everitt, Robeson Bailey, Herbert Agar, Herschel Brickell, Wallace Stegner, Fletcher Pratt; (center) Gorham Munson, Bernard DeVoto, Theodore Morrison, Robert Frost, John Gassner; (front) Mary Stegner, Helen Everitt, Kathleen Morrison, Eleanor Chilton

Last night Frost gave the best lecture I have ever heard him give. His mind was seething and rolling with metaphors and humor, and he was exhausted when he was finished. He seemed to feel it was his last talk at Bread Loaf. He said that like a drowning man, he could remember everything in his life, and to hear him, one believed him.

He said he would follow his usual custom and make up some poems on the spot. It was the most remarkable performance I have ever seen. He talked on in the direction of an idea, all around it, and then said, "Here is a poem," and very slowly, changing a few words, but for the most part going ahead as one would on paper, he made his poem, and it was a good poem. He called it "Dark, Darker, Darkest." Life is *dark* because life, this bright foam that catches the light, is flowing forever and ever into insanity, into poverty. Life is *darker* because man doesn't know how to play the stops on mankind well enough to change the situation. We must advance in a broad front and we don't know how to turn to the poor and the insane. Life is *darkest* because, perhaps, we're not meant to do anything about it. Frost said he wanted life so much he hadn't time to play with dead things; man hasn't time.

—*Charles H. Foster,*
  JOURNAL (1938)

His talks were larded with unfounded allusions to his own "badness" and to behavior not proven by fact. All this accompanied the wit and wisdom of his usual Bread Loaf talks. Leisure time brought other problems. Bernard De-Voto, Herschel Brickell, Robeson Bailey, and their wives conspired to walk with him, and supply his late-breakfast needs of a raw egg and milk diluted with coffee. Couples played endless sets of doubles tennis, doggedly fought and exhausting to Robert's partner, whose life depended on no double faults and no missed balls. His moods were unpredictable. Brilliant talk before the fire of an evening at the faculty cottage often ended in abrupt departure, leaving his colleagues uncertain of the true reason—perhaps a distasteful argument or a fancied slight; more often the need for a solitary five-mile walk on the road toward the mountains.

—*Kathleen Morrison,*
  ROBERT FROST: A PICTORIAL CHRONICLE (1974)

*Archibald MacLeish arrives at
Bread Loaf in good humor, 1938*

*Theodore Morrison, Robert Frost,
Archibald MacLeish, 1938 (BDV)*

At MacLeish's reading, Frost sat near the back. Early in the proceedings he found some mimeographed notices on a nearby chair and sat rolling and folding them in his hands. Now and again he raised the roll of paper, or an eyebrow, calling the attention of his seat mates to some phrase or image. He seemed to listen with an impartial, if skeptical, judiciousness. About halfway through the reading he leaned over and said in a carrying whisper, "Archie's poems all have the same *tune.*" As the reading went on, to the obvious pleasure of the audience, he grew restive. The fumbling and rustling of the papers in his hands became disturbing. Finally MacLeish announced, "You, Andrew Marvell," a tour de force that makes a complete thirty-six-line poem out of a single sentence. It was a favorite. Murmurs of approval, intent receptive faces. The poet began. Then an exclamation, a flurry in the rear of the hall. The reading paused, heads turned. Robert Frost, playing around like an idle, inattentive boy in a classroom, had somehow contrived to strike a match and set fire to his handful of papers and was busy beating them out and waving away the smoke.

Those who knew Frost of old laughed and shook their heads over him. Those who did not know him that well thought his bonfire the comic accident he made it seem. But later, over in Treman, a circle of people gathered around MacLeish and persuaded him to read his new radio play, *Air Raid.* There he was, still on center stage, and there was Frost again in the audience, on the periphery—a thing he could not stand.

In *Air Raid* the announcer, waiting with the inhabitants of a nameless town for the coming of the planes, repeats several times the dry refrain, "We have seen nothing and heard nothing." Some of the people in Treman Cottage that night, not paying much attention or not comprehending, could have made a similar report. One was myself. Another was Charles Curtis, gifted with an enviable capacity for enjoying a party, who went smiling around through the whole evening remarking on how wonderful Bread Loaf was, what good talk, wonderful people, wholehearted good times. But others, including DeVoto, interpreted every rattle of ice in a glass, every cough and murmur, as sight or sound of war.

For Frost was quite deliberately trying to break up the reading. His comments from the floor, at first friendly and wisecracking, became steadily harsher and more barbed. He interrupted, he commented, he took exception. What began as the ordinary give and take of literary conversation turned into a clear intention of frustrating and humiliating Archie MacLeish, and the situation became increasingly painful to those who comprehended it. Once, DeVoto got up and went outside and walked around the house to get over his agitation. When he came back, the inquisition was

Robert Frost and Avis DeVoto, 1938 (BDV)

still going on, MacLeish patiently going ahead, Frost nipping and snapping around his heels, and now and then sinking his teeth in with a savage quick bite that looked playful and was not. People sat where they had been trapped, and looked into their drained glasses and did not quite dare look around.

Eventually DeVoto, who more or less agreed with Frost's opinion of the play, but who completely sympathized with MacLeish, being systematically humiliated by a man he enormously respected and would not reply to, said something. No one who was there seems to remember exactly what he said—something like, "For God's sake, Robert, let him read!" Hardly more than that—not enough to catch the attention of the ones like Charles Curtis who were enjoying the literary evening. But a rebuke, and one did not rebuke Jahweh.

It does not appear that Frost replied at once, or directly. But shortly he elected to take offense at something—DeVoto remembered it as his taking personally a derogatory remark that was meant for Stephen Spender. He said something savage, got up and went out on the arm of the cheerfully oblivious Charles Curtis. The reading went on, lamely but with relief, to its end, and people escaped to their rooms.

—*Wallace Stegner,*
THE UNEASY CHAIR: A BIOGRAPHY OF
BERNARD DEVOTO (1974)

Robert Frost, Archibald MacLeish,
Theodore Morrison, 1938 (BDV)

The conversation [at Treman] shifted . . . into little eddies
and I went over to see how Frost was stirring the waters. I
sat next to Frost on a davenport and after a time Archie
came over and sat on the arm of it. Frost had one arm
around me and as more drinks were drunk and the discussion arose Archie balanced himself with an arm around my
shoulder. With Frost's arm around my back and Archie's
around my neck and with both arguing and almost meeting before my nose, I felt at least physically in the center
of American poetry. Frost said that it made him mad when
"a young squirt" like Spender gave what he had worked on
all his life a phrase and tried to take the credit for it. "I'm
going to England and spank Spender." "Jesus H. Christ,
Robert," said Archie, "you're the one who ought to be
spanked. You're the foundation and we all know it." "I'm
an old man. I want you to say it, to say it often. I want to
be flattered." Archie said that it wasn't that he wanted
flattery. It was perfectly natural to want to get recognition
for what you had started. Archie then tried to make the
conversation less personal and Frost said "God-damn
everything to hell so long as we're friends, Archie." "We
are friends, Robert."

—*Charles H. Foster,*
JOURNAL (1938)

I should like to believe the poet gets an equivalent assurance in the affections of the affectionate. He has fitted into
the nature of mankind. He is justified of his numbers. He
has acquired friends who will even cheat for him a little
and refuse to see his faults if they are not so glaring as to
show through eyelids. And friends are everything. For why
have we wings if not to seek friends at an elevation?

—*Robert Frost,*
FROM HIS PREFACE TO BREAD LOAF ANTHOLOGY
(1939)

ROBERT FROST TO KATHLEEN MORRISON
[c. September 1938]

Dear Kay:

I try you with a pencil to see if a change of tool won't give me the release that a change of paper sometimes does. I am like an ocean that in its restlessness may have brought up every imaginable shape to the surface, but won't be satisfied till it brings up the sea serpent. You two rescued me from a very dangerous self when you had the idea of keeping me for the whole session at Bread Loaf. I am still infinitely restless, but I came away from you as good as saved. I had had a long lover's quarrel with the world. I loved the world, but you might never have guessed it from the things I thought and said. Now the quarrel is made up. Not that it ought to matter to anyone but me, but I can't help hoping it matters a little to my friends. The turning point for the better was on that Sunday when I seemed to behave so much worse. Stanley King's charge against me was ingratitude. It will be a sensitive subject with me the rest of my life. I must be careful to avoid even the appearance of ingratitude. I am grateful to you two for your ministrations. Never doubt me. Let us pray the sea-serpent I feel so big with and about may prove to be poetic drama.

Others to whom I should take this opportunity to acknowledge indebtedness for my relative restoration are Herschel Brickell, Bob Bailey, Fletcher Pratt, Gassner, Strauss, Stegner and those two literary girls Hassell and Negli, in about that order. Hershell and Bob lead all the rest. I save Benny for a complete list by himself. There I think my obligations are met in form and my character for the moment vindicated. . . .

Kathleen Morrison, 1938 (BDV)

Kathleen Morrison (right) chats with Helen Everitt and Edith Mirrielees, 1938 (Courtesy Rae Eastman)

ROBERT FROST TO LOUIS UNTERMEYER
[Boston, November 28, 1938]

. . . This year I have worked hard in the open, and I think it has done me good. My secretary has soothed my spirit like music in her attendance on me and my affairs. She has written my letters and sent me off on my travels. It is an unusual friendship. I have come to value my poetry almost less than the friendships it has brought me. I say it who wouldnt have believed I would ever live to say it. And I say it with a copy of The Independant containing my first published poem on the desk before me. I was thrust out into the desolateness of wondering about my past whether it had not been too cruel to those I had dragged with me and almost to cry out to heaven for a word of reassurance that was not given me in time. Then came this girl stepping innocently into my days to give me something to think of besides dark regrets. My half humorous noisy contrition of the last few months has begun to die down. You have heard a lot of it and you are hearing it still a little here. I doubt if it has been quite dignified. I am told I am spoken of as her "charge." It is enough to be. Lets have some peace. You can figure it out for yourself how my status with a girl like her might be the perfect thing for me at my age in my position. I wish in some indirect way she might know the way I feel for her.

ROBERT FROST TO LOUIS UNTERMEYER
[*Boston, November 28, 1938*]

. . . Be moderately sorry for a poor old man of iron will.
Nothing I do or say is as yet due to anything but a strong
determination to have my own way. I may show as sick,
but it is for practical purposes. I dont know what I deserve
for a nature like mine. I was boasting to David [McCord]
this very day that I was clever enough to beat my nature.
Did he suppose I wasn't?

Well among the things I don't deserve but hope to get
is what I am about to propose from and for you. If you
consent to do it you will be doing more than one thing to
make my immediate future a joy forever. Not to beat about
the bush a page longer it is: Come to Bread Loaf and team
up with me in poetry criticism four or five days a week for
the two weeks of the Conference. You could go home
over the week end and I could go with you. We would
make the poetry consultations and clinics a joint stunt to
the nation. I got up this idea and Ted Morrison took to it
like live bait. I needn't go into my mixture of motives
except to say that they are all honorable by now. I am
growing more and more honorable every time the moon
comes safely through an eclipse. . . .

*1939 Faculty: (rear) Fletcher Pratt, Gorham Munson, Herbert
Agar, Richard Brown, Bernard DeVoto, Robeson Bailey, Herschel
Brickell; (center) John Gassner, Louis Untermeyer, Robert Frost,
Edith Mirrielees; (front) Mrs. John Gassner, Inga Pratt, Kathleen
Morrison, Eleanor Chilton, Mrs. Robeson Bailey*

At the poetry clinics Untermeyer would read a poem submitted by a conferee. The author remained mercifully anonymous, and everyone was free to criticize the technique, form, and content of the poem, with no holds barred. While reading a poem Untermeyer's voice occasionally sputtered out, but his wit and humor generally managed to put everyone at ease for a good discussion. He referred to the conferees as "a nest of singing birds," although he and Frost were well aware that many of the birds sang badly, that some were sentimental or crabbed, and that even the old birds were sometimes more concerned with staying snugly in their nest than in singing or flying. Much of the poetry read at the clinics was wretchedly conventional.

On one occasion Untermeyer read a sonnet and everyone tore it to shreds. It was full of cliches, sententious sentiments, high-flown rhetoric and inflated diction, and was in every way a poor imitation of conventional love lyrics. This time, Untermeyer said, he would break the rule of anonymity. He was sure the author wouldn't mind. The poet was William Shakespeare. Untermeyer had read one of Shakespeare's lesser known sonnets. There was a stunned silence. Someone asked to have the poem read again. Then the conferees gradually retreated from their severe criticism. They found many little literary gems they had missed with the first reading. Afterwards Frost and Untermeyer chuckled over how easily people can be intimidated by established literary reputations.

—*Peter J. Stanlis,*
"ACCEPTABLE IN HEAVEN'S SIGHT: ROBERT FROST AT BREAD LOAF, 1939–1941," IN FROST CENTENNIAL ESSAYS, VOL. 3, EDITED BY JAC THARPE (1978)

1940 Fellows pose with Theodore Morrison and Louis Untermeyer: (rear) Eudora Welty, John Ciardi, Brainard Cheney, Edna Frederickson, Untermeyer; (front) Marian Sims, Morrison, Carson McCullers. (Courtesy Virginia Spencer Carr)

FORTIES

I . . . remember her somewhat awkward, angular way of moving, those glasses of straight gin, and that air of secret, bemused, withdrawn self-communion that she wore much of the time. She was my first personal contact with a confirmed devotee of the grotesque, and I found her very interesting, but not easy to know . . . she seemed to me a twilight figure, old beyond her years, bizarre, everything about her just a little crooked, and hence interesting, but not necessarily what I would have liked to be myself.

> —*Wallace Stegner,*
> IN VIRGINIA SPENCER CARR, THE LONELY
> HUNTER: A BIOGRAPHY OF CARSON MCCULLERS
> (1975)

Louis Untermeyer and Carson McCullers, 1940

My one clear memory of her is of descending a flight of stairs at the Bread Loaf Inn in the company of Richard Brown, the assistant director. There was a pug-nosed little girl with black bangs at the foot of the stairs reading the bulletin board. I said to Dick Brown, "My God, whose *enfant terrible?*" And he said, "That's Carson McCullers." Then we drew back into the alcohol fumes that purified us.

> —*John Ciardi,*
> IN VIRGINIA SPENCER CARR, THE LONELY
> HUNTER: A BIOGRAPHY OF CARSON MCCULLERS
> (1975)

Friends of us both first brought Eudora Welty to visit me three years ago in Louisiana. It was hot midsummer, they had driven over from Mississippi, her home state, and we spent a pleasant evening together talking in the cool old house with all the windows open. Miss Welty sat listening, as she must have done a great deal of listening on many such occasions. She was and is a quiet, tranquil-looking, modest girl, and unlike the young Englishman of the story, she has something to be modest about, as this collection of short stories [*A Curtain of Green*] proves. . . .

She loves music, listens to a great deal of it, all kinds; grows flowers very successfully, and remarks that she is "underfoot locally," meaning that she has a normal amount of social life. Normal social life in a medium-sized Southern town can become a pretty absorbing occupation, and the only comment her friends make when a new story appears is, "Why, Eudora, when did you write that?" Not how, or even why, just when. They see her about so much, what time has she for writing? Yet she spends an immense amount of time at it. "I haven't a literary life at all," she wrote once, "not much of a confession, maybe. But I do feel that the people and things I love are of a true and human world, and there is no clutter about them. . . . I would not understand a literary life."

. . . She has never studied the writing craft in any college. She has never belonged to a literary group, and until after her first collection was ready to be published she had never discussed with any colleague or older artist any problem of her craft. Nothing else that I know about her could be more satisfactory to me than this; it seems to me immensely right, the very way a young artist should grow, with pride and independence and the courage really to face out the individual struggle; to make and correct mistakes and take the consequences of them, to stand firmly on his own feet in the end. I believe in the rightness of Miss Welty's instinctive knowledge that writing cannot be taught, but only learned, and learned by the individual in his own way, at his own pace and in his own time, for the process of mastering the medium is part of a cellular growth in a most complex organism; it is a way of life and a mode of being which cannot be divided from the kind of human creature you were the day you were born, and only

in obeying the law of this singular being can the artist know his true directions and the right ends for him.

Miss Welty escaped, by miracle, the whole corrupting and destructive influence of the contemporary, organized tampering with young and promising talents by professional teachers who are rather monotonously divided into two major sorts: those theorists who are incapable of producing one passable specimen of the art they profess to teach; or good, sometimes first-rate, artists who are humanly unable to resist forming disciples and imitators among their students. It is all well enough to say that, of this second class, the able talent will throw off the master's influence and strike out for himself. Such influence has merely added new obstacles to an already difficult road. . . .

. . . But there is a trap lying just ahead, and all short-story writers know what it is—The Novel. That novel which every publisher hopes to obtain from every short-story writer of any gifts at all, and who finally does obtain it, nine times out of ten. Already publishers have told her, "Give us first a novel, and then we will publish your short stories." It is a special sort of trap for poets, too, though quite often a good poet can and does write a good novel. Miss Welty has tried her hand at novels, laboriously, dutifully, youthfully thinking herself perhaps in the wrong to refuse, since so many authoritarians have told her that was the next step. It is by no means the next step. She can very well become a master of the short story, there are almost perfect stories in this book. It is quite possible she can never write a novel, and there is no reason why she should. The short story is a special and difficult medium, and contrary to a widely spread popular superstition it has no formula that can be taught by correspondence school. There is nothing to hinder her from writing novels if she wishes or believes she can. I only say that her good gift, just as it is now, alive and flourishing, should not be retarded by a perfectly artificial demand upon her to do the conventional thing. It is a fact that the public for short stories is smaller than the public for novels; this seems to me no good reason for depriving that minority.

—*Katherine Anne Porter,*
INTRODUCTION TO A CURTAIN OF GREEN BY
EUDORA WELTY (1941)

The game that outdid all others happened once a year when teachers and members at the Writers' Conference, employees and staff of the Inn, and townsfolk all came to the Homer Noble Farm for a battle royal. The diamond was marked out on our stubbly hayfield, sometimes using one or two of the granite boulders to mark the bases. It was Robert's custom to inspect the field on the morning of the game, and he nearly always decided that one of the rocks, usually the biggest and most obstructive, must be buried to lessen the danger of accident. At noon he would set forth with pick and shovel, outwearing and outlasting fellow workers twenty years or more his juniors. On one occasion he so exhausted himself that his batting performance during the game did not come up to his expectations. He hid his chagrin by disappearing into the woods, to be lured out by a sympathetic teammate. Choosing sides for the players was a touchy business. Robert, as one of the captains, felt imposed upon if he had to accept too many women for his team. And which side was to have the great catcher, Fletcher Pratt, member of the Conference staff, historian, and science fiction writer? Which was to have the swiftest base runner, or a visiting celebrity such as James Farrell, the novelist, or the cricket-playing poet Auden?

 —Kathleen Morrison,
  ROBERT FROST: A PICTORIAL CHRONICLE (1974)

Robert Frost, swinger of birches, at the annual softball game, 1940s

There was some effort to find tennis opponents for Robert Frost, and since he couldn't play singles, doubles were arranged. Kay Morrison and Frost were to oppose Louis Untermeyer and me. It was understood among us that Frost was to win one set. Louis and I—though neither of us was any good—generally won the first set, and then threw the second. Louis could not be restrained from making remarks, which Frost ignored, about giving Frost the set. Afterwards Frost would say, "I don't know what it is about Louis. He starts well but can't sustain it." Untermeyer, who prided himself on his virility as much as Frost, had to keep quiet.

 —Richard Ellmann (1986)

Robert Frost, playing tennis with (note) a net, 1940s

One of the social highlights during each Writers' Conference was the softball game played in an afternoon on the boulder-strewn meadow on the lower end of the Homer Noble farm. The staff, the conferees, famous visiting writers, and occasionally guests at the Inn, divided into two teams. Great care was taken that the best players should be on Frost's team, thus increasing the odds that his team would win. Frost disliked having women players, so they were not chosen for his team. Conferees with cameras recording the occasion called forth his silent ire and wrath. Fletcher Pratt, who was reputed to have been a prize fighter, was generally the plate umpire, and his gestures in calling strikes and balls, and in declaring base runners out or safe, were histrionic, and provided many hot arguments and witty comments.

Benny DeVoto and Frost were generally the two outstanding players. DeVoto's rambunctious character came out sharply during the softball games. He would lay down a bunt along the third base line. Then, after reaching first base ahead of the ball, counting successfully on the ineptitude of the fielders, he would keep running to second, then on to third, always a few strides ahead of the ball, then in a mad dash home, climaxed by a slide that began a good ten feet before he reached the plate, with the cheers of supporters and the jeers of opponents ringing him around the bases. Thus, on several occasions he turned a soft bunt into a home run. Once in his slide to the home plate he tore his trousers from ankle to knee and had to play the rest of the game with safety pins holding his pants together. . . .

One incident humiliating to Frost occurred, which illustrated why he did not like to play softball with women on the teams. Frost hit a liner into left field and tried to stretch it into a double. The outfielder threw the ball in a long arching fly back to the second baseman, Laura Brooks, a hefty, solid girl, who stood in the base path between second and first, blocking Frost's path to the bag. As he ran toward second base Frost saw her standing with her gloved hand outstretched waiting for the ball to descend. He stopped, perplexed by how to get around her to second base. She caught the ball with one hand, turned around, and casually tagged Frost. Fletcher Pratt had run out almost to the pitcher's mound, and with elaborate gestures he shouted Frost out, waving him to the sidelines. Sheepishly, Frost left the field. To be tagged out thus by a mere girl was almost too much for him. Had the second

baseman been a man Frost would undoubtedly have knocked him over to reach the bag. It was very difficult to play to win when women players required chivalrous behavior by their male opponents.
—*Peter J. Stanlis,*
    "ACCEPTABLE IN HEAVEN'S SIGHT: ROBERT FROST
    AT BREAD LOAF, 1939–1941," IN FROST
    CENTENNIAL ESSAYS, VOL. 3, EDITED BY
    JAC THARPE (1978)

We had arranged to have a baseball game, as was the annual custom. Captains had been appointed, sides chosen up. Frost and I were on opposite teams.

"Now, Bud," DeVoto advised me in advance of the contest, "you'd better let Robert's side win." I asked him why. He said, "If it doesn't, he'll chuck the conference."

I allowed for prejudice. It had been agreed once that DeVoto was to be Frost's official biographer. Not strangely, in view of their characters, the two had fallen out and there existed between them now, if not actual enmity, then something close to it.

On the field I began to believe DeVoto was right. Frost, though not young, was a pretty fair player, a point incidental to his complete and passionate involvement as a contestant. He argued about balls and strikes. He protested calls at the bases. Chin out, red-faced and furious, he kept confronting the umpire, waving wild arms as if ready to swing.

Watching, I wondered. Here on this otherwise peaceful afternoon, during an hour that was supposed to be fun, over a game the result of which could mean nothing, how could wisdom be so foolish? How could a man be so great and so small? Was hot concern over trifles an ingredient of greatness?

Frost's side won the game, and he came to the faculty cottage in high good humor.
—*A. B. Guthrie, Jr.,*
    THE BLUE HEN'S CHICK (1965)

Bernard DeVoto is flanked by Josephine Saxton and Mark Saxton outside the Little Theatre, 1940s (JWM)

At least during the 1930s and 1940s, everything ran at such a pace, everyone worked so hard and went to bed so late, that only will power held them together till the end. People of less than heroic fiber got sick, caught colds, got hung over, had accidents, sprained their ankles, ran into doors and blacked their eyes, fell in love, had quarrels, developed phobias and paranoias, so that every morning it was harder to get up and go forth to teach when duty's bugle blew. More than one staff member, trying to see clearly enough to pack his bag on the last morning, blessed fate and the management that the Conference lasted only two weeks. One added day would have left staff, Fellows, and customers only quivering puddles of protoplasm.

Nevertheless, from this combination of Plato's Academy and Walpurgisnacht the customers more often than not went home thrilled and stimulated and overflowing with ambition and ideas; the Fellows left knowing what they needed to do to get a start on their careers, and knowing some people who were ready, willing, and strategically placed to help them; the professionals went back to their offices purged and refreshed, perhaps with a new novelist or two on their string; and the staff members who were college teachers dispersed to their several campuses full of readiness for the autumnal renewal under the elms.

That was when there were still elms. That was when the world was young. It was never younger for Benny DeVoto than during the last two weeks of August in the 1930s and early 1940s, when he was doing what he liked to do and did well, among people he liked to work with, in a place that he liked. It was as close as he ever got to being an insider, a leader with a constituency that he could have confidence in, a teacher who instructed not only his students but his colleagues. If it was Theodore Morrison and his wife, Kathleen, who were primarily responsible for pulling the Conference together and holding it together against all the multiple strains of Depression, war, talent, genius, temperament, neurosis, and propinquity, DeVoto helped define it, and it helped define him. Probably he never thought in such terms, but it was totally appropriate that this belligerently American intelligence should have been influential in the creation of the writers' conference, an institution as native to America as Rotary or universal free education.

—*Wallace Stegner,*
THE UNEASY CHAIR: A BIOGRAPHY OF
BERNARD DEVOTO (1973)

(Top) Ted and Kay Morrison at the annual square dance; (center) A. B. Guthrie, Jr. and partner; (bottom) Ed Dragon dancing, Philip Cohen clapping, Dan Dragon fiddling, 1941

William Sloane, Robert Frost, John P. Marquand, 1941

1941 Fellows: (rear) Theodore Roethke, L. Sprague DeCamp, Robert Richards, Cedric Whitman, Charles Edward Eaton; (front) Constance Robertson, Theodore Morrison, Vivian Parsons, Mari Tomasi (Courtesy L. Sprague DeCamp)

Apart from the faculty, Ted Roethke made the most lasting impression on me. He was a large man, both in height and bulk, and moved around rather awkwardly, uneasily, I might say, in his big body, and conveyed both shyness and underlying strength, even aggressiveness, contemptuous as he was of the poets who did not believe in his fastidious use of form. I know he respected Frost, but he seemed wary of him as perhaps a too formidable competitor, for Ted was somewhat older than I and somewhat nearer to Frost's age. Perhaps it was simply that Frost threatened to be an overpowering and engulfing presence, and I noticed that Frost did not particularly warm to Roethke as a person either.

I was fortunate that Ted felt that he could be somewhat more himself with me, and we became good friends in so far as such a complicated person could offer his friendship. We had many talks and walks together, and he would invite me up to his room to talk about poetry. It was there that I learned how morbidly sensitive he was. The slightest noise seemed to upset him, and he went so far as to tell me he could not stand the ticking of the clock which he took from his desk, wrapped in a heavy towel, and tucked far back in his closet. He was the only Fellow who had brought a bulging briefcase of his reviews and press clippings, and he would pull them out and read them to me for as long as he thought he could hold my attention. This surprised me since he had already received a considerable amount of

recognition, and I was again made acutely aware of his underlying insecurity and uneasiness. He seemed to admire, and perhaps envy a little bit, my ability to move around more freely and to enjoy the world. Since I took an interest in the girls and went dancing in the evening, he would be particularly triumphant when he beat me at ping-pong which he took far more seriously than I did and which, I suppose, was a compensation for him, one that I did not resent. My lasting impression of him is of a big, baggy, bearlike man, hanging around the edges of groups—in some ways a figure of pathos—and yet I, at least, knew that he was a true poet and that he would one day have an important reputation.

—*Charles Edward Eaton* (1986)

The incident that made the most impression on me [in 1941] was when I showed around a copy of my first published novel, *Lest Darkness Fall,* which had come out a few months before. Old Robert Frost picked up the copy, glanced at it, and walked off with it. When I said something to Pratt about getting it back, he expressed horror. Well then, I said, I'll offer Frost a trade, my book for a copy of one of his books of verse. Oh, no, said Pratt; he would replace my book at his own expense. So I dropped the matter.

—*L. Sprague DeCamp* (1985)

Poets, 1941: (rear) Edward Weismiller, Theodore Roethke, William Carlos Williams, Louis Untermeyer, Robert Frost, Theodore Morrison; (front) Charles Edward Eaton, Richard Ellmann, Cedric Whitman

On Saturday, August 23 [1941], Williams and Floss arrived at the Bread Loaf Writers' Conference . . . where Williams delivered a talk that same evening. Again, his speech stressed the need for a new measure and therefore a new reality which would be able to resist the daily lies of the papers and the radio to which millions were each day subjected. He did not stay at the conference long, apologizing to Louis Untermeyer that he definitely had to be back home for his medical practice by Monday. But the real reason he was anxious to say his say and then clear out was the dark presence of Robert Frost, who refused to attend Williams' lecture even though he was conspicuously present at Bread Loaf, sitting in his cabin only half a mile away. . . .

. . . Williams was beginning to measure up too much like one of those heavyweight contenders Frost so much distrusted, and so now—in the summer of '41—he made it a point not only to stay away from Williams' reading but to tell his students to do the same.

One of those he warned away was Charles Eaton, who had been invited to the conference that summer by Frost himself. Williams was no real poet, he told Eaton. All he really wrote were snippets of poems, things like "The Red Wheelbarrow." And, puritan that he was, he warned Eaton that there were stories circulating that Williams was some kind of Lothario. In spite of the warning, Eaton did go to the Little Theatre for Williams' talk and found himself instinctively liking the man. Williams was not physically imposing in the way Frost could be, he thought, but he did find him charming, "very generous with his time and enthusiasms," outgoing, and genuinely interested in what others had to say in a way Frost was definitely not. What particularly struck Eaton was that, though his own poetry was so different from Williams', Williams could still take the time to read and to praise it.

—*Paul Mariani,*
WILLIAM CARLOS WILLIAMS: A NEW WORLD
NAKED (1981)

ROBERT FROST TO LOUIS UNTERMEYER
[Boston, January 4, 1941]

Why don't I take advantage of this season of gladness on earth as it is in heaven to pour out my resentment against you once more for not wearing the same front to your listening audiences as you wear to your reading audience in the article on Yeats Pound Hillyer and Fearing in the current Yale Review? You are the only brains we've got in the criticism of poetry. You are neither a poet spoiled to make a critic nor a poet who had to turn critic in revenge on the Muses for having failed him, nor a professor. You have the poetry in you express and implicit, you have the philosophical and psychological apparatus, and you have the magnanimity. And the rest has been added unto you. I dont want you showing carelessly on the lecture platform as of indifferent and questionable intellectual rank. You read some of the best poems of our time when you were here at Harvard: and they were your own: but you apologized for them and deprecated them. I wasnt the only one who was angry at you for your sin against yourself. And then you joke too much. Im sure. Im sure. Fifty percent too much—seventy five percent. People who tell you otherwise are deceiving you and possibly themselves also. You have a cause to maintain. You have easily the best critical powers in our day. I am not asking you to carry them any way but easily. But there are times and places where you must take thought not to damage your position of authority by clowning. Clown with your friends clown at home clown at Bread Loaf (on the Tennis court and in Information Tease). But for the confusion and confounding of your enemies and mine I wish I could insult you into an almost punless high literary dignity for the lectures you have it in you to better America with. Sometimes I wonder if you respect your audiences enough considering your political origins. I dont want you to respect the masses too much—just enough. You can lift them to anything you please with your platform skill.

But I linger too long in the negative side of this letter. Go the platform way to perdition if you will. What is one soul lost to me? I write only from a fresh access to pride in you on reading your article in The Yale Review. Let us rest in that and make the most of great things that no little thing can take away from much. . . .

Louis Untermeyer clowns with Helen Everitt and Frances Curtis, 1941 (Courtesy L. Sprague DeCamp)

William Sloane, Louis Untermeyer, Robert Frost, 1946 (JWM)

Only once during my directorship was I called on to take a stand in a matter involving sex, and I think it showed the parties concerned in a light at least as naif as I was myself. A certain pleasant gentleman was not only a frequent visitor to the Conference, but a benefactor as well. A friend and sponsor of his asked me whether I would disapprove, or whether the College would take it amiss, if the gentleman entertained his mistress overnight at the Inn. In the face of this odd request I said that the question should not have been put to me; that if it was, I could give only one answer as an officer of a College I thought expected conservative morals. The gentleman should have acted according to his own judgment and not asked for a blessing in advance. What the upshot was I did not inquire.

—*Theodore Morrison,*
    BREAD LOAF WRITERS' CONFERENCE: THE FIRST
    THIRTY YEARS (1976)

ROBERT FROST TO LOUIS UNTERMEYER
[Ripton, Vt., July 18, 1945]

Before the poet in you amid the many movements of his mind gets to imagining there is anything more to these precautions for peace at Bread Loaf than meets the eye, let me fall all over myself to assure you there is absolutely nothing more. Certain gossip that has seeped into circles here from the direction perhaps of the Rockwell Kents, though not in the least malicious, was mistaken enough to need correction and has left a condition it is just as well to be careful about. Esther's attempt to drag Bread Loaf into the story for the bad publicity may have caused a slight flurry among the Middlebury College trustees. I wouldnt put it past her to be trying to think up right now what next she can legally do to you or anyone connected with you to express her feelings. I dont mean anyone is much afraid of her legalities. Still for the sake of the institution you can see Ted's object in wanting to protect our stained glass windows with a screen of wire netting. Nobody can say a word against Mary [Mary Jane Gaffney, writer of short stories] coming as an enrolled member. She has standing as a writer. The fee wont break you. And once she's here she can be your guest at the table or at Treman and she and you can pair up for doubles against your old rivals as of old. Oh Gee isn't it fun being discreet at last. . . .

Untermeyer exhibits his tennis style, mid-1940s

Helen Everitt, Wallace Stegner and Mary Stegner, and Joseph Moneyway stand before the Little Theater, c. 1946

1946 Faculty and Fellows: (rear) Robert Frost, Robert Bordner, Graeme Lorimer, Andrew Glaze, Wallace Stegner, Rudolph Kieve, Theodore Morrison, Eugene Burdick, William Sloane; (front) Mrs. Burdick, Kay Morrison, Helen Everitt, Mary Stegner

Faculty party at Treman Cottage, 1940s

Evenings were a fitting completion of the days. If there was an evening lecture, either by a regular or a visitor, most attended, if not out of interest then out of sheer solidarity. But afterward they found themselves again sprawling in Treman's worn wicker arguing the lecturer's points or rehashing theory or trading notes on the Conference madwoman (there was always one), or with astonishing generosity and unselfishness promoting some newly discovered talent among the Fellows or the customers. Or they played poker, or made a game of throwing ice picks at the pocked kitchen door, or settled down to soul-searching with highballs in hand. I can remember vignettes from those evenings as clearly as I remember anything: Eudora Welty sitting worshipfully at the feet of Katherine Anne Porter after a reading, Truman Capote holding himself conspicuously aloof from Louis Untermeyer after Untermeyer had lectured on contemporary poetry and called T. S. Eliot a writer of society verse, Carson McCullers in her starched, white boys' shirt deep in talk with W.H. Auden—and deep in my last bottle of bourbon, which I had been saving for Sunday, when the liquor store in Brandon would be closed. I can remember the night one

of the Fellows, a boy just invalided out of the Royal Air Force after forty-seven bombing missions, lifted somebody else's bottle and hid it under his coat and took it to his room and went to bed with it, and to sleep; and how one of the staff, keeping an eye on him, went quietly over after a while and rescued the bottle and pulled the blankets up over the kid and tiptoed out.

That sort of evening. Sometimes, while the conscientious tried to read manuscripts in their rooms upstairs, to which every word and laugh penetrated, and while the snakebit lay down to recover, others stood with their arms around one another in the hall and sang barbershop under the baton of Louis Untermeyer, dominated always by the beautiful *basso cantante* of Colonel Joe Greene, editor of the *Infantry Journal,* and at least once with the assistance of the black soprano Dorothy Maynor and her accompanist, Arpad Sandor. I do not take seriously DeVoto's complaint about the glee-clubbers. Often I was one of them, and they were magnificent.

—*Wallace Stegner,*
    THE UNEASY CHAIR: A BIOGRAPHY OF
    BERNARD DEVOTO (1974)

Truman Capote, a few years after his appearance at Bread Loaf, in the famous publicity portrait used for Other Voices, Other Rooms, *1948*

On my vacation [from *The New Yorker*] I went to the Bread Loaf Writers' Conference—I was only about seventeen. I never liked Robert Frost's poetry and during the course of a conversation he got the idea that I felt rather indifferent toward him. He gave a reading, and while he was reading, a mosquito bit my ankle and I bent to scratch my ankle and sort of slumped over. It looked like I'd fallen asleep, and Robert Frost, who was standing at this podium reading, suddenly slammed his book shut and threw it at me all the way across the room. It missed me but he said, "If that's the way *The New Yorker* feels about my poetry, I won't go on reading," and he stomped out of the room. He then wrote a letter to Harold Ross at *The New Yorker* saying, "How can you send out such a disrespectful person to represent you." Harold Ross—with whom I was actually quite friendly—wanted an explanation as to what had happened and I said, "Well, I really don't need to give any explanation because I was there on my own, it was my vacation, it had nothing to do with *The New Yorker*." So I left the magazine for about six months but then I went back.

> —*Truman Capote,*
> IN CONVERSATIONS WITH CAPOTE, EDITED BY
> LAWRENCE GROBEL (1985)

1945 Faculty and Fellows: (rear) A. B. Guthrie, Jr., Col. Joseph I. Greene, E. Louise Mally, William Sloane, Richard Brown, Walter Havighurst; (center) Elizabeth Abell, Helen Everitt, Louis Untermeyer, Edith Mirrielees, Theodore Morrison, Catherine Drinker Bowen, Robert Frost; (front) Fletcher Pratt, Inga Pratt, Kay Morrison, Gilley

In August of 1945, when I was sixteen, I went to the Bread Loaf Writers' Conference at the old wooden inn outside Middlebury in Vermont. Frost had been associated with the Writers' Conference from the beginning, and he was my main reason for going. The year before, I had spent my first year at prep school, and I had met an English teacher named Hyde Cox who knew Robert Frost, who quoted his conversation, and who told me about Bread Loaf. Aspirant writers could spend two weeks there in the summer, listening to lectures, workshopping, sometimes being read and criticized by professionals; there, you could catch a glimpse of Robert Frost.

At fourteen, I had decided to become a poet; I worked on poems two or three hours every day after school. I collected rejection slips from *The New Yorker* and *The Atlantic,* and when I was sixteen began to publish in little magazines—very little magazines: *Trails, Matrix,* and *Experiment.* I was exhilarated; surely book publication and undying fame would follow as the night the day; Bread Loaf would accelerate matters. . . .

The first night at Bread Loaf we heard a speech of welcome by the director, Theodore Morrison. We gathered in a large lecture hall where I sat next to a row of French doors. As Morrison talked—the history and purpose of Bread Loaf, what to expect in our two weeks—my eyes wandered over the listeners, wondering which of these people were writers I knew about. I was keeping my eyes out for Frost, hoping for a glance at the man who made great poems. Looking casually to my right, through the glass doors, I saw him. He was walking with two friends, Frost a little ahead, his mouth moving humorously as he talked. The ground outside sank away, and Frost, approaching the lecture hall uphill, appeared to be rising out of the ground. His face was strong and blocky, his white hair thick and rough. He looked like granite, some old carved stone like the menhirs in Ireland that I saw in *National Geographic,* but gifted to walk and speak. Through the window I watched as his mouth moved with talk, and the faces of his companions broke into laughter.

But I had no mind, at sixteen, for his companions. I had seen the great poet, the maker of "To Earthward," and "After Apple-Picking." He was palpable, he was human, he was alive in my time. I felt light in my head and body. Merely seeing this man, merely laying startled eyes upon him, allowed me to feel enlarged. My dreams for my own life, for my own aging into stone, took on reality in the stern flesh of Robert Frost, who rose out of a hill in Vermont.

—*Donald Hall,*
    THEIR ANCIENT GLITTERING EYES (1992)

Except for a couple of casual encounters I hardly knew Bernard DeVoto at the time [1945]. A difficult man, a curmudgeon, given to extremes and tantrums, he made me uneasy, and uneasier still because he was an authority on the early West, a student with knowledge undoubtedly far beyond mine even in application to the limited years I'd researched. Fortunately, I didn't know that in a sense I had stolen his subject, and was writing the kind of novel he had long wanted to write and perhaps would have written already but for a growing shakiness of faith in himself as a writer of fiction.

He sat with a group of us on the porch of Cherry Cottage on the first day . . . and I thought, while he proclaimed the eternal truth on all manner of subjects, how ugly he was. He was a trifle under average height and had a bow in his upper spine, yet suggested animal power. Glasses dimmed but somehow exaggerated belligerent eyes set in a square face that could have been called hangdog save for his immense and articulate vitality. His mouth kept working under a nose that nature had shoved in, with the result that his nostrils were like those of a man seen supine.

After he had gone I said, "Without an umbrella he'd drown in the rain."

I shan't forget the rebuke. Robeson Bailey, then a professor of English at Smith, made an answer that mildness made stinging: "Here on the mountain," he said, "we don't talk of appearances."

In later years I came to admire DeVoto and we grew to be close friends. Outrageous he would always be and, often, difficult. He bristled when crossed. Carried away on the tide of an idea or argument, he spouted extremes that reflection toned down and made plausible in his writing, vigorous and valorous though his writing was. As a teacher and speaker he was wont to bully students and audiences. He would have fought a bear.

But his behavior was all compensation, a bluff to conceal his compassion, a counter, one suspected, to an abiding uncertainty, to a self-diminishment that the man's self wouldn't let be diminished. Under that outward protection was another personality, a sturdy one to be sure, but one smiling and agreeable and generous, quick to help and to praise when praise was in order.

Another man might have resented my usurpation of his Western preserve, might have cried down through vexation the kind of a novel he'd had in mind before me. Not DeVoto. He read *The Big Sky* in manuscript and promptly beat all his drums to promote it.

A. B. Guthrie, Jr. and Bernard DeVoto, 1948 (JWM)

Character, once it is known, alters countenances; and when I look back now I do not see the face on the porch of Cherry Cottage. I see Benny DeVoto, the whole man, and in glad company with the ancient dead whom we both know, we again sail together down the wide Missouri.

—*A. B. Guthrie, Jr.,*
THE BLUE HEN'S CHICK (1965)

BERNARD DEVOTO TO WILLIAM SLOANE
[July 5, 1949]

William Sloane, John Ciardi, Bernard DeVoto, 1947. (JWM)

It is still an absolutely dead sure thing that I will not go [to Bread Loaf] but other pressures as powerful as yours are being applied to me. . . . Probably I will still be unalterably refusing to go when I drive into the yard of Treman and start bellyaching about Fletcher's martinis. . . . The truth is I mortally hate the place, its hysterias, its psychoses, its doublebitted axes, its miasmas, blights, poisons, obsessions, shuck mattresses, dining room regulations, Ophelias, Lady Macbeths . . . Pistols, Olsens, Johnsons, somnambulists, insomniacs, and most of all, by Christ, its glee-clubbers. The truth is, further, that it terrifies me and infects me with manias, depressions, and blue funks. Beyond that is the further truth that there are increasingly acute reasons why I should not come, and beyond that is the concentric truth that I always have the best time of the year when I am there.

1947 Faculty: (rear) Robeson Bailey, Julie Sloane, Richard Brown, Josephine Saxton; (center) Walter Prichard Eaton, Edith Mirrielees, William Sloane, Theodore Morrison, Bernard DeVoto, Robert Frost; (front) Fletcher Pratt, Mrs. Eaton, Mark Saxton, Helen Everitt, Joseph Kinsey Howard, Kay Morrison (JWM)

Chick Guthrie and Joseph Kinsey Howard, 1947 (JWM)

Joseph Kinsey Howard, Robert Frost, Arnold Lott, 1947. (JWM)

With his death the West lost one of its few writers of the first rank and one of its most valuable citizens. He had elected to stay in the West, as most writers who are born there do not. For any writer the decision means a constant expenditure of energy resisting the forces which have transformed the West from an intensely individualistic society to one that puts a survival value on conformity, from the most cosmopolitan of American sections to one parochially assertive of its orthodoxies. For Joe Howard, who was born a fighter, an instinctive member of minorities, and a champion of the exploited and the oppressed, it meant a tumultuous and frequently bitter life. There would be no point in recalling here the details of the career that led the novelist A. B. Guthrie, Jr., to say of him when he died, "We have lost our conscience." Or in recalling details of the vigilantism with which a society inimical to the critical spirit fought back. Enough to say that he made himself heard, that castles and causes which had mercilessly assailed him came to solicit his support, that he won through to a position of acknowledged leadership and power. When *Montana, High, Wide and Handsome* was published in 1943, you could buy it in some places in Montana only by such a back-room transaction as was required some years ago to buy a good novel in Boston. By the time its author died eight years later he came closer to being the spokesman of the West than any other writer has ever been. Indeed few writers of our time have so deeply or so visibly stamped their impression on their own place.

Thus summarized, it seems a triumphant career but Joe Howard had no sense of triumph: he had scars. His friends were aware of a deep melancholy in him, a deep loneliness, and he died a very tired man. American literature at large has no concern with the private pain in which books are forged, and cannot be troubled by the suspicion and contempt with which the West surrounds the practice of letters, so long as fine books come of it. There should be some concern, however, when a distinguished writer dies just as his talent reaches full maturity.

—*Bernard DeVoto,*
INTRODUCTION TO STRANGE EMPIRE BY
JOSEPH KINSEY HOWARD (1952)

John and Judith Ciardi during a party in the barn, late forties (JWM)

John Ciardi lectures on "How Does a Poem Mean," late 1940s (JWM)

One evening at Bread Loaf Mr. Frost was reading his poems and talking about them. He was often a sort of horse trader in ideas. He seemed to pull out a conceptual stick to whittle while he talked *around* the idea he was trading for, rambling off in what seemed to be indirection, only to turn and surprise the idea from behind. It could be a great performance, and that night's was one of his greatest.

His conceptual stick for the occasion was "technical tricks": he wanted to tell us about some of his. He read a poem, paused to ask the audience in what meter it was written, and then had fun scolding those who did not know it was in hendecasyllabics. A bit later he interrupted a reading to say he was "a synecdochist by profession," and went on to have his fun with those who did not know which trope a synecdoche is, or even that it is a trope. So he went on. He pointed out rhyme pairings in which he took special pleasure. He paused to underline some of what he called his "bright ideas" for the management of the poem. He had things to say about "the tune" of this poem and that. He was well cast in the role of the master craftsman and he was having a good time.

I had been watching a sweet elderly lady in the second row. She had been giving signs of increasing agitation as the talk went on. The applause had hardly died down when she was on her feet, waving her arm furiously for attention, and spilling out the question she had been repressing (if it could be called a question) even as she called for attention. "But, Mr. Frost," she cried, "*surely* when you are writing one of your *beautiful poems, surely* you can't be thinking about"—and here her voice slurred the dirty words— "about *technical tricks!*"

Mr. Frost put his hands together, the spread fingers touching tip to tip, looked owlish for a moment, and then leaned forward into the microphone and said in a playfully gravelly bass: "I *revel* in 'em!"

—*John Ciardi,*
DIALOGUE WITH AN AUDIENCE (1963)

Frost attended some of the poetry workshops, conducted outdoors by Louis Untermeyer after lunch. When Frost was present we learned to tremble. Whatever poem was up for discussion that day, Frost was liable to be cutting, sarcastic, dismissive. The day when Untermeyer chose to read and discuss my poems was a day Frost didn't come; I was relieved. One day Frost took over the workshop all by himself. He chose a young woman's poem to read aloud, and asked for comments. A few people said a few fatuous things; only the brave or the stupid would lay themselves open to Frost's wit. He dismissed the fatuities with a cast of his forearm. Then he said, "Who *wrote* this poem?," his voice heavy with disgust. The young woman—I remember she was small, attractive in the Cambridge manner, married to a Harvard graduate student—acknowledged authorship, looking deliberately stalwart. *"No,"* said Frost, "I mean, who *really* wrote it?" There was silence, bewilderment. After a long pause, while Frost held to the sides of the podium with evident anger and stared at the audience as if he dared anyone to speak, the woman spoke again. "I wrote it," she said, "and I don't know what you're talking about."

"You didn't write it," Frost said, and waved the typed page in the air. "You know who wrote it?"—his voice pronounced the name with the heaviest sarcasm he could summon, and he could summon sarcasm as well as anyone: *"T.S. Eliot!"*

—*Donald Hall,*
THEIR ANCIENT GLITTERING EYES (1992)

Robert Frost and Shad, late 1940s

1949 Faculty: (rear) Bernard DeVoto, William Sloane, A. B. Guthrie, Jr., Richard Brown, John Ciardi, William Raney, Frank Campbell; (center) Edith Mirrielees, Robert Frost, Catherine Drinker Bowen; (front) Kay Morrison, Julie Sloane, Inga Pratt, Fletcher Pratt, Helen Everitt, Judith Ciardi

One day, talking with him on the porch, I sat with a young woman from Bryn Mawr and her mother, both good looking. Frost rocked and spoke laconically yet wittily, proud and strong, delighted to hold his audience. We sat in the breeze, late afternoon, late summer, three of us looking at one of us, waiting for the words he would utter, and I was aware—as at times of love, of triumph, and of catastrophe—of the moment as I lived it. He asked me about my school, and about where I would go to college. Then Frost, who had gone to Lawrence High School and fitfully to Dartmouth and Harvard, disparaged higher education. At the time I felt uncomfortable and did not know why: He was one-upping me, because *he* hadn't needed a diploma but *I* did. He could not help but make himself out to be better than any male around him, even if the male was sixteen.

 —*Donald Hall,*
  THEIR ANCIENT GLITTERING EYES (1992)

It's one thing to hear the notes in the mind's ear. Another to give them accuracy at the mouth. Still another to implicate them in sentences and fasten them to the page. The second is the actor's gift. The third is the writer's.

 —*Robert Frost,*
  FROM REMARKS FREQUENTLY DELIVERED AT
  BREAD LOAF

John Ciardi, around 1950

Isaac Asimov, as he appeared on the jacket of
Pebble in the Sky, *1950 (Courtesy Isaac Asimov)*

FIFTIES

Among the important men of the faculty [in 1950] was Fletcher Pratt, and it was he who had urged me to attend. [Asimov's first novel, *Pebble in the Sky,* had been issued the preceding January, and he attended the Conference as a paying student.]

I arrived at Bread Loaf on August 16, 1950 . . . Pratt was there, of course. Also William Sloane, a publisher who had authored two well-thought-of science-fiction novels, and Catherine Drinker Bowen, a popular historian.

Present in addition was John Ciardi, tall, slim, with a shock of dark hair and an incredibly majestic nose that would have made it possible for him to play Cyrano without makeup. He had a beautiful bass voice that was delightful to listen to. He was a poet and when he lectured on poetry there was no use in his trying to distinguish between good poetry and bad poetry. When *he* read poetry, it all sounded good. . . .

. . . It was at Bread Loaf, I think (though possibly at Annisquam, three weeks earlier), that someone came to me, shook my hand vigorously, and said, "Congratulations."

"On what?" I said.

"On keeping your name. It takes courage to insist on being called Isaac."

"Not at all," I said, offended. "I *like* the name."

And every time after that, this man who loved my bravery called me nothing but "Zack," a nickname I despised. . . .

. . . The faculty at Bread Loaf recognized my established writer status and didn't lump me together with the other students. Bill Sloane, without warning, called me to speak on the nonhuman heroes of science fiction, and I gave a one-minute impromptu speech that went over well.

Then, on August 26, I helped out in the session that was designed to teach interviewing by allowing myself to serve as the subject of an interview. I was told by the faculty to answer briefly, and to interpret questions narrowly and literally, so that the students would learn how to ask questions properly.

One student, a dentist in real life (as I recall), after it had been established that I did quite a bit of writing, asked how much money I made in this way.

I hesitated, and then said, "About as much as I make at my job as an instructor."

He laughed and said, with what I took as a sneer, "That's all?"

I would have answered angrily, but Pratt intervened, and scolded him for his impoliteness to someone who was trying to be of service to them.

There were still three days to go, but one of the students was driving back to Boston that day and invited me to come with him, and on impulse, I went. The dentist's remark was the deciding factor, I think.

—*Isaac Asimov,*
IN MEMORY YET GREEN (1979)

1950 Faculty: (rear) Fletcher Pratt, Richard Wilbur, William Raney, John T. Fischer, Richard Brown, Mark Saxton, William Sloane; (center) Robert Frost, Catherine Drinker Bowen, Theodore Morrison, John Ciardi; (front) Inga Pratt, Barbara Rex, Kathleen Morrison, Josephine Saxton, Betty Finnin, Julie Sloane

Elizabeth Spencer is from North Mississippi and I am from Central Mississippi, so there needed to be a modest coincidence to bring us together. This occurred. Elizabeth came as a student to Belhaven College in Jackson and was unerringly made president of the Belhaven Literary Society; it was the year I published my first book, and I lived right across the street facing the College. Elizabeth made a telephone call to ask if I'd please step over to a session of the Literary Society so they could meet a real writer and seek my advice. It would have been unneighborly to stay home.

I met then a graceful young woman with a slender, vivid face, delicate and clearly defined features, dark blue eyes in which, then as now, you could read that Elizabeth Spencer was a jump ahead of you in what you were about to say. She did as nice Southern girls, literary or unliterary, were supposed to do in the Forties—looked pretty, had good manners (like mine, in coming when invited), and inevitably giggled (when in doubt, giggle). But the main thing about her was blazingly clear—this girl was serious. She was indeed already a writer.

As a matter of fact, she was all but the first writer *I'd* ever met, and the first who was younger than I was. (The other was Katherine Anne Porter.) Elizabeth offered me my first chance to give literary advice. But my instinct

protected us both. This free spirit, anybody could tell, would do what she intended to do about writing. What else, and what better, could a writer know of another writer? It was all I was sure of about myself. I imagine she was glad not to get advice.

Instead of advising each other, we became friends. To leap over something like a decade's difference in age proved no more trouble to either than crossing Pinehurst Street. It wasn't long before Elizabeth herself, with degrees from Belhaven and Vanderbilt, published her own first book, the novel *Fire in the Morning*: she'd gone right on her way as she'd known she would, and as she always has. . . .

It would have been as reckless to predict for Elizabeth as it would have been to offer her advice, and for the same good reason. Indeed, how *could* I have guessed, for one thing, that a schoolgirl so fragile-looking (though she went with a determined walk that made her hair bounce) could have had so much *power* to pour into her stories? Without any sacrifice of the sensitivity and the finely shaded perceptions we expect of her, her cool deliberateness to pull no punches will time after time take the reader by surprise. . . .

—*Eudora Welty*,
FOREWORD TO THE STORIES OF ELIZABETH
SPENCER (1981)

1950 Fellows: (rear) Thaddeus
Ashby, Roger Eddy, Jose Pena;
(front) Mary Elizabeth Witherspoon,
Robert Lucas, Elizabeth Spencer.
(Courtesy M. E. Witherspoon)

I was thirty-one, a housewife with two small children, in 1950. As a novelist I'd worked in almost total isolation (but with incredible confidence) until then. *Somebody Speak for Katy* went "over the transom" three times before Dodd, Mead accepted it on the fourth try. Then came the fellowship. I arrived at Bread Loaf full of myself, scornful of status (including my own), iconoclastic toward all heroes. That didn't stop me from feeling proud to find the Fellows warmly integrated with the staff at Treman Cottage. I had my first martinis there, served up in pimiento cheese glasses. I sat on the floor singing folk songs, soaking up a sense of democratic fellowship, and was only mildly disenchanted to discover that the Fellows had kitchen detail. The disenchantment deepened slightly when I heard the publisher William Sloane, who was on the staff, putting down somebody in absentia. I said to him quite sincerely, "Well, maybe he's not as intelligent as you are, but . . ."

"Intelligent!" he said emphatically. "He's not even as intelligent as *you* are . . ."

"Wait a minute!" I exploded, spluttering, and as I was spluttering, I caught a glimpse of Richard Wilbur's sensitive, blushing face and downcast eyes. He was presumably embarrassed for us both. The publisher and I, however, had built a bridge with our impulsive confrontation, and both of us went away wiser.

—*Mary Elizabeth Witherspoon* (1986)

Theodore Morrison was special to me, not as a hero, but as a friend. Not only had he said kind things to me about my book; he simply radiated the real. I felt he had no neurosis to hide, no excess ego to spend, and that he lived by his own standards. I had this feeling, too, about Catherine Drinker Bowen, about Elizabeth Spencer, whom I greatly admire, and about Richard Wilbur, with whom I went on a picnic. A very nice young fellow, Richard Wilbur. He is two years younger than I, with an Ivy League background. On a Sunday, halfway through the Conference, we were both invited on an outing by John Fischer of *Harper's*, who had his wife and children with him and who thought we might be missing our own families. For me it was life-saving; there had been too much intensity, too much pressure all week long, and suddenly I was relieved of it, out in the wilds on a stream much like those I was used to in the Smoky Mountains.

Richard Wilbur and I went rock-hopping in the stream. Almost immediately he stooped to his haunches to study a fault in the rock; then he made some remark I thought too academic, and I teased him about it. He said, "One must always verbalize, I think."

I thought rebelliously, Must one? Like Eliza Doolittle, I had had nothing but "words, words, words" for a week and was desperately in need of a little silent communion with the natural. Later on, I wrote a poem about that interchange, which I enclose. Richard Wilbur never saw the poem, nor would he have recognized himself, I'm sure, if he had; but I am grateful to him for the inspiration.

—*Mary Elizabeth Witherspoon* (1986)

Middlebury River, main branch

Rock-Hopping With an Intellectual

Lank-haired boy with inward eyes,
toes flaunting themselves through your sneakers,
don't speak.
You move with an air of moving, and your
bare toes lie,
for your body is cramped with consciousness.
Come ride with the eddying leaf, bend with the branch,
burn with the boulder's warmth, and lie
seeking the sky through lace and lattice-work.
If you must learn, then trace with your finger
the thin, whitened fault in the rock,
and wonder. But know this as you do:
you cannot crowd infinity into a bowl of bone.
If you must startle the stream with your
poor crippled fragments of sound, then
follow its flow round the bend, out of sight,
and leave me behind, submissive to mystery,
a being blended bone with stone,
mind cupped contented in the palm of sense.
—*Mary Elizabeth Witherspoon* (1950)

One afternoon Elizabeth Spencer and I, both being from the Deep South, were invited to the summer home of Donald Davidson, a member of Vanderbilt University's literary "Fugitive" group. It was a pleasant interlude, and the Davidsons could not have been kinder to us, but I got the distinct impression we were being warned against the politics at Treman Cottage. It was the year of Joe McCarthy's Wheeling, West Virginia, speech, the decade of the Silent Generation, but Bread Loaf wasn't silent. Neither was it radical, however; it was simply open—that is, within the bounds of moderation. When a visiting radical with a genial, weathered face and a booming voice, Malcolm Ross, began a protest song about man's basic right to overthrow his government, I glanced at Mr. Morrison's face and found him looking thoughtful and amused. When the protest song was finished, one of us began an old Methodist hymn, the other followed suit, the group joined in, and the subject was changed. I can't remember whether that was the day the Lattimores were there, but I have a poignant mental picture of the three of them (Owen Lattimore, his wife and son) sitting silently in the corner, looking sad, like refugees in a temporary sanctuary. Whether the picture is true, I can't say; I didn't have a chance to get to know them.
—*Mary Elizabeth Witherspoon* (1986)

(Above) The old marble walkway beneath towering roadside maples may have disappeared when the state highway was widened and "safer" concrete walks installed, but blessedly the vista past Maple cottage (right) has not

1952 Faculty: (rear) Richard Brown, Lincoln Barnett, Judith Ciardi, Jessamyn West, William Sloane, Rachel MacKenzie, Eric Swenson, Robert Frost, Richard Wilbur; (front) John Ciardi, Inga Pratt, Theodore Morrison, Julie Sloane, Kathleen Morrison; (front) Fletcher Pratt

Robert Frost and Frank O'Connor at the Frost cabin, 1952
(Sprague Holden)

As soon as classes ended at Harvard, Kelleher drove O'Connor and Stan up to Bread Loaf for the writers' conference, where O'Connor was to be the guest speaker on August 23 [1952]. As they were crossing Vermont, somewhere beyond White River Junction, O'Connor suddenly gave an imperious command: "Stop at the nearest pub." When John informed him that in rural Vermont there was no such thing, he responded with the verdict "Barbarism!" The next day John took them to Ripton, near Bread Loaf, to meet Robert Frost. Richard Wilbur, the poet, was with Frost that morning, and found him worried about what poem he should "say" for Mr. O'Connor. He needn't have worried. Frank, in his most Yeatsian cadence, introduced the subject: "Ah, that poem of yours, Mr. Frost, 'Stopping by Woods on a Snowy Evening.'" He began to recite it. Frost interrupted. "No, no, no! That's not how you say it!" and began his own rendition, which Frank interrupted with "No, no, Mr. Frost! You're ruining your own poem." Later, the two posed for Stan's camera.

 —James Matthews,
  VOICES: A LIFE OF FRANK O'CONNOR (1983)

Ted and Kay Morrison with Robert Frost, 1955 (JWM)

John Ciardi, early 1950s

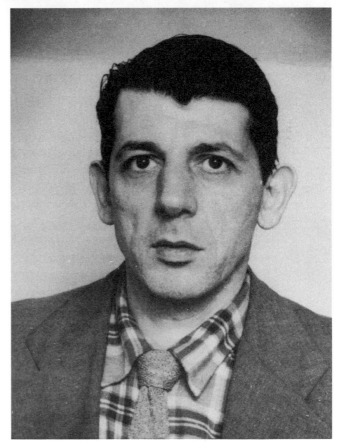

I was not intimate with Frost; I could not pretend to that. He was kind to me over many years but I cannot speak as one intimately acquainted. I speak as an admirer. And I had the privilege of knowing him, usually at the Bread Loaf Writers' Conference, for about 25 years. Away from Bread Loaf, I'd see him here and there when he came to lecture. I admire his poetry—I've had an enormous charge out of it—and admire the man. I do not think of Frost as many people do, as a white-haired old saint. He was not a white-haired old saint. He could in season be a mean old son-of-a-bitch. That's part of the man's energy. The best way I've found to say it (and I mean it as an admiration): he had a magmatic mass at his core. He burned at a higher heat than is commonly known. When this man erupted, it produced the glories. It was Mount Frost, the volcano. But volcanos also have their sulfurous sidestinks.

—*John Ciardi,*
"CIARDI ON FROST: AN INTERVIEW," BY EDWARD CIFELLI, IN FROST CENTENNIAL ESSAYS, VOL. 1, EDITED BY JAC THARPE (1974)

Frost [was] a man who was punctilious in his ritual. He liked to decide when a door was to be opened, and nothing would get his back up sooner than to have somebody push in against a door he would rather keep closed. For many years at Bread Loaf I kept my distance. I didn't want to thrust myself upon him. We had little conversations now and then, but always I was an extremely junior member of whatever was going. There were many people around who had known him longer and much better. But when I was appointed director of the conference some 15 or 16 years later, I got a letter from him. I suspect that Kay Morrison prompted the letter. As nearly as I recall it, he began with "Dear John, You read my poems, I read yours, what's this about your asking if"—I had a poem in which I said "does God believe in me?"—and Frost said, "There you are, the fair-haired boy, director, professor, publisher, poet, asking questions like that." He's half kidding. He's being playful, friendly, but the real occasion of the letter was the fact that he signed it "Robert," which was his way of saying, "All right, you may now call me Robert, instead of Mr. Frost." And it was a ritual arrangement: *he* would say when. I was, of course, grateful for the letter. I hadn't pushed against his door; he had opened it. I flew down to Florida, to West Miami Beach to interview him for *Saturday Review* on his 80th birthday, and we had long discussions there. I put up at the local hotel, took him out to dinner. He absolutely insisted on paying the dinner check, and when I went to pay the motel check, he paid it. I pointed out that Good

1953 Faculty: (rear) William Sloane, Lincoln Barnett, Rachel MacKenzie, May Sarton, Richard Brown, Eric Swenson; (middle) Inga Pratt, Julie Sloane, Robert Frost, Kathleen Morrison, Theodore Morrison, John Ciardi; (front) Willie Ley, Fletcher Pratt, Rowland Sturges (Above) Ciardi and Frost, late 1950s

Heavens, I was on the *Saturday Review* expense account; there was no need for it. He said, "You came down to see me, and you are my guest. That's the way I was brought up."

—*John Ciardi,*
"CIARDI ON FROST: AN INTERVIEW," BY EDWARD CIFELLI, IN FROST CENTENNIAL ESSAYS, VOL. 1, EDITED BY JAC THARPE (1974)

1955 Faculty: (rear) Bernard DeVoto, William Sloane, John Ciardi, A. B. Guthrie, Jr.; (center) Rachel MacKenzie, Fletcher Pratt, Theodore Morrison, Robert Frost, Inga Pratt; (front) Judith Ciardi, Lincoln Barnett, Mary Moore Maloney, Kay Morrison, May Sarton (JWM)

It was the morning of the opening of the conference in 1955. As Crumb editor and bookstore manager, I had to help Tom Donovan out at the Front Desk. (The conferee-administration ratio was lower then.) Dick Brown, the assistant director, had put his shoulder out and wasn't on the mountain. Midmorning Kay Morrison came by the Front Desk to ask where the waiters were. It was a good and pertinent question. They weren't anywhere. The Director of Food Services had forgotten to hire them and Dick hadn't been around to nudge him. In those days waiters were Language School students who wanted to hang around for a couple of weeks and earn free board and room (no tuition) by waiting on tables. They weren't considered to be members of the conference. Somehow Food Services managed to round up an assorted lot and the day was saved. But it was a rocky start—by late afternoon the Inn manager gave a scream, jumped out the switchboard window and didn't show up again until the next day. Temperamentally he never seemed right for the job.

I decided that if I ever had a chance my first administrative priority would be "Do it yourself." Two weeks later—no cause or consequence—I was Assistant Director. I decided waiters should be Bread Loafers—contributors or auditors. As I recall, they got room and board as under the old arrangement. In the ways of the Business Office they just weren't charged tuition. They applied to me for a waitership and I took their applications of the ones I wanted over to Lois Thorpe, the Bread Loaf dietician. The form required a picture in the upper right corner—that's how Lois judged character. "He'll be trouble, but what the heck." Women had to be 5/3, 110 pounds. I remember the statistic because it seemed so strange. Necessary because it was the minimum size Food Services said was needed to carry trays. Affirmative Action 1956. The Business Office was delighted not to have to be bothered. Food Services bore the budget. I got some of Bread Loaf's liveliest. We were all happy.

By 1959 John had raised enough money to establish one scholarship, and Frost said we had the damnedest hierarchy he'd ever heard about outside Britain.

—*Paul Cubeta* (1990)

Theodore Morrison and John Ciardi, 1955 (JWM)

Ted Morrison with Fletcher and Inga Pratt, 1955 (JWM)

John Ciardi, May Sarton,
Ted and Kay Morrison, 1955 (JWM)

I was a fellow in 1956 and my memories are sharp but selective. John Ciardi was the big cheese, no doubt about that, and he ruled the roost amiably and firmly. He was at the zenith of his fame, I suppose, having just roasted Anne Lindbergh in *The Saturday Review.* I particularly remember a session in which he read with great dramatic effect in that wonderful operatic basso of his, "Homage to Mistress Bradstreet." At that point I knew nothing of John Berryman and still less about his poetry, and Ciardi's reading was a blaze of fire in the sky. Bill Sloane was still the best reader of novel mss. and he gave me not only sage advice on my second novel but put me in touch with editors who could be interested in my work. I never knew how he managed so well, because, as everyone who knew him said, he drank more gin every day than most could have drunk in a week. But every morning he was as bright and clear as the youngest person there. Merle Miller and I first met that session and became good friends for the rest of his life. He was a lively performer on the Bread Loaf stage, and his sessions always drew enthusiastic crowds. Some of the other faculty were less expert onstage, but nearly all appear to have been good in tutoring.

Robert Frost was still living nearby and came now and then for an evening with the faculty and fellows, but he always demanded to be treated like royalty and generally was; this had the effect of making him virtually unapproachable to younger, less eminent writers. Ted Morrison and his wife hovered over Frost as if he were a prize Easter egg, and discouraged mortals from contact with him. But for some reason he took a brief shine to me at Treman one night and went off into a corner to find out all about me. I had written one book only and was just a shade over thirty, and had little interesting to say to him but he wanted me to tell him about my newspaper days, which

for some reason fascinated him. The only thing I remember him saying, probably one of those things he said all the time, was "the only thing a big wheel is good for is to roll." I didn't much like him or his arrogance, but if possible the Morrisons were worse. On the other hand, I liked Catherine Drinker Bowen immensely and thought she wore her learning lightly. Another sweet old man was Bruce Lancaster, who was there with his elderly wife; they were kind to everyone but always seemed a little shocked at the drinking and general air of abandon in Treman.

Bud Guthrie also was very agreeable but rarely sober. The focus of everything for faculty and fellows was Treman. Customers were banned, and often cruelly pilloried behind their backs. Fellows were invariably told they had no duties to perform except to make the martinis before lunch and dinner. There were many martinis daily but the six of us had no difficulty keeping up with them since vermouth was not encouraged. Otherwise fellows were treated with the same respect given the faculty. Despite the good food, Merle, my wife and I drove into Middlebury often at night to have dinner and see a movie. The atmosphere tended to be claustrophobic and there was a certain tyranny about being at Treman all the time. Since I was then teaching at a small college in Virginia, I had had about as much claustrophobia as I could handle. We even went to other small towns in the area to find movies we hadn't seen.

The general atmosphere was pleasant, and there was the stunning Vermont countryside, so green after the hot spell we had just come from down in the south. The conference was exciting in its way and, certainly for me, it was valuable both to meet established older writers and to have them read my work. They were always generous to me.

—*Paxton Davis* (1990)

(Top) 1956 Faculty: (rear) Robeson Bailey, William Raney, Max Steele, Paul Cubeta; (seated) William Sloane, Bruce Lancaster, Merle Miller, Kay Boyle, A. B. Guthrie, Jr., Robert Frost, Mildred Walker, Leonie Adams, Catherine Drinker Bowen, John Ciardi (Left) Faculty reception (Above) Robert Frost "says" a poem, late 1950s

1957 Fellows: (rear) May Swenson, Mrs. Drohan, Leonard Drohan; (front) Richard Moore, Alma Brodie, Jane Mayhall, Dan Wakefield, Joseph Dever, Mrs. Gottlieb

My initiation . . . occurred in 1957, when I was awarded a Fellowship. . . . I went that first summer to the literary mountain in Vermont from an ovenlike apartment in Greenwich Village, and soon was happily intoxicated by the fresh mountain air, the presence of older writers I had admired in print but never seen in the flesh, and the excellent martinis that taste even better and have less painful after-effects in that elevated northern climate. In those days it was the duty of the fellows . . . to oversee the mixing of martinis for the staff, a function whose importance was explained by a gentleman who served that year as "Dean of Fellows." He told us: "Liquor is the handmaiden of literature."

I have never disputed that adage, and it is an especially good one for a writers' conference, where there is almost continuous talk and socializing. A basic and fairly common public misunderstanding about the writers' conference is that people go there to write. But that is one activity that never goes on—there isn't time. You can write when you get back home. That summer as a fellow I don't think I wrote anything but a couple of postcards to my far-off, stifling friends in New York, and I was perfectly content to drink, talk, discuss, listen to lectures, laugh, sing, read, joke, eat, walk, paddle a canoe, and climb part way up one small mountain. It was one of the best times I'd had since my Boy Scout days at Camp Chank-tun-ungi in Indiana.

—*Dan Wakefield,*
"CONFESSIONS OF A SUMMER CAMPER
(LIT'RY DIVISION)" (1966)

John and Judith Ciardi (right)
pose with conferees outside the Library

Robert Frost in the Little Theatre, late 1950s

During one fairly typical session at Bread Loaf [in 1957], the high point for some of the conferees was a talk by Kay Boyle on the work of Beckett. Yet some of the audience sat through that particular lecture with a look of stunned confusion that suggested they were listening to a talk on hydraulics. Those who were bored or bewildered by Beckett, however, perked up a few days later when the platform was adorned by a writer of slick magazine fiction who addressed himself to the demands of the market place. This master of the slick serial continued voicing the same concerns in the workshop sessions he conducted, and he seemed unable to finish a sentence without mentioning a sum of money. He also had a habit of spicing his talk with the "in" nicknames of the various magazines he had written for, and his monologues sounded something like this: "I remember the time I sold a short-short to *Cosmo.* . . . There was a wonderful lady over there in fiction who went to *Good House,* and eventually was hired by *Ladies Home.* At any rate, times have changed, and a serial that once would only bring four might be sold in today's market for as high as seven-five."

During one of this man's market reports, some of us got to giggling in the back of the auditorium. One of the Fellows that year, a Boston Irishman named Joe Dever who has written not only novels, biography and journalism, but also a scathing satirical short story about a writers' conference (titled "A Quick Trip to Butternut") raised his hand and was recognized by the lecturer.

"Dever!" said our marketing expert. "You're a writer—what do you wish to add?"

Dever stood, militarily proud, and said in a ringing voice:

"I just wanted to tell you about the time I sold a short story to *Commonweal* for $35."

It brought down the house—or at least that part of the house inhabited by those of us who were accustomed to the miniature scales of little magazine payment.

—*Dan Wakefield,*
"CONFESSIONS OF A SUMMER CAMPER
(LIT'RY DIVISION)" (1966)

John Ciardi, late 1950s

I was a Fellow at Bread Loaf in 1957. My first book of poems had been published by Scribner's the year before, and I brought with me the manuscript of my second book, which Rinehart & Company subsequently published. Robert Frost was there, and Fellows were invited to consult him. He agreed to read my manuscript and comment. Should his word be favorable, I planned of course to suggest it for the jacket. The manuscript came back to me with a note—but was it positive or negative? Frost wrote: "It reeks of poetry." No, I didn't show this to my editor, but comforted myself with the thought: "Better than no smell at all."

—*May Swenson* (1986)

1959 Staff: (rear) Richard Gehmann, William Sloane, Hollis Summers, William Raney, {?}, Ralph Ellison, {?}, William Meredith, Paul Cubeta; (front) {?}, Nancy Hale, Robert Frost, John Ciardi, {?}.

In a photo staged by Alfred Eisenstaedt, a group of young Bread Loafers (including Anne Sexton, in white dress) sit at the feet of Robert Frost in the meadow behind Treman Cottage, 1959 (Courtesy Dartmouth College Library Special Collections/By Permission of Time, Inc.)

ANNE SEXTON TO CAROLINE KIZER
[Newton Lower Falls, Massachusetts, July 24, 1959]

. . . I am going to study with Roethke this summer as I have received the Robert Frost Fellowship at Bread Loaf. He probably won't like my work. And there we'll be (you and me) with our Cal and our Ted, not liking our work enough (sobbing in our own private caves of womanhood and kicking at the door of fame that men run and own and won't give us the password for). . . . Perhaps not. Perhaps we can exchange famous poets' admiration, back and forth as if it were coin or old or solid. Eh? . . .

The spring before William Sloane, who had been teaching a fiction workshop at Rutgers, spelling John Ciardi, had suggested to me that I come up to Bread Loaf the next summer [1959] as a waiter. He also asked Douglas Davis (a graduate student in art history then whose wife worked at the Rutgers University Press which Sloane directed, and now long-time art critic at *Newsweek*). I drove up to Vermont with Doug—and on our arrival we settled in to our rooms which were upstairs above the dining room at the Inn. The arrangement was that we served three meals a day, and the rest of the time we could attend lectures, swim, read, whatever, and at night, unlike the paying guests, we could drink with the staff at the main staff residence and bar.

For a nineteen year old, who considered himself a vaguely Bohemian literary type (without ever having done much more than help edit the *Anthologist,* the Rutgers literary magazine, and take a writing workshop or two) this was clearly the way to live. At meal times we worked fairly hard at our service (I've never forgotten the art of carrying a tray that I acquired that summer), and the rest of the time was mostly pleasure. Some of the staff came to us, such as George Barker, the British poet, who always seemed to be lounging on the beds in our rooms, particularly on the bed of Parker (forget his last name) from North Carolina, a willowy young fellow my age to whom Barker had obviously taken a liking. Most of the time we waiters were out of our rooms except to sleep, getting to know the writers on staff.

One of those was Ralph Ellison, with whom I've been friends ever since. It was in fact Ralph's presence that led me to create a minor incident one night up at the Snow Bowl. We were having a staff party and a lot of beer was drunk, with a mountain of cans piling up in the large trash barrel in the middle of the room. Someone started singing folk songs, and pretty soon someone started up "Old Black Joe." I became incensed that someone would sing such a song in Ralph's presence and I leaped up and knocked over the huge trash bin full of beer cans, effectively ending the party. Big conscience, big drunk!

There was marijuana too, though few people knew much about it in those days. A beautiful young blond woman from Jersey City, of all places, daughter of a Democratic party chief, drove up in a Morgan, and was always passing around joints (which I had discovered the summer before at Rutgers, when a girl in our crowd who was dating a jazz musician in New York City brought some back for all of us). One afternoon after lunch we were getting quite stoned, about five or six of us waiters, when Bill Sloane came up with Robert Frost and a photographer from *Life* named Alfred Eisenstaedt and told us that Eisenstaedt wanted to take photographs of us with Frost. He marched

"*One more picture, Mr. Frost!*"

us across the road and into the field, where we sat, stoned, in a circle around Frost, and giggled, and he asked us, "Children, why are you laughing? You're not laughing at me, are you?" Oh, no, we said, we're just happy at the day!

Most of the time went like this, though there were some darker moments, such as the late night when a few of us waiters were drinking in town and drove back up the mountain very late, about three in the morning, and decided we'd go to Treman for one last drink—we barged into the darkened living room, flipped the light switch, and there on the sofa were Richard Gehman, the freelancer, and Anne Sexton. . . .

"Hi, fellows," Sexton said, obviously quite high, waving to us from her reclining position on the sofa.

On another dark evening the wild, wire-haired daughter of a New York literary agent took me behind the barn, a cold wind swept over us, and she revealed to me that she was a witch! We took off our clothes and went for a swim in the pond. I don't remember what happened after that.

This summer at Bread Loaf did bewitch me. It was my first full dose of the literary life, life with writers and editors and agents, and though it was another twenty years before I began to publish fiction that time at Bread Loaf drifted now and then into my thoughts. Bill Sloane, John Ciardi, my earliest mentors, they made a good time for a Jersey boy with illusions and dreams!

—*Alan Cheuse* (1989)

Serving the faculty table, 1960

Nancy Hale and Richard Yates, 1960

SIXTIES

I was 20 [in 1960], entering my senior year at Boston College. I had won *The Atlantic*'s college contest in fiction. Bread Loaf had awarded its more-or-less designated *Atlantic* contest fellowship in fiction to Linda Tanner, who came from Fort Smith, Arkansas, and was, not to put too fine a point upon the matter, a cookie. Until I saw her, I couldn't figure out why the Loafers had given her the fellowship, while I had to sling hash in the dining room to earn my keep. After I saw her, I concluded why they had, and the reason was not far to seek. Alas, Linda would have none of me.

Nancy Hale read my stories, which were not very good. But that evened things out—she wasn't, either. Allen Drury autographed a copy of one of his clunkers for my parents, who thought highly of it. Robert Frost autographed his collected poems for them, too. I thought he was pretending when he didn't recognize the young fellow who picked him up in Cambridge and round-tripped him to BC each year for his Humanities Series appearances, but of course he wasn't—he was just rude.

The best writer in the hills where Justin Morgan's horses romped that year was Edward Lewis Wallant, whose first novel—*The Human Season*—was about to appear. He had received the Guggenheim on which he would write, I think, *The Pawnbroker,* and during which he would die, in Rome. What a nice man he was, and what a wonderful writer. Samuel "Chip" Delaney roomed across the hall from me—he later published some sci-fi, and then I lost track of him—and one night after refreshments confided that white people smelled funny to him. Thus emboldened, I told him he was the first Irish jig I'd ever met. One of the paying guests was a garrulous big fat lady who wore décolleté blue flowered dresses, and when I cleared her luncheon plate one day—chicken à la king—the slimy fork dropped off the plate just as she stopped talking in mid-sentence; never since have I been so relieved to find a messy fork in my jacket pocket.

I came home from Bread Loaf that year with a new dent in the door of the red and grey '53 Olds Holiday coupe and no adequate response when my father appraised that and my first scragliassed attempt at a mustache and summed up his opinion by remarking: "Well, you look as though you had a good time." I had learned, though it took me several more years to understand it, that writers' conferences are a colossal waste of time, unless you go for the carousing, in which case it makes a lot more sense to skip the conferring and go out carousing. And I had met a lady who seemed to me then to be very mature—I suppose she was thirty or so, a mere child by my terms of today—who quite solemnly assured me in the Green Mountain summer moonlight that of course I was a writer, if I wished to be. And I believed her. I wish I could remember her name. I owe her a bouquet.

—*George V. Higgins* (1985)

1961 Faculty: (rear) Howard Nemerov, Richard Yates, William Hazlett Upson, William Sloane, Louis Rubin, William Raney, Bernard Asbell, John Frederick Nims, Paul Cubeta; (front) John Ciardi, Nancy Hale, Robert Frost, Eunice Blake, Dudley Fitts. (PC)

Robert Frost, 1960 (JFS)

For whatever it's worth, there was the occasion of, I think, the dumbest question ever asked a distinguished speaker following a lecture. One year at Bread Loaf, Frost came up from his farm for an afternoon give-and-take. As you know, he had published a number of books called Selected Poems, Collected Poems, Complete Poems, and as time went by he would do a new book and there would be a new edition of this Complete Poems or Collected Poems. When he finished reading one afternoon, someone arose and said— (in this context, I guess she had been in the bookstore and seen all these different books, and books are expensive, and she didn't want to spend her money foolishly)—she said, "Mr. Frost, is it safe to buy the Complete Poems *now?*" I've never seen Frost so nonplussed in my life! He shook his head, as if someone had just belted him. He didn't lose his composure, but I guess he was expressing disgust more than amazement. I guess he had had enough experience in not being really stunned by human stupidity. He shook his head and leaned into the microphone and said, "I don't give a damn whether you buy the book or not."

Another occasion I think was a little odd and rather endearing. At the end Frost began to go deaf. But he was too proud to wear a hearing aid. He didn't like to wear glasses though he needed them to read. When you're in your 80's, you begin to be in your 80's. Nevertheless, he had his sense of pride, and he wasn't going to wear a hearing aid. Therefore, at the end of a lecture, at Bread Loaf, I would sneak up behind him, field the questions from the floor, and shout them into his right ear, which was his good one. And he accepted this without any objections. Somehow this arrangement was less obvious than a hearing aid. And it soothed his pride.

But, you see, unless you have these little quirks and cantankers, what have you got to go on when you get that old? I never knew Frost in his prime, but from what I've read and from photos I've seen, he was an extraordinarily powerful man. We hate to give up our stubbornness and identity. Who wants to decline into old age without railing against it a bit?

—*John Ciardi,*
    "CIARDI ON FROST: AN INTERVIEW," BY EDWARD
    CIFELLI, IN FROST CENTENNIAL ESSAYS, VOL. 1,
    EDITED BY JAC THARPE (1974)

Robert Frost makes himself available for pictures and autographs,
1961 (PC)

The faculty social hour at Treman Cottage, early 1960s

Richard Frost, Bob Huff, and I shared a cottage [in 1961]. . . and we made so much noise that some little old ladies complained to Ciardi in the middle of the night once. He got up and came over to our cottage to tell us to shut up. When he'd done that, he found out we'd been telling limericks, and it was our laughter that had disturbed the old folks. John sat down and began his own recitation. It was an astounding performance—he went on for what seemed like, and I think literally was, hours. Of course, the old ladies couldn't complain again under the circumstances.

I remember being unable to understand how anyone could write both poetry and novels. I couldn't get my head around a novel to write, so I asked Howard Nemerov how he did it. He shrugged and said, "All you need is a novel

idea." He was right. Years later I had an idea that would fit in nothing but the form of a novel, and I wrote it off without a hitch. . . .

Dudley Fitts was my critic. At one of our sessions he mentioned that when he was teaching at Cheshire Academy he used to read the *Morning Record* of Meriden, Connecticut. I told him that was my home town paper and I'd first published my poems in Lydia Atkinson's poetry column, "Pennons of Pegasus," when I was a high school student. He laughed and said, "My wife and I used to read that column aloud every Wednesday morning and begin the day with a hearty laugh." I told him I had no idea I'd had such a distinguished audience, and I was pleased he'd been familiar with my work for so long.

—*Lewis Turco* (1985)

I met Robert Frost that summer . . . I recall he came to Treman in the evening and sat in an armchair with a shawl over his knees. I recall being astonished at the super sophistication of the staff and fellows: no one except John Ciardi seemed to pay any attention at all to him. But that there was great awareness of Frost was clear if one looked clearly at what was happening. The conversation and drinking and walking about was as usual, but there was a clear line of demarcation over which no one stepped: a semicircle around Frost's chair. And everyone was careful to pretend indifference to Frost. It was a form of fright.

I stood at the edge of the circle staring at Frost, who looked very lonely. John went to him and said something, and then came toward me. He said something like, "Why don't you go and talk with him? He's being ignored." But I was too timid. John left, I continued standing, until I heard Frost mutter, "Won't someone talk to me?" I gathered up my courage and went over to introduce myself.

I sat down at his side and said, "What will we talk about?" He answered, "You start." So I told him a story about a woodchuck that had chased my wife once in Connecticut. He responded by telling me something about his adventures the first time he had gone to England. Soon we were joined by two young women, sisters whose names I forget. . . . We talked with Frost almost the whole evening. Almost no one else interrupted the whole time.

Almost no one. Our little group of four was talking, and John was looking on, when one of the waiters knocked at the door, asked for John, and requested permission of him to bring in the other waiters who wanted to sing Frost a song. Ciardi asked Frost if it would be all right, Frost acceded, and the waiters came in, gathered round us in a semicircle, and sang—to the tune of "Hernando's Hideaway"—"Whose woods these are I think I know. . . ." The chorus was "Ole!" I know this has entered legend, and I'm told people (including Marvin Bell, if I'm not mistaken) maintain the incident occurred in other years, but it happened in 1961 in Treman House.

—*Lewis Turco* (1985)

Frost arrived in style for cocktails in his honor. "Cocktails?" he snorted. "Doesn't anyone drink good old New England rum?" No one did; and he turned down scotch, rye, bourbon, and likewise soft drinks. I had what he wanted— Old Newburyport—and dashed up to my room and fetched it. Made his day. Mine, too.

—*Martin Dibner* (1986)

Robert Frost, 1961 (PC)

Beyond the stacked porches of Maple Cottage lies the prospect of Bread Loaf Mountain

He loved to sit after an evening, with a circle of people on the floor while he sat in a chair and played the wise man, usually reciting lines of stories he had practiced and rehearsed for purposes of his own. He tended to pick up a little motif and play it for a year or so, and if you heard him on several occasions you would hear him repeating himself, always as if it had just come to him. But after all, he was called on to perform in public so often he had to have— what shall I call it?—some standardized "Material" to use over and over. I've had to play the same game myself at times, running my mouth through long-since memorized impromptus.

A sad story about the decline of a great man occurs—I think it was the last time or almost the last time I saw him,

his last year at Bread Loaf. He announced that he wasn't strong enough to do the full program he had done in the past, and he said he would either come up and give an afternoon talk, or he would autograph the books people had bought. Either would take an afternoon's work. People had bought so many books that we elected to satisfy them by getting the books signed. And there were crates of them. We used my office . . . and stacked them up there and had a little chain going. One person would take the books out of the crate and hand them to Kay Morrison who was Frost's confidant, advisor, general factotum, secretary, arranger of everything, a marvelous person, and she would look at the names on the slip of paper inserted in the book and remind Frost of any relationship that might exist—

that's so-and-so's grandson, you know, and you ought to mention such-and-such—and Frost would write that in the book, and I would take it out from under him and hand it to somebody else to put in a box. It got to be a long session on a sunny, warm, lazy afternoon. Frost took off his coat and sat there in suspenders, and from time to time somebody would bring him a lemonade as I had prearranged, and he would sit and reminisce for a while, and it was very *en famille* and friendly, and finally he got through the stack of books and was just reminiscing about this, that, and the other. As a matter of fact, I think we were talking about his marvelous dog, a border collie named Gilly, as we started out the door.

This is, I think, a slightly funny story, a rather sad story, about the decline of a great man. The point may well be that he is a great man, and the decline happens to us all. Frost had spent so much time on stage that it was at least partly possible to say that except in very intimate and relaxed circumstances, he was never *off* stage. He was always playing the role he had learned to perform, a rather coy one at times. . . .

As we came out of the office that afternoon he caught sight of one small, white-haired lady coming through the door, and suddenly he turned off the conversation about Gilly or whatever it was and said, waving his hands in the air, "And I'll *tell* them in Washington." Then he turned to that little old lady from Dubuque and raised his voice and with a kind of false heartiness said, "Oh, hello there!" And he picked up this Washington theme he had suddenly thrown in the air. He *snowed* that poor old gal. Here she was in the presence of the great man in a blizzard of blither. He walked her around the corner, and she went one way, and he went out the door, still waving and performing: "You can be sure I'll *tell* them when I get down there." Pontificating, he took three steps and turned to me and in a totally different voice said, "Who the hell's that?" He wasn't kidding himself, in a way. He liked to play the role. He relished it.

All I'm saying is that he was an extremely complicated man and it was something of a revelation to see this little quirk in his character. It doesn't lessen the mountain or lessen the heat of the eruption. Remember this is a man of 85 or 86. He would never have played that role that way some years earlier. Reserve judgment until you get to be 85 or 86 and see what you have left to go on.

—*John Ciardi,*
"CIARDI ON FROST: AN INTERVIEW," BY EDWARD CIFELLI, IN FROST CENTENNIAL ESSAYS, VOL. 1, EDITED BY JAC THARPE (1974)

Maple Cottage

For Robert Frost, in the Autumn, in Vermont

All on the mountains, as on tapestries
Reversed, their threads unreadable though clear,
The leaves turn in the volume of the year.
Your land becomes more brilliant as it dies.

The puzzled pilgrims come, car after car,
With cameras loaded for epiphanies;
For views of failure to take home and prize,
The dying tourists ride through realms of fire.

"To die is gain," a virgin's tombstone said;
That was New England, too, another age
That put a higher price on maidenhead
If brought in dead; now on your turning page
The lines blaze with a constant light, displayed
As in the maple's cold and fiery shade.
    —*Howard Nemerov,*
      THE BLUE SWALLOWS (1967)

Robert Frost stands in the door of his cabin, 1962 (Kathleen Morrison)

"The only certain freedom's in departure."
    —*Robert Frost,*
      "HOW HARD IT IS TO KEEP FROM BEING KING
       WHEN IT'S IN YOU AND IN THE SITUATION," IN
      THE CLEARING (1962)

Nelson Algren and Bread Loafers depart the Little Theatre, 1963

Nelson Algren's hard to kill. When he was around, he was feisty, funny, resilient, and until his 60's—when he wearied of the fight to gain the respect that his lesser, more polite contemporaries gathered with ease—prolific. He left us a significant body of work, much of which was out of print for some time. But more to the point, he wrote well. He wrote brilliantly, especially in *A Walk on the Wild Side*, and *The Man With the Golden Arm*, which are, to my mind, his best, most artistically successful books. His language lasts: the voice of an Algren story or novel is unmistakably his, as permanently, flat-out American as Twain's and Crane's and more authentic than Hemingway's. There's a combination of layered and compressed writing (a truly rare combination of virtues; writers usually have one or the other) that reminds me of Eudora Welty and William Kennedy at their best. . . .

I was lucky enough to know Nelson when I was young. Childless, he took a lot of young writers under his wing (Terry Southern, Bruce Jay Friedman, numerous others), providing fatherly protection, encouragement and example all at once. I was a 23-year-old pipefitter in Concord, N.H., who hadn't gone to college but had written a novel that, despite a few striking paragraphs here and there, was quite simply awful. I took off work for a week and lugged my manuscript to the Bread Loaf Writers' Conference in Vermont, where Algren was on the staff, more or less. (John Ciardi, the director, thought less; Algren thought more.) He read my manuscript, as he was paid to do, quickly located those few striking paragraphs and pointed them out to me and made it clear that I was supposed to do the rest myself (and what more can an apprentice writer ask of a master, anyhow?). But meanwhile, he said, since I had wheels and we were stuck up here on this mountain surrounded by writers drinking sherry with their little fingers in the air, and since he, like Jack Kerouac, didn't drive, why didn't I take him to Middlebury for a beer and then maybe we'd go on to visit his pal Paul Goodman, who had a summer place somewhere nearby? We did, and that was the end of my tour at Bread Loaf, more or less.

Algren in person was a lot like his books—large-hearted, funny, angry, lonely. He spoke the truth to power wherever he met power (and he saw injustice where most people preferred to see only good intentions gone awry, which made him no friend to bourgeois academics and intellectuals: he trusted a brutal, racist Chicago cop more than a suburban Republican banker). To those of us who loved him, he could sometimes seem perversely self-defeating: he was unable to resist any chance to tweak the beard of somber authority.

 —*Russell Banks,*
  FROM THE FOREWORD TO A WALK ON THE WILD SIDE BY NELSON ALGREN (1990)

1963 Fellows and Scholars: (rear) Arno Karlen, Richard Underwood, Paris Leary, William Wetmore, Fleming Blitch, Charles Rose, Alan Levy; (front) Barbara Overmyer, Nancy Sullivan, Joan Didion

1963 Faculty: (rear) Paul Cubeta, Robert Pack, Brock Brower, John Hawkes, John Frederick Nims, Nelson Algren, Walter Ross, William Sloane; (front) Hollis Summers, Cornelia Otis Skinner, John Ciardi, Eunice Blake, William Raney, Mark Harris

One late August evening, I happened through a parlor at the office end of Bread Loaf's main building. The critic Elizabeth Drew sat at an empty card table, her back to the croquet lawn. She did not look up, as I took a comfortable chair and began to read a book, passing the time until dinner.

I had never talked to Miss Drew, but I knew her tragic story: how she had escaped during World War II to the United States, bringing her daughter to safety by accepting a position in a New England college, and then how the girl had darted into a quiet street and been killed by a car. As a young woman, unmarried and childless, I probably appreciated the irony more than the pain.

Suddenly John Ciardi appeared in the door. With his disheveled hair, his energy and robustness, he seemed at once vulnerable and intimidating. He boomed, "Can anyone here play bridge?" It was obvious that he had been on a mission to scout out two more players after the originals failed to show. Ciardi looked at me, and I felt my heart jump. I had played dormitory bridge and not even much of that. Surely I couldn't be drafted to play with the stars of the conference, who were as likely to be crafty with cards as they were with sentences.

Before long, a fourth person joined us, a young woman I think, and the draw determined that Ciardi and I were partners! Whether by residual wisdom, pure luck, or terror, I managed to play without making a fool of myself. In fact, Ciardi and I were due to clinch total victory when, in the final hand, I won the bid—two no-trump! What could be worse than having to play while Ciardi sat back as the watchful "dummy"? Somehow I managed to make the bid, and as we got up from the table, everyone smiled and thanked each other for the good game.

I watched as Ciardi went out the door and over the lawn to the main road. He and his wife and numerous children lived in a house across the way, and he was hurrying back to get them for supper in the big dining room. Just then a long sleek car roared up the slope from the direction of Middlebury. It never braked at the sight of buildings or people, but even before it got past Ciardi he had assumed a posture of defiance, raised his arm as if to throw something, and begun to bellow. I don't remember if he used profanity, but in effect he yelled, "Slow down! We've got children here!"

After the car disappeared up the road toward Texas Falls, he fumed his way home. I turned, and the parlor was empty. Had Elizabeth Drew lingered long enough to see Ciardi, to hear him rail against the absurdity of accidental death?

—*Jean Lawlor Cohen* (1990)

In the 1960s the walk past the Annex was maple-shaded

William Sloane autographs a book, 1966

1964 Faculty: (rear) William Sloane, Howard Nemerov, Dan Wakefield, Brock Brower, Robert Pack, Paul Cubeta, William Raney; (front) John Ciardi, Eunice Blake, Nancy Hale, Shirley Jackson, David McCord

In 1940, as trade manager of then Henry Holt & Co., a trim young man named William Sloane, who looked like the president of some recent Princeton graduating class, published my first book of poems in an act of editorial benevolence I then believed to be no more than my due. Fifteen years later, the same William Sloane, as director of Rutgers University Press, and looking like the president of a less recent Princeton graduating class, published my *As If, Poems New and Selected.* At lunch just before the latter publication, Sloane was jovial but wry.

"In 1940," he began, forming his words around the stem of his pipe, "I squandered a modest but accountable sum of Henry Holt's money on a first book by a lean and hungry young poet. From the meager resources of the University Press, I am about to squander a second sum to publish the selected poems of a not-so-young, not-so-lean, but probably still hungry poet. In an effort to justify this extravagance, I have read the manuscript and in it I discover that not one of those first poems on which I squandered Henry Holt's money struck that poet as good enough to be included in the selected poems."

Bill liked preambles. He finished this one, fussed with his pipe, got it going, and moved to his point. "How," he said, "am I to justify my handling of the money once entrusted to me by Henry Holt? How am I to justify my

present handling of the Press's funds? And what sort of an editor does that make me?"

"Let me start," I said, "by suggesting the word 'genius.' You are the sort of editor who can recognize talent even when it isn't there."

Over the years, Bill liked to return to this bit of banter in which he ruefully confessed his gullibility while implying my sly entrapment of his good nature. Yet, even in play, he was touching a serious side of himself. I was moved to dismiss that first book as juvenilia and to sweep those poems under the carpet. Bill was forever moved to ask himself what he had done, why he had done it, and if he had done it well enough. I have never known a man so dedicated to the idea of giving a consistent shape and purpose to his life.

It was never a case of being prostrate before his own image. It was a modest thing, almost, I felt, a sense of curatorship, of discharging his debt to many good men from whose example he had shaped his own sense of purpose. Bill sought to give shape to his life as a novelist gives shape to his book, which is to say in answer to some ideal sense of form.

—*John Ciardi*,
INTRODUCTION TO THE CRAFT OF WRITING BY
WILLIAM SLOANE (1979)

Some time after my novel *Lea* had been published, I had been invited to a party in Greenwich Village. Among the guests was this large, impressive-looking man with the attention-getting voice and the imperial head. I didn't know it was John Ciardi until someone introduced me to him. I can't recall exactly what he said, but in the next few moments I learned—to my astonishment—that he had read and liked my novel. Somewhere in the course of our brief conversation, he said something about ". . . having you up on the hill next year."

I had heard of Bread Loaf, but I made no connection between John Ciardi's words and that remote, rather exotic place. It was more a rumor than a reality to me. "Having you up on the hill" struck me as an invitation of some sort, but what it made me imagine was a high feudal bastion somewhere in New Jersey. I figured that some time in the indefinite future, a drawbridge would be let down and the Epsteins would clatter into the Ciardi keep for a dinner replete with saffron soup and trenchers of bread to be thrown to the dogs that growled beneath the table.

Grace Schulman, the poet, happened to be present at the same party, and some minutes later she approached me and said, "I suppose you realize you were being invited to the Bread Loaf Writers' Conference." I answered no, I hadn't realized anything of the sort, and I was sure she was wrong. But I did write a letter to John Ciardi and asked if his words could possibly mean what Grace Schulman thought they meant. I got an immediate response confirming that understanding, and I could expect additional information to follow shortly. That August, or the following one, I was on the staff of the Bread Loaf Writers' Conference.

It was on that first visit that I began to gather the first of my Ciardi impressions. I remember the pink Cadillac. I remember John saying that he wanted to be the first poet in the United States to own a pink Cadillac. I was among the first to arrive at Bread Loaf that year, and also among the first was Charles Jackson, author of *The Lost Weekend*. I remember sitting at the inn in Middlebury with John Ciardi and Charles Jackson, hoisting a few and talking (actually listening, mainly, to Ciardi) and thinking to myself: *You, this is you, sitting here with this world-famous poet and this novelist, whose novel had been made into a movie starring Ray Milland! If you live to be a hundred, you will never fully absorb the wonder of it!*

But time adjusts all perspectives, and while I came to know these men as men, I was prophetic in supposing I would never fully absorb the wonder of that evening. That first occasion has secured for itself a timeless corner in my head, and when I wish to recover that inimitable moment I think of Ciardi and Jackson and Epstein imbibing in that mythic inn. The unlikeliness of it all touches the lift-off button, and for a brief time I find myself once again

Seymour Epstein, 1965

floating in a gravity-less universe where all laws of probability have been cancelled and Epstein has been alchemized into another essence, one that permitted a free mingling with John Ciardi and Charles Jackson. That alchemizing effect has never left me in all the subsequent years I attended Bread Loaf.

John was not a man of easy, one-on-one exchange. In retrospect, I realize that [our first] conversation . . . was almost entirely anecdotal and impersonal. It was, as I remember, mainly about the mechanics and finances of an itinerant poet. But when that first year's conference got under way, I had the opportunity of seeing John Ciardi as the numbers around him increased from two to ten to a hundred, and with that increase came an increase in charm, wit, and illuminating facets of the man as poet and raconteur. In time, I evolved the theory of numbers in the case of John Ciardi. One-on-one produced next to nothing in the way of Ciardi music, but as the numbers increased so did the Ciardi resonance, until the full diapason was sounded in a lecture hall with every seat occupied. This observation of Ciardi is not meant to be invidious. I liked and admired the man, although I did find it impossible to get close to him. It was simply the way he was. Imperious, generous, charming, and gregarious—but only in numbers.

—*Seymour Epstein* (1988)

On the front porch of Treman Cottage, 1968: identifiable are Walter Goodman, John Williams, Peg Martin, Seymour Epstein, Diane Wakoski

1965 Faculty: (rear) William Lederer, William Sloane, Seymour Epstein, Brock Brower, Richard Ellmann, Walter Goodman; (center) John Frederick Nims, Eunice Blake, John Ciardi, Nancy Hale, Chard Powers Smith; (front) Edward Martin, Henry Rago, Charles Jackson, Robert Pack

Standing Close to Greatness   *John Ciardi chats with Bread Loafers after a lecture, mid 1960s*

His eyes shine like an expensive car.
His voice is distant and clear, like the Greek Islands. We move
around him as if someone were writing his name
all the time.
He forgives us our excessive love.

We do need the great ones, who brush their teeth
and never spit and who it is hard to think of
wanting a word.

O they are important for looking down as they do.
It is not true
that in the bathroom they act like anyone else.
They act great.

Still we know, we know,
for every object of universal acclaim
there must be others highly respected and fussy
who never heard the name
and snort and grumble when they tell us so.
    —*Miller Williams,*
        THE BOYS ON THEIR BONY MULES (1983)

John Ciardi and William Hazlett Upson

Poetry Dignitary

He lectures, palms extended on the air,
Much like the pope to bless St. Peter's Square.
Heaps laurel on his bumpy brow benign;
Chants, "Acres of Parnassus, and all mine!"
    —John Frederick Nims,
      OF FLESH AND BONE (1967)

Seymour Epstein and Maxine Kumin during a fiction presentation in the Little Theatre, 1969

One of the things that Bread Loaf has taught me was that I could teach. This was almost as stunning a revelation as the revelation that I could write. Perhaps even greater, since writing had always presented itself as an endowment having little to do with formal education. You either could or couldn't and the only way to find out was to try. Teaching was something you did after a sizable portion of your life had been dedicated to being taught. Since I had read extensively and chaotically but hadn't much more than a few years of college night school, I never even considered the possibility of becoming a teacher. It was a turn of fortune as remote as the stars.

Fredson Bowers, the eminent Shakespearean scholar and the husband of Nancy Hale, herself a Bread Loaf staff alumnus, suggested to me one Bread Loaf season that I would make a good teacher of creative writing. Fortunately for me, that opinion coincided with the presence of John Williams, another Bread Loaf staffer, who was heading up at the time the graduate writing program at the University of Denver. One thing led to another and John invited me for a year's stay at the university as a visiting lecturer. That

year extended to eighteen. I retired two years ago as a full professor. I who hadn't even taken an undergraduate degree!

Another Bread Loaf miracle!

I guess I shared with every ex–Bread Loafer an almost extra-terrestrial sensation as I would wind my way up the mountain, passing signs of Bread Loaf's proximity. I did it for so many years, and although the potency eventually dissipated, it never completely vanished. Some residue of the original magic was there to be tasted with each year's approach. For me it is comparable to the magic of childhood, where everything is proof against diminishment and decay. Disillusion can set in, but the disillusion is the result of not having your accomplishments live up to your expectations, not having a success commensurate with your dreams. Bread Loaf stands apart from these realities. Bread Loaf allows you to tunnel back to a pristine time, as childhood is a pristine time, a time when reality has not yet begun to make its inevitable encroachments.

—*Seymour Epstein* (1988)

Bread Loaf Inn, early 1960s

Robert Pack, 1965 (PC)

Looking back, I begin to realize how difficult those years were, the middle and late sixties; anyone who could afford a ballpoint pen or a typewriter was allowed to think of himself as a poet or a novelist; talent and craft were suspect, more often than not described as "elitist," a curse-word of the period; and literacy was thought by many to be a species of corruption, a loss of innocence or a kind of damnation. It was, alas, a hysteria to which a few staff members, who should have known better, surrendered. And yet in those difficult years, somehow Bread Loaf managed to survive, even to thrive, against the pressures of mediocrity. I'm afraid that it took me some time to realize that, at Bread Loaf, at least, the mainstay against the encroachment of that old enemy was John Ciardi himself.

To all appearances, he was an unlikely mainstay. He was always around, but he seemed to be not intimately connected with the running of the Conference itself. I saw him (and I see him now) sitting, night after night, at the large table in the living room at Treman, playing cribbage, first with Doc Klompus and later with Miller Williams, drinking his bourbon steadily and almost soberly; in the late afternoons, throwing a Frisbee to his German Shepherd, Dippy, a dog that seemed almost as much a loner as John himself; or perfecting his stroke by swinging a golf club against the undriveable meadows of the Bread Loaf fields. He seemed to me almost indifferent to what went on around him.

He was not, of course.

Somehow, without being told, he knew everything that went on. That seemingly indifferent eye was always the first to see when a student (or for that matter a staff member) might begin to crack under the incremental intensity of the Conference; and the voice that could be brusque and impatient in casual encounters seemed always to know exactly what to say to calm the raw nerve or to steady the teetering psyche. With an irascibility that was almost sentimental, he protected the privacy of the staff and the dignity of the students; and if there were privileges accorded to any, they were the privileges of talent rather than rank. The essential kindness of the man was not displayed casually, as a social grace; thus it sometimes went unperceived. But it was there always, in an extremity of need.

Appearances do not always deceive, but often enough they do; for appearances are what we make of things that sometimes we do not understand. I think I first began to allow my friendship with John Ciardi when I realized that his occasional brusqueness with acquaintances, and even friends, was the mask that tries to disguise affection and an innate shyness; and when I realized that the salient quality of the man's character was loyalty.

John Williams, 1960s

He was loyal to his own past, to the circumstances in which he was born and from which he emerged, perhaps more determined by them than he wished to be; he was loyal to his friends, to their strengths as well as their weaknesses, knowing that the one is always necessary to the other; and perhaps above all, he was loyal to the art he practiced, the principles of that art, and to the integrity of his work. However posterity may judge the ultimate worth of his own work (if, indeed, posterity has any business making such a judgment), it cannot but admit him into the select company of those who are essential to the stubborn and somehow miraculous persistence of civilization.

—John Williams,
"LOOKING FOR JOHN CIARDI AT BREAD LOAF," IN
JOHN CIARDI: MEASURE OF THE MAN, EDITED BY
VINCE CLEMENTE (1987)

Picnic on the West Lawn, 1966

Roundtable in the Little Theatre

On Treman porch, late 1960s: Lewis Turco, {?}, {?}, Dan Wakefield, Sy Epstein, Judson Jerome

It is hardly the monetary motive alone that brings us to these affairs. One could always sit home and make as much money as the conference pays by daily application to the typewriter. The excuse to escape from this routine is of course one of the benefits offered by the conference (an excuse that every writer is constantly on the lookout for) and the temptation is increased by the fact that many of these summer conclaves are staged in extremely pleasant locations like Vermont, Colorado and Cape Cod. Spending a week or two in the mountains or at the seashore, and getting paid for it while talking about writing, is a happy prospect for an author who has sweated out most of the year contemplating the view of his typewriter keys. But I suspect that even this dividend is not the deepest attraction that the conference holds for the professional writer.

The truth, as usual, is rather embarrassing. Perhaps I can best suggest it by explaining that serving on the staff of a summer conference is one of the only opportunities I know for a writer to enjoy the sort of status in a temporary community that is comparable in the outside world to the status of, say, baseball players and television panelists. Like the pro instructor at a ski resort, the professional writer at a summer conference is surrounded by people who in general admire what he does and would like to be able to perform in the same medium with skill—if only as a weekend skier, or an occasional contributor to *The Saturday Evening Post* or *Kenyon Review.* The pro in such a setting enjoys a rare form of regard. He may not be well-liked, or even particularly liked at all, but at least attention is paid.

Perhaps the staff members are the ones who should actually pay to go to the conference.

—Dan Wakefield,
"CONFESSIONS OF A SUMMER CAMPER
(LIT'RY DIVISION)" (1966)

Dan Wakefield, Robert Pack, and Diane Wakoski chat in the Barn, 1966

John Aldridge, 1965

Dan Wakefield chats with a Bread Loafer following his lecture, 1966

John Ciardi and Robert Pack, mid-1960s

Inside the faculty lounge, mid-1960s: Dan Wakefield, John Williams, William Sloane, Walter Goodman

Advice to Poets Whose Lines Run on
in Pursuit of Free Expression but Who
Suffer from the Pathetic Fallacy and
Who Peter Out, Whose Form Lacks
Animation and Whose Spirit Cannot
Keep It Up, to Try Using an Iambic Line,
Alliteration, Even Writing a Sonnet, in
Service to Your Muse

But no one writes iambic verse these days,
You say. Your random meter's limp, so try
To join your beats and let rhyme soothe the ways
Urania can make you soar. For why
Would you erect a loose form that your Muse
Cannot ascend? Submit! True potency
Must serve her needs. Stroke her caesura, bruise
Her Bacchic breast in bold embrace, and see,
She will rejoin by handing you a line—
God's "I Am that I Am," flaming your ears,
Whispering your enjambment is divine
For play, your assonance blasts her to tears.
Coupling in climax, your technique could blow it
Without care where you put your extra foot, you poet!
—*Robert Pack,*
Waking to My Name (1980)

View of the south meadow from the Inn

Dan Wakefield, 1970 (RL)

John Ciardi holds forth, late 1960s

Between classes, late 1960s

During one of my stays at Bread Loaf, a promising young writer who had published his first story in *The Hudson Review* knocked out an angular foreign gentleman who contributed travel articles to *The Saturday Evening Post.* I can't remember the issue that started the battle, but I am sure it was unimportant in itself and that the conflict was as inevitable as it was literary. After all, how often does a *Hudson Review* man have the opportunity to floor a *Saturday Evening Post* man?

Most of the conflicts, however, are restricted to the writer's more traditional weapon—words. One poet, speaking in a workshop against the principles espoused by another poet on the staff, got so worked up with his own eloquence that he ended the hour by marching over to the rival poet and exclaiming: "What you need is a good analysis!"

The lady writers, too, are capable of doing literary battle, though sometimes their wrath is expressed in terms more feline than bookish. At one evening party I was listening to two lady writers discuss a third, who had made the mistake of being the first to leave.

"Where's Miriam?" said the first lady writer.

"Oh, she just made her exit, looking very grand, as usual."

"Well, she keeps herself marvelously," said the first lady writer. "I understand she puts cold cream on every night before bed. I only wish *I* had the time for that."

If the rivalries at a writers' conference often occur along literary lines, so does the romance. If you happen to be hard at work on a novel inspired by Joyce, Proust, and Svevo, it is difficult to walk hand in hand into the sunset with a girl who is carrying a well-thumbed copy of *The Carpetbaggers.* By the same token, a girl who has brought to the conference a thin sheaf of poems influenced by Robert Lowell is not likely to greet the dawn with a man who is working on "A History of the Kiwanis Club in Ohio."

Happily, the kindred souls are quickly able to spot one another, and soon the conference settles down to its cliques and controversies that make up a world, a society within a society. It all sounds terribly frivolous, but surely we who are writers or want to be deserve our own convention or annual picnic as much as the National Association of Manufacturers and the Eastern Star, complete with serious lectures and seminars that are followed by cocktails, gossip, shoptalk, corny jokes and the stimulating aura of literary, political and romantic intrigue. Though not announced in the catalogue or advertised in the literary columns, those are the elements that help make the summer writers' conferences continue to flourish. I know this view is scorned by the serious literary folk, and I can only hang my head and plead: After we've worked so hard for the bread, let us enjoy the circus.

—*Dan Wakefield,*
"CONFESSIONS OF A SUMMER CAMPER
(LIT'RY DIVISION)" (1966)

Judson Jerome chats with William Lederer and others outside the Little Theatre, 1967 (RL)

In 1967 John Ciardi invited me to join the staff at Bread Loaf, and again in 1968. This was an opportunity I'm afraid I blew. The experience completely changed my prejudices about writers' conferences. The few appearances I had made at such gatherings had convinced me that they were no more than occasions for the untalented to gather autographs of the dubiously glamorous; but the quality of both the student and staff writers at Bread Loaf was impressive; moreover, the social contacts were at least educational and of genuine benefit to the careers of many. I attended every workshop and found myself learning as much as I taught from such regulars as John Frederick Nims, Miller Williams, Hollis Summers, Robert Pack, and of course, Ciardi.

But they were heady times—and the times had gone to my head. In addition to serving their serious purposes, the

Bread Loaf sessions are for many occasions for partying and philandering, activities I participated in as eagerly as I did the workshops and lectures. I earned enough of a reputation in that regard to receive a warning along with my invitation to return, but my indulgences in 1968 turned out to be even more extensive than they had been the year before. The walls of the buildings at Bread Loaf are paper thin, and though John and the management had no desire to regulate morals, they demanded a discretion I failed to muster.

I can think of a lot of excuses, but they won't stand up in court. 1968 was one of the watershed years of our century. The assassination of Martin Luther King had brought the nation close to revolution. Then the assassination of Robert Kennedy at the crest of a brawling, bitter, multi-sided contention for the Democratic nomination.

1967 Faculty: (rear) Edward Martin, John Aldridge, Miller Williams, Seymour Epstein, William Hazlett Upson, Henry Simon, John Frederick Nims (middle) William Sloane, Camille Davied, Archibald MacLeish, John Ciardi, Susan Hirschman, Judith Ciardi; (front) Judson Jerome, John Williams, Robert Pack, William Lederer (RL)

Then, while we were at Bread Loaf, Russia's invasion of Czechoslovakia. We went home from Bread Loaf to the news of the Democratic Convention in Chicago and all the violence which surrounded it. Black power. The counterculture. Drugs. Communes. I was wearing my hair shoulder length and making inflammatory speeches on campuses around the country. I had had an article accepted by *Life,* "The System Really Isn't Working," which was launching me on a new career as a social and education reformer—and I was a little crazy with it all. And in my mind, licentious behavior was somehow mixed up with political radicalism, part of the agenda for the emerging counterculture.

Once I asked John for permission to bring a woman student into Treman, the drinking cabin from which

students were excluded. He was in the midst of one of his eternal gin rummy games with his good friend "Doc," the staff doctor, and he refused me curtly. Later I told him I didn't mind the refusal so much—but, I asked, why the tone? I thought we were by then old friends. "Don't get too near a psychic buzz saw," he said. All of us learned to be wary of a volatile and unpredictable personality.

—*Judson Jerome,*
   "JOHN CIARDI REMEMBERED," JOHN CIARDI:
   MEASURE OF THE MAN, EDITED BY VINCE
   CLEMENTE (1987)

1968 Faculty: (rear) Edward Martin, John Frederick Nims, Seymour Epstein, Miller Williams, William Lederer, John Aldridge; (center) Dan Wakefield, Hollis Summers, Eunice Blake, John Ciardi, Judith Ciardi, John Williams; (front) William Sloane, Lewis Turco, Judson Jerome

Robert Pack (RL)

John Frederick Nims (RL)

The old bookstore, late 1960s

William Kotzwinkle . . . was married during the 1968 Conference, in a setting out in the woods, I believe (I was not at the ceremony). He read one of his stories to a group of us one night—I think it was titled *Maria* or a name like that—and it was beautiful, clearly the best story read at the Conference. We were in the same cottage. I had brought my typewriter along to do some writing and he did, too. Seems to me we were writing in separate rooms, our typewriters back to back but separated by the wall, and I could hear his typewriter clatter as we both wrote, almost as if the machines were holding a conversation.

I remember Harry Crews playing the guitar, singing country songs—magnetic, hell-raising, yet you sensed an underlying and brooding sensitivity. John Ciardi reveled in the role of mentor and director. He played the part of gadfly during all-night drinking and talking sessions, brilliant. He put a price tag on a lot of things, including his own poetry. One night, he said: "I once earned more money speaking in one night in Texas than my father did in a year." I remember Bill Lederer as having a slight stammer which only added to the drama of his talks. He was warm, friendly, generous, sensitive to young writers. He also appeared troubled about something in his life. Of all the people I met there, I cherish the memory of him most, although I knew him only fleetingly, and he most likely doesn't even remember me.

I remember Hollis Summers as being unfailingly kind and gracious. And John Frederick Nims introducing me to his wife as the subject of what was and still is one of my favorite poems, *Love Poem* ("My clumsiest dear, whose hands shipwreck vases").

Going to Bread Loaf was for me like being shot out of a cannon into a world I did not know existed. I did not come from an academic background, had never known established writers or hung around with writers. I did some writing, a lot of beer drinking, remained on the fringes, and returned to earth after two weeks. I was very glad to go to Bread Loaf and very glad to return to the real world.
—*Robert Cormier* (1986)

John Frederick Nims, X. J. Kennedy, David Wagoner, 1966

I remember Miller Williams after an evening reading being approached by a Bread Loafer and being told, "That wasn't bad," and Miller replying, "It wasn't supposed to be." I remember Isaac Asimov getting up almost violently and bolting as far away as possible from anyone who put a match to a cigarette. I remember him saying something to the effect that I must teach him how to create fully dimensioned characters, and my thinking that I would be happy to try it if he would teach me how to make even a fraction of what he made on his writing. I remember John Nims standing on the lecture platform and exchanging furious invectives with Henry Rago, the then editor of *Poetry* magazine. As I recall it, each man was thoroughly convinced of the other man's need of extensive psychiatric treatment. I remember the curious clicking sound coming from the next door apartment, which I knew was occupied by David Wagoner and his wife. The source of the sound proved to be a pet turtle that Mrs. Wagoner kept in the

bathtub. I remember Maxine Kumin taking out a group of people for a mushroom hunt and their returning to Treman, spreading their mycological finds on a sun-splashed counter of the kitchen. How strangely vivid that scene has remained.

I remember the first time I met Harry Crews, whose beetling brow and deep-set eyes and ferocious muscles made me wonder what I would do if I were ever confronted with a crisis of candor. I asked myself what I would do if Harry were to say to me, "Sy, I want you to level with me . . ." As a matter of fact, he did ask me that by force of circumstances. He was there as a fellow and I had read his manuscript. At the interview, I was as nervous as he was. I don't remember what I said to him then, but I do know that I have come to admire his writing greatly, even though we are as opposite in style and subject as two writers can be.

—*Seymour Epstein* (1988)

I wanted to publish about as badly as any man has wanted to do anything *ever*. Today I lust after an audience. I wish I were widely, widely read. I wish the audience of people who read and like my work were eight times as big as it is. I wrote fifteen years without any approval at all. I was rejected by everybody in the country and nobody ever mentioned anything about talent in the letters they wrote back to me. In the form rejection slips, nobody ever said a word about talent. I used to dream when I was as old as twenty-five or twenty-six that one of my novels (of course I'd written four novels by that time which had been rejected), I used to dream that one of my novels had been published; and dream while I was asleep this tremendous joy and celebration and the rest of it and then wake up literally humiliated, crushed, depressed, stricken that I was still where I was. . . . Now I have six novels and in my personal life it's done nothing. I always somehow assumed that it would. It hasn't.

—*Harry Crews,*
IN "ARGUMENTS OVER AN OPEN WOUND: AN INTERVIEW," BY V. STERLING WATSON, PRAIRIE SCHOONER (SPRING 1974)

Maxine Kumin, 1970 (FG)

Harry Crews, lawn party, 1970 (FG)

Suppose you asked, "Did I think writing could be taught?" Now this has been hashed over time out of mind. And I don't think you ever change anybody's mind about it. I don't know whether writing can be taught or not. Just let me go on record as saying that when I work—with people in the university who think they want to write fiction, I think of myself only as what a very fine editor would be—I'm a reader. I read their work and give my best reaction to it. I say to them, "I believe this, I don't believe this, this seems too quick, this is whatever, the language is garbled, or whatever." I give them my best reaction, and from my reaction, the best reading I can give the piece, the writer is free to go and do whatever he wants to do with this work, including nothing. I have never told anybody, "Go and do this: add another character." Every writer up to a certain point needs a reader. . . . Let me cite Ralph Ellison. In an interview in *Harper's,* he said he thought it was important for a writer to be around other writers *particularly* when he was young, because when he was young he was developing that fund of craft out of which he would draw for the rest of his life—almost a direct quotation, and that marvelous "fund of craft"—I love that. I don't think anybody's ever hurt by knowing too much about his art.

—*Harry Crews,*
IN "ARGUMENTS OVER AN OPEN WOUND: AN INTERVIEW," BY V. STERLING WATSON, PRAIRIE SCHOONER (SPRING 1974)

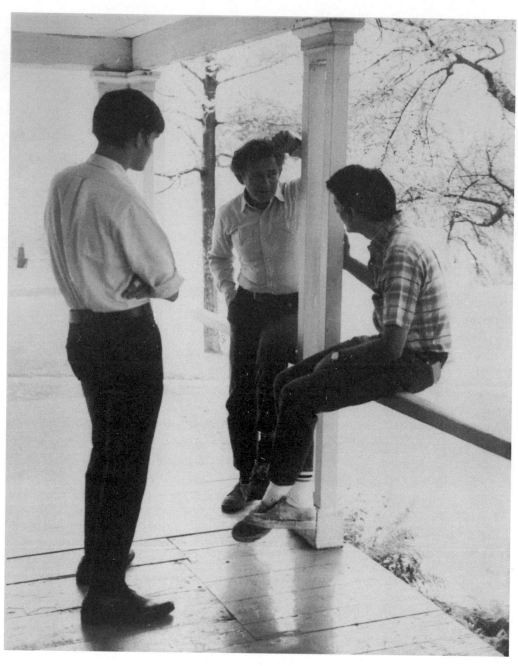

*Norman Mailer chats with
Bread Loafers, 1967 (RL)*

I remember Norman Mailer preparing his audience for a reading from his recently published *Why Are We in Vietnam.* He prefaced the reading with a mini-lecture on the uses of obscenity in literature, making the point that four-letter words were verbal substitutes for physical violence, and that he used them frequently and imaginatively not for their own sake but for the sake of mirroring the violent times in which we lived.

I was sitting at the rear of the Bread Loaf lecture hall during this lengthy prologue, and I noticed four women in religious garb sitting toward the front. It was, I remembered, a practice on the part of some southern convent to send a few of its sisters to the conference each year. That was one of the prizes offered by the order for particularly meritorious members. So there, if you please, was one of those situations that only Bread Loaf could produce: Norman Mailer about to embark on a reading of his latest work with the promise that it will be well-spiked with four-letter words, and there were four nuns sitting primly at attention.

Would they get up in a body and walk out when he began? Would they drift out one by one? Or would they cover their ears and refuse to hear? What they actually did was sit there throughout the R-rated lecture, still primly at attention—except for the one that I noticed nodding off from time to time, snapping back to consciousness so that she could heed well the uses of obscenity in literature.

—*Seymour Epstein* (1988)

The Little Theatre, late 1960s

I was a poetry fellow in 1967 and stayed at Cornwall cottage, with William Caldwell and Douglas Davis, and I read my poetry in the Little Theater one night, along with Doug Davis, Jim Whitehead, and Shane Stevens. Archibald MacLeish came up to give a talk. . . . Later, at Treman, I heard him tell some good stories about his friend Carl Sandburg. When Norman Mailer came up for a weekend guest appearance, he arrived about 10 P.M. on a Friday night. I was in the kitchen at Treman—working my way through a bottle of Jack Daniel's—when Mailer came in to get his first Bread Loaf drink. "My god, it's the man himself," I said to myself. Once he had his drink, he turned around to face me and said, "I'm Norman Mailer," I introduced myself, and we shook hands. He asked me where I was from. I told him I lived in a small town out in the cornfields but worked in Chicago. *Why Are We in Vietnam* had just been published. I told Mailer I hadn't read it yet but I had seen a review of it—in galley proofs—written by my friend and coworker at Encyclopedia Britannica, Joseph Epstein. He was very interested and asked me what Epstein had written about the book. I told him the review was a good one. He seemed pleased, saying he wouldn't have believed that Epstein would be too kind.

Mailer asked me some questions about myself and then I asked him what he thought of the current situation in the heavyweight boxing division, which was at that time a mess, what with a dozen boxers vying with each other to take over Ali's crown which was, I believe, taken away from him due to his dodging the Army. Anyway we talked about the relative merits of Joe Frazier, Jimmy Ellis, and others. I remember that Mailer liked Thad Spencer, a boxer whom few can recall now. Some other people, realizing that Mailer had arrived, started to push into the kitchen and I said to Mailer, "Nice talking with you." Someone asked him a question, something about how he liked John Updike or had he read such and such a book by some guy from Chile. Mailer smiled and mumbled something or another. Then he asked, "Are there mushrooms around here?" I had seen many mushrooms on my walks in the woods. "There are lots of them down by the river." "What kinds?" Mailer said. "Oh, red ones and yellow ones, and kind of whitish-gray ones with spots." Mailer laughed and nodded his head as I made my way out of the kitchen.

The next evening, before Mailer read from *Why Are We in Vietnam,* he talked briefly on language and that the four-letter words in the book were necessary, as the characters would use those words. "I will say some words that will no doubt offend some of you," he warned, "and I will wait for anyone who does not want to hear these words and would like to leave." Everyone more or less glanced around to see who, if anyone, would get up and depart the Little Theater. I saw two nuns leave, and perhaps one or two elderly folks. My experience—limited as I am not a Catholic—is that nuns don't run from anything. Anyway, some of those fantastic dirty words made a lot of people twitch a bit, all of whom were trying to remain emancipated and casual as sliced tomatoes at a businessmen's lunch.

—*Dave Etter* (1986)

In the summer of 1969, at Ciardi's invitation, I joined the staff of the Bread Loaf Writers' Conference. . . . It was the first of seven seasons for me there, all stamped with Ciardi's sometimes formidable presence. Sometimes, on drizzly afternoons, a group of us would stump out to forage for mushrooms, which abound in late August in Vermont. I can still hear John, who punctuated most lunches with a call for silence in the dining hall in order to make his announcement: "The Witch of Fungi will lead a mushroom walk at three o'clock." It became our custom to fry these comestibles in the staff kitchen to accompany the cocktail hour.

I can't remember whether John was an eater or avoider of our exotica. But, judging from [one] poem and from his general zest, I think he partook. . . . He was a charismatic reader of his own poems, filling the hall with acolytes and admirers, holding them spellbound with his easy articulation. My favorites were his tribal poems: "Three Views of a Mother," in which he describes his mother foraging for wild mushrooms and himself sitting across the table from her, helping to clean them, is surely a classic. Then there was "Elegy," which begins: "My father was born with a spade in his hand. . . ." Best of all, I remember Ciardi reciting, from the cycle dedicated to Judith, "Men marry what they need. I marry you . . ." to a hushed gathering, and how I went away in a kind of trance, thinking that poems could say so much in such gorgeously constraining ways. John Ciardi was the first poet who alerted me to the oral-aural possibilities of the public performance. He did not dramatize, he did not embarrass; he simply spoke the lines and they lodged themselves in my head so that I may always have them, in his tone of voice.

— *Maxine Kumin,*
"John Ciardi and the Witch of Fungi," in
John Ciardi: Measure of the Man, edited by
Vince Clemente (1987)

Maxine Kumin, 1970 (FG)

John Ciardi confronted by flower child, 1970 (FG)

The long walk to Tamarack Cottage

John Ciardi outside the Little Theatre, late 1960s

John Ciardi, Arno Karlen, William Cole, 1969

I knew John's wits well before I met the man. His wits and his wit I met first in the pages of *The Saturday Review*. The man I met at the Bread Loaf Writers' Conference, in 1969. I'd been asked, at the suggestion of my friend and fellow poet, Miller Williams, to be the Conference Physician. John Ciardi's wits, I learned, fit the man—both were writ large, both were full of ambiguities and of grace, and both were in indelible ink. John was on center stage at Bread Loaf: it was *his* conference and I was privileged to sit in on the endless evening and early morning conversations that took place in Treman cottage, where the faculty gathered to drink and talk. I learned quickly that alcohol was the prime social lubricant and that its application began early in the day: just before noon, Bloody Mary's were available to the faculty (and the physician); drinks also were served before dinner and after the evening lecture (about 9 P.M.), all in Treman and all in the best company. It was only half-facetiously that, as I got to know John, I made him an offer: we'd work out a research protocol which would consist of drawing "liver function tests" from the blood of those attending Bread Loaf, doing this before and after the conference—our findings might need corroboration by liver biopsies, again done before and after the bouts at Treman had taken place. I was turned down, with grace and good humor, and another promising research paper went by the boards. Ah, the writers that were there during the three summers I served as physician: Miller Williams, John Frederick Nims, William Meredith, Maxine Kumin, Isaac Asimov, Diane Wakoski, William Sloane, Robert Pack, Barry Hannah, James Whitehead, and many others. It was a privilege to hear these writers and others in daily workshop sessions as well as evening readings from their work. In the Theatre, I heard John hold the rapt attention of us all as he discussed "Valediction Forbidding Mourning" by John Donne and "The Eve of St. Agnes" by John Keats. The discussion was all the more remarkable for John's never using notes and quoting huge stretches of the poems from memory. And the readings from his own work were likewise incomparable. I was also privileged to be at Bread Loaf at John's last lecture, the year he left Bread Loaf: it was a time of sadness because John had devoted so many years of his life to the Conference. Late August, to this day, brings with it a certain nostalgia for the fireplace and camaraderie of Treman—and the words, words, words of the place.

I remember one evening in particular: everyone had gone to bed except John, Harry Crews and me. John was holding forth on any subject offered up by the Muse of Treman. Often the Muse offered up limericks, but etymology was beginning to seize John's imagination and we were introduced to the sweep of linguistics as we threw logs on

John Ciardi

the fire and toasted whomever seemed appropriate. Harry had noted that the pulse in one of the arteries around his ankle was intermittently irregular. I did a brief physical exam and gave a brief lecture on the physiology of ventricular premature contractions (which can be a normal variant or can be exacerbated by sleep deprivation and alcohol). About four A.M., the three of us decided we were hungry, so we lit out for the Director's house next door, made for the kitchen, and John concocted something out of eggs and a variety of leftovers and canned goods: I remember only that it tasted wonderful. And that I slept hard.

    —*John Stone,*
      "JOHN CIARDI: HIS WIT AND WITNESS," IN
      JOHN CIARDI: MEASURE OF THE MAN, EDITED BY
      VINCE CLEMENTE (1987)

1970 Faculty: (rear) Galway Kinnell, Judith
Ciardi, Perry Knowlton, Miller Williams, Dan
Wakefield, Edward Martin, Harry Crews; (center)
John Frederick Nims, Maxine Kumin, William
Sloane, John Ciardi, Joanna Foster; (front) John
Williams, Shane Stevens, William Meredith (FG)

John Ciardi discusses the theology of poetry
with a conference member, 1970 (FG)

SEVENTIES

Young Nun at Bread Loaf

Sister Elizabeth Michael
has come to the Writers' Conference.
She has white habits like a summer sailor
and a black notebook she climbs into nightly
to sway in the hammock of a hundred knotted poems.
She is the youngest nun I have ever known.

When we go for a walk in the woods
she puts on a dimity apron that teases her boottops.
It is sprigged with blue flowers.
I wear my jeans and sneakers. We are looking
for mushrooms (chanterelles are in season)
to fry and eat with my drinks, her tomato juice.

Wet to the shins with crossing
and recrossing the same glacial brook, a mile
downstream we find them, the little pistols,
denser than bandits among the tree roots.
Forager, she carries the basket.
Her hands are crowded with those tough yellow thumbs.

Hiking back in an unction of our own sweat
she brings up Christ. Christ, that canard!
I grind out a butt and think of the waiting bourbon.
The sun goes down in disappointment.
You can say what you want, she says.
You live as if you believe.

Sister
Sister Elizabeth Michael
says we are doing Christ's work, we two.
She, the rosy girl in a Renoir painting.
I, an old Jew.
    —*Maxine Kumin,*
        OUR GROUND TIME HERE WILL BE BRIEF (1982)

Dan Wakefield's lecture on literary craft reaches a higher plane when his Muses (Maxine Kumin, Peg Martin, John Frederick Nims) unexpectedly descend to lend a hand, 1970s (EB)

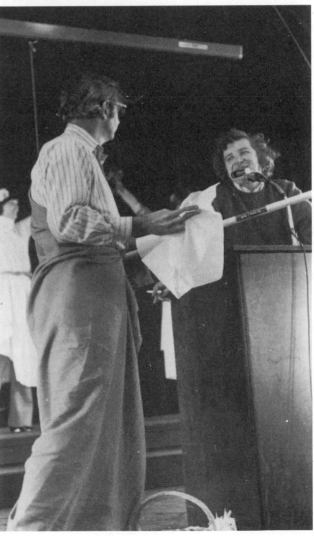

I was a student at Connecticut College for Women between 1967 and 1969, studying under William Meredith, and I had won the student poetry prize two years in a row. Bill Meredith told me about Bread Loaf, and I think with his support Connecticut College helped pay for me to go—because my parents would never have paid for me to go to a place like that! I wasn't allowed to go to school where there were guys, and I wasn't allowed to go to a school on my own—I had to go where my older sister went. So I went to Bread Loaf for the first time in 1969, and fell in love with the community of writers and with the Vermont landscape. All these people talking about *nothing* but writing, forcing *me* to think about writing! I aspired to this great society with its magical set of people. The faculty was distant and god-like, sitting at their separate table in the dining room. They were the stars—and we were supposed to watch and admire them. I don't remember any minorities there. And I think the first Hispanic person I met at Bread Loaf was Judith Ortiz Cofer, when she was the librarian in the mid-eighties.

As a teacher, William Meredith was very quiet; he always had that smile, so that you didn't know what was behind the smile—whether he was annoyed, or interested, or whether he was being ironic. But he had a way of just letting the class *happen,* of making a comment and letting it take its own way. Yet you always felt as if he knew where it was going. A very dreamy kind of teacher. Bill Meredith was almost shy in class. Sometimes you had to lean forward to hear what he was saying. At Connecticut College he really encouraged and cultivated me. Back then I was very different, not Americanized—almost an off-the-boat girl. And he really encouraged Gayl Jones, who was in college with me; we shared a writing prize, and she later came to Bread Loaf on a scholarship. The year he was off he brought June Jordan to replace him—and she taught a course about "Revolution and Literature"! I could believe that Meredith was listening to women, listening to minority women, and really encouraging us to have a voice. If it hadn't been for him, I wouldn't have thought of going off to be a writer. Sure, I was writing and writing in high school, with some of those English teachers who encourage you and who you never forget. But once I got to college I didn't know what I was going to do. As a freshman I took creative writing from him, not knowing if I was going to survive with all these glamorous people, older upperclassmen. All I can remember is that soft tone of voice you had to lean forward to hear. And those big eyes. But this ironic smile. I didn't quite understand him; I was a little afraid of him yet I trusted him. And he took time with me.

At Bread Loaf I didn't have Bill Meredith as my conference reader because he was my teacher at Connecticut College. I chose to be read by John Frederick Nims; I don't

know why, I just chose. Nims was nice to me because he was very interested in Spanish culture, with his translating. He asked a lot of questions about Spanish poetry and about various words. But when it came time to talk about my own poetry, Nims was harsh and I felt really bad. Years later when he accepted one of my poems for *Poetry* magazine, he wrote me and said, "You really surprised me. These are good poems. How did you do it?"

I remember Ciardi's lectures being very, very good, and Nims's were my favorites. (They later became part of a lovely textbook of his, *Western Wind.*) I remember Harry Crews being absolutely riveting. I didn't grow up in this country in the fifties, but I imagine that what Elvis Presley must have been to a little small-town bobby-sox girl, Harry Crews was to a bunch of literary beatniks at Bread Loaf. He totally galvanized the imagination of his audience. You never knew what was going to happen. He used to come out from behind the lectern to talk, and he used

John Frederick Nims critiques the poetry of Julia Alvarez, 1972 (EB)

Harry Crews commands the dance floor, 1972 (EB)

to do this sort of Elvis Presley hip-thrust, keeping time to his lectures. He was wonderfully crazy. I remember a group of nuns used to sit in the front taking notes and he'd be up there doing this thrusting-of-his-hip stuff. That first summer I stayed up in the Annex dormitory, on a women's floor, of course. On one side of my room was a nun. On the other side of me was this woman who came up from New York City with a bunch of suitcases—she came *to dress* and strut her stuff. And of course the first night she and Harry hooked up. On the one side I had absolute silence from the nun. And on the other side they used to keep me up all night—they were something *wild.* I'd go into the bathroom to brush my teeth and bump into Harry coming out grinning crazily, half naked.

Even with Harry Crews nightly in the hallway, and John Frederick Nims discouraging me with his marginal pencil notes, it didn't totally sink in—because I not only fell in love with Bread Loaf that year, I also fell in love. I had gone to convent schools and then to staid old Connecticut College. When I met this guy I had stardust in my eyes. And he was probably baffled by me—because I was totally attached to him and totally celibate! And that combination just didn't work at Bread Loaf. If you had a crush on someone of course you slept with him. Meanwhile, Harry Crews was next door making all that racket. Here I was in

this world where people were so talented and wild and crazy and hedonistic. I wanted to be like them but none of my training prepared me for it. I was closer to the nun, in terms of where I was coming from, and who I didn't want to be close to. And I had this guy deliver me at eleven or something to my door and he couldn't understand what was going on. I remember on the last day sitting on the lawn waiting for a bus to come take us away, and I was waiting for him to talk about our future. And so I said, are you going to write me, don't you want my address? He said, "I think I should tell you that I'm engaged to this girl back home." I couldn't believe it—and the doors of the bus were opening and everyone was scurrying to get in, and I was heartbroken.

Still, everything was changed; during my two weeks of Bread Loaf I had gone down to the Middlebury College admissions office and asked for an application. They said that the new applications weren't printed yet, that I would have to wait until later in the fall. I said I didn't want to go next year—I wanted to go *now.* They interviewed me, and I think they were impressed with how passionate I was for this place: how soon could I get my transcript and two letters of recommendation up here? I called people from a pay phone in downtown Middlebury (charging it to my parents, of course). A few weeks later we were down in New

*Galway Kinnell leads a
poetry clinic, 1970 (FG)*

William Meredith, 1971 (FG)

*Crews' fiction class in the
barn, 1973 (EB)*

1971 Faculty: (rear) Robert Pack, Alfred Balk, Miller Williams, William Meredith, William Sloane; (center) Diane Wakoski, Judith Ciardi, John Ciardi, Maxine Kumin, Joy Anderson; (front) Ezekiel Mphahlele, John Williams, Edward Martin, Seymour Epstein, Isaac Asimov, Shane Stevens (Jonathan Aldrich)

York packing the car to go to Connecticut College and they called me up and said that I was in.

So I came to Middlebury and studied under Bob Pack. He was the very opposite of Bill Meredith as a teacher, as I later learned. Bob was this feisty little guy; he was like a lighter you flick up and the spark comes up, and you could see his mind working as he tried to best whatever had just been said. He was such a dynamo in his class, always jumping out of his chair and getting really excited about things. And there was also Bread Loaf for the next two summers—so I wouldn't have to go back to that repressive environment—I would get a job working at the snack bar at Bread Loaf for both the School of English and the

Writers' Conference. Then after I graduated I kept going back, with all sorts of jobs. One summer I even worked in the kitchen as a dishwasher. Then, maybe a year after I graduated I decided to go to a graduate writing program. I ended up at Syracuse. And every summer, or almost every summer, there would be Bread Loaf.

The years all flow together now—I had a scholarship in 1979, a fellowship in 1986, and then was a staff associate for a few years. But back in the earliest years I remember Robert Hayden as being in the Meredith mold, a modulated and quiet delivery, that almost blind man—you didn't think he was going to make it to a reading. Miller Williams was very funny and entertaining. And Diane

Picnic on the West Lawn, 1971 (EAM)

Dining room scholar Carolyn Forché checks the faculty table, 1970 (FG)

Wakoski was such a presence. For some reason in 1972 she invited me to a sort of alternative party in her room given by alternative people. I don't know whether it was because I was Hispanic or what, because I didn't even know her. And I remember hearing Archibald MacLeish read. . . . I mean, he was an *old, old* man, with connections going back to Bread Loaf in the thirties! I remember hearing him read and telling stories about Bread Loaf, how Robert Frost always detracted attention from his readings, coughing or moving around in his seat, or lighting something on fire. At some point in MacLeish's reading, there was a peal of thunder and his words were drowned out. And MacLeish stopped and looked up through the ceiling at the sky and called, "Stop that, Robert!"

—*Julia Alvarez,*
INTERVIEW (1990)

John Ciardi with Isaac and Gertrude Asimov outside the Little Theatre, 1972; Gary Margolis in background (EB)

1972 Faculty: (rear) Joy Anderson, John Ciardi, Miller Williams, John Frederick Nims, James Whitehead, Isaac Asimov, Seymour Epstein, Diane Wakoski; (center) Robert Hayden, Harry Crews, Judith Ciardi, Robert Pack, Jonathan Aldrich; (front) William Lederer, John Williams (EB)

John Ciardi presides over the Round Table, with Alfred Balk, John Williams, William Sloane, and Miller Williams, 1971 (EAM)

Nothing particular was scheduled for the final meeting in the Little Theatre—students could talk about anything. Sandy Martin opened the proceedings and answered the first questions and suggestions, but Ciardi was feeling fully recovered from his cold and kept getting up to the lectern to add to whatever Sandy said. Finally, he just stayed there once, to take the next question, and Sandy stood off to one side, saying nothing more, but obviously listening and caring.

At first the questions and suggestions were about procedures. Couldn't the clinics be started the first week instead of the lectures? Couldn't they be broken up into small discussion groups? Wouldn't it be possible to set up a beer bar in the Barn now that the Vermont drinking laws had changed? There were many more such ideas, most all of which seemed sensible to me, but for most of which Ciardi gave some reason why it couldn't be done.

Then one young student stood up to make a statement. "There's a hierarchy here," he said, "and some of us resent it." "But how does that affect you?" asked Ciardi. "Don't you get to attend whatever classes you want? Don't you have as much chance to speak up as any other person? If you choose to superimpose a hierarchy on yourselves, what can *we* do about it? The hierarchy seems to be in your mind." "No," the student said. "It's also right there in the bulletin, where it lists the kinds of participation. That's what establishes the idea of a hierarchy to begin with. And it doesn't seem right that there should be different kinds of us here."

Then another student spoke up. "Some of us applied too late to be contributors, but we brought our manuscripts anyway. And some of the staff, like Bill Meredith, would read the poems and talk with us about them, but—" "They shouldn't do that!" interrupted Ciardi. "I've made it a firm rule that no student may give a staff member a manuscript directly. They must all go through the office." "Well, I'm sorry if I got anyone in trouble. But what if they like you and *want* to read it?" "You are trying to swindle the conference," said Ciardi. "Not of the money, I don't mean that. But of the teacher's time, which someone else has paid for." Then he paused. "I'm sorry, but it's necessary for me to growl a little. I must protect my staff from the arm-grabbers." He gripped his left wrist and tugged at it savagely to indicate what he meant by the arm-grabbers. "They grab at you to read their manuscripts. They insist that you come to their readings. I used to sit in this lecture hall and listen to one person read after another. I was dying to have a drink, but I didn't want to be rude and get up and leave.

Barry Hannah and Laurie Colwin, 1971 (Jonathan Aldrich)

Laurie Colwin at Johnson Pond, 1972 (EB)

Until finally I needed a drink bad enough, and then I got up and was rude and did leave."

"We could set up a bar over there in the corner," said a student, and everybody laughed, Ciardi too.

Then Miller Williams spoke up. "I'm a great believer in equalitarianism," he said, "but there has to be some structure to the teaching process. And besides, any order here is an order of merit; it depends on the degree of excellence and experience in writing."

Then one of the waiters stood up. He was slightly built, very young, with long blond hair, wearing faded, patched blue denim. Ciardi nodded to him to speak, but instead of speaking from where he was, the waiter walked down to the lectern. Ciardi stepped aside to let him use it. "I want to make my point as calmly as possible," he said calmly, "because I realize that your first reaction is naturally to be antagonized by any questioning of the authority set up here. It seems to me that the statement just made by Miller Williams reflects a kind of arrogance that dominates and harms this conference. It seems to me that nothing very worthwhile will ever happen here until you"—and he looked directly at Ciardi as he said this, but he meant the whole staff—"until you recognize that you have just as

1971 Fellows: (rear) William Crawford Woods; (center) Charles Flowers, Elaine Kraf, Barry Hannah, Wendy Kindred; (front) Eleanor Glaze, Michael Stevens. (Credit: Jonathan Aldrich)

much to learn from me as I do from you." There was a reasonable, gentle quality to his manner that emphasized the effrontery of what he was saying, like a parent reasoning things out very calmly with a child.

Ciardi gave a chuckle, did remain calm, almost seemed to enjoy it. "You mean," he said to the young waiter, "that you know just as much about writing as I do?" "Yes," the boy said thoughtfully, "in a way I do. About writing, and about other things. All of us"—he indicated the audience—"have as much to teach you"—indicating the staff—"as you have to teach us."

Ciardi began to answer calmly, but his tone became angrier as he spoke. "If I haven't more to give you than you have to give me, then you're being cheated here. I have no sense of being arrogant about this. I feel you are part of an over-encouraged generation—encouraged to feel that you are very special. And you're not very good listeners." The boy stood there, sharing the lectern with Ciardi, hands in his back pockets, watching him with a faint smile. He tilted his head to one side, perhaps to indicate that he was in fact listening, perhaps to look like Christ on the cross, or maybe just to keep the hair out of his eyes.

When Ciardi finished, Bill Meredith stood up. "I really have to object to that, John. Writing has changed a good deal in recent years, and there may very well be a way that we have much to learn from the young today. We are novices of different kinds. One thing we must learn to cultivate is their generosity of spirit—" "I haven't seen all that much generosity of spirit this afternoon," said Ciardi, and people laughed, tension momentarily released. . . .

. . . Ciardi waved the boy aside impatiently and indicated he should go back to his seat, which he did. Ciardi took full possession of the lectern, hunched forward over it, and began to speak seriously. "What we have to teach you and you have to learn from us is technique. I believe in the maestro system. To learn to write poetry you must learn to move easily in harness, to use Frost's metaphor. You must learn the discipline of the harness. Before you can fly a plane you need to know how to use the controls. Before you can play the piano you must practice the scales. This emphasis on learning the craft of writing has always been part of the Bread Loaf tradition. This conference has been going on for many years; it doesn't chop itself down and grow anew every year. Any apparent hierarchy of Bread Loaf is to some extent a sense of trusteeship. I feel I am trustee for a number of ghosts—Frost, Theodore Morrison, Bernard DeVoto, Fletcher Pratt, Joe Green, and there are others, but you won't have known them."

There is a long silence. Then a bearded student in a straw hat stood up in the back. "This is really just therapy for us, isn't it?" he asked. "All this letting us sound off? Nothing is going to change, is it?"

Shane Stevens got up. "It may be therapy for you, but it's punishment for us. I move we adjourn." Laughter, then applause that sounded somehow—well, *grateful*—and everyone got up as if to leave, but many lingered to discuss it all more informally.

I drifted toward the back and sat down next to Judith Ciardi, who was waiting in case John wanted to go to the Barn and have a cup of coffee with her. "Do they really have this kind of masochistic session at the end of each year?" I asked her. "Oh, last year was much worse," she said. "Galway Kinnell had the kids all worked up about Vietnam and there was a whole lot of the generation-conflict thing. This year was bad, but at least it wasn't so angry."

"*Is* there a chance anything will change? Does he listen at all?"

"Each and every suggestion mentioned here has been discussed at least seventy-five times," she said.

"Doesn't it upset him?"

"Oh, no. It gives him a chance to sound off and he loves it. He'll go back to the house now and do the crossword puzzle."

—*Rust Hills,*
"WE BELIEVE IN THE MAESTRO SYSTEM,"
AUDIENCE 2, NO. 3 (MAY/JUNE 1972)

Miller and Diane Williams, David Madden, and Robert Pack on the way to the dining hall, 1972 (EB)

Miller and Diane Williams with John Ciardi, 1972 (EB)

Shane Stevens, 1970 (FG)

Colleagues, over coffee, in the Barn, 1972 (EB)

Marvin Bell and conferee, 1973 (EB)

Poetry discussion group with Marvin Bell, 1973 (EB)

I was living in Moretown, Vermont, while teaching a trimester at Goddard College during its freaky period. I got notes from a couple of people saying they'd be at the Bread Loaf Writers' Conference and I should come over for a visit. Of course, I'd heard about the conference but I'd never been to it. I was from a small town, and I'd grown up thinking that being a writer must be wonderful, but I didn't know what a writer did, exactly. I'd seen *pictures* of the Bread Loaf Writers' Conference, and it seemed that the writers were all pretty successful, famous people even if they weren't. And so I drove down in 1972 on what turned out to be the first day of the last conference with John Ciardi as Director. It was raining hard, and cold. I stayed about a half day, and I was invited to go over to the inn for lunch. I remember sitting with the faculty at tables that were perpendicular to the other tables and raised on a dais. It also seemed to me that the best-looking waiters and waitresses were assigned to the faculty table. I felt the hierarchy in evidence. Later I went back over to Treman. John Ciardi and Miller Williams were sitting over on the window seat behind the cribbage table, drinking Bloody Marys. Others were huddled next to the fireplace because of the cold day. I said hello to the people I knew and then it was time to go on my way.

But I did meet Bob Pack. I stopped in at the bathroom in the Barn, and in he came, and we said hello. We were aware of each other's work—but I don't remember being aware of the fact that he had been named director for the 1973 conference. But later he called and invited me back to teach at the next session. So I came back. After seeing what Bread Loaf was like in the Ciardi era, and after reading Rust Hills' article about Ciardi's penultimate session when it all hit the fan, I spent a lot of time in the barn, with the waiters and others. And I played a lot of tennis—I had just discovered the game, and would have played until midnight. I tried to do everything—the waiters would read at midnight and *I would be there*—just racing all over, meeting people and being thrilled by the occasion, and I got myself very worn down. Then I stayed up all night with Harry Crews over at Treman. Harry was already sick. I caught it—but figured I'd just hide out in my room for a couple of days, get it out of my system. After a few days Bob Pack came over to see me and I was too sick to stand—so he had me carted off to Porter Medical Center in Middlebury, for what would be two days, and after which I would return to finish the conference. But on my way out to the hospital—it was the Watergate summer—I called out, "You won't have Marvin Bell to kick around anymore!"

—*Marvin Bell*,
INTERVIEW (1990)

Donald Justice, 1975 (EB)

View of Tamarack cottage and the primary range from Maple cottage (EB)

Rendering the scene, 1975 (EB)

Tamarack lawn, looking north (EB)

Marvin Bell conducts a poetry group on the caretaker's lawn, 1976 (EB)

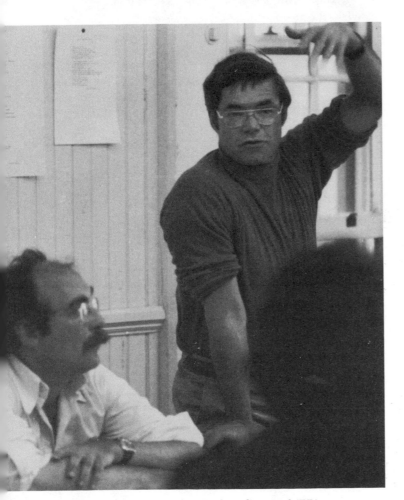

Lawrence Raab listens as Robert Pack teaches, 1976 (EB)

As a veteran of the pleasure of Vermont's Green Mountains in August . . . I wish to exhort you: despite the swirl of shared literary performances, do not fail to wander and pause so you can fix the landscape in your memory—perhaps to bring back later as metaphor in your poems and stories. The fields and woods will be brimming with flowers in bloom: fireweed, black-eyed Susans, purple vetch, bird's-foot trefoil, tiger lilies, hawkweed, asters, chickory, thistle, purple loosestrife, daisy fleabane, small sundrops, Joe-pye-weed, wood sorrel, and jewelweed. The names themselves are a cornucopia of delights. And here on the mountain, following the constellations of the zodiac on a clear night, one can become dizzy with stars. Chances are good at this time of the year that we will get our first display of northern lights. The sense of awe, both wonder and dread, that comes from the feeling of human finitude in the essence of cosmic space, ties us to our first ancestors, and reminds us of our mere creaturehood, our vulnerability, and thus our need for language to assert our momentary presence on this planetary stage. This world of lights and images, witnessed and named, is indeed the theater, as Stevens says, in which we play out the obscure dramas of our lives—in fields such as these, perhaps, and under this very sky. . . .

—*Robert Pack,*
FROM A WELCOMING ADDRESS AT BREAD LOAF

Others knew him longer and more intimately. I offer this account of friendship in the knowledge that it is representative—that many have been touched as I, and share in the general loss. We met on Tuesday, April 16, 1974. He came to Bennington, Vermont, on a reading tour; he and his wife, Joan, arrived for dinner at our house.

My first impression of Gardner remains: a short, pot-bellied, pipe-smoking man, with a high-pitched voice and rapid rate of utterance, pontificating splendidly and if by rote. His eyes were red-rimmed, his white hair lank; he made his entry two hours late. It was not his fault, in fact; it was Albany Airport's, and the fog's. But somehow, in the ensuing years, there would always be some such disruption: a car would fail to start or end up in a ditch, a snowstorm would come out of nowhere, a wallet would be lost. Joan Gardner wore expensive clothing and fistfuls of jewelry; the novelist wore blue jeans and a black leather vest. He emptied a quart of vodka before he sat to eat.

I saw him often in such situations later; they are hard to avoid. Fame brings a constant, admiring assault, a request from civil strangers to be brilliant or outrageous or at least informed. It wears one down and forces one to substitute a mask for face; sooner or later, they fuse. This is doubly a danger for the writer, since privacy is the sine qua non of his work and he has had no training in the actor's life.

. . . For three years thereafter, we saw each other continually. Our families grew close and have remained that way. His presence was a gift. He ballyhooed my work in public and berated it in private. Day in, week out, we wrangled over prose. There was nothing polite or distanced about his sense of colleagueship; if he hated a line he said so, and if he hated a character he said so all the more loudly. At this remove it's hard to remember what we discussed at such length: profluence, *energeia*, walnut trees. I spent three days hunting through graveyards and telephone books in order to prove that Sherbrooke with an *e*—the surname of a character—would be more likely than Sherbrook without. He came up with a whiskey bottle spelled Sherbrook; I pointed to a Sherbrooke township south of Montreal. We cotaught classes and founded [the Bennington] summer writing program together. . . .

. . . Novelist, poet, critic, playwright, librettist, scholar, translator, fabulist—at forty-nine years old, he had the exuberance and protean energy of men not half his age. He was involved in the theater, in music, woodworking, publishing, teaching, painting—any number of pursuits and none of them casual or slapdash. His paintings were intensely seen; his boxes and furniture served. I remember dropping by his house in Bennington to find so many bookshelves fabricated in one day that I thought the pipe smoke he stood wreathed in had caused my eyes to blur. He did seem, somehow, multiple. The first musical selection of the Memorial Service on East Main Street in Batavia—the town in upstate New York where he was born and buried—was a cassette of John and his son, Joel, performing on their French horns. They played "Amazing Grace."

—*Nicholas Delbanco,*
INTRODUCTION TO
STILLNESS AND SHADOWS
BY JOHN GARDNER (1986)

The cathedral-like barn
and rickety chairs, unaltered
since the 1940s (EB)

John Gardner answers
post-lecture questions
in the Little Theatre,
1975 (EB)

John Irving, 1975

*Conferees relax on the lawn, mid
1970s (EB)*

I was at Bread Loaf for nine years beginning in 1975. I had met Bob Pack after his reading at the University of Iowa—I was teaching at Iowa then—and there was a party afterward at Marvin and Dorothy Bell's and I met him, and he invited me to teach at the conference. I remember the first three years especially because it was then that I was writing *The World According to Garp*. Back then I certainly felt fortunate to have a good job, teaching at the Iowa Writers' Workshop; it was an honor, especially for a writer whose books hadn't sold anything. *Setting Free the Bears* had sold about eight thousand, *The Water-Method Man* about twenty-five hundred, and *The 158-Pound Marriage* had sold under two thousand. But teaching at Iowa never seemed to be very *special*. I'd been a student there from 1965 through 1967 and when I returned it was just a teaching job that was better than other teaching jobs—it was a graduate school and you had a lot of time to yourself.

But Bread Loaf was the first place that really gave me an *audience*. Compared to the first three, *Garp* was a long and complicated book for me. It doesn't seem long for me now because my books have gotten longer and more complicated. But *Garp* was a big undertaking, what with my full-time teaching and coaching responsibilities. And it was put together very piecemeal over a long period of time, in every which way, all out of order. The anxiety: I had no idea how long a reader was going to spend on that novel. He might be reading it over a month, or six weeks. As the years in making it went on—it got up to three or four—I thought, You know this story so well but what about someone who's only reading twenty pages a night—how are they going to stay with it? Are they going to remember this 400 pages later? I really needed to know that it was working. I can't overemphasize the importance of needing some confidence at a time when other people aren't doing a whole lot to give it to you. It's awfully easy to have confidence in yourself when people are patting you on the back all the time, and when they've obviously seen that you've done something well. It's not that easy to sustain confidence in yourself when nobody's reading you. The Bread Loaf response—and I don't mean from the audience in the Little Theater, clapping, but from the other writers, the faculty and fellows and scholars—the obvious excitement from the people at Treman to that work in progress was a real confidence giver. I never had anything else that was so central as that. I could really feel that support. It was very important.

One of the stupidest things that nonliterary journalists ask me is this: they all want to know now that one is famous or commercially successful if there is a kind of specter looking over my shoulder, as if having an audience suddenly turns one conscious of the audience and makes one want to please it. It is such a naive question; it can only be conceived by someone who's never written a book. The truth is, the opposite is true. The time you agonize about your audience is when you don't have one, when you think, *God—who's reading me? Is anyone getting this? Is there anyone out there? Am I being clear? Do they understand it?* Once there's an audience you stop thinking about it. You just take something that gnaws at you and you forget it. Then you say, enough people are buying my books. I don't care if anyone else does. That's it. It is an advantage. It is a luxury.

I don't think I'll ever forget the earlier time—I still have written more books in the condition of being unknown than I have being known. I wrote four books catch as catch can. I've only written three with a little space around myself; it's easier. I think the response of the audience at Bread Loaf, and especially of Bob Pack's clear fondness and admiration for my writing, was on a level with getting my first novel published as a confidence builder. I want to emphasize that strongly. I really took it very personally how much he supported me.

—*John Irving,*
INTERVIEW (1990)

Tim O'Brien's fiction discussion group on the porch at Treman Cottage, 1970s (EB)

Tim O'Brien critiques a short story with a conferee, 1976 (EB)

You can tell a true war story by the questions you ask. Somebody tells a story, let's say, and afterward you ask, "Is it true?" and if the answer matters, you've got your answer.

For example, we've all heard this one. Four guys go down a trail. A grenade sails out. One guy jumps on it and takes the blast and saves his three buddies.

Is it true?

The answer matters.

You'd feel cheated if it never happened. Without the grounding reality, it's just a trite bit of puffery, pure Hollywood, untrue in the way all such stories are untrue. Yet even if it did happen—and maybe it did, anything's possible—even then you know it can't be true, because a true war story does not depend upon that kind of truth. Absolute occurrence is irrelevant. A thing may happen and be a total lie; another thing may not happen and be truer than the truth. For example: Four guys go down a trail. A grenade sails out. One guy jumps on it and takes the blast, but it's a killer grenade and everybody dies anyway. Before they die, though, one of the dead guys says, "The fuck you do *that* for?" and the jumper says, "Story of my life, man," and the other guy starts to smile but he's dead.

That's a true story that never happened.
—*Tim O'Brien,*
   "HOW TO TELL A TRUE WAR STORY,"
   THE THINGS THEY CARRIED (1990)

Spotlit in the Barn by the sun (EB)

Toni Morrison's lecture, 1976 (EB)

Authors arrive at text and subtext in thousands of ways, learning each time they begin anew how to recognize a valuable idea and how to render the texture that accompanies, reveals or displays it to its best advantage. The process by which this is accomplished is endlessly fascinating to me. I have always thought that as an editor for twenty years I understood writers better than their most careful critics, because in examining the manuscript in each of its subsequent stages I knew the author's process, how his or her mind worked, what was effortless, what took time, where the "solution" to a problem came from. The end result—the book—was all that the critic had to go on.

Still, for me, that was the least important aspect of the work. Because, no matter how "fictional" the account of these writers, or how much it was a product of invention, the act of imagination is bound up with memory. You know, they straightened out the Mississippi River in places, to make room for houses and livable acreage. Occasionally the river floods these places. "Floods" is the word they use, but in fact it is not flooding; it is remembering. Remembering where it used to be. All water has a perfect memory and is forever trying to get back to where it was. Writers are like that: remembering where we were, what valley we ran through, what the banks were like, the light that was there and the route back to our original place. It is emotional memory—what the nerves and the skin remember as well as how it appeared. And a rush of imagination is our "flooding."

Along with personal recollection, the matrix of the work I do is the wish to extend, fill in and complement slave autobiographical narratives. But only the matrix. What comes of all that is dictated by other concerns, not least among them the novel's own integrity. Still, like water, I remember where I was before I was "straightened out."

—*Toni Morrison,*
   "THE SITE OF MEMORY," INVENTING THE TRUTH:
   THE ART AND CRAFT OF MEMOIR, EDITED BY
   WILLIAM ZINSSER (1978)

Toni Morrison and conferee, 1976 (EB)

On the Inn veranda, Gail Godwin, Stanley Elkin, and Hilma Wolitzer chat with a conferee, 1978 (EB)

Seymour Epstein and Hilma Wolitzer in a Barn classroom, 1974 (EB)

Nancy Willard, 1975

Four years after my first time at Bread Loaf, as a scholar, I returned in 1974 as a fellow, a little less nervous than before and with my first novel just published on August 8th. It was *Endings,* and I remember the date distinctly because I was done out of a review in *Newsweek.* They had interviewed and photographed me and it was all ready to go. Then Nixon resigned—and I got bumped along with a lot of other stories. Still, I had the great pleasure of going down for lunch to Middlebury with Hilda Gregory and Carole Oles and Linda Pastan, and we picked up a *Time* magazine. It ran a lovely review of the book—they ordered champagne and we read it breathlessly. And when we came back there were other friends waiting on the porch of Cherry cottage with a bottle of wine. What a tremendous feeling of celebration and of support!

I'm almost positive that 1974 was also the year that John Gardner was late getting to the conference, and Sandy Martin asked me and Francine Prose, who had been a fellow the year before and who was now an associate, to handle John's first discussion group. And I had never taught anything, anywhere. It was a Horatio Alger story—I was there to stop the horse! I had no idea how one led a discussion group, but because I love to talk so much it wasn't hard to find out how to do it. It was a lovely experience; I actually *enjoyed* it, it was lively, Francine and I interacted well with the group. And at the end of the conference, at the final cocktail party, Sandy Martin gave me a check for a hundred dollars. I didn't want to take it—you shouldn't get paid for something that's so much fun. But something else wonderful had happened during the conference. When John Gardner finally showed up, he came to my reading. I had been very, very nervous about reading my work in public and felt quite ill beforehand—I didn't know whether I'd faint or throw up or have a heart attack or do something else to disgrace myself besides the reading itself. And I think that because John was there in support of a fellow, on an afternoon when a lot of staff people tended to take naps, was wonderful. At the end he stood up and said, "Bravo." That he had such an enthusiastic and public response cured my stage fright instantly. I had to pull my own fingers away from the podium—I would have read for the rest of the day. It felt *very* good. And he continued to be very supportive.

A lot of what I've learned from teaching has been from teachers here like John Gardner, Harry Crews, Maxine Kumin, Bob Pack—watching how other people taught with generosity, that nice balance of charity and honesty . . . which doesn't mean you lie to the writer—it's important to be honest about the student's work, but without destroying an ego in the process. Now there's something I say at the beginning of every workshop: the purpose of our being here is revision, not suicide.

—*Hilma Wolitzer,*
INTERVIEW (1990)

Southernly bird's-eye view of Bread Loaf campus, 1970s

Mark Strand, 1976 (EB)   *George P. Elliott, 1976 (EB)*   *Stanley Plumly, 1978 (EB)*   *Carolyn Forché, 1978 (EB)*

Geoffrey Wolff, 1978 (EB)   *Francine Prose, 1974 (EB)*   *Stanley Elkin, 1978 (EB)*

Northernly bird's-eye view of Bread Loaf campus, 1970s

Robert Pack, 1978 (EB)

Marvin Bell, 1978 (EB)

May Swenson, 1976 (EB)

As the core faculty has aged, the sports have come and gone. Tennis was the first. I used to bring a different novelty T-shirt every year, and one year it said, "Bread Loaf Tennis Conference." But it was possibly during my first year at Bread Loaf that I was on the tennis court playing doubles. Peter Sears was also there—he was a very slick tennis player, a lot of fun to play with. I had to serve and the sun was in my eyes. I wasn't that good a tennis player, and I was a terrible server as it was. So Peter took off his old Blue Seal Feeds cap and gave it to me to keep the sun out of my eyes. Then, when I tried to give it back he said, "No, you look good in it, you should keep it." So I was wearing it teaching a class up in the barn—I was also wearing a work shirt that I wore a lot in those days—and I had a cup of coffee in my hand, and the official conference photographer, Eric Borg, happened to snap it. Later I guess I saw the picture, and since I needed one to run with a column I was writing for the *American Poetry Review,* I used it. And that's how I came to be identified with Blue Seal. I often thought I should write the company. . . .

After tennis, running took over. May Swenson's companion showed us all how to run a mile back in 1976, and I did it. Then, Gary Margolis got me interested in marathoning. We would go for a jog down the highway toward Ripton, and Gary had just run in the Boston Marathon from the back of the pack with a friend. Gary convinced me that I could train up to it, and I ended up running in the Honolulu Marathon in December 1979, and then I ran Boston from the back of the pack, to get my son started, in April 1980. By then, running had taken over, and there were a lot of us running here at Bread Loaf. Gary and I conceived of the idea of the Bread Loaf Writers' Cramp Race. The idea was that you had to run down the highway to the turnoff for the Homer Noble Farm, and then run up the road to Robert Frost's place, and kiss the sign, and then turn around and run back. Of course it's a vicious, uphill gravel-surface climb. However, there were subordinate rules; one was that if you didn't feel like going all the way you didn't have to. They would give out Bread Loaf T-shirts to the winners. The idea was to have it the morning after the dance—indeed, in the beginning it was held at a fairly early hour so that people couldn't even get to sleep. And there were no rules against throwing up. John Gillespie once said that "Any writer who can't run three and a half miles with a hangover doesn't belong here."
—*Marvin Bell,*
INTERVIEW (1990)

(center) Richard Ford and Terrence Des Pres, 1976 (EB)

(Above) Linda Pastan, (above right) Carolyn Forché, and
(right) Ellen Bryant Voigt, 1976 (All EB)

I don't believe [that writing can't be taught]. In my opinion, nobody would ever say that about painting or about composing. The teaching of musical composition has been going very well since at least Bach and probably centuries earlier. Vienna was what it was because of brilliant teachers like Papa Hayden, Mozart, Beethoven, and so on. In art nobody has ever condemned Cezanne for taking students. But there is a notion, which has to do with the romantic hero image, that writing is pure genius, and you can't teach it. The basic problem with the [*Harper's*] article attacking Bread Loaf, then, is that it begins with the premise that a writing workshop has to be a fraud, because writing can't be taught. Bread Loaf, in fact, has been going for a very long time and has a very good record of helping extremely talented writers to become solid artists.

—*John Gardner,*
"AN INTERVIEW WITH JOHN GARDNER," BY
JUDSON MITCHAM AND WILLIAM RICHARD,
NEW ORLEANS REVIEW (SUMMER 1981)

[Something I mind] is the notion that Bread Loaf is run by stars, and that there's a great distance between the contributors, that is to say, the students, and the stars who teach the courses. In fact, most of the stars at Bread Loaf came up through the so-called ranks. Linda Pastan, a famous poet now, began as a student, became a fellow, that is, an assistant to one of the instructors, and then became an instructor herself. John Irving and Tim O'Brien also worked their way up, and I think it's fair to say that those people who began as contributors and ended up as teachers at Bread Loaf became the fine writers they became at least partly because of the superb teaching they got at Bread Loaf. Not exclusively. Linda Pastan studied with James Dickey at the University of Virginia. James Dickey, at his best, is probably as good a poetry teacher, teacher of the writing of poetry, as America has ever seen. But although I would grant that much of what Linda got she got from James Dickey in classes, I think she also got help at Bread Loaf.

What happens at Bread Loaf, far more than at any other conference, I think, is that the selectivity process tends to bring in young writers at the point when they're almost ready to publish but have some little problem that needs fixing. Usually the people I teach . . . and I teach about twenty novelists and short story writers every year, when I go (I've only taught off and on there) . . . the writers that I get are either people who used to publish regularly and have lost it somehow—they fell out of style or went sentimental or lost their old editors and never found new ones, or something—or else they're first rate beginning

Bread Loafers relax on the Inn veranda, 1976 (EB)

writers who still have a couple of mistakes to get rid of in their writing. In the two weeks they spend at Bread Loaf those people are learning the little things they need to become well published writers. Then, of course, what happens after that is that the people they have met at Bread Loaf help them. One of the comments [one often hears is] that Bread Loafers are always praising each other, that John Gardner writes a blurb on Irving's book, Irving writes a blurb on O'Brien's book and so on. That's all true, but it sounds more like nepotism than in fact it is, because, for instance, Irving wrote on O'Brien when O'Brien was a Bread Loaf fellow, not a famous writer yet. That's the usual situation, Bread Loaf teachers helping Bread Loaf writers just getting started. That's how it happened that I began promoting and defending Susan Shreve, who wrote *Children of Power.* She started as a contributor and is now a teacher at Bread Loaf, a very fine short story writer and novelist. Susan Shreve showed me work, and we went over it, I told her what I thought was wrong, and so on. Bread Loaf helps young writers in other ways, of course. At Bread Loaf we introduce people to agents and editors who come to visit. It's almost the only workshop where that's an important part of the program, arranging for young writers to talk in a social situation with editors and agents. Anyway, once the novel is accepted I, of course, wave the flag and say "finest novelist since Tolstoy" or something. From a distance it looks like nepotism, but in fact I'm not writing blurbs for John Irving now; he no longer needs me. What we're doing, in giving support to new novelists, is continuing the teacher-student relationship—the help—after the Bread Loaf two weeks. I think that's something to be boastful about rather than ashamed of.

—*John Gardner,*
"AN INTERVIEW WITH JOHN GARDNER," BY
JUDSON MITCHAM AND WILLIAM RICHARD,
NEW ORLEANS REVIEW (SUMMER 1981)

John Gardner confers with Ron Hansen, 1979 (David Stanton)

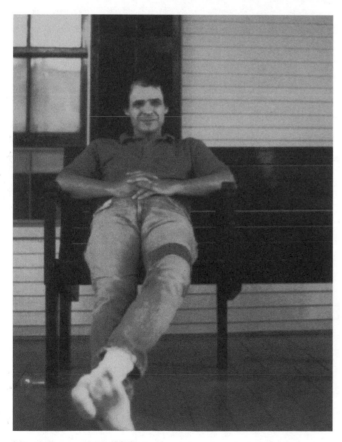

Tim O'Brien, 1985 (JOC)

Tim O'Brien, George Murphy, and Robert Pack, early 1980s

EIGHTIES

One of the unquenchable memories for anyone who attended the Bread Loaf Writers' Conference in the late 1970s and the early 1980s was of an exalted continuing debate, or colloquy, concerning the moral and artistic functions of fiction. This colloquy was carried on between an established master of the writing craft and a young novelist just coming into his renown.

The established master was the great teacher and philosophical novelist John Gardner—whose works included *The Sunlight Dialogues* and *October Light.* The emerging artist was Tim O'Brien—who in 1978 had won the National Book Award for his Vietnam War novel *Going After Cacciato.*

Their debate never presented itself as a debate, but more as a series of motifs and responses in a gorgeous suite of ideas. Here's how it usually unfolded: First John Gardner, all pink and platinum, looking like a minor medieval saint, would take the lectern and preach an unforgettable sermon about fiction as a test of Good against Evil: fiction that creates myths a society can *live* instead of die by, metaphor that becomes reality as we read and therefore implies a moral accountability on the part of the artist. Then a few mornings later would come Tim O'Brien, ballcapped, bomber-jacketed and chain-smoking, looking less like a medieval saint than a captured pilot.

Tim's own lecture, while never structured as a reply to Gardner's, often had the resonances of sympathetic and respectful dissent. Serious fiction was indeed about a test of virtue, for O'Brien—but instead of Good against Evil, he advocated a test more ambiguous and filled with risk: the test of one virtue in fateful opposition to another. For Tim O'Brien the constant virtue was always Courage. In place of John Gardner's redemptive public myths, Tim seemed to image stories as redemptive private dreams— redemptive for the writer as well as the reader.

"Soldiers are dreamers," said Siegfried Sassoon, and Tim O'Brien was in a position to know this. *Going After Cacciato* was about dreaming, as Doris Grumbach wrote—dreaming in the presence of war and the pursuit of peace, and elevating the dream to a kind of theology. The imagination itself was sacred.

Finally, in place of John Gardner's metaphoric truth, Tim called for the lie, but a sublime and magical lie, a lie that rose above falsehood and into a realm in which the boundaries of fantasy and the actual were forever blurred, but in which a higher, healing truth stood purified and revealed. And not even merely healing: "Stories," he told us over and over again, "can save our lives."

—*Ron Powers* (1990)

1981 Faculty: (rear) Tim O'Brien, Bob Pack, Ron Powers, Bill Matthews, Geoffrey Wolff, Terrence Des Pres, Mary Morris, Howard Nemerov, Pamela Hadas, Bill Stafford; (middle) Bob Houston, Stanley Elkin, Marvin Bell, Linda Pastan, Carole Oles; (front) Hilma Wolitzer, David Bain (EB)

1980 Faculty: (rear) Tim O'Brien, Bob Houston, Michael Arlen, {?}, Stanley Plumly, Ron Powers, Pamela Hadas, Steve Orlen, Sy Epstein, Ron Hansen; (middle) Nancy Willard, Linda Pastan, Judy Moffett, Gail Godwin, Howard Nemerov; (front) Hilma Wolitzer, Marvin Bell, Bob Pack, Mally Cox-Chapman (EB)

CALL FOR AN OPEN CONFERENCE

To the Editor:

A grass-roots movement is afoot to declare an "open" writers' conference at Bread Loaf. To those of us who are spearheading the movement, this has been no easy decision. We believed in the bright promise of Robert Pack and have worked hard to support his administration. But many questions have arisen over the past months. Questions such as, "What's a dactyl?" and "How do you think up all those metaphors and similes, anyway?" Accordingly, the proponents of an "open" writers' conference are urging that Robert Pack make the statesmanlike gesture of releasing his fellowgates (not to mention his scholargates and contributorgates) to support the candidates of their choice. After all, every thinking person realizes that New Hampshire is a long, long way away.

We who believe in an "open" conference are loyal to the principles of our great party. (In fact, if Pack had managed to produce a few great parties, he might not be in this mess.) Unfortunately, Pack has acted without rhyme or reason in failing to place party interests first. All of us are aware that Robert Pack is not his Administrative Director's keeper; nevertheless, the continuing front-page exploits of Stanley Bates have been a major liability to Pack's political base. Put bluntly, Bates is a hell-raiser and a wild and crazy guy. While his antics may make amusing copy for the media, those of us who are concerned for the conference's viability wince at his every public utterance: "When you've seen one waiteroid, you've seen 'em all" certainly does not reflect the Bread Loaf policy on minority groups. Worse still is Bates's recently disclosed practice of accepting ten percent of every Bread Loaf faculty member's royalties—without bothering to register as an agent. This of course has earned him the nickname, in the press, of "re-Bates." Is this the image we want for the most powerful free writers' conference in the world?

An open conference is the only answer.

—*The Crumb* (August 14, 1980)

BLOODLESS PURGE ENDS SCANDAL

All roads in and out of Bread Loaf were closed for two hours yesterday as the Middlebury College secret police conducted a "purge of reactionary, counter-revolutionary" elements within the writers' community. Numerous local "trouble makers" were rounded up and put on a plane for Iowa City. When asked if the action was a response to what has been known as Stanleygate, Bread Loaf Director Robert Pack looked coolly at this reporter and said, "We have no, as you call them, Stanleygates. We have only fascist imperialist bloodsuckers." Meanwhile, ultra-rightist Ron

The Inn veranda (pre-railings, access ramp, and across-the-street flagpole) (EB)

Powers, thought to be the organizer of the "open conference" movement, was seen walking eastward toward the mountains and New Hampshire. Tim O'Brien and others dressed in green tennis shorts were seen tracking Powers, following a trail of Hershey wrappers. When asked of his intentions, O'Brien stated, "I'm going to catch a tory."

—*The Crumb* (August 16, 1980)

Landscape with Self-Portrait

A shading porch, that's open to the west
Whence the weather comes, and giving on a lawn
Won from the meadow where the hay's been baled
In cubes like building blocks of dusty gold,
And further down, through trees, the streaming creek
With three still pools by passagework
Of rapids and rills in fretted rhythms linked;

And on the porch the life-defeated self
And reciprocating engine of reverie
Translating to time the back and forth of space,
The foot's escapement measuring the mind
In memories while the whole antic machine
Precesses across the floor and towards the edge
And has to be hitched back from time to time;

And there to watch the tarnished silver cloud
Advancing up the valley on a wind
That shudders the leaves and turns them silverside
While shadows sweep over stubble and grass,
And sudden the heavy silver of the first
Raindrops blown slanting in and summer cold
And turning continuous in silver strings;

And after that, the clarified serene
Of the little of daylight that remains to make
Distinct the details of the fading sight;
The laddered blue on blue of the bluejay's tail,
The sweeping swallows low above the swale
Among the insect victims as they rise
To be picked off, and peace is satisfied.
　　—*Howard Nemerov*,
　　　WAR STORIES (1986)

*(Top) Howard Nemerov, Treman porch, 1982 (DHB); (facing)
The Treman lawn, which provided a setting for his "Landscape
with Self-Portrait"; (above) nearby, the porches of Bridgman and
Cornwall cottages (EB)*

Gail Godwin and Hilma Wolitzer, 1982 (DHB)

Bob Reiss, Chase Twichell, and Ann Hood, 1987 (DHB)

Bob Shacochis and Amy Hemple,
1985 (DHB)

Sue Ellen Thompson and
David Huddle, 1984 (DHB)

1985 Faculty: (rear) Tom Gavin, Tim O'Brien, Bob Houston, Ron Hansen, Wyatt Prunty, Mark Strand, Bill Matthews, Hilma Wolitzer, Sydney Lea, Richard Tillinghast; (center) Carole Oles, Donald Justice, Marvin Bell, Robert Pack, Linda Pastan, Ellen Schwamm; (front) Joyce Johnson, Judy Moffett, Nancy Willard, Francine Prose, David Bain (MSD)

. . . You can get used to anything, even your life.

Have you noticed the perversity of old people? How they insist on what appears to you to be small, pointless martyrdoms, how they almost invariably eschew comfort and small gains? This one attends a dentist who hasn't kept up; that one will not eat French food. Their habits are not loyalties, they are superstitious, some customized mumbo jumbo of accommodation, set in their ways as children, warding off risk by never taking one and putting their faith in the locks and deadbolts of ritual and habituation.

Middle age is nothing like that. It puts its faith in the law of averages, which is what it still has in common with youth. What it has in common with old age, of course, is the beginning of an unpleasant consciousness of the body. Aches and pains like echoes in reverse, the mimic noises of the bones and flesh without any apparent stimulus. What it does not have in common with either is a certain privileged smugness, almost brave, almost heroic, status by dint of staying power.

If one stands on ceremonies they are one's own ceremonies.

For myself I am no longer vain of my appearance. If I'm flabby—flabby? I'm gross, I'm gross with grocery—I consider what it would cost me to alter my stats. Hard work,

exercise, the bad breath of diets, a will power in the service of some will not my own, some sleek and glossy Overwill, what strangers might like to look at, playing some other guy's gig and force-feeding myself into youthful images so alien—that I would probably feel comfortable only on Halloween. Your real dirty old man rarely looks his age. I'd as soon purchase a toupee or have my face lifted, my teeth capped, my shoes shined. . . .

Understand me. Swim laps, lay off the smokes, restrict your salt intake. If your motive is health, getting right with the underwriters, if you're sick and tired of sick and tired, I'm all for you. But good shape? At *our* age?

I made this holy silver-wedding-anniversary vow. If some lady in a strange town, really great-looking, really intelligent, nice and not a hooker, nice and not crazy, should ever come up to me at a party and say, "Hey look, I figure, a swell guy like you, you're a happily married man with this nifty family I wouldn't hurt for the world and I expect absolutely nothing in return, absolutely nothing, it's just that gross, middle-aged guys old enough to be my father happen to turn me on. So what do you say, sailor, when it's over it's over, strictly goodbye-dear-and-amen-here's-hoping-we-meet-now-and-then, meanwhile everything my treat, what do you say, my place or yours?" Well, I'll be honest. I would almost certainly have to think about it. I'll be more than honest. It hasn't come up and I no longer expect that it will.

So, in my case, middle age is at least partly ascetic, in the sense that however okay it may now be deemed to be to come out of the closet—Paunch Power!—and however seemly and respectable it may yet become even to die, it is mostly a piecemeal withdrawal of expectation. It's too late to learn to ski with impunity. I shall never go into the wet suit or snorkel the seas. I shall never break the bank at Monte Carlo, and learning Chinese is out of the question. Neither do I expect to be asked to spy for my country and I'll never solo. Nor will I handicap the ponies or get the knack of reading sheet music. I have almost given up hope of ever receiving a standing ovation.

But that's all small potatoes. Never my area of competence or concern. *Ski?* Even as a kid it hurt my hands to make snowballs and I'd catch cold pulling my sled and what do I care about breaking the bank at Monte Carlo? I wouldn't know what to give the *croupier.*

They're strengths in disguise, could be, these holes in my training. They free up obsession and shut distraction off at the pass. All the things I won't do, or can't, focus my options, allow me to service only my necessities. They tunnel my hope and—well, it's like this. As people get older they cease taking polls. More certain of their own, they're not so interested in other people's opinions. When fantasy flies out the window reality comes in at the door.

He's not a bad fellow, Reality. Quite nice, really, when you get to know him. For every pipe dream he takes away he leaves an energy, some increment of measured confidence just as heady as the diffuse, winner-take-all vanities of the young. And you *do* grow negligent of appearances; you do better; you grow *weary* of them, of all the reflected stances. You take less offense in mirrors and, like sums done in the head, narcissism becomes an inside job.

Like most writers, I've always wanted a best seller. Nothing spectacular: eleven weeks, say, at number seven or eight on the *New York Times Book Review* best-seller list would do me, maybe ten minutes including breaks for commercials at the end of a major talk show, and David Levine to do my caricature. Perhaps an honorary degree from a minor major university. Modest, you see, bucking for average as these things go. (Indeed, as they go every day.) I'm working on a new novel now [*George Mills*], perhaps the best, certainly the longest, I've ever written, but I doubt it will happen. I don't write it off—this is the world, everything happens—but I wouldn't bet on it. For now it's enough to do the work, to use my craft *for* my craft, and let the icing take care of itself. Leave me to Heaven, I say, and soak in my middle years as cynical and comfortable and unselfconscious as a man in his tub.

—*Stanley Elkin,*
"Turning Middle Aged,"
TWA Ambassador (1981)

A portrait of Stanley through his friends: Tim O'Brien, Hilma Wolitzer, and Linda Pastan listen to an imitable Elkin anecdote, 1985 (MSD)

John Gardner and Teddy prepare to leave Bread Loaf, 1982 (DHB)

Carolyn Forché and John Gardner lead waiters and conferees in "Amazing Grace," 1982 (DHB)

John Gardner and Susan Thornton, 1981 (DHB)

Ten years ago at Bread Loaf, when I'd written no more than a handful of poems, a sketch of an old woman from the village I grew up in, and several anguished letters about the artist's role in society, I worked up my nerve to approach John Gardner, then one of the more colorful and controversial figures in the literary world. A short, stocky man, with long white hair and bright blue eyes, he could be found most days holding court in the barn, the informal gathering place. But he was alone the afternoon I asked him to look at my sketch.

"I'll read," he said in a weary voice, "till I get bored."

My heart pounded. A man who would write thirty books in a short lifetime, including *Grendel,* a novel destined to outlive our age; who'd read many of the great works in twenty-seven different languages; who shook up the literary community with *On Moral Fiction,* his scathing attack on some of our most-respected writers—surely such a man would tire quickly of my work. He read my first paragraph and motioned me to sit down.

"You're a writer," he said simply, then continued reading.

Gardner read a few more pages, suggesting some changes, and then he sat back in his chair, lit his pipe, and started talking to me. He talked for the next four and a half hours, patiently giving me instructions about the sacred nature of my art, the religious devotion it requires of its servants. I will not presume to say that what passed between us was a moment of election, nor can I remember many of the specifics of his discourse. What stays with me is the care and attention he showered on a twenty-two-year-old apprentice to the craft. He was serious, intense: writing was everything to him. And that day I decided to dedicate my life as well to the art. Whatever success I may achieve with the pen I owe in large measure to Gardner.

I was to see him only once more, five years later, the first summer I worked at Bread Loaf. A recent beating from some churlish critics had left him smarting. But he was as generous as ever toward younger writers; and if he was less than responsible as a lecturer, still his workshops were brilliant. He'd completed a new story as well as a translation of the Sumerian epic, *Gilgamesh,* and he was full of life. At 4:30 one morning I heard him sing "Frankie and Johnny" as only a Welshman can sing such a ballad.

One month later he was dead, killed in a motorcycle accident at the age of forty-nine. Like many others, I felt as if Death had cheated the world again; John Gardner had so much yet to give.

—*Christopher Merrill* (1987)

Afternoons, when staff people take a hike up the mountain, or run a Middlebury errand, or just sit somewhere in the shade with friends, Gardner would station himself in the big barn, the central meeting place, and be available to anyone who wanted his help. This was, I think, a point of honor with him. . . .

I've seen Gardner steady as noon sun, giving himself with tribal care to any person with the guts or smarts to seek him out, and many did; sometimes it would look like a raid. I have also seen him join the rest of us at 5:30 for cocktails on the lawn or, if it rained, in the barn. And then go on after the evening reading and drink deep into the night. How much alcohol gets consumed at Bread Loaf is an astronomer's guess, and it's not that Gardner drank more than most, but that with him it was an *anabasis,* a march into the next day's dawn, and mainly for this reason: he loved, sought out, maybe really needed, community of talk. Not every night, but enough, he'd engage in discussion, excitement would spread like a message from the capitol, and a small knot of writers, equal in thought, equal in drink, would gather to fathom Gardner and themselves. Literature, politics, God, no subject smaller would do, and off things would go, Gardner as orator, sophist, inquisitor by turns, talking on and on, elated with ideas and the sport of it, playful, earnest, sometimes as if possessed—and all the time he, like the others around him, would be sipping away, in Gardner's case mainly gin, not noticing how much or how fast it went down. This sort of event wasn't unusual among members of the conference, but Gardner was different in that he'd seldom just stop. The lateness of the hour seemed to mean nothing to him, perhaps because in his other life, as a working writer, his habit was to start writing at midnight and keep on until five or six in the morning. As long as there could be talk, those Bread Loaf nights, there would be, and much of it was very fine. It could also lead to drunken nonsense, of course, but at his best Gardner could be a little like Socrates at the symposium, talking real philosophy, drinking everyone else under the table. . . .

. . . The last time I saw Gardner was departure time, Sunday morning, the end of the 1982 session at Bread Loaf. My son and I were loading our bike onto its trailer and Gardner came over to give us a hand. Then we said goodbye and he was gone. Speaking of his work the year before, he'd said: "When you look back there's lots of bales in the field, but ahead it's all still to mow." The rural metaphor was typical of him; so was the ambition, the natural look forward.

—*Terrence Des Pres,*
"ACCIDENT AND ITS SCENE," THE YALE REVIEW
73, NO. 1 (OCTOBER 1983)

John Gardner, 1982 (JOC)

Theodore Morrison returns to Bread Loaf, 1985, shown above on the Treman porch with Jack Bridgman and Robert Pack (DHB)

Theodore Morrison pauses in front of the Bread Loaf Inn for his last time, 1985 (DHB)

Many words have gone forth from Bread Loaf into print, and many of them distinguished words. And many people have felt themselves humanly enlarged and fortified by the experience of "the mountain."
　—*Theodore Morrison,*
　　Bread Loaf Writers' Conference: The First
　　Thirty Years (1976)

No great writer ever became one in isolation. Somewhere and some time, if only at the beginning, he had to experience the excitement and intellectual ferment of a group something like this.
　—*John Ciardi,*
　　Introductory Remarks at Bread Loaf (1958)

Lining up for a picnic lunch are David Hadas, Wyatt Prunty, Hilma Wolitzer, David Huddle, and Howard Nemerov, among others (DHB)

Yet another beige meal: William Jefferson, Sue Ellen Thompson, Chris Merrill, Tim O'Brien, John Irving, Brendan Irving, Carol Houck Smith, Pamela Hadas, Robert Finch (DHB)

Galway Kinnell and Carolyn Forché compare schedules on the Treman Porch, 1983 (DHB)

The commitment to achieve graceful form, to master a craft, and thus to be worthy of the Muse, always has needed the re-enforcement of a tradition that honors serious art and a community that supports the process of learning. Bread Loaf seeks to be such a community, simply by bringing together writers of all ages who are eager to listen to one another, to exchange ideas, and to benefit from the experience of those whose careers have preceded them on the road, one hopes, toward literary immortality.

—*Robert Pack,*
    INTRODUCTORY REMARKS AT BREAD LOAF

Stanley and Joan Elkin, 1982 (JOC)

Marvin Bell waits for his mail at the Inn (JOC)

Stanley Elkin was one of the funniest of the faculty members with his acerbic wit. Back when no two workshops in the same genre met at the same time, often you would get sixty or seventy people in your workshop, depending on how popular you were. Stanley was popular and often had a full room. One year . . . he knew that out of that whole crowd someone was sure to leave once the workshop got going. You know, even if one person leaves, you feel insulted. So Stanley had a plan. He was in a wide classroom—the room stretched off to his left and his right, full of people. About twenty minutes into the workshop, sure enough, a young guy sitting way over on the far side decided to leave. He got up, started tiptoeing and stepping over people, but of course stepping *on* them and whispering, "Excuse me . . . excuse me." And Stanley just stopped talking. He sat there silently. He let this guy trip over ankles the length of the room, and finally get to the door, and just as the kid got his hand on the doorknob and opened the door, Stanley called out in that loud way of his, "How do you like me so far, fella?"

Stanley was famous for collecting small soaps from motels, but his passion was beyond the bounds of sanity. He would take small soaps from anywhere. It's possible that airlines started using soap dispensers because Stanley, when he was flying, would go into the lavatories and steal all the little soaps. He had a huge collection. Once I knew that Stanley was a soap freak I would save them during the year, especially when I was in exotic places like Marrakesh or Tangier. Whenever Stanley was going to give a lecture or a reading I would get in there first and put a soap or two up on the lectern. And he would come in, and in a pleased way—without acknowledging it to the audience—he would put the soap in his pocket and begin his talk. Occasionally I would get enough soap during the year and dump it all in a bookbag and send it off to Stanley without a note. Then I'd get back a note from him: "Send more soap." But after a while Stanley was spoiled. Whenever I would see him when we would first arrive at Bread Loaf, he would say, "Where's my soap?" And it got so I had to shake hands with him with a soap in my hand. One time I was giving him soaps when Geoffrey Wolff came along—and it turned out that Geoffrey Wolff saves motel soaps, and he was jealous. So I had to start parceling them out. Then, one year, Jerome Charyn went up to Stanley and asked him if he saved soap. "I save fortune cookie fortunes," Charyn said. So I reached into my wallet and pulled out a fortune—I had a bunch of them. He was so amazed—he kept saying, what if I'd asked for this or that? He never forgot it.

—*Marvin Bell,*
INTERVIEW (1990)

Donald Justice strikes a pose for Blue Argo, mid-1980s (DHB)

Concert in the Bread Loaf Barn

Writing makes the exact man.

—Mrs. Snow

Four or five o'clock, late summer
around us like a cocoon, gauzy and intimate;
The sunlight of late afternoon plays
in the corner of The Barn upon a worn piano
covered with a sheet, silent as snow descending
like the memory of scales on white keys.

Mr. Justice contemplates silent keys
under the sheet's white shade, perhaps recalling summer-
idle days, the hand of Mrs. K descending
on his shoulder, a time when his fingers learned intimacy
at the price of fifty cents each week, a prophesy cast on a
childhood piano.
And his hands hover above the blank white sheet, a smile
plays

with the corners of his mouth. He will attempt to play
over the cover; an exercise in memory, a lark across the keys.
Still, for a time, he postpones the first chord, while the piano
beckons, teases. He looks around, full of secrets, cautious
of summer
stillness—then his fingers dance—a lively intimation
of a time when time was still harmony, not money.

It was an exercise requiring further practice, a descent
into memory, a difficult exercise, played
through as if by someone else, overheard in barn intimacy,
to him it seems full of mistakes, out of key.
Repeat it now, no one was listening, summer
hums in our ears. And his hand moves, moving across the
piano

and slowly the keys grow brighter to the touch, although
pianissimo.
No longer can he bear the disguise; his hands descend
upon the sheet, fling it to the summer-
warmed floor, and he plays!
identifying himself to the poetry police as the key
suspect, a lyric poet. What else? A man of intimacy,

and when you go, it is there, towards the intimacy
of music. I am the soprano, fanning herself near the piano,
a poet practicing her scales, my thumbs slip clumsily over
the keys.
As you leave The Barn, we few with the new instruments,
descend
into our soft chairs, novices, playing
the two strings—this summer, this summer,

While the sunlight of late afternoon descends
sweetly behind the green mountains to the music played
by the exact man, this August, this summer.
—*Pamela Ditchoff*

(1) Advice to Poets

Never write about poetry.
Never, never write about poetry.
Never, ever write about poetry.
Never, never. Don't
write about poetry. Never
about poetry. Never, never.
Don't ever. (Write about poetry.)
You must never, never write
about poetry. Never, ever do it.
(Write about poetry.) Never.
Not even once. Never twice.
I'm warning you. Never write
about poetry. The poetry police
said never write about it,
and that's good enough for me.

(2) There's More

Don't write about your father.
It's been done. Don't write about
your mother. It's been done.
Don't write about love. They
did it. Never mind history. They
did it. Keep off nature. They all
already did it. They wrote about
everything, in every way possible.
They wrote about art and war.
They wrote aubades and elegies.
They wrote epithalamiums
and odes, and they wrote in all
the stanzas there ever were.
They used refrains before you.
They used rhymes before you.
They exhausted free verse.
It's dead now. They said so.
When the poetry police
say not to do a thing anymore,
you don't do it. Anyway,
the poetry police will tell us
when it's time for poetry.
For now, it's been done.
  —Marvin Bell,
    "AT THE WRITERS' CONFERENCE," NEW
ENGLAND REVIEW 14, NO. 1 (FALL 1991)

Marvin Bell (foreground) and Ron Powers, 1983 (DHB)

Two pages of poets: (Clockwise from left) Robert Pack, 1985 (JOC); Marvin Bell, Donald Justice, and Wyatt Prunty on the Treman lawn, late 1980s (DHB); George Murphy, Sue Ellen Thompson, Sydney Lea, and Chris Merrill, 1985 (DHB)

(Clockwise from right) William Matthews (BA); Linda Pastan, Wyatt Prunty, and William Hathaway, 1983 (DHB); Deborah Digges, Mark Jarman, Robin Behn, and Philip Levine, 1986 (DHB)

Joyce Carol Oates and husband Raymond Smith are introduced to faculty members at Treman by Jay Parini, 1986 (DHB)

Nancy Willard, Eric Lindbloom, and Lore Segal, mid-1980s (DHB)

1986 Faculty (rear) {?}, David Huddle, Paul Mariani, Wyatt Prunty, Don Axinn, Bob Houston, Ron Powers, Nick Delbanco, Ed Hirsch, Bob Reiss, William Matthews, David Bain; (center) Ellen Pall, Lore Segal, Linda Pastan, Donald Justice, Philip Levine, Joyce Johnson, Lynn Sharon Schwartz, Francine Prose; (front) Alice Fulton, Tim O'Brien, Dan Wakefield, Robert Pack, Nancy Willard, Carole Oles, Tom Gavin (MSD)

Fun

for Michael Collier

You wish to sleep, to close your window to the singing,
But you can't it's so sweet;
The whoops, the hard blues piano
Tumbling drunk and forgetful
    out of the barn door.

So you listen to what the the revelers wish to state:
We need *baby, baby, babies*
(The rest of the lyrics are mumbled),
And we can be better than the person
    who stood earlier
At the cocktail party, dying
With a drink in his hands.

That wasn't really us floats through the window.
Here we are: listen.
And the piano barks,
The voices tighten and yap,
Tickling the night with *what the hell.*

                    Bread Loaf, August 1986

   —*Cornelius Eady,*
     The Gathering of My Name (1991)

1986 Fellows: *Michael Cunningham, {?}, Don Mitchell, {?}, Margot Livesey, Tom Swiss, {?}, {?}; (front) Deborah Digges, Michael Collier, Ken Smith, Kathleen Lawrence (DHB)*

1987 Faculty: *Paul Mariani, Ron Powers, Bob Reiss, Steve Bauer, Bob Houston, Bill Matthews, Mark Jarman, Liz Arthur, David Huddle, Joyce Johnson, Donald Justice, Jay Parini, Wyatt Prunty; (middle) Francine Prose, Linda Pastan, Hilma Wolitzer, Marvin Bell, Nancy Willard, Lore Segal; (front) Ron Hansen, David Madden, Bob Pack, Tim O'Brien, Julia Alvarez, David Bain, Carole Oles (MSD)*

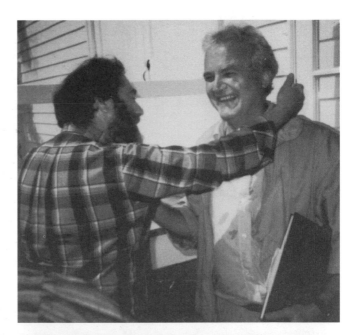

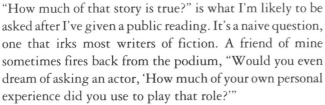

(Clockwise from above) Tim O'Brien, late 1980s; Marvin Bell greets Russell Banks, 1988; Linda Pastan, Lore Segal, Donald Axinn, 1986 (All DHB)

"How much of that story is true?" is what I'm likely to be asked after I've given a public reading. It's a naive question, one that irks most writers of fiction. A friend of mine sometimes fires back from the podium, "Would you even dream of asking an actor, 'How much of your own personal experience did you use to play that role?'"

But the autobiographical question interests me. . . . Thirty years of reading serious fiction and 20 years of trying to write it haven't cured me of my own naive curiosity about what's true and what isn't in a good story. . . . So I'm ready to try to answer a reader—or listener—who might be similarly wondering about something in a story of mine. Perhaps perversely, in the eyes of most of my brother and sister fiction writers, I feel honored, rather than bemused, by my audience's curiosity.

But in most cases, providing an answer would be a tough assignment for me. When I start writing a story, it's usually based on something I lived through, but as I'm writing it, I quickly forget what actually happened. That kind of truth is useful to me only as a starting point in my thinking about a story. Even though I begin with personal experience, I'm tinkering with it from the first words I set down. When I finish writing—finish the last of the ten to twenty-five or thirty drafts that it takes for me to feel that I've done all I can for my story—my memory of the truth of what happened has been clouded by my many alterations of it. . . .

—*David Huddle,*
"STORY-TRUTH," THE WRITING HABIT: ESSAYS (1990)

NINETIES

Forty-three years old, and the war occurred half a lifetime ago, and yet the remembering makes it now. And sometimes remembering will lead to a story, which makes it forever. That's what stories are for. Stories are for joining the past to the future. Stories are for those late hours in the night when you can't remember how you got from where you were to where you are. Stories are for eternity, when memory is erased, when there is nothing to remember except the story.

—*Tim O'Brien,*
    "SPIN," IN THE THINGS THEY CARRIED (1990)

Tim O'Brien, Richard Jackson, Ellen Bryant Voigt, 1990 (DHB)

Reunion at Treman: Hilma Wolitzer, Ellen Bryant Voigt, and Linda Pastan reminisce with William Meredith, 1990 (DHB)

Jennifer Egan, Bob Pack, Ted Conover, at Larch Well reception, 1990 (DHB)

John Irving and Janet Turnbull greet Jack Bridgman, 1990
(DHB)

We do not invent language. We inherit it. Language has its own genius which recreates itself through our use of it. We are the means by which it grows and keeps itself alive. Like a god, it speaks through us and survives us. Our minds are created by language; our thinking is made possible by the structure it provides, just as our bodies know only what our senses are capable of perceiving. And if we give ourselves to the language, embracing it, cherishing it word by word, we may take on something of its grandeur and its majesty. I want to say that we receive its "grace," for we enter into the community of mind that crosses time and place, containing them. Every true poem, by its very nature, is a celebration of its inheritance—the language—which is never ours, though we, in our passing, partake of its ongoing grace.
—*Robert Pack,*
INTRODUCTORY REMARKS AT BREAD LOAF

The End of Summer School

At dawn today the spider's web was cold
With dew heavy as silver to the sight,
Where, kicked and spun, with clear wings befouled,
Lay in the shrouds some victims of the night.

This morning, too, as if they had decided,
A few first leaves came loose and drifted down
Still slopes of air; in silence they paraded
Their ominous detachment to the lawn.

How strange and slow the many apples ripened
And suddenly were red beneath the bough.
A master of our school has said this happened
"Quiet as grass can ruminate a cow."

And now the seeds go on their voyages,
Drifting, gliding, spinning in quiet storms
Obedient to the air's lightest laws;
And where they fall, a few will find their forms.

And baby spiders, on their shining threads,
The middle air make glisten gold all day;
Sailing, as if the sun had blessed their roads,
Hundreds of miles, and sometimes out to sea.

This is the end of summer school, the change
Behind the green wall and the steady weather:
Something that turns upon a hidden hinge
Brings down the dead leaf and live seed together,

And of the strength that slowly warps the stars
To strange harbors, the learned pupil knows
How adamant the anvil, fierce the hearth
Where imperceptible summer turns the rose.
  —*Howard Nemerov,*
   THE NEXT ROOM OF THE DREAM (1962)

ROSTER:
BREAD LOAF WRITERS' CONFERENCE

1 9 2 6

Faculty:

John Farrar, *Director*
Edward Davison
Robert M. Gay
Doris Halman
Harriet Monroe
Grant Overton

Speakers:

Owen Davis
William McFee
Honore Willsie Morrow
Isabel Paterson

1 9 2 7

Faculty:

John Farrar, *Director*
Hervey Allen
Herbert Gorman
Addison Hibbard
Burgess Johnson
Edith Mirrielees

Speakers:

Achmed Abdullah
Harry Payne Burton
Floyd Dell
Philip Dunning
Robert Frost
Susan Glaspell
Jean Wick

1 9 2 8

Faculty:

John Farrar, *Director*
Joseph Auslander
Wilfred E. Davison
Robert M. Gay
Grant Overton
Margaret Widdemer

Speakers:

Maxwell Aley
Stephen Vincent Benét
Sinclair Lewis
Henry Maule
Jean Wick
Otis Wiese

1 9 2 9

Faculty:

Robert M. Gay, *Director*
Hervey Allen
Edith Mirrielees
Gorham Munson
Edward Weeks
Margaret Widdemer

Speakers:

John Farrar
Robert Frost
Samuel Merwin
Joel E. Spingarn
Louis Untermeyer

1 9 3 0

Faculty:

Robert M. Gay, *Director*
Hervey Allen
Walter Prichard Eaton
Edith Mirrielees
Theodore Morrison
Gorham Munson

Speakers:

John Farrar
Samuel Merwin
Lee Simonson
Edward Weeks
Margaret Widdemer

1 9 3 1

Faculty:

Robert M. Gay, *Director*
Hervey Allen
Lee Wilson Dodd
Edith Mirrielees
Theodore Morrison
Gorham Munson
Margaret Widdemer

Speakers:

Donald Davidson
John Farrar
Claude Moore Fuess
Clayton Hamilton
Samuel Merwin
William Hazlett Upson
Edward Weeks

1 9 3 2 *

Faculty:

Theodore Morrison, *Director*
Bernard DeVoto
Lee Wilson Dodd
Walter Prichard Eaton
Robert Hillyer
Gorham Munson
Margaret Widdemer

Speakers:

John Farrar
Dorothy Canfield Fisher
Archibald MacLeish
David McCord
William Hazlett Upson
Edward Weeks

1 9 3 3

Faculty:

Theodore Morrison, *Director*
Bernard DeVoto
Walter Prichard Eaton
Raymond Everitt
Gorham Munson

Speakers:

John Farrar
Dorothy Canfield Fisher
Sinclair Lewis
Archibald MacLeish
Edward Weeks

1 9 3 4

Faculty:

Theodore Morrison, *Director*
Hervey Allen
Fanny Butcher
Bernard DeVoto
Walter Prichard Eaton

Speakers:

Maxwell Aley
John Farrar
Dorothy Canfield Fisher
Archibald MacLeish

Fellows:

Catherine Drinker Bowen
Lauren Gilfillan
Josephine Johnson
Scott O'Dell
Frances Prentice

Visitors:

Irving Fineman
Alexander Laing
Owen Lattimore

1 9 3 5

Faculty:

Theodore Morrison, *Director*
John Mason Brown
Gladys Hasty Carroll
Bernard DeVoto
Helen Everitt
Raymond Everitt
Gorham Munson
Julia Peterkin
John Crowe Ransom
George Stephens

Speakers:

Stephen Vincent Benét
John Farrar
Gilbert Seldes

Fellows:

Shirley Barker
Howard Fast
Robert Stallman
Isabel Wilder

Visitors:

Robert Frost
Philip Wheelwright

1 9 3 6

Faculty:

Theodore Morrison, *Director*
John Mason Brown
Bernard DeVoto
Helen Everitt
Raymond Everitt
Robert Hillyer
Josephine Johnson
Edith Mirrielees
Julia Peterkin

Speakers:

John Farrar
Robert Frost

Fellows:

Robeson Bailey
Edward Crook
Eleanor Delamater
Janet Johl
Marie Luhrs
George Marion O'Donnell
Hope W. Sykes
Anthony Wrynn

Visitors:

Shirley Barker
Allene Corliss
Kimball Flaccus
Alexander Laing
Lee Simonson
Louis Untermeyer

*Administrator, 1932–1955: Richard Brown

1 9 3 7

Faculty:

Theodore Morrison, *Director*
Eleanor Chilton
Bernard DeVoto
Helen Everitt
Raymond Everitt
Paul Green
Edith Mirrielees
Gorham Munson
George Stephens

Speakers:

Herbert Agar
Elmer Davis
James T. Farrell
Robert Frost
Archibald MacLeish
Louis Untermeyer

Fellows:

Helen Card
Robert Francis
Mary F. Hunt
Ira Nelson
Inez Oellrichs
Fletcher Pratt
James Still

Visitors:

Eleanor Chilton
Josephine Johnson

1 9 3 8

Faculty:

Theodore Morrison, *Director*
Herschel Brickell
Eleanor Chilton
Alan Collins
Bernard DeVoto
Helen Everitt
Raymond Everitt

Robert Frost
John Gassner
Merritt Hulburd
Gorham Munson
Fletcher Pratt
Wallace Stegner

Speakers:

Herbert Agar
Archibald MacLeish
Louis Untermeyer

Fellows:

Elizabeth Davis
Charles Ford
Charles Foster
Harriet Hassell
Josephine Niggli
Wellington Roe
Theodore Strauss
Arthur Tourtellot

Visitors:

Josephine Johnson
Lee Simonson

1 9 3 9

Faculty:

Theodore Morrison, *Director*
Herschel Brickell
Eleanor Chilton
Alan Collins
Bernard DeVoto
Raymond Everitt

Robert Frost
John Gassner
Edith Mirrielees
Gorham Munson
Fletcher Pratt
Louis Untermeyer

Speakers:

Herbert Agar
Lambert Davis
Walter Prichard Eaton
Archibald MacLeish
John P. Marquand
Wallace Stegner

Fellows:

Holmes Alexander
Anne Einselen
Marian Jones
Elizabeth Marion
Samuel French Morse

Visitors:

William Sloane
Lawrance Thompson

1 9 4 0

Faculty:

Theodore Morrison, *Director*
Herschel Brickell
Eleanor Chilton
Alan Collins
Walter Prichard Eaton
Helen Everitt
Barbara Fleury

Robert Frost
John Gassner
John P. Marquand
Edith Mirrielees
Fletcher Pratt
Wallace Stegner
Louis Untermeyer

Speakers:

Herbert Agar
W. H. Auden
Katherine Anne Porter

Fellows:

Brainard Cheney
John Ciardi
Edna Frederickson
Carson McCullers
Marian Sims
Eudora Welty

Visitors:

Helen Grace Carlisle
Bernard DeVoto
Robert Evans
James Still

1 9 4 1

Faculty:

Theodore Morrison, *Director*
Naomi Burton
Philip Cohen
Alan Collins
Frances Woodward Curtis
Bernard DeVoto
Walter Prichard Eaton

Helen Everitt
Barbara Fleury
Robert Frost
John Gassner
John P. Marquand
Fletcher Pratt
Louis Untermeyer

Speakers:

William Carlos Williams

Fellows:

L. Sprague DeCamp
Charles Edward Eaton
Vivian Parsons
Robert Richards
Constance Robertson
Theodore Roethke
Mari Tomasi
Cedric Whitman

Visitors:

Merrill Moore
Gorham Munson
Wallace Stegner

1 9 4 2

Faculty:

Theodore Morrison, *Director*
Philip Cohen
Alan Collins
Walter Prichard Eaton
Helen Everitt
Raymond Everitt
Barbara Fleury

Robert Frost
John P. Marquand
Edith Mirrielees
Fletcher Pratt
Wallace Stegner
Louis Untermeyer

Fellows:

Harriet Ball Hale
Dilys Bennett Laing
Elizabeth Gregg Patterson
Winfield Townley Scott

1 9 4 3

Faculty:

Theodore Morrison, *Director*
Philip Cohen
Alan Collins
Frances Woodward Curtis

Helen Everitt
Raymond Everitt
Walter E. Havighurst
Fletcher Pratt

Speakers:

Elizabeth Drew

Fellows:

Betty Middlebrook
Virginia Sorenson
Betty Wason

1 9 4 4

Faculty:

Theodore Morrison, *Director*
Philip Cohen
Alan Collins
Helen Everitt
Raymond Everitt

Robert Frost
Edith Mirrielees
Fletcher Pratt
Wallace Stegner
Louis Untermeyer

Speakers:

Catherine Drinker Bowen
Helen Harkness Flanders
Arthur K. D. Healy

Fellows:

Elizabeth Fisher
Laura Loudon
Catherine Pomeroy Stewart

Others:

Truman Capote
William Sloane

1 9 4 5

Faculty:

Theodore Morrison, *Director*
Catherine Drinker Bowen
Alan Collins
Bernard DeVoto
Walter Prichard Eaton

Helen Everitt
Robert Frost
Col. Joseph I. Greene
Walter E. Havighurst
Edith Mirrielees

Fletcher Pratt
William Sloane
Louis Untermeyer

Speakers:

Richard Wright

Fellows:

Elizabeth Abell
A. B. Guthrie, Jr.
E. Louise Mally

1 9 4 6

Faculty:

Theodore Morrison, *Director*
Alan Collins
Helen Everitt
Robert Frost
Col. Joseph I. Greene
Graeme Lorimer
Fletcher Pratt
William Sloane
Wallace Stegner
Louis Untermeyer

Speakers:

Walter Prichard Eaton
William Hazlett Upson

Fellows:

Robert Bordner
Eugene Burdick
Jean Byers
Esther Carlson
Andrew Glaze
Rudolf Kieve

Visitors:

Robeson Bailey
Warren Beck
Marshall Best
W. N. Chambliss
Conrad Richter
George F. Whicher

Others:

William Styron,
    student

1 9 4 7

Theodore Morrison, *Director*
John Ciardi
Alan Collins
Bernard DeVoto

Faculty:

Helen Everitt
Robert Frost
Joseph Kinsey Howard
Edith Mirrielees

Fletcher Pratt
Mark Saxton
William Sloane

Speakers:

Walter Prichard Eaton
Karl Shapiro

Fellows:

Cal Cain
David Davidson
Charles Guthrie
Henry Hornsby
Frederick Morton

1 9 4 8

Faculty:

Theodore Morrison, *Director*
John Ciardi
Bernard DeVoto
Helen Everitt
Robert Frost

A. B. Guthrie, Jr.
Fletcher Pratt
Mark Saxton
William Sloane

Speakers:

Gerald Warner Brace
Frank Campbell
William Lederer
Frederick Melcher
Louis Untermeyer
William Hazlett Upson

Fellows:

Maxwell Arnold
H. O. Austin
Frank Campbell
Margaret Coit
Henry Hornsby
Rachel MacKenzie
Robert Mende

Visitors:

Robert Bordner
Oscar Williams

1 9 4 9

Faculty:

Theodore Morrison, *Director*
John Ciardi
Bernard DeVoto
Helen Everitt
Robert Frost
A. B. Guthrie, Jr.
Edith Mirrielees
Fletcher Pratt
William Sloane
William Hazlett Upson

Speakers:

Catherine Drinker Bowen
Frank Campbell
Nannine Joseph

Fellows:

Lucy Herndon Crockett
Andrew Geer
Firman Houghton
Caroline Iveyh
William Lederer
Arnold S. Lott
Robert Mende
Sylvia Shirley
Richard Spong
Era Bell Thompson

Visitors:

Robeson Bailey
Robert Bordner
Eugene Burdick
Alan Collins
Alfred Edwards
William Raney
Catherine Pomeroy Stewart

1 9 5 0

Faculty:

Theodore Morrison, *Director*
Catherine Drinker Bowen
John Ciardi
Betty Finnin
Robert Frost
Nannine Joseph
Fletcher Pratt
William Raney
Barbara Rex
Josephine Saxton
Mark Saxton
William Sloane
Richard Wilbur

Speakers:

Lincoln Barnett
John Mason Brown
John T. Fischer
Owen Lattimore
Mark Van Doren
Max Wylie

Fellows:

Thaddeus Ashby
Roger Eddy
Robert Lucas
José Pena
Elizabeth Spencer
Mary Elizabeth Witherspoon

Visitors:

Robeson Bailey

Others:

Isaac Asimov

1 9 5 1

Faculty:

Theodore Morrison, *Director*   Josephine Saxton
Lincoln Barnett   Mark Saxton
John Ciardi   Richard Scowcroft
Rachel MacKenzie   William Sloane
Fletcher Pratt   Richard Wilbur
May Sarton

Speakers:

John Mason Brown
Robert Frost
Arthur Schlesinger, Jr.
Wallace Stegner
William Hazlett Upson

Fellows:

Doris Davis
Robert De Vries
Jane Eklund
Hoke Norris
O. William Pierce

Visitors:

Col. Joseph I. Greene

1 9 5 2

Faculty:

Theodore Morrison, *Director*   Fletcher Pratt
Lincoln Barnett   William Sloane
John Ciardi   Eric P. Swenson
John T. Fischer   Jessamyn West
Rachel MacKenzie

Speakers:

Ian Ballantine
Robert Frost
Frank O'Connor

Fellows:

Eugenie Clark
Mary Moore Malony
John Secondari
Will Thomas

1 9 5 3

Faculty:

Theodore Morrison, *Director*   Fletcher Pratt
John Ciardi   May Sarton
Rachel MacKenzie   William Sloane
Frank O'Connor   Eric P. Swenson

Speakers:

Lincoln Barnett
Robert Frost
Willy Ley
Wallace Stegner

Fellows:

Nathaniel Burt
Noel Clad
Ruth Harnden
Richard Kraus
Clay Putnam
Edgar Rosenberg

1954

Faculty:

Theodore Morrison, *Director*
Saul Bellow
John Ciardi
Alan Collins
Louis M. Lyons

Rachel MacKenzie
Fletcher Pratt
William Sloane
Eric P. Swenson
Richard Wilbur

Speakers:

Lincoln Barnett
Robert Frost
Willy Ley
Alfred Steffrud
William Hazlett Upson

Fellows:

Jerry Allen
Eaton G. Davis
Whitfield Ellison
Melvin B. Tolson

1955

Faculty:

Theodore Morrison, *Director*
John Ciardi
A. B. Guthrie, Jr.
Rachel MacKenzie
Fletcher Pratt

Adrienne Rich
Richard H. Rovere
May Sarton
William Sloane

Speakers:

Lincoln Barnett
Bernard DeVoto
Robert Frost
William Hazlett Upson

Fellows:

Stefanie Blank
Ruth Goodwin
Clinton Seeley

1956 *

Faculty:

John Ciardi, *Director*
Leonie Adams
Catherine Drinker Bowen
Bruce Lancaster

Rachel MacKenzie
Merle Miller
Fletcher Pratt
William Sloane

Speakers:

Robert Frost
Louis M. Lyons
Winfred Van Atta

Fellows:

Wilbur Cross III
Paxton Davis
Evans Harrington
Herbert Kenny
Mrs. Leon Levine
Robin White

1957

Faculty:

John Ciardi, *Director*
Leonie Adams
Eunice Blake
Kay Boyle

A. B. Guthrie, Jr.
Nancy Hale
Stewart Holbrook
William Raney
William Sloane
Mildred Walker

Speakers:

Lincoln Barnett
Catherine Drinker Bowen
Robert Frost
David McCord
Winfred Van Atta

Richard Wilbur

Fellows:

Alma Brodie
Joseph Dever
Leonard Drohan
Gerald Gottlieb

Jane Mayhall
Richard Moore
May Swenson
Dan Wakefield

1958

Faculty:

John Ciardi, *Director*
Leonie Adams
Eunice Blake
Catherine Drinker Bowen
Daniel Curley
Nancy Hale

Bruce Lancaster
John Frederick Nims
William Raney
Berton Roueché
William Sloane

Speakers:

Carl Carmer
Robert Frost
Theodore Morrison
William Hazlett Upson

Fellows:

Bernard Asbell
John Farris
Dan Jaffe
John Lydenberg
Anthony Ostroff

John H. Randall III
Robert Sward
Edward Tripp
Joan Williams

*Administrator, 1956–1964: Paul Cubeta

1 9 5 9

Faculty:	Speakers:	Fellows:	Scholars:	Others:
John Ciardi, *Director*	Robert Frost	Elizabeth Baker	Nancy Means Wright	Alan Cheuse
George Barker	Theodore Morrison	Robert Hutchinson		Douglas Davis
Eunice Blake	William Hazlett Upson	George Lea		
Ralph Ellison	Dan Wakefield	Irene Orgel		
Richard Gehman	Richard Wilbur	Anne Sexton		
Nancy Hale				
William Meredith				
William Raney				
William Sloane				
Hollis Summers				
Walter Magnes Teller				

1 9 6 0

Faculty:	Speakers:	Fellows:	Scholars:	Others:
John Ciardi, *Director*	David Blumenstock	Robert Burch	John Engels	George V. Higgins
Bernard Asbell	Charles E. Feinberg	Martin Dibner	Sylvester Leeks	
Eunice Blake	Dudley Fitts	X. J. Kennedy	John Medelman, Jr.	
Allen Drury	Robert Frost	Claire McAllister	Gloria Oden	
Richard Gehman	Stewart Holbrook	Anthony Robinson	Eugene O'Donnell	
Nancy Hale	Theodore Morrison	Arthur Roth	Avodah Offit	
Louis W. Koenig	William Hazlett Upson	Edward Stephens	Paul Olsen	
David McCord		Irene Warsaw	Guy Owen	
John Frederick Nims			Robert Richie	
Mark Saxton			Edward Wallant	
William Sloane			John A. Williams	
			Richard Yates	

1 9 6 1

Faculty:		Speakers:	Fellows:		Scholars:
John Ciardi, *Director*	John Frederick Nims	Robert Frost	Charles P. Breen	Milton Kessler	A. R. Ammons
Bernard Asbell	William Raney	Theodore Morrison	David Delman	Lewis Turco	Leonard Casper
Eunice Blake	Louis Rubin	William Hazlett Upson	Richard Frost	Milton White	James Chace
Dudley Fitts	William Sloane	Dan Wakefield	Frank Hercules	Miller Williams	Cynthia Gilbert
Nancy Hale	Richard Yates		Kaye Starbird		John Gilgun
Howard Nemerov			Jennison		R. Leslie Gourse
					Robert Huff

1 9 6 2

Faculty:		Speakers:		Fellows:	
John Ciardi, *Director*	Nancy Hale	Robert Frost		William Crawford	William Melvin Kelley
Eunice Blake	David McCord	Theodore Morrison		George Cuomo	Donald St. George Reeves
Margaret Cousins	John Frederick Nims	Frederick Nichols		Robert Hutchinson	Barbara Robinson
Richard Ellmann	William Raney	Cornelia Otis Skinner		Gary Jennings	John Woods
Dudley Fitts	William Sloane	William Hazlett Upson			
	Richard Yates				

1 9 6 3

Faculty:	Speakers:	Fellows:	Scholars:	Others:
John Ciardi, *Director*	Dudley Fitts	Fleming Blitch	Barbara Overmeyer	Russell Banks
Nelson Algren	Theodore Morrison	Joan Didion	Charles Rose	
Eunice Blake	Cornelia Otis Skinner	Arno Karlen	Nancy Sullivan	
Brock Brower	William Hazlett Upson	Paris Leary		
Mark Harris		Alan Levy		
John Hawkes		Edward P. Stafford		
John Frederick Nims		Ruth Stone		
Robert Pack		Richard Underwood		
William Raney		William Wetmore		
Walter Ross				
William Sloane				
Hollis Summers				

1 9 6 4

Faculty:		Speakers:	Fellows:	Scholars:
John Ciardi, *Director*	Shirley Jackson	Theodore Morrison	John Bleibtreu	Elling Eide
Eunice Blake	Howard Nemerov	William Hazlett Upson	Jerome Charyn	David Ray
Brock Brower	Robert Pack		Mary Durant	
Stanley Elkin	William Raney		Burton Hersh	
Dudley Fitts	William Sloane		Romulus Linney	
Nancy Hale	Dan Wakefield		Mark Mirsky	

1 9 6 5 *

Faculty:	Speakers:	Fellows:	Scholars:	Others:
John Ciardi, *Director*	Dudley Fitts	Claude Brown	Helen S. Chasin	Julia Child
Eunice Blake	Theodore Morrison	Catherine Crary	Adassa Frank	
Brock Brower	Chard Powers Smith	Kristin Hunter	Donn Pearce	
Richard Ellmann	William Hazlett Upson	Justin Mamis	Marguerite Taussig	
Seymour Epstein		David Shapiro		
Walter Goodman		Ralph Lee Smith		
Nancy Hale		Octavia Waldo		
Charles Jackson				
William Lederer				
John Frederick Nims				
Robert Pack				
Henry Rago				
William Sloane				

*Administrator, 1965–1978: Edward Martin.

1 9 6 6

Faculty:

John Ciardi, *Director*
Eunice Blake
Brock Brower
Seymour Epstein
X. J. Kennedy
William Lederer
John Frederick Nims
William Sloane
David Wagoner
Dan Wakefield
John Williams

Speakers:

Lewis Dralle
William Hazlett Upson

Fellows:

F.M. Esfandiary
Richard Koiner
Robert Kroetsch
Hal Levitt
James McCormick
Jay Neugeboren
Marvin Schiller
Charlene Talbot
Diane Wakoski

Scholars:

Hal Bennett
Stanwood Bolton, Jr.
Christopher Bursk
Florence M. Hecht
Leo Skir

Others:

Julia Child
Joy Williams

1 9 6 7

Faculty:

John Ciardi, *Director*
John Aldridge
Camille Davied
Seymour Epstein
Judson Jerome
William Lederer

John Frederick Nims
Robert Pack
Henry W. Simon
William Sloane
John Williams
Miller Williams

Speakers:

Archibald MacLeish
Norman Mailer
William Hazlett Upson

Fellows:

William Caldwell
Douglas Davis
Dave Etter
Hannah Green
Arona McHugh
Margaret Ritter

Audrey Soracco
Shane Stevens
Joyce Varney
Stephen Walton
James Whitehead
Gerald Zeigerman

Scholars:

William Hassebrock
Paula S. Paige

1 9 6 8

Faculty:

John Ciardi, *Director*
Eunice Blake
Seymour Epstein
Judson Jerome
William Lederer
John Frederick Nims
William Sloane
Hollis Summers
Lewis Turco
Dan Wakefield
John Williams
Miller Williams

Speakers:

Edmund S. Muskie

Fellows:

Joy Anderson
Jay Bell
Richard Braun
Helen S. Chasin
Robert Cormier
Harry Crews
Roy Friedman
Diana Green
Roger Hall
John Morressy
Robert Mueller
Thomas Taylor
Paul Tyner

Scholars:

Alvin Aubert
Edward Brash
Linda Caffiano
John Conron
Harold E. Donn
William Kotzwinkle
Herbert W. Martin
Nita Regnier
Henry Van Dyke

Others:

Vassar Miller

Visitors:

Archibald MacLeish

1969

Faculty:

John Ciardi, *Director*
Harry Crews
Seymour Epstein
Joanna Foster
Andrew Glaze
Arno Karlen
Maxine Kumin

William Meredith
John Frederick Nims
Peter Schrag
William Sloane
John Williams
Miller Williams

Fellows:

Nora Levin
Charles Newman
Dan Potter
Mary Shumway
William Sleator
Jonathan Strong
Wendy Watson
Alan Weiss

Scholars:

William E. Doreski
Carolyn J. Gaiser
Elizabeth H. Harris
Adolph Hoehling, Jr.
Johanna Kaplan

Rodger Kingston
Delores Netzband
David Rabe
Lin Root
David H. Steinglass

Others:

Julia Alvarez
Richard Jackson
Leon Stokesbury

1970

Faculty:

John Ciardi, *Director*
Harry Crews
Joanna Foster
Galway Kinnell
Perry Knowlton
Maxine Kumin
William Meredith

John Frederick Nims
William Sloane
Shane Stevens
Dan Wakefield
John Williams
Miller Williams

Fellows:

James Burke
Gary Gildner
Conrad Hilberry
Bernard Kaplan
Sharon Bell Mathis
Michael Mewshaw
Barbara Murphy
Elizabeth Scott

Catherine Anderson
Paulette Bates
Margaret Colliton
William V. Davis
Adelle Diamond
Philip Dow
Mary Elder
Richard Jackson

Scholars:

Bennett Kremen
Thomas Lux
Glenn Meeter
Harold R. Ober
Carole Oles
Linda Oliver
Joseph Pillitteri

Lauren Shakely
Zona Silverstein
James Tipton
Hilma Wolitzer

Others:

Julia Alvarez

1971

Faculty:

John Ciardi, *Director*
Isaac Asimov
Alfred Balle
Seymour Epstein
Maxine Kumin
William Meredith
Ezekiel Mphalele

Eleanor Nichols
Robert Pack
William Sloane
Shane Stevens
Diane Wakoski
John Williams
Miller Williams

Speakers:

William Lederer
Ellen Levine

Fellows:

Charles Flowers
Eleanor Glaze
Barry Hannah
Edward Hannibal
Wendy Kindred
Elaine Kraf
Michael Stephens
William Crawford Woods

Scholars:

Laurie Colwin
James N. Hall
Shael Herman
Gayl Jones
Lin Lifshin
James Morgan
Joe Shea

Others:

Rust Hills

1972

Faculty:

John Ciardi, *Director*
Joy Anderson
Isaac Asimov
Harry Crews
Seymour Epstein
Robert Hayden
William Lederer

John Frederick Nims
Robert Pack
William Sloane
Diane Wakoski
James Whitehead
John Williams
Miller Williams

Fellows:

Richard Allen
William Amidon
David Freeman
Julie Gilbert
David Madden
Mary Walker

Scholars:

Bruce R. Guernsey
Bruce H. McAllister
Gordon T. Osing
Susan M. Singer
William Valgardson
Gloria van Scott
David Clifton Walker

Others:

Julia Alvarez

Visitors:

Marvin Bell

1 9 7 3

Faculty:

Robert Pack, *Director*
Joy Anderson
Marvin Bell
Vance Bourjaily
Harry Crews
George P. Elliott
Seymour Epstein
Walter Goodman
Anthony Hecht
Maxine Kumin
Peter Schrag
Lore Segal
Mark Strand

Speakers:

Georges Borchardt
Brock Brower
Anatole Broyard
Diane Divoky
Perry Knowlton
James Landis
Ellen Levine
William Meredith
Morris Philipson
Anne Sexton
Wendy Weil

Fellows:

Lillie D. Chaffin
Calvin Forbes
Alan Goldfein
Andrew Goldstein
Katie Letcher Lyle
Marcia Newfield
Francine Prose
Lawrence Raab
Karen Swenson

Scholars:

Joe David Bellamy
George Briggs
Christopher Brookhouse
David Evans
Gerald Murphy
David Jeddie Smith
David Charles Tillinghast

1 9 7 4

Faculty:

Robert Pack, *Director*
Marvin Bell
Rosellen Brown
George P. Elliott
Seymour Epstein
John Gardner
William Gass
Walter Goodman
Anthony Hecht
Lore Segal
Mark Strand
Mona Van Duyn

Associates:

Lawrence Raab

Speakers:

Richard Marek
Stephen Sheppard
George Starbuck
Jarvis Thurston

Fellows:

Alvin ben-Moring
David Black
Daniel Halpern
Judith Minty
Maureen Mylander
Thomas P. Nugent
Linda Pastan
Carmen Rinaldo
Ira Sadoff
Robert Siegel
Hilma Wolitzer

Scholars:

Gary Corseri
Hilda Gregory
Rolly Kent
Colleen McElroy
Joan Norris
Catherine Petroski
Suzanne Rioff
Bryna Taubman

1 9 7 5

Faculty:

Robert Pack, *Director*
Marvin Bell
George P. Elliott
Seymour Epstein
John Gardner
Walter Goodman
Anthony Hecht
John Irving
Donald Justice
Maxine Kumin
William Meredith
Lore Segal
Nancy Willard

Associates:

Maureen Mylander
Linda Pastan
Lawrence Raab
Hilma Wolitzer

Speakers:

James Landis
Richard Marek
David Price
Richard Selzer

Fellows:

Kelly Cherry
Carl Dennis
Stephen Dunn
Tom Gavin
Gwen Head
Tim O'Brien
Nancy Winslow Parker
James Reiss
Dave Smith
Doris Smith
Bryan Wolley

Scholars:

Charles Butterfield
Tess Gallagher
Marianne Gingher
Susan Mikhell
Mary Morris
Judy Moyer
Jack Porter
John Ronan
Muriel Spanier
Connie Stapleton
William Zaranka

Visitors:

Joseph Brodsky
John Frederick
Nims

1 9 7 6

Faculty:	Associates:	Speakers:	Fellows:	Scholars:	Visitors:
Robert Pack, *Director*	Tim O'Brien	Robert Brustein	Donald Bredes	James Atlas	Georges Borchardt
Marvin Bell	Linda Pastan	James Landis	Sue Ellen Bridgers	Laurel Blossom	Brock Brower
Stanley Elkin	Lawrence Raab	Richard Marek	Terrence Des Pres	Marguerite Bouvard	John Gardner
George P. Elliott	Hilma Wolitzer	Jarvis Thurston	John Engels	Mary Crow	Walter Goodman
John Irving			Carolyn Forché	David J. Dwyer	Hilda Gregory
Donald Justice			Richard Ford	Carol Frost	Galway Kinnell
William Meredith			Carol Muske	Rachel Hadas	Carole Oles
Toni Morrison			Gregory Orr	Beatrice Ann Hawley	
Lore Segal			David St. John	Alice Hoffman	
Mark Strand			Susan Richards Shreve	Cleopatra Mathis	
May Swenson			Leon Shtainmetz	David Milopky	
Nancy Willard				Edward Mooney	
Geoffrey Wolff				Priscilla Hadley Price	
				Margaret A. Robinson	

1 9 7 7

Faculty:	Associates:	Speakers:	Fellows:	Scholars:	Visitors:
Robert Pack, *Director*	Terrence Des Pres	Daniel Halpern	Donald Chankin	Richard Grayson	Georges Borchardt
Marvin Bell	Richard Ford		Joseph DiPrisco	Michael Hefferman	Paul Gray
Stanley Elkin	Tess Gallagher		Laura Gilpin	John McKernan	Daniel Halpern
John Gardner	Tom Gavin		David Huddle	Dannye Romine	Richard Marek
John Irving	Carol Muske		Gail Kessler	Jane Smiley	John Frederick Nims
Maxine Kumin	Tim O'Brien		Sydney Lea	Elizabeth Spires	
William Meredith	Ira Sadoff		George Marlen	Donna Stein	
Toni Morrison			Marilynne Roach	Mary Swander	
Charles Simic			Raymond Sokolov	Jonathan Webster	
Mark Strand			Ellen Bryant Voigt	Susan Wood	
Nancy Willard			Blanche Willoughby		
Geoffrey Wolff					
Hilma Wolitzer					

1 9 7 8

Faculty:	Associates:	Speakers:	Fellows:	Scholars:	
Robert Pack, *Director*	Richard Ford	Judy Blume	James Applewhite	Anthony Abbott	Emily Lambert
Marvin Bell	David Huddle	Nancy Evans	Dorothy Gallagher	Arlene Biggs	Robert Louthau
Stanley Elkin	Ira Sadoff	Kathy Fury	Don Hendrie, Jr.	Beth Brown	John Morgan
George P. Elliott	Susan Richards Shreve	Walter Goodman	Charlotte Koplinka	Jane Butler	Greg Pape
John Gardner	Ellen Bryant Voigt	Richard Marek	Gregory Maguire	Philip Cioffari	Douglas A. Pike
Gail Godwin			Gail Mazure	Glenndale Defoe, Jr.	David Rosner
Howard Nemerov			Judith Moffett	Scott Edelstein	Annieliese Schultz
Linda Pastan			Craig Nova	Carol Rita Henrickson	Todd Shasser
Stanley Plumly			Ellen Schwamm	Joan Johnson	Candice Ward
Nancy Willard			Allen Weir		
Geoffrey Wolff			Meredith Sue Willis		
Hilma Wolitzer					

1 9 7 9 *

Faculty:	*Associates:*	*Speakers:*	*Fellows:*	*Scholars:*
Robert Pack, *Director*	Terrence Des Pres	David Godine	Michael Angellela	Linsey Abrams
John Gardner	David Huddle	Walter Goodman	Donald E. Axinn	Julia Alvarez
Gail Godwin	Judith Moffett	Paul Gray	Mally Cox-Chapman	John M. Barrett
John Irving	Steve Orlen	Hilda Gregory	Sara Ann Friedman	James Bennett
Donald Justice	Ronni Sandroff	David Hadas	Carol Frost	Christopher Bursk
David Madden	Ellen Bryant Voigt	Jean Naggar	Pamela Hadas	Marilyn Coffey
Howard Nemerov		Eileen Schnurr	Ron Hansen	Meg Dodds
Tim O'Brien			Larry Heinemann	Mary Ellen Donovan
Linda Pastan			Robert Houston	Robert Dunn
Stanley Plumly			Judith Moffett	Lynn Emanuel
Lore Segal			Carole Oles	Robert A. Hedin
Nancy Willard			Steve Orlen	Alan Hines
Geoffrey Wolff			Carolyn Polesi	Joan Kobin
			Ron Powers	Bernard Meredith
			Mary Robinson	Karen Petrovich
			Sanford J. Smoller	Nancy Rubin
				Diane Stevenson
				Carolyne Lee Wright

1 9 8 0

Faculty:	*Associates:*	*Speakers:*	*Fellows:*	*Scholars:*
Robert Pack, *Director*	Mally Cox-Chapman	Michael Curtis	Elizabeth Arthur	Deborah Burnham
Michael Arlen	Pamela Hadas	David Godine	Patricia Baehr	Suzanne Doyle
Marvin Bell	Ron Hansen	Paul Gray	David Haward Bain	Frank Faulkner
Stanley Elkin	Robert Houston	Jean Naggar	Suzanne Berger	Kay Baker Gaston
Seymour Epstein	Judith Moffett	Nat Sobel	Michael Blumenthal	Andrew Hudgins
John Gardner	Steve Orlen		James Bowden	Kevin McIlvoy
Gail Godwin	Ron Powers		Ambrose Clancy	James Paul
Howard Nemerov			Deborah Clifford	David Schloss
Tim O'Brien			William V. Davis	Howard Smith
Linda Pastan			Paul Mariani	Janice Lee Smith
Stanley Plumly			David Martin	Karen Haas Smith
Nancy Willard			Judy Mearian	Sharon Smith
			Mary Morris	Rennard Strickland
			Bob Reiss	Julia Thacker
			Marcia Southwick	Daniel Thrapp
			Stephen Tapscott	Eric Trethewey
			Nancy Thayer	Edward Zorensky
			Stephanie Tolan	
			Susan Wood	

*Administrator, 1979–   : Stanley Bates.

1 9 8 1

Faculty:	Associates:	Speakers:	Fellows:	Scholars:
Robert Pack, *Director*	David Haward Bain	Georges Borchardt	Steven Bauer	Diane Benedict
Marvin Bell	Terrence Des Pres	Michael Curtis	Jared Carter	Lady Borton
Stanley Elkin	Pamela Hadas	Peter Davison	Margaret Coel	Teresa Cader
John Gardner	Ron Hansen	Paul Gray	Peter Cooley	Michael Collier
John Irving	Robert Houston	Maria Guarnaschelli	Stephen Corey	Steven Cramer
Erica Jong	Paul Mariani	Joyce Johnson	Page Edwards	Cornelius Eady
William Matthews	Mary Morris	Woody Klein	Roland Flint	Sandra H. Flowers
Howard Nemerov	Carol Oles	Esther Newberg	Reginald Gibbons	Alvin Handelman
Tim O'Brien		Nat Sobel	Stephen Hunter	Sharon Lerch
Linda Pastan		Alice Turner	Brana Lobel	Caroline Marshall
Ron Powers			Tom McDonugh	Florri McMillan
William Stafford			Betsy Sachs	Lynn O'Malley
Geoffrey Wolff			Gjertrud Schnackenberg	Deborah Pope
Hilma Wolitzer			Eleanora Tate	Joyce Renwick
			David Traxel	Marieve Rugo
			Bruce Weigl	Kenneth Smith
			Meg Wolitzer	Lisa Steinman

1 9 8 2

Faculty:	Associates:	Speakers:	Fellows:	Scholars:
Robert Pack, *Director*	David Haward Bain	Dominick Abel	Joanne Bario	David Baker
Marvin Bell	Terrence Des Pres	David Godine	Greg Barron	Leslie Boone
Jerome Charyn	Page Edwards	Maria Guarnaschelli	Douglas Bauer	Judith Ortiz Cofer
Stanley Elkin	Carolyn Forché	Joyce Johnson	Diane Benedict	Robert Cording
John Gardner	Pamela Hadas	Stanley Lindberg	Pat Crickenberger	Mary Hood
Gail Godwin	Ron Hansen	Peter Stitt	Robert Finch	Diane Lefer
William Matthews	David Huddle	Jane Warth	Mark Harris	Nancy Mairs
Howard Nemerov	Sydney Lea		Ben Howard	William McDonald
Tim O'Brien	Mary Morris		Howard Kohn	Mary Pope Osborne
Linda Pastan	Carole Oles		Gary Margolis	James Shepard
Ron Powers			Catherine Petroski	James Simmerman
Mark Strand			Wyatt Prunty	Robert Stewart
Hilma Wolitzer			Ira Rosen	Laurie Stroblas
			Sherod Santos	Philip Szcubeleck
			David Small	Sue Ellen Thompson
			Susan Snively	Gary Zebrun
			Richard Tillinghast	
			William Zaranka	

1 9 8 3

Faculty:	*Associates:*	*Speakers:*	*Fellows:*	*Scholars:*
Robert Pack, *Director*	David Haward Bain	Mally Cox-Chapman	Clare Bell	Sandra Alcosser
Marvin Bell	Page Edwards	Michael Curtis	Michael Brondoli	Agha Shahid Ali
Jerome Charyn	Robert Finch	David Godine	Scott Bunn	Julia Alvarez
John Irving	Carolyn Forch)	Paul Gray	Ron Carlson	Michael Cunningham
Galway Kinnell	Pamela Hadas	Howard Kohn	Elizabeth Einstein	Trip Gabriel
William Matthews	Ron Hansen	Paul Mariani	Rick Fields	Peter Gordon
Howard Nemerov	David Huddle	Jean Naggar	Eric Goodman	Amy Hempel
Tim O'Brien	Sydney Lea	Betsy Sachs	William Hathaway	Margot Livesey
Linda Pastan	Mary Morris		Ursula Hegi	Gardner McFall
Ron Powers	Carole Oles		Edward Hirsch	William McGowan
Robert Stone	Wyatt Prunty		T. R. Hummer	Faye Moskowitz
Nancy Willard	Bob Reiss		Richard Jackson	Sarah Provost
Hilma Wolitzer			Joyce Johnson	Bob Shacochis
			Susan Mitchell	Arthur Smith
			Ellen Pall	Sharon Sheehe Stark
			James Shepard	Thomas Swiss
			Jim Simmerman	Jami Lynn Wolf
			David Wojahn	

1 9 8 4

Faculty:	*Associates:*	*Speakers:*	*Fellows:*	*Scholars:*
Robert Pack, *Director*	Elizabeth Arthur	Rob Cowley	Charles Baxter	Miriam Berkley
Marvin Bell	David Haward Bain	Page Cuddy	Lady Borton	Patricia Clark
Jerome Charyn	Steven Bauer	John Elder	Alice Fulton	Stephen Dowdall
Nicholas Delbanco	Robert Finch	David Godine	Emily Grosholz	Elizabeth Evans
Stanley Elkin	Thomas Gavin	Ellen Levine	Richard Hawley	Kathy Fagan
Donald Justice	Pamela Hadas	Dan Menaker	Richard Kenney	David Graham
William Matthews	Ron Hansen	Eileen Schnurr	Craig Lesley	Kathleen Lawrence
Linda Pastan	Robert Houston		Nancy Mairs	Irene McKinney
Ron Powers	David Huddle		Jay Parini	Maris Nichols
Francine Prose	Joyce Johnson		Meredith Pierce	Jean Nordhaus
Mark Strand	Carole Oles		Tom Sleigh	Nicholas Samaras
Nancy Willard	Wyatt Prunty		Sharon Sheehe Stark	Linda Svendsen
Hilma Wolitzer	Bob Reiss		Chase Twichell	Bruce Weber
	Richard Tillinghast		Norman Williams	
			Baron Wormser	

1 9 8 5

Faculty:

Robert Pack, *Director*
Marvin Bell
Stanley Elkin
Donald Justice
Paul Mariani
William Matthews
Tim O'Brien
Linda Pastan
Ron Powers
Francine Prose
Mark Strand
Nancy Willard
Geoffrey Wolff
Hilma Wolitzer

Associates:

David Haward Bain
Thomas Gavin
Ron Hansen
Robert Houston
David Huddle
Joyce Johnson
Sydney Lea
Judith Moffett
Carole Oles
Jay Parini
Wyatt Prunty
Ellen Schwamm
Richard Tillinghast

Speakers:

Stanley Bates
Page Cuddy
David Godine
Paul Gray
Elizabeth Grossman
Wendy Weil

Fellows:

James Brown
Martha Collins
Lynn Emanuel
Ben Green
Kent Haruf
Amy Hempel
Alan Hines
Andrew Hudgins
Mark Jarman
Fred Kaplan
Faye Moskowitz
Mary Pope Osborne
Bin Ramke
Bob Shacochis
Nancy Tilly
Eric Trethewey
Leslie Ullman

Scholars:

Victoria Amador
Barri Armitage
Randolph Bates
Robert Boswell
Jim Clark
Perry Glasser
Kathleen Hill
Gregg Hodges
Sharyn Layfield
Lynda Leidiger
Antonya Nelson
Peter Nelson
Lynn O'Malley
Hilda Raz
Louis Skipper
Katherine Soniat
Norman Stock
Marly Swick
Donna Tepper

1 9 8 6

Faculty:

Robert Pack, *Director*
Nicholas Delbanco
Donald Justice
Philip Levine
Paul Mariani
William Matthews
Tim O'Brien
Linda Pastan
Ron Powers
Francine Prose
Lynne Sharon Schwartz
Lore Segal
Dan Wakefield
Nancy Willard

Associates:

David Haward Bain
Alice Fulton
Thomas Gavin
Edward Hirsch
Robert Houston
Mark Jarman
Joyce Johnson
Mary Morris
Carole Oles
Ellen Pall
Wyatt Prunty
Bob Reiss

Speakers:

Michael Curtis
Betsy Davidson
David Godine
Arnold Goodman
Elise Goodman
Joyce Carol Oates
John Pickering
Alice Turner

Fellows:

Sandra Alcosser
Julia Alvarez
Jamie Callan
Michael Collier
Michael Cunningham
Deborah Digges
Cornelius Eady
Philip Graham
Rolly Kent
Kathleen Lawrence
Margot Livesey
Don Mitchell
David Shields
Janice Lee Smith
Kenneth Smith
Thomas Swiss
Alan Weisman

Scholars:

Lynn Arditi
Robin Behn
Brian Cochran
Andre Dubus III
Ann Fletcher
Wanda Fries
Joyce James
Richard Lyons
Judson Mitcham
Elaine Mott
Daniel O'Brien
Barbara Penn
Gerald Shapiro
Judith Slater
Lew Steiger

1 9 8 7

Faculty:	Associates:	Speakers:	Fellows:	Scholars:
Robert Pack, *Director*	Julia Alvarez	Lisa Bain	Agha Shahid Ali	Gail Adams
Marvin Bell	Elizabeth Arthur	Russell Banks	Don Belton	Penelope Austin
Nicholas Delbanco	David Haward Bain	Philip Church	Mark Childress	Andrea Barrett
Donald Justice	Steven Bauer	John Elder	Judith Ortiz Cofer	Jane Bradley
David Madden	Ron Hansen	Robert Finch	Steven Cramer	Ellen Drew
Paul Mariani	Robert Houston	David Godine	Eloise Bradley Fink	Katherine Ellison
William Matthews	David Huddle	Maria Guarnaschelli	Philip Gerard	Laura Fargas
Tim O'Brien	Mark Jarman	Maura High	Marianne Gingher	John Howland
Linda Pastan	Joyce Johnson	Richard Jackson	Mark Hertsgaard	Martin McGovern
Ron Powers	Carole Oles	Don Mitchell	Ann Hood	Tom Miller
Francine Prose	Jay Parini	Amy Pastan	Christopher Leland	Patricia O'Brien
Lore Segal	Wyatt Prunty	Hilda Raz	Walter Mead	Scott Olsen
Nancy Willard	Bob Reiss		George Murphy	Helen Schulman
Hilma Wolitzer	David St. John		Jean Nordhaus	Ingrid Smith
	Sharon Sheehe Stark		Samuel Pickering	Ron Smith
			Arthur Smith	Bill Wadsworth
			Michael Spence	Michele Wolf
			Sue Ellen Thompson	

1 9 8 8

Faculty:	Associates:	Speakers:	Fellows:	Scholars:
Robert Pack, *Director*	Julia Alvarez	Lisa Bain	Judith Baumel	Adrienne Bond
Russell Banks	David Haward Bain	Michael Curtis	Robin Behn	Bruce Bond
Nicholas Delbanco	Carol Frost	David Godine	Christopher Buckley	Robert Bradley
Donald Justice	Thomas Gavin	Maura High	Henri Cole	Bill Brown
Philip Levine	Richard Hawley	T. R. Hummer	Katherine Ellison	Stacey Chase
Paul Mariani	Ann Hood	Ellen Levine	Carole Glickfeld	Andrew Cox
William Matthews	David Huddle	Jean Naggar	Barbara Haas	Chard deNiord
Tim O'Brien	Richard Jackson	William Pritchard	Lesley Hazleton	Normandi Ellis
Linda Pastan	Mark Jarman	Ellen Bryant Voigt	John Hildebrand	Ed Falco
Ron Powers	Joyce Johnson		Garrett Hongo	Peter Liotta
Francine Prose	Jay Parini		Marie Howe	Janice Marino
Lynne Sharon Schwartz	Wyatt Prunty		Alice Mattison	Connie Porter
Nancy Willard	Bob Reiss		Keven McIlvoy	Jan Reynolds
Hilma Wolitzer	Sharon Sheehe Stark		Reginald McKnight	Suzanne Rhodenbaugh
			Don Metz	Clare Rossini
			Katherine Soniat	Michael Ruhlman
			Garrett Weyr	Pamela Schirmeister
			Robert Wrigley	Janet Singleton
				Douglas Whynott

1 9 8 9

Faculty:

Robert Pack, *Director*
Marvin Bell
Rosellen Brown
Nicholas Delbanco
David Huddle
Donald Justice
William Matthews
Tim O'Brien
Linda Pastan
Ron Powers
Lore Segal
Ellen Bryant Voigt
Nancy Willard
Hilma Wolitzer

Associates:

Carol Frost
Thomas Gavin
Marianne Gingher
Richard Hawley
Ann Hood
Robert Houston
Richard Jackson
Margot Livesey
Don Mitchell
Carole Oles
Wyatt Prunty
Bob Reiss
James Shepard
Sharon Sheehe Stark

Speakers:

Jim Atwater
Lisa Bain
David Godine
T. R. Hummer
James Landis
Francine Prose
Carol Houck Smith

Fellows:

David Baker
Andrea Barrett
Rick Bass
Ted Conover
Joseph Duemer
Tony Eprile
Frank Gaspar
Marie Howe
Jane LeCompte
Phillis Levin
Jean McGarry
Christopher Merrill
Hilda Raz
Susan Rosowski
Helen Schulman
Katharine Stall
Stuart Stevens
Julia Wendell

Scholars:

Michelle Boisseau
Dina Coe
Sheila Dietz-Bonenberger
Lucia Getsai
Mary Grimm
Susan Holahan
Monty Leitch
Brian McCormick
Walter Mosley
Chad Oness
Joyce Renwick
Chris Spain
David Tammer
Michael Taylor
Donna Trussell

1 9 9 0

Faculty:

Robert Pack, *Director*
Marvin Bell
Rosellen Brown
David Huddle
John Irving
Donald Justice
Paul Mariani
Tim O'Brien
Linda Pastan
Ron Powers
Ellen Bryant Voigt
Nancy Willard

Associates:

Andrea Barrett
Ted Conover
Ann Hood
Robert Houston
T. R. Hummer
Mark Jarman
Margot Livesey
Jean McGarry
Reginald McKnight
Carole Oles
Bob Reiss
James Shepard

Speakers:

Lisa Bain
David Baker
Virginia Barber
Michael Curtis
David Godine
Camille Hykes
Richard Jackson
Gary Margolis
Francine Prose

Fellows:

Brian Berkey
Larry Brown
Rand Cooper
Gerard Gormley
Eddy Harris
Juan Herrera
Marie Howe
Brigit Kelly
Roger King
Edward Kleinschmidt
Jeanne Larsen
Dorianne Laux
Melissa Lentricchia
Geoffrey O'Gara
William Olsen
Leon Stokesbury
Susan Swan
Gary Young

Scholars:

Kim Addonizio
Andrea Hollander Budy
Kevin Clark
Michael Conniff
Jennifer Egan
Nancy Eimers
Ann Finkbeiner
Matthew Furbush
Sharon Hashimoto
Charlotte Holmes
David Lynn
Richard Neumann
Chad Oness
James Solheim

1 9 9 1

Faculty:

Robert Pack, *Director*
Nicholas Delbanco
Ron Hansen
David Huddle
Philip Levine
Paul Mariani
William Matthews
Tim O'Brien
Linda Pastan
Ron Powers
Francine Prose
Ellen Bryant Voigt
Nancy Willard
Hilma Wolitzer

Associates:

Andrea Barrett
Larry Brown
Judith Ortiz Cofer
Carol Frost
Emily Grosholz
Richard Hawley
Amy Hempel
Ann Hood
T. R. Hummer
Richard Jackson
Mark Jarman
Margot Livesey
Jean McGarry
Don Mitchell
James Shepard

Speakers:

Virginia Barber
Emilie Buchwald
Michael Curtis
David Godine
Walter Goodman
Camille Hykes
Joyce Johnson
James Landis
Jay Parini
Sallie Sheldon

Visitors:

William Meredith

Fellows:

Angela Ball
Claire Bateman
Geraldine Connolly
Mark Cox
Tracy Daugherty
Philip Deaver
Chard deNiord
Pamela Frierson
Brett Lott
Jill Allyn Rosser
Dennis Sampson
Steven Schwartz
Dinitia Smith
Stephen Stark
Susan Straight
Richard Terrill

Scholars:

Julian Anderson
Peter Chilson
Pamela Ditchoff
Geoffrey Douglas
Meg Files
Tony Grooms
Emily Hammond
Ann Harleman
Dianna Henning
Seaborn Jones
Marshall Klimasewski
Jessica Neely
Ionna Veronika Warwick
Therese Witek

1 9 9 2

Faculty:

Robert Pack, *Director*
Rosellen Brown
David Huddle
Donald Justice
William Matthews
Tim O'Brien
Jay Parini
Linda Pastan
Ron Powers
Francine Prose
Mark Strand
Ellen Bryant Voigt
Nancy Willard
Hilma Wolitzer

Associates:

Andrea Barrett
Larry Brown
Judith Ortiz Cofer
Michael Collier
Carol Frost
Richard Hawley
Ann Hood
Richard Jackson
Margot Livesey
Gary Margolis
Don Mitchell
Jean Nordhaus
Bob Reiss
Helen Schulman
Dinitia Smith
Stephen Stark

Speakers:

Virginia Barber
Nicholas Clifford
John Elder
Robert Finch
David Godine
Robert Houston
Camille Hykes
Gail Lawrence
Eileen Schnurr
Carol Houck Smith
Richard Wilbur

Fellows:

Pinckney Benedict
Bruce Bond
Teresa Cader
Jeff Danziger
Judith Hall
James Harms
Ehud Havazelet
Pam Houston
Laura Kasischke
James Kilgo
Judson Mitcham
Antonya Nelson
Leila Philip
Connie Porter
William Roorbach
Nicholas Samaras
Jack Stephens
Elaine Terranova

Scholars:

Cynthia Atkins
Gerard Donovan
Mary Edsall
Jack Hayes
Maurice Kilwein-Guevara
Lisa Knopp
Lynne Kuderko
Beth Livermore
Susan Luzzaro
Lee Martin
Dorien Ross
Donna Stein
Constance Warloe
Phillip Welch

NOTES

P. 5: Brewster Baldwin, "Notes on the Geology of Vermont, an Ancient Continental Margin," Middlebury College, 1977; Baldwin, "Geology of Vermont," *Earth Science* 35, no. 3; Parker E. Calkin, "Surficial Geology of the Middlebury 15' Quadrangle, Vermont," *Report to the State Geologist,* 1965; George H. Perkins, *Report of the State Geologist* 7, 1909–1910; Bradford E. Van Diver, *Roadside Geology of Vermont and New Hampshire,* 1987; **pp. 5–6:** Abby Hemenway, *Vermont Historical Gazetteer,* 1868–1891.

Pp. 6–7: "a Puritan"; "My sister": Joseph Battell, undated statements (1860s), Swift Folder, Sheldon Museum, Middlebury, VT; "sleigh rides": Joseph Battell, *Yankee Boy from Home,* 1863, 205; "We would": Joseph Battell, undated statement, op. cit., 7; "Unfortunately": *Yankee Boy,* 214; "Dear Cornelia": Joseph Battell to Cornelia, 5/16/66, Sheldon Museum; "staggeringly juvenile": Theodore Morrison, *Bread Loaf Writers' Conference: The First Thirty Years,* 1976, 2; West Brattleboro: *Yankee Boy,* 225; **p. 7:** "Inverness": *Yankee Boy,* 114; "I had": Ibid., 124–125; "This is": Ibid., 103–104; **p. 8:** "Perhaps we are": Joseph Battell to Philip Battell, 8/30/66, Swift Papers (1863–1869), Sheldon Museum; "by the aid": *Middlebury Register,* 7/25/66; "with several"; "the situation": Ibid., 8/29/66; **pp. 8–11:** "the fountainhead": George Perkins Marsh, *Man and Nature,* reprint 1965, ix; "Every middle-aged": Ibid., xvii; "Even now": Ibid., ix; "Some folks": Thomas E. Boyce, "Notes on the Bread Loaf Inn and Its Founder," 1930, Middlebury College Library (MCL); "They lie": Boyce to Hazel Scott, 7/20/24, MCL; "could often"; "He was above"; "sitting for hours": Clara K. Curtis, "Joseph Battell, An Appreciation," 1939, MCL; "he lived": Elsa Rauer, "Recollections of Joseph Battell," MCL; "What are you": Boyce, "Notes on Bread Loaf Inn and Its Founder," MCL; "He loved": Curtis, op. cit.; **pp. 11–12:** "incredible": Federal Writers' Project, WPA, *Vermont: A Guide to the Green Mountain State,* 1937, 273; downtown Middlebury: Glenn M. Andres, *A Walking History of Middlebury,* Sheldon Museum, 1975; "timber butchers": *Middlebury Register,* 2/26/15; **p. 12:** Joseph Battell's death: Rauer, op. cit.; *Middlebury Register,* 2/26/15, 3/5/15, 3/26/15; Boyce: Boyce, "Re The Work of T. E. Boyce for Joseph Battell," c. 1924, MCL; Inn sale and BLSE: George K. Anderson, *Bread Loaf School of English: The First Fifty Years,* Middlebury College, 1969, 9–10. A number of other papers and letters relating to Joseph Battell are at MCL and Sheldon; *Middlebury Register,* which contains many references to the Inn beginning in 1866, is bound at Sheldon.

P. 13: "in a sort": *Selected Letters of Robert Frost* (ed. Lawrance Thompson), 1964, 148f.; Robert Frost–Wilfred Davison correspondence: Ibid., 261; Cather: Anderson, op. cit., 21, 42, 135.

Pp. 15–16: "He has taken"; "arranging love": John Farrar, *The Literary Spotlight,* 1925, 185–194; **p. 31:** "Farrar was": Charles Norman, *Poets and People,* 1972, 9–12.

Pp. 16–18: "We went": Margaret Farrar to Theodore Morrison, 1975, MCL; "The people": Harriet Monroe, *Poets and Their Art,* 1926; "because everybody": Margaret Farrar, op. cit.; "eyes . . . bright": John Farrar, op. cit., 214; **pp. 19–20:** "There was": Margaret Farrar, op. cit.; "Events, some polite": Achmed Abdullah, *The Cat Had Nine Lives,* 1933, 4–5; *Selected Letters of Stephen Vincent Benét* (ed. Charles A. Fenton), 167–168; "from so meager": Charles A. Fenton, *Stephen Vincent Benét,* 1958, 222–223, 305; **pp. 20–21:** "I know": Edward Weeks, *My Green Age,* 1973, 260; "the industry": Carl Van Doren, *Sinclair Lewis: A Biographical Sketch,* 1933, 35–36; "The 1920's": Edward Weeks, "The

Schooling of an Editor," *New York Public Library Bulletin* 54, no. 6.

Pp. 21–22: "The main thing": Robert Gay to Robert Frost, 1/16/29, in Lawrance Thompson, *Robert Frost: The Years of Triumph,* 684; "unpleasant verbal": Ibid.; "mistreatment": *The Family Letters of Robert and Elinor Frost* (ed. Arnold Grade), 1972, 115–116, 128; "Have a cigar": Theodore Morrison, op. cit., 66; "Taste changes": Robert Hillyer, *A Letter to Robert Frost,* 1937, 4; **pp. 23–24:** "In time": Edward Weeks, "The Schooling"; "There was": Weeks, *My Green Age,* 261–262; "I am left": *Selected Letters of Robert Frost* (ed. Thompson), 365–366; "a much": *Literary Correspondence of Donald Davidson and Allen Tate* (ed. J. T. Fain and T. D. Young); "settled wagers": *Bookman* 73, 247; "If anyone": Allen Tate, BLSE lecture, 1940; see Peter Stanlis, "Acceptable in Heaven's Sight: Robert Frost at Bread Loaf," *Frost Centennial Essays,* vol. 3 (ed. Jac Tharpe), 1978, 256; **pp. 24–25:** *Boston Herald,* 6/15/31; *Boston Globe,* 6/15/31; **p. 25:** "I had plenty": Morrison, op. cit., 10.

Pp. 27–28: "I shall feel": Morrison to Margaret Widdemer, MCL; "I think": Morrison to John Farrar, MCL (there is a great deal of other correspondence about the 1932 session at MCL); "the conference is": Robert Gay to Morrison, 4/8/32, MCL; "It is a source": Paul Dwight Moody to Morrison, 12/4/31, MCL; "traditional forms": Morrison, *The First Thirty Years,* 13; **p. 28:** "he had solved": Catherine Drinker Bowen, Edith Mirrielees, Arthur M. Schlesinger, Jr., Wallace Stegner, *Four Portraits and One Subject: Bernard DeVoto,* 1963, 12; "Bernard DeVoto": Ibid., 3; **pp. 29–30:** "a writer": Morrison, *The First Thirty Years,* 13; "I don't": Morrison to Paul Dwight Moody, MCL; see 1932 folder for other correspondence; "the country": Morrison to Paul Dwight Moody, MCL; near-cancellation: Morrison, *The First Thirty Years,* 16–17; **p. 30:** Morrison and Frost: Ibid., 66–67; **pp. 30–31:** Dorothy Thompson, *I Saw Hitler,* 1932, 3, 13–14; "After the evening"; "an extraordinary": Morrison, *The First Thirty Years,* 17–18.

Pp. 31–33: "When we can": Wallace Stegner, *The Uneasy Chair,* 1974, 408; "sort of pater": *Chicago Daily Tribune,* 9/8/34; "to present"; "perhaps the first": *Southern Writers: A Biographical Dictionary,* 349; "progress down": *Chicago Daily Tribune,* 9/8/34; "I think": John Farrar to Morrison, MCL; "to be a writer": Morrison, *The First Thirty Years,* 47; "In the ten": *Letters of Bernard DeVoto* (ed. Wallace Stegner), 1975, 203; "a fury": Stegner, *The Uneasy Chair,* 409; "She is"; "the best looking": *Chicago Daily Tribune,* 9/8/34.

Pp. 33–34: Frost and Ransom: Thomas Daniel Young, "Our Two Worthies," *Frost Centennial Essays,* vol. 3 (ed. Jac Tharpe), 1978; "So many stories": see *The Crumb,* 1935; "Just call"; "She was": Morrison, *The First Thirty Years,* 49–50; Howard Fast: telephone interview, 3/5/87; **p. 36:** "wobble down": Morrison, *The First Thirty Years,* 67; **pp. 36–37:** "This novel": see *Author's Guild Bulletin,* Summer 1989, 14; "Although I read": James T. Farrell, "How Studs Lonigan Was Written," *The Frightened Philistines,* 1945, 84; "my recollection": Morrison, *The First Thirty Years,* 21; "Back with": Emily Clark, *Innocence Abroad,*

1937, 268–269; "If he ": Morrison, *The First Thirty Years,* 21; **p. 38:** "the best neglected": *New York Times,* 7/16/87.

Pp. 39–42: "I expect": *Selected Letters of Robert Frost* (ed. Thompson), 470; Kathleen Morrison and Robert Frost: see Kathleen Morrison, *Robert Frost: A Pictorial Chronicle,* 1974, 5–20; Lawrance Thompson and R. H. Winnick, *Robert Frost: The Later Years,* 1976, xv–xvi, 1–10; Stegner, *The Uneasy Chair,* 202–211; Donald G. Sheehy, "The Poet as Neurotic: The Official Biography of Robert Frost," *American Literature* 58, no. 3 (October 1986); these sources were augmented by several background interviews, 1985–1991; "I've had a"; "They weren't really": Frances Fox Sandmel, journal, 1938, provided to Theodore Morrison, MCL; "the best lecture": Charles H. Foster, "Robert Frost at Bread Loaf," *Frost Centennial Essays,* vol. 1, 71; "badness": Kathleen Morrison, op. cit., 18; Stegner, *The Uneasy Chair*; "Frost told me": Thompson and Winnick, op. cit., 8; **pp. 40–42:** "Mr. Morrison": Sandmel, op. cit.; "I hear": Theodore Morrison, *The First Thirty Years,* 52; Stegner and DeVoto: Wallace Stegner and Richard W. Etulain, *Conversations with Wallace Stegner on Western History and Literature,* 1983, 27–29; "Of all the poets"; "He seemed to": Stegner, *The Uneasy Chair,* 206; "Ted Morrison asked": Thompson and Winnick, op. cit., 371; see also Stegner, *The Uneasy Chair,* 206–207, and Theodore Morrison, *The First Thirty Years,* 69–70; **pp. 42–44:** "unusual friendship": *Selected Letters of Robert Frost* (ed. Thompson), 483–484; South Sea island: Stanley Burnshaw, *Robert Frost Himself,* 1986, 83; "Come to Bread Loaf": *Selected Letters of Robert Frost* (ed. Thompson), 483–484; "of the cloak": Stanley Kunitz, *Twentieth Century Authors.*

Pp. 45–46: "Jackie Mackie": Suzanne Marrs, *The Welty Collection,* 1988, 157; "Monsieur Boule": *Writers at Work IV* (ed. George Plimpton), 1976, 286; "because it": Kunitz, op. cit.; Welty's rejections: Marrs, op. cit.; **pp. 46–47:** "Its interest": *New Republic,* 7/28/40; "Whose enfant"; "the first living": John Ciardi interview, 1/85; "found the great"; "He wrote": John Holmes, "John Ciardi, Tufts Poet," *The Tuftonian,* 12/55; Porter: Robert Van Gelder, "Katherine Anne Porter at Work," *New York Times Book Review,* 4/14/40; "a pleasant": Peter Stanlis, op. cit., 268; "Auden was": Ibid., 267.

Pp. 49–52: "Everyone was": Ibid., 304–305; "Who do you": Kathleen Morrison, op. cit., 20–21; "When I use": Stanlis, op. cit., 306; "higher literary": *The Letters of Robert Frost to Louis Untermeyer* (ed. Untermeyer), 1963, 1/4/41; "Bread Loaf would": Charles Edward Eaton to author, 12/11/86, MCL; "One day while"; "Frost was politely": Stanlis, op. cit., 306–307; "He would invite"; "I was not": Eaton, op. cit.; see also Paul Mariani, *William Carlos Williams: A New World Naked,* 1981, 452–454; "I really wanted": Kunitz, op. cit.; "He was": Eaton, op. cit.; "of all things": Donald Hall, *Remembering Poets,* 1978 (enlarged later in *Their Ancient Glittering Eyes,* 1992); **pp. 52–53:** Whitman: Theodore Morrison letters, MCL, and *The Letters of Bernard DeVoto* (ed. Stegner), 112–113; "I recall him": Brendan Gill, *Here at The New Yorker,* 1975, 317; "after Untermeyer": Stegner, *The Uneasy Chair,* 124; Capote version: *Conversations with Capote,* 1985 (ed. Lawrence Grobel); **p. 54:** "It was Fletcher's": Theodore

Morrison, *The First Thirty Years,* 85; "Excellent as writing": *American Mercury,* 10/37; **pp. 55–56:** "When Frost came": Donald Hall, *Remembering Poets,* 1978, 48; "The only": Ibid., 51; "All those first": A. B. Guthrie, Jr., *The Blue Hen's Chick,* 1965, 170; "read *The Big Sky*": Ibid., 190; "The practice": Ibid., 188–189; "I wondered": Richard Wright, *Black Boy,* 1945, 217–218; "to enlighten": Michel Fabre, *The Unfinished Quest of Richard Wright,* 1973, 287; "I expected": Donald Hall to author, 10/30/89; "I found": Fabre, op. cit., 289.

Pp. 59–61: "confronted by": Walter Havighurst to author, 9/29/85; "We need": Theodore Morrison to Havighurst, 1/29/46, MCL; "has hated me": Stegner, *The Uneasy Chair,* 229; "Robert, you've": Thompson and Winnick, op. cit., 446; "DeVoto picked": Edward Cifelli, "Ciardi on Frost: An Interview," *Frost Centennial Essays,* vol. 1 (ed. Tharpe), 481; "It was team": *The Letters of Bernard DeVoto* (ed. Stegner), 51–52; "No misunderstanding": *Harper's,* 11/47; **pp. 61–62:** "I had the shaky": Harvey Breit, "Talk with A. B. Guthrie, Jr.," *New York Times Book Review,* 10/23/49; "Her genius": *The New Yorker,* 4/5/80; "impressive": Theodore Morrison, *The First Thirty Years,* 75; "superior history": Kunitz, op. cit.; "With his death": Joseph Kinsey Howard, *Strange Empire,* 1952, 3–4; "in a characteristic": Wallace Stegner, *The Uneasy Chair,* 410–411; **pp. 62–63:** "you know": *Paris Review* 2, 42; "turning largely": Theodore Morrison to President Samuel S. Stratton, 10/7/46, MCL.

Pp. 63–65: "Fear and suspicion": Owen Lattimore, *Ordeal by Slander,* 1950, 186, 188; "[W]ould the air": Theodore Morrison, *The First Thirty Years,* 91; "I am not a judge": Theodore Morrison, "Introduction of Owen Lattimore," BLWC 1950, MCL; Sloane and FBI: Athan G. Theoharis and John Stuart Cox, "A Tale of Two Authors: J. Edgar Hoover, Political Censor," *Author's Guild Bulletin,* Summer 1989; Untermeyer's "loyalty": Burnshaw, op. cit., 81–82; **pp. 67–68:** "the politics": M. E. Witherspoon to author, 11/12/86; "This kind of": Kunitz, op. cit.; "Along the pasture": Elizabeth Spencer to author, 12/11/85; "There are": Kunitz, op. cit.; "His personal elegance": Theodore Morrison, *The First Thirty Years,* 75; interview, 1985; "was life-saving": M. E. Witherspoon to author, 11/12/86 and 11/26/86; **pp. 68–69:** "I had to give": May Sarton to author, 9/13/85; "I was not": Ibid.

Pp. 69–71: "Over twenty"; "It was a time"; "The obvious successor": Theodore Morrison, *The First Thirty Years,* 92; interviews and letters to author, 1985–1986; "In Treman's": Stegner, *The Uneasy Chair,* 377.

Pp. 73–74: "it is going": John Ciardi to Stephen A. Freeman, 11/20/55, MCL [Note: as spotty as the administrative documentation is for the Morrison era, one may find a rich array of correspondence about the BLWC among the Paul M. Cubeta papers at MCL, 1955–1964]; "It's much too": Ciardi to Paul M. Cubeta, 2/1/56, MCL; "a man who": Cifelli, op. cit., 479; interviews, 1/85; "Each will be": Ciardi to Cubeta, 2/14/56; **pp. 74–75:** Treman: Paxton Davis to author, 2/20/89; "As a newspaperman": Herbert A. Kenny to author, undated letters, 1989; Ciardi absent in Rome: Ciardi to Cubeta, 4/8/56, 7/20/56, MCL;

"I specialize": *New York Times,* 9/26/88; **pp. 76–78:** "For many years": William Sloane to Ciardi, 5/27/55, MCL; "an offensively": *Saturday Review,* 1/12/57; "I am not yet": *Saturday Review,* 3/9/57; "the rhubarb": Cubeta to Stephen A. Freeman, 6/12/57, MCL; Cronin report: *St. Louis Post-Dispatch,* 9/21/57.

P. 78: "All I do": Ciardi to Cubeta, undated letter, early 1958, MCL; "Scratch Phil Roth": Cubeta to Ciardi, 6/13/58, MCL, and see Cubeta to Ciardi, 1/19/61, MCL; "the dumbest question": John Ciardi, interview, Key West, 1/85, and Cifelli, op. cit., 483–484.

Pp. 79–80: "All I wanted": *Writers at Work IV* (ed. Plimpton), 400; "I thought": Ibid., and *Contemporary Authors,* New Revision Series, III, 491; "The most important": *Writers at Work IV* (ed. Plimpton), 402; Holmes warned Kumin: Elaine Showalter and Carol Smith, "A Nurturing Relationship: A Conversation with Anne Sexton and Maxine Kumin, April 15, 1974," *Women's Studies* 4 (1976), 121–122; "He worked": *Writers at Work IV* (ed. Plimpton), 406; "How silly": *Anne Sexton, A Self-Portrait in Letters* (ed. Linda Gray Sexton and Lois Ames), 1977, 72; "I am going": Ibid., 82; **pp. 80–82:** "Letter just received": Ciardi to Sloane and Cubeta, 5/8/59, MCL; "something of a": Cubeta to Ciardi, 2/2/59, MCL; "I was intrigued": Ralph Ellison, *Shadow and Act,* 1964; "A mountain": Alan Cheuse to author, 11/88; "I never had": Cubeta to George Starbuck, 9/17/59, MCL; "I am beginning": *Anne Sexton: A Self Portrait in Letters* (ed. Sexton and Ames), 83.

Pp. 82–84: "Chance to putter": Ciardi to Cubeta, undated letter, April 1960, MCL; "I wish": Cubeta to Ciardi, 5/4/60, MCL; "Ciardi leaves": Cubeta to William Raney, 2/14/62, MCL; Yates: John Ciardi, interview, Key West, 1/85, and Bread Loaf administrative files, 1962; "Getting Kennedy": Ciardi to Cubeta, undated letter, March 1961, MCL; Julia Child: Julia Child to author, 11/13/87, and Stegner, *The Uneasy Chair,* 426; **pp. 84–85:** Turco's experiences: Lewis Turco to author, 9/12/85, 9/19/85; "At the end": John Ciardi, interview, Key West, 1/85, and Cifelli, op. cit., 484.

Pp. 88–89: "the poet of the": *New Republic,* 5/4/42; Nelson Algren and Russell Banks: Banks, Foreword to Algren's *A Walk on the Wild Side,* 1989; **p. 89:** little girl: Leslie Garis, "Didion and Dunne: The Rewards of a Literary Marriage," *New York Times Magazine,* 2/8/87, and *Writers at Work V* (ed. Plimpton), 342–343; "I didn't realize": Ibid.; "a sense of": Ibid., 344; "I wanted": Ibid., 347; "When I finished": Ibid., 346; "hard drinkers"; "I just tended": Ibid., 345; **pp. 89–91:** all material on Robert Pack from interviews, 1987–1990.

Pp. 91–92: Shirley Jackson: Lenemaja Friedman, *Shirley Jackson,* 1975; "from time to time": Gill, op. cit., 228; "She became": Ibid., 246–247.

Pp. 94–95: "It treated": Diane Wakoski to author, 12/16/86, and Wakoski, "Dionysian Memories," *John Ciardi: Measure of the Man* (ed. Vince Clemente), 1987; "It's slightly": Lewis Turco to author, 9/19/85.

Pp. 95–96: "I went off": Doris G. Bargen, *The Fiction of Stanley Elkin,* 1980, 221; Seymour Epstein: Epstein to author, 1988; pp. 96–97: "Once, in 1968": Judson Jerome to author, 1988, and Jerome, "John Ciardi and I," *Negative Capability* 7, nos. 3 and 4, 58; "Later in the": Ibid., 60; "We can all": Ibid., 60–61, and compare to Jerome, "Ciardi Remembered," *John Ciardi: Measure of the Man* (ed. Vince Clemente), 1987, 135–140.

Pp. 97–98: Mailer and *Armies*: Hilary Mills, *Mailer: A Biography,* 1982, 298–300; "My god": Dave Etter to author, 11/26/86 and 12/15/86; Ciardi and Martin: Interviews with John Ciardi, 1985, Edward Martin, 1990, and a number of other faculty members and fellows; "as a girl": *St. Louis Post-Dispatch,* 3/3/68; "who was probably": Freeman to Ciardi, 4/3/68, with clipping attached, MCL; "Hers is in fact": Ciardi to Freeman, 4/5/68, and see Ciardi to Martin, 4/5/68, MCL, as an indication of how unimportant the matter was to Ciardi.

Pp. 98–99: "among the most": Vassar Miller to author, undated letter, 1989; "magnetic": Robert Cormier to author, 12/12/86.

P. 99: "Say it with flowers": *Contemporary Authors,* New Revision Series, XXI, 227; "By the end": *Contemporary Authors,* Autobiography Series, VIII, 216; Kumin and Sexton: see Anne Sexton notes above; "I can still hear": Maxine Kumin, "John Ciardi and the Witch of Fungi," *John Ciardi: Measure of the Man* (ed. Vince Clemente), 1987, 132; "A poem": from a lecture at Bread Loaf; Julia Alvarez: interview, 10/90; "the band showed": Dave Etter to author, 11/26/86 and 12/15/86.

Pp. 101–102: "the men in the": sixties troubles: John Ciardi, interviews, 1/85; Martin and flower child: Edward A. Martin, "Frost Heaves," *Middlebury College News Letter* 43, no. 3; "Looking back": John Williams, "Looking for John Ciardi at Bread Loaf," *John Ciardi: Measure of the Man* (ed. Vince Clemente), 1987, 128; "His deepfelt comments"; "a Marlon Brando"; "the look of a street"; "History is"; "Let the story": Alan Caruba, "Bread Loaf 1970: Boot Camp for Writers," *Publishers Weekly,* 9/21/70; p. 103: "He gave me": Hilma Wolitzer, interview, 8/90.

Pp. 104–109: "It has been fairly easy": Stegner, *The Uneasy Chair,* 411; "the kids would"; final clinic; Ciardi and Martin break: remarkably, interviews with John Ciardi in 1/85, follow-up correspondence, and interviews with Edward A. Martin in 1990 and with other staff members present substantially agree with L. Rust Hills, "We Believe in the Maestro System," *Audience* (May–June 1972); the accounts differ not in content but in interpretation—which of course ranges widely; p. 107: "When you want"; "to get things right": John Ciardi, interview, 1/85; Ciardi's angry reading was verified by three Bread Loafers present; Ciardi to Armstrong, 8/2/72, MCL.

P. 108: "Exit line": several versions exist—the one here was in circulation in 1972; "I have nothing": John Ciardi, interviews, 1/85; Robert Pack, interviews, 1990.

Pp. 110–111: "The famous": Hilda Gregory, "A Green Time," *Prairie Schooner* 47, no. 3, 204; "I heard this": Carol McCabe, "The Plot Was Thin but, Oh, Those Characters," *Middlebury College News Letter,* Summer 1975, 36; "He looked": Dan Johnson to author, 9/89; "gravelly and": Katie Lyle, "Confessions of a Bread Loaf Fellow 1973," MS, MCL; "she seemed very": Anthony Hecht to author, 9/21/85; "surrounded": Lyle, op. cit.; "We sit still": Gregory, op. cit., 204.

Pp. 111–113: "Only a few": Hecht, op. cit.; "Gardner had a crewcut": Raymond Carver, Foreword to John Gardner, *On Becoming a Novelist,* 1983, xiii–xiv; "It was a": Ibid., xiv; Mona Van Duyn: Marvin Bell, interviews, 8/89, 8/90; "Give me six": Linda Pastan, interview, 8/90.

Pp. 114–117: John Irving quotations: John Irving, interview, 8/90; Tim O'Brien quotations: Tim O'Brien, interview, 8/90; "She whispered": Hilma Wolitzer, interview, 8/90; "a bad man": Geoffrey Wolff, Bread Loaf reading, 1976; Wolff's reading: Marvin Bell, interview, 8/90; "a philosopher": Ibid.

P. 119: Pack and Martin split: interviews with Robert Pack and Edward A. Martin, twelve years later, continue to exhibit their "philosophical differences" in running a writers' conference. The differences really boil down to personality and approach. When they are contrasted with the much more public (and actively publicized) problems between Martin and Ciardi, it seems fitting to let sleeping nuances lie.

P. 126: Irving's reservations: John Irving, conversation, 8/83, and interview, 8/90.

P. 127: "We read five": John Gardner, "How Does One Know If One's a Writer," 1981 lecture MS, MCL, substantially the same as in Gardner, *On Becoming a Novelist,* 1983.

P. 129: "Our talks (good)": John Ciardi to author, 1/25/85.

Pp. 129–131: "When . . .": The first respondent to answer all correctly will win a jug of Douglas Orchard (Shoreham, VT) cider, a package of Cream Hill lamb chops, and a Bread Loaf T-shirt; decision of the editors is final.

P. 137: Robert Frost, "The Doctrine of Excursions: A Preface," *Bread Loaf Anthology,* 1939.

ACKNOWLEDGMENTS

This book has been a long time in coming, and I am in the debt of many people for encouragement, aid, and advice extended along the way. Bread Loaf's three great directors, Theodore Morrison, John Ciardi, and Robert Pack, who together represent more than sixty-five years of involvement with the conference, were generous in granting me time for interviews and patient in answering my many follow-up queries. In particular, I must single out my friend and colleague Robert Pack, whose enthusiasm and support were invaluable. Bob's faith and energy are remarkable, as anyone who knows him can attest. My gratitude is boundless.

Carol Knauss, secretary to the Writers' Conference, with her generosity, intuition, and indefatigable nature, has been helpful and inspirational in a thousand ways in the twelve years of our friendship.

Ellen Levine, literary agent and friend, maintained her always infectious enthusiasm during the many twists and turns of this project.

A number of members of the Middlebury College community deserve special thanks—especially Nicholas Clifford, historian and novelist, whose support while serving as college provost made some of this book's research, and indeed its very publication, possible. John McCardell, president of the college, has been supportive throughout. Michael Schoenfeld, Ronald Liebowitz, and Ron Nief each extended many courtesies. I would also like to thank David Ginevan, Bruce Peterson, and Olin Robison. Edward Martin of the Middlebury English Department was also extremely helpful. I think it should be added here that none of the above persons, serving in various official capacities at Middlebury, sought to influence anything that I was to write, nor indeed did anyone even ask to see the manuscript until the final version was turned over to The Ecco Press; this book was begun

years before I moved to Vermont and joined the Middlebury faculty (adjunct and part time), but from the moment I began teaching, there was never even a hint of pressure to tell the Bread Loaf story in a particular way. Some of the above officials may disagree with interpretations presented in the text, which is their right—but each has contributed to the spirit of academic and scholarly freedom I've experienced at Middlebury since 1987.

Many members of various library staffs have aided in many ways. I'm grateful for the help I received at the New York Public Library and the Brooklyn Public Library during the early years of research. The superb research staff at Middlebury College's Egbert Starr Memorial Library aided in many ways; Robert Buckeye, director and curator of Middlebury's Abernethy Collection of American Literature, has never flagged in his enthusiasm and resourcefulness, nor has Kay Lauster, his assistant. Polly Darnell, director of the Sheldon Museum in Middlebury, Vermont, was always a great help.

I am grateful to the scores of Bread Loafers who contributed recollections in the form of letters, articles, interviews, photographs, and published or unpublished work—including narrative poems. My thanks go out to them all, particularly those whose contributions were graciously allowed to be quoted at length; many publishers, too, extended courtesies in allowing reprint of material under their control. (The copyright acknowledgments are included elsewhere, although of course there were many others whose contributions are evident in the narrative text.)

Marvin Bell has been generous in allowing a poem from his cycle, "At the Writers' Conference," to be used as this book's introduction and in allowing the cycle to be excerpted elsewhere in the documentary section. His comments on the manuscript were extremely helpful. I am equally thankful for the friendship and counsel of Paul Mariani, who offered many valuable suggestions. Deep thanks, also, must go to Ron Powers, Don Mitchell, Tim O'Brien, John Irving, Wallace Stegner, Steven Bauer, Bob Reiss, and Mally Cox-Chapman for particular moments of inspiration along the way.

The Windham Foundation, of Grafton, Vermont, was generous in supporting a summer-long block of undisturbed research time. I salute the important work it does in preserving New England traditions and heritage. This book was written using primarily the Wordstar word-processing program; at one point during the project, Wordstar International graciously updated my program, which I hereby acknowledge with thanks.

A comprehensive list of all the people who also aided significantly in this project would go on for many pages. I apologize for not including them here, knowing they will understand. But I would like to thank Leo Hotte, caretaker of the Bread Loaf Inn, for his many insights into the history of the place and his explanations of how it is kept going. Another good friend, the gifted photographer Tad Merrick, supervised all of the laboratory work on my suitcase of photographs and old negatives.

Daniel Halpern, poet and director of The Ecco Press, must receive my fulsome thanks for seeing the merit of this book. Ecco's Christopher Kingsley, Cathy Jewell, Steve Hill, John Fuller, and Mary Elizabeth Allen have shown skill and diplomacy in negotiating it through the publication process. Thanks also to Richard Oriolo for following my baffling design ideas and improving them so well, and to Katherine Streckfus for her fine copyediting job.

Finally, no word of this book would have been possible without the sublime support of Mary Smyth Duffy, my partner in life, who aided in many hours of research, who heard every word of the narrative as it developed and who offered uncountable improvements, who helped carry on during many daunting reverses, and whose capable editorial sensibility and intuitive artist's eye helped give shape to the documentary section of this book, with its numerous photographs and editorial extracts. Truly, no aspect of this project escaped her. My gratitude for her help and inspiration, in fact, would fill the Champlain Valley all the way to the brim of Bread Loaf Mountain.

—DAVID HAWARD BAIN
Shoreham, Vermont
February 1993

Grateful acknowledgment is hereby given to the following individuals and publishers for use of excerpts of previously copyrighted material:

Phoebe-Lou Adams (Weeks): *My Green Age* (Atlantic Monthly Press), (c) 1973 Edward Weeks; **Isaac Asimov:** *In Memory Yet Green* (Doubleday), (c) 1979 Isaac Asimov; **Russell Banks:** introduction to Nelson Algren's *A Walk on the Wild Side*, first published in *The New York Times Book Review*, November 26, 1989, (c) 1989, 1990 Russell Banks; **Marvin Bell:** "At The Writers' Conference," *New England Review* (Fall 1991), (c) 1991 Marvin Bell; **Myra, Benn, and John L. Ciardi:** *Dialogue With an Audience* by John Ciardi (Lippincott), (c) 1963 John Ciardi; introduction to William Sloane's *The Craft of Writing* (Norton), (c) 1979 John Ciardi; **Dartmouth College Library:** Robert Frost to Kathleen Morrison, (September) 1938; **Nicholas Delbanco:** Introduction to *Stillness and Shadows* by John Gardner, (c) 1986 by Nicholas Delbanco; **Pamela Ditchoff:** "Concert in the Bread Loaf Barn," (c) 1989 Pamela Ditchoff; **Doubleday and Company:** column by John Farrar in *The Bookman* (November 1926), published by Doubleday, Doran and Company; "Foreword" by Eudora Welty, *The Stories of Elizabeth Spencer*, (c) 1981 Eudora Welty; **Cornelius Eady:** "Fun," from *The Gathering of My Name* (Carnegie Mellon), (c) 1991 Cornelius Eady; **Stanley Elkin:** "My Middle Age," from *Pieces of Soap* (Simon & Schuster), (c) 1992 Stanley Elkin; **Estate of James T. Farrell** (c/o International Creative Management, Inc.): *The Frightened Philistines* (1945), (c) James T. Farrell; **Estate of Robert Francis and University of Massachusetts Press:** *The Trouble With Francis*, (c) 1971 Robert Francis; **Estate of Louis Untermeyer and Harcourt, Brace, and Company:** *From Another World* by Louis Untermeyer, (c) 1939 Harcourt, Brace, and Company, renewed 1969 Louis Untermeyer; **A. B. Guthrie, Jr.:** *The Blue Hen's Chick* (McGraw-Hill), (c) 1965 A. B. Guthrie, Jr.; "Introduction" by Katherine Anne Porter, *A Curtain of Green* by Eudora Welty (c) 1941 Eudora Welty; **Rust Hills:** "We Believe in the Maestro System," *Audience* (May/June 1972), (c) 1972 L. Rust Hills; **Henry Holt and Co.** and the Estate of Robert Frost: *Selected Letters of Robert Frost*, ed. Lawrance Thompson, (c) 1964 Lawrance Thompson and Holt, Rinehart and Winston; *The Letters of Robert Frost to Louis Untermeyer*, (c) 1963 Louis Untermeyer and Holt, Rinehart and Winston; **Houghton Mifflin Company:** *Anne Sexton: A Self-Portrait in Letters*, edited by Linda Gray Sexton and Lois Ames, (c) 1977 Linda Gray Sexton and Loring Conant, Jr., executors of the will of Anne Sexton; **David Huddle:** "How Much of This Story is True?", from *The Writing Habit: Essays* (Peregrine Smith), (c) 1991 David Huddle; **Judson Jerome:** "Poetry and Personality," from *John Ciardi: Measure of the Man*, ed. Vince Clemente (Arkansas), (c) 1987 Judson Jerome; **Maxine Kumin:** "John Ciardi and the Witch of Fungi," from *John Ciardi: Measure of the Man*, ed. Vince Clemente (Arkansas), (c) 1987 Maxine Kumin; **Paul Mariani:** *William Carlos Williams: A New World Naked* (McGraw-Hill), (c) 1981 Paul Mariani; **Christopher Merrill:** "Bread Loaf: Age and Quality," (c) 1988 Christopher Merrill; **Middlebury College and the Abernethy Collection of the Starr Memorial Library:** manuscripts by Thomas E. Boyce, Clara Curtis, and Elsa Rauer, letters of Theodore Morrison and Robert M. Gay, held by the Abernethy Collection of the Starr Memorial Library; Theodore Morrison, *Bread Loaf Writers' Conference: The First Thirty Years*, (c) 1976 Middlebury College Press; **Judson Mitcham and Bill Richard:** "Conversation with John Gardner," *New Orleans Review* (Summer

1981), (c) 1981 Judson Mitcham and Bill Richard; **Toni Morrison:** "The Site of Memory," from *Inventing the Truth: The Art and Craft of Memoir* (ed. William Zinsser) (Houghton Mifflin), (c) 1987 Toni Morrison; **Howard Nemerov:** "Landscape With Self-Portrait," from *War Stories* (University of Chicago Press), (c) 1987 **Howard Nemerov; "The End of Summer School," from** *The Next Room of the Dream* (University of Chicago Press), (c) 1962 Howard Nemerov; "To Robert Frost, in Autumn, in Vermont," from *The Blue Swallows* (University of Chicago Press), (c) 1967 Howard Nemerov; **New American Library, a division of Penguin Books USA Inc.:** *Conversations With Capote* by Lawrence Grobel, (c) 1985 Lawrence Grobel; **The New York Times Company:** "Confessions of a Summer Camper (Lit'ry Division)," by Dan Wakefield, *New York Times Magazine,* July 31, 1966 (c) 1966 The New York Times Company; **John Frederick Nims:** "Poetry Dignitary," from *Of Flesh and Bone* (Rutgers), (c) 1967 John Frederick Nims; **Tim O'Brien:** "How to Tell a True War Story," from *The Things They Carried* (Houghton Mifflin), (c) 1990 Tim O'Brien; **Robert Pack:** "Advice to Poets . . .", from *Waking to My Name* (Johns Hopkins), (c) 1980 Johns Hopkins University Press; Introductory remarks at Bread Loaf, published in "Musings on Language, Craft and Community: Welcoming Remarks by Robert Pack at the Bread Loaf Writers' Conference, 1974-1984" (Middlebury College), (c) 1984 Robert Pack; **Ron Powers:** introduction to Donald E. Axinn lecture by Tim O'Brien, Middlebury College, 1990, (c) 1990 Ron Powers; **Ruth Page Schorer:** *Sinclair Lewis: An American Life* (McGraw-Hill), (c) 1961 Mark Schorer; **State University of New York Press:** *Family Letters of Robert and Elinor Frost,* ed. Arnold Grade, (c) 1972 State University of New York Press; **Wallace Stegner:** *The Uneasy Chair: A Biography of Bernard DeVoto* (Doubleday), (c) 1973, 1974 Wallace Stegner; **John Stone:** "John Ciardi: His Wit and Witness," from *John Ciardi: Measure of the Man,* ed. Vince Clemente (Arkansas), (c) 1987 John Stone; **Janice Farrar Thaddeus, Alison F. Wilson, and Curtis Farrar:** *The Literary Spotlight* (Doubleday, Doran), (c) 1925 John Farrar; **Ticknor & Fields:** *Their Ancient Glittering Eyes,* (c) 1992 Donald Hall; **Time-Warner, Inc.:** photograph of Robert Frost at Bread Loaf, 1959, by Alfred Eisenstaedt, published in *Life,* 1959, (c) 1959 Time Incorporated; **University of Nebraska Press and V. Sterling Watson:** "Interview with Harry Crews," by V. Sterling Watson, *Prairie Schooner* (Spring 1974), (c) 1974 University of Nebraska Press; **University Press of Mississippi:** "Ciardi on Frost," ed. Edward Cifelli, *Frost Centennial Essays,* v. 1 (ed. Jac Tharpe), (c) 1974 University Press of Mississippi; Peter J. Stanlis, "Acceptable in Heaven's Sight: Robert Frost at Bread Loaf, 1939-1941," *Frost Centennial Essays,* v. 3 (ed. Jac Tharpe); (c) 1978 University Press of Mississippi; **Viking Penguin, a division of Penguin Books USA, and Maxine Kumin:** "Young Nun at Bread Loaf," from *Our Ground Time Here Will be Brief,* (Viking), (c) 1982 Maxine Kumin; **Meg Werner:** "Albert Fletcher Remembers," *Mountain Top Memories* (self-published), (c) 1975 Meg Werner; **John Williams:** "Looking for John Ciardi," from *John Ciardi: Measure of the Man,* ed. Vince Clemente (Arkansas), (c) 1987 John Williams; **Miller Williams:** "Standing Close to Greatness" (new revision) from *The Boys on Their Bony Mules* (Louisiana State University Press), (c) 1983 Miller Williams; **Mary Elizabeth Witherspoon:** "Rock Hopping With an Intellectual," (c) 1950, 1993 Mary Elizabeth Witherspoon; **Yale University Press:** "Accident and Its Scene" by Terrence Des Pres (*Yale Review* Autumn 1983), (c) 1983 Yale University; *Stephen Vincent Benét* by David Fenton, (c) 1958 Yale University Press.

All of the above are reprinted by permission.

Finally, acknowledgment is also gratefully rendered to the individual authors who responded to queries with long letters of narrative, which were used both in the narrative and documentary sections. Particular thanks go to **Alan Cheuse, John Ciardi, Jean Lawlor Cohen, Robert Cormier, Paul Cubeta, Paxton Davis, L. Sprague De Camp, Martin Dibner, Charles Edward Eaton, Richard Ellmann, Seymour Epstein, Dave Etter, George V. Higgins, May Swenson, Lewis Turco, and Mary Elizabeth Witherspoon;** their longer extracts are identified in the documentary section by the year date in parentheses. These contributions are their own property and as such may be deemed to be in copyright by them.

PHOTOGRAPHY CREDITS

With the exception of those photographs identified as being included courtesy of the owning institution or individual, it may be assumed that all others are held by Middlebury College or the editors. For the sake of brevity of captions, most photographic credits are identified by initials, the key for which follows: BDV: Bernard DeVoto; JWM: Jarvis Woolverton Mason; JFS: John F. Smith, Jr.; PC: Paul Child; RL: Roger Lewis; FG: Frank Gohlke; EAM: Edward A. Martin; EB: Erik Borg; JA: Jonathan Aldrich; DHB: David Haward Bain; MSD: Mary Smyth Duffy; JOC: Judith Ortiz Cofer; BA: Blue Argo. Those photographs not credited regrettably resisted all attempts to trace their origins.

INDEX

DATE DUE

FEB 11 2006